ON THE BATTLEFIELDS OF THE COLD WAR

victor israelyan

ON THE BATTLEFIELDS OF THE COLD WAR

a soviet ambassador's confession

foreword by melvin a. goodman
translation edited and revised by stephen pearl

the pennsylvania state university press   university park, pennsylvania

Publication made possible with a grant from
the Earhart Foundation.

Library of Congress Cataloging-in-Publication Data

Israelyan, Victor Levonovich, 1919–
On the battlefields of the cold war : a Soviet ambassador's confession / Victor L. Israelyan.
p.   cm.
ISBN 978-0-271-05847-4 (pbk : alk. paper)
1. Soviet Union—Foreign relations—1945–1991.
2. World policies—1945–1989.
3. Cold War.
4. Israelyan, Victor Levonovich, 1919–
I. Title.

DK282 .I84 2003
327.47'0092—dc21   2003009371

Copyright © 2003 The Pennsylvania State University
All rights reserved
Printed in the United States of America
Published by The Pennsylvania State University Press,
University Park, PA 16802-1003

It is the policy of
The Pennsylvania State University Press
to use acid-free paper. Publications on uncoated stock satisfy the
minimum requirements of American National Standard for Information
Sciences—Permanence of Paper for Printed Library Material,
ANSI Z39.48-1992.

Frontispiece: The Cold Warrior, Ambassador Victor Israelyan,
makes a statement at a press conference in the
Palace of Nations in Geneva in 1985.

To the eternal memory
of my father, Levon, and my mother, Yevgenia

CONTENTS

Foreword by Melvin A. Goodman IX

Preface XV

1 Training for the Cold War 1

2 The First Collisions of the Cold War 23

3 Stalin Is Dead. What Next? 36

4 Sowing the Seeds of Hatred in Hungary 53

5 The Khrushchev Style of Diplomacy 66

6 Thaws and Frosts 86

7 On the Diplomatic Sidelines 106

8 The Battlefield, the UN 126

9 The Soviet Union's 105th Veto 143

10 The Cold War on the Middle East Front 159

11 China—A New Front in the Cold War 175

12 Time to Go Home 198

13 The Soviet Diplomatic Headquarters at Smolenskaya Square 236

14 An Uneasy Truce in the Cold War 259

15 The Apotheosis of the Cold War 299

16 Marking Time 325

17 The Beginning of the End of the Cold War 347

18 Feigned Friendship 366

19 Farewell to the Cold War 384

Conclusion 397

Index 403

FOREWORD BY MELVIN A. GOODMAN

History, including the history of international relations, inexorably moves forward, and students of history must have autobiographies and memoirs that look back in order to understand the past and anticipate the future. Over the past ten years, we have learned a great deal about the rise and fall of the Soviet Union from the memoirs of President Mikhail Gorbachev, Foreign Minister Eduard Shevardnadze, Ambassador Anatoly Dobrynin, and Politburo member Yegor Ligachev, the second most powerful Communist leader during the dramatic changes of the Gorbachev era and one of the last substantial true believers in communism. Such memoirs shed a great deal of light on Soviet policymaking during the Cold War, but they are also selective and self-serving on key issues and do not convey the challenges and frustrations of everyday life in the Soviet system from the bureaucratic trenches. With Ambassador Victor Israelyan's memoir, *On the Battlefields of the Cold War*, we have not only a memoir that provides an inside look at the Soviet foreign ministry but also a searing and probing examination of how the Kremlin conducted its foreign policy and how it treated its own diplomats and policy players.

Ambassador Israelyan's rich and distinguished career as a physician, diplomat, scholar, and professor spanned more than five decades until Foreign Minister Shevardnadze forced his retirement with a series of trumped-up charges. During the 1970s and 1980s, Israelyan was one of the Soviet Union's leading diplomatic specialists in arms control and disarmament. In 1973, as a member of Foreign Minister Andrei Gromyko's staff, he served on a small task force that attended Politburo meetings during the October War between Israel and the nations of Egypt and Syria. His account of the war, published in 1995, was the first Soviet record of crisis management inside the Kremlin. *Inside the Kremlin During the Yom Kippur War* remains the best documentary evidence available to scholars and students of what happened inside the Politburo during times of crisis; it recorded Soviet assessments of United States policy that were free of dogma and Politburo exchanges on international security that were devoid of Marxist-Leninist ideology. We learned a great deal about Soviet foreign policymaking from this book.

Ambassador Israelyan was unlike his foreign ministry colleagues in many ways. He was not Russian but Armenian; he lacked the typical distrust of the West and was more open to the international community. He was a diplomat and a scholar immersed in the complexities of international discourse and partial to the use of diplomacy to solve international problems. He was critical of the confrontational style of the Soviet foreign ministers of the Stalin and Khrushchev eras and he was pragmatic in his own approach to problem solving. Israelyan believed in arms control and encouraged Soviet acceptance of confidence-building measures and verification to achieve breakthroughs in disarmament. He was part of a small community of arms control specialists in the foreign ministry who were largely unknown to anyone in the United States, except the arms control community in Washington.

In this fascinating memoir of his career, we learn about the trials and tribulations of a high-level Soviet bureaucrat who has his own views on foreign policy and who was present during the worst days of the Cold War and the beginning of the transition that led to a series of arms control agreements and the loosening of Soviet control over Eastern Europe. Israelyan occasionally tried to offer his own views on important foreign policy matters, but his foreign counterparts warned him that they wanted the official Soviet position, not the unconventional views of an enlightened Soviet official. And not being wise to the world of espionage and clandestine collection of information, he was surprised to be upbraided by his Soviet masters who had learned that he had been candidly critical of Soviet actions in some of his remarks to foreign dignitaries.

At his best, Ambassador Israelyan provides authoritative views of the major turning points in Soviet foreign policy. He describes the key events that led to the increased diplomatic isolation of the Soviet Union, the decline in the credibility of the Soviet leadership, and the worsening of Soviet-American relations. He recalls his surprise in learning from future Soviet party boss and then Soviet ambassador to Hungary Yuri Andropov that the uprising in Budapest had not been organized and orchestrated by the Western powers. In tracing the Soviet invasions of Czechoslovakia in 1968 and Afghanistan in 1979, Israelyan refers to Czechoslovakia and Afghanistan as major turning points that created significant cynicism within the Soviet apparatus itself, with key bureaucratic players never understanding the need for the use of military force near Soviet borders.

If his doubts about Hungary were latent in 1956, he became more vocal in 1968. In a particularly revealing chapter, Ambassador Israelyan describes the invasion of Afghanistan as the event that both marked the "doom of our Soviet socialist system" because of its misguided "urge to impose on other peoples an alien and unacceptable political regime" and proved to be a watershed in Soviet-American relations, sharply dividing the previous decade of détente from the ensuing years of containment and confrontation.

At the same time, it is noteworthy that Israelyan was surprised by the key events in Afghanistan, not attaching any importance to the coup in Kabul in 1978 and even challenging his diplomatic colleagues who argued that "there was great trouble in store" for Moscow in Afghanistan. The Soviet invasion of Afghanistan the following year was a greater surprise to Israelyan, but other high-ranking Soviet officials were also out of the decision-making loop. Serendipitously, the ambassador was hospitalized in December 1979, when the Soviet invasion took place, and the Soviet ambassador to the United States, Anatoly Dobrynin, was in a neighboring ward. The news of the invasion shocked both of these senior diplomats, which meant that the Kremlin had not even bothered to consult its ambassador in Washington for his view of the invasion's impact on the Carter administration and Soviet-American relations. Both men were alarmed by this fateful decision, not knowing that the Politburo had made a complete strategic reappraisal in the fall of 1979 and that a rump group of Politburo members then decided in November on invasion before year's end.

The October War of 1973 was another turning point of sorts in Soviet-American relations because the unexpected U.S. declaration of a nuclear alert near war's end dealt a major blow to Soviet-American relations and introduced the nuclear card for the first time since the Cuban missile crisis. Ambassador Israelyan has written about the war elsewhere (*Inside the Kremlin During the Yom Kippur War*, 1995), but here he adds important details to his earlier work. He provides a candid assessment of the Politburo's criticism of the Arab decision to go to war and its shock at the decision of the United States to issue a nuclear alert (Defense Condition III). Egypt and Syria had clearly defied the Kremlin in resorting to war, and the paramount consideration for the Politburo was to ensure that the war did not damage Soviet-American relations. (Washington, for that matter, was unhappy with the start of the war because it began in the midst of the Watergate crisis for the Nixon administration.)

Some Soviet officials actually wanted to match the U.S. alert status, particularly KGB chief Andropov and Defense Minister Andrei Grechko, but Secretary General Leonid Brezhnev and Prime Minister Aleksei Kosygin prevailed and simply failed to respond to the U.S. nuclear alert, which had been the responsibility of national security adviser Henry Kissinger and not President Richard Nixon. Israelyan's memoir provides an arresting commentary on the limits and constraints on Soviet policy in the Middle East during a major crisis. His analysis is a useful antidote to those Americans who exaggerated the ability of the Soviet Union to project power in the Third World during the Cold War.

At a celebration commemorating the October Revolution, which happened to coincide with the end of the October War, Ambassador Israelyan noticed that the only Soviet official who did not join the circle offering congratulations to the leadership for the solution to the crisis was Marshal Sergei Akhromeyev, who clearly believed that the United States had intimidated Moscow, resorting to the threat of force—even nuclear force—to win a major diplomatic triumph. Thus, the ambassador had identified a future opponent of the reforms of the Gorbachev era, since it was Akhromeyev who opposed many of the arms control agreements of the 1980s and the unilateral Soviet troop withdrawal from Central Europe in 1989. In the wake of the abortive coup against President Mikhail Gorbachev in August 1991, Marshal Akhromeyev, who was a fan of James Fenimore Cooper and referred to himself as the "last of the Mohicans," committed suicide when it was certain that the coup would fail.

There is a wonderful humanity to Victor Israelyan's work. He goes behind the major decision-makers in the Kremlin and offers perceptive biographic and demographic profiles of the men (there were no women) in the foreign ministry and the policy apparatus. In addition to impressionistic portraits of such key figures as foreign ministers Aleksandr Shepilov, Gromyko, Shevardnadze, and Andrei Kozyrev, there are descriptions of the bureaucratic landscape, including a new generation of foreign ministry officials who were brought in following the death of Josef Stalin and those who were introduced with the surprising arrival of Shevardnadze in 1985. Ambassador Israelyan provides a candid description of the foreign ministry's unhappy reaction to the Shevardnadze appointment, believing that a rank amateur from the Caucasus would not be able to keep Soviet diplomacy on the tracks. His opposition to the Shevardnadze appointment may have played some role in the way Shevardnadze forced the resignation of his fellow countryman from Tbilisi, Georgia, although the ouster was far more ugly and tawdry than circumstances required.

For the first time, we begin to see the complex demographics within the foreign ministry during the Cold War, which included a liberal and pro-Western community that supported arms control negotiations with the United States in the 1970s and 1980s and the Prague Spring reform movement in Czechoslovakia in the 1960s. Israelyan introduces us to such "Americanists" as Dobrynin, Roland Timerbayev, Oleg Grinevsky, Yuly Vorontsov, and Alexander Bessmertnykh, who at one time or another held important positions in the Soviet embassy in Washington or with the Soviet delegation at the United Nations and opposed such Soviet decisions as the deployment of SS-20 missiles and the invasion of Afghanistan. All of them were communists but also pragmatists, who wanted to remove ideology from decision-making in Soviet national security policy.

Finally, Victor Israelyan's *On the Battlefields of the Cold War* is a work of great courage and honesty in a field that is often dominated by self-aggrandizing and self-serving accounts of international security. The ambassador is willing to acknowledge policy blunders in the Soviet system and personal faults in his own conduct; he is an excellent student of diplomatic history and also records American errors in judgment along the way. With a non-traditional background in medicine, perhaps it is no surprise that the ambassador is sensitive to the need for greater international stability and security for all nations. As an author of a dozen books in Russian and English on diplomacy and international relations, Israelyan has a sense of balance and fairness that is the hallmark of a professional historian. Finally, with great clarity and eloquence, he has provided a memoir that opens the door to nearly fifty years of diplomacy between the two superpowers that dominated the period of the Cold War. He describes himself as an "ordinary civil servant who labored in the trenches in the middle tier of the Soviet apparatus," but his memoir is the rewarding work of an extraordinary and humane man who helps us to understand some of the reasons for the collapse of the Soviet Union and the international instability that followed in its wake.

PREFACE

As God would have it, I lived in a country that was in the midst of a tragic social-economic experiment. The goal was to build a new society, a society with neither poor nor rich, oppressed nor oppressors, where justice prevailed over inequality. The country that declared such noble goals achieved great accomplishments. By putting the lives of 27 million of its sons and daughters on the altar of victory, it helped to rid the world of the menace of fascism. It was the first country to successfully explore space. So powerful did this country become that by the latter half of the twentieth century it was recognized as one of only two superpowers determining the face of the modern world. At the same time, monstrous crimes were committed in this very same country; monstrous crimes against its own citizens, including mass murders and terrible infringements of human rights and freedoms. This is what gave rise to the label "evil empire"—a label that reverberated with shame throughout my country. I personally felt this shame, knowing that I shared the responsibility for the crimes and violations.

Nonetheless, I was a believer in the experiment, and to the best of my ability I served the system that had been created to support that experiment. Over the course of my forty years of service in the Foreign Ministry I gained a reputation among my colleagues and partners in negotiations as a knowledgeable diplomat. My service was appreciated highly; I was awarded nearly twenty governmental orders and medals, a state prize, ranks, and other decorations. Hundreds of times I sat in conference halls, negotiating at tables beneath a plaque bearing the name of the Union of Soviet Socialist Republics, and I always felt proud and honored to be representing the interests of such a great country. In the end, however, the Soviet experiment collapsed under the weight of its contradictions. And the irony for me was that I was a casualty of these contradictions, forced to resign in shame after having always tried to fulfill my duties.

I resolutely oppose those of my countrymen, including my fellow diplomats, who shift responsibility for the Soviet evil exclusively to the leaders. No doubt the leaders must bear a lion's share of the responsibility, since they were, so to speak, directing the show, but the others—party functionaries, bureaucrats, diplomats, military officers, scientists, artists, and more—participated in this show. Surely some played greater roles than others, and many did so out of fear, but it is important that each Soviet citizen realize and admit his or her share of the responsibility.

Memoirs are worthless if their authors attempt to present themselves as angels. I hope, therefore, that I do not belong to the unfortunately large group of former Soviet functionaries (party and governmental "apparatchiks," bureaucrats, diplomats, and others), who have written memoirs in which they try to convince their readers that during their sometimes stellar careers they always saw the errors and blunders of the Soviet leadership. Some of them belonged to the very leadership they now criticize, and yet we are supposed to believe that they apparently stood firm against these errors, but alas in vain. This seeming opposition did not prevent these men from climbing the ladder of service, for some were elected as delegates to the Supreme Soviet, some became members of the Party's Central Committee, and some even became CPSU secretaries, being assigned to prestigious and important posts all along the way. In actuality, any noticeable opposition would not have been tolerated and would have resulted in strict punishment in the totalitarian Soviet state. Some authors, for example, former CPSU functionaries, claim to have sympathized with the "Prague Spring" and yet they advanced in the apparatus precisely because they had participated in its suppression. After the disintegration of the USSR, Politburo members who once headed the KGB in Soviet republics claimed to be champions of human rights and fighters for democratic freedoms. We shall leave it on their conscience.

It is important that we have firsthand accounts from those who held the highest leadership positions in the Soviet Union. Less recognized, but equally interesting and important, are the ordinary civil servants who labored in the trenches—the middle tier of the Soviet State apparatus. I myself belonged to this tier; and therefore, it is what I have concentrated on in writing my memoirs.

In the summer of 1991 I was invited by the Fulbright Foundation to teach a course on Soviet foreign policy at Pennsylvania State University. I accepted this invitation with pleasure; but when I left Moscow for the United States in the days of the August 1991 coup, I could not imagine that I was leaving a country that soon would cease to exist. So sudden was the Soviet collapse that I had to alter the course I was teaching at the time. Continuing to hold forth on the foreign policy of a nonexistent state somehow seemed inappropriate. In the years that followed I was invited many times to lecture and to participate in conferences. Invariably, the one subject I was always asked to speak about was the Soviet collapse. Why had it happened? Even today I find it impossible to fully explain the fall of the Soviet state. I do not even attempt such an explanation here. Rather my aspiration is to bring to life, as best I can, one part of the Soviet experience to which I devoted all my life. I cannot claim to be objective but I have tried to be as evenhanded as possible in the hope that future observers will have one more piece of the puzzle as they seek to understand the tragedy that was the Soviet experiment.

On the pages of this book, I mention many names—friends and colleagues, diplomats of the former Soviet Union and other countries. I am grateful for their cooperation and even confrontation during the Cold War years. Writing this book, I enjoyed the essential help and friendship of a young American, Peter Potter, my editor at Penn State Press. Peter and my son Karen made possible the publication of this book.

1
TRAINING FOR THE COLD WAR

Save Humanity from the Epidemic of War

I did not set out to become a diplomat. Since childhood I had been fascinated by the medical profession. My father was a successful pediatrician in Tbilisi, the capital of Georgia, the city where I was born in 1919 and spent my early years. He loved his work and tried to instill that feeling in me, and my decision to enter one of the best medical schools of the country, the First Moscow Medical Institute, was therefore only natural, I suppose. A successful and enthusiastic student, I intended to devote myself to research in the area of bacteriology. It was my dream to find ways to protect humanity from diseases that took millions of lives. My idols were the German Robert Koch, the Frenchman Louis Pasteur, and the Russian Ilya Mechnikov, the great bacteriologists. I studied their research with great interest.

I completed the five-year course in June of 1941. The finals on obstetrics and gynecology were scheduled for June 25. However, the preexamination fever was suddenly interrupted. On Sunday, June 22, Stalin's deputy Vyacheslav Molotov announced that Germany had attacked the Soviet Union. Although it was a sunny weekend, the streets of Moscow were strangely silent as anxiety and alarm swept through the city. Further preparations for the finals were out of the question. The students were asked to complete their studies as soon as possible and prepare for the beginning of war. Upon receiving my medical diploma at the end of June I left for the recruiting office in Tbilisi to which I had been assigned. It was the first week of the war. Despite Molotov's assurances that the enemy would be immediately driven from Soviet territory, the Germans advanced deep into the country. Though the route of my four-day trip from Moscow to Tbilisi went nowhere near the front line, signs of war were already apparent. The train did not run according to schedule and was delayed at stations, jammed with passengers, who had suddenly been forced to leave their homes. Consternation reigned as we wondered why the Germans had attacked us.

In Tbilisi I rushed to the recruiting office where I enlisted in July of 1941 as a private in a newly formed infantry regiment. Not having had any military training, I frequently found myself in tight spots and did everything wrong, drawing severe reprimands and punishment from my superiors and sneers from my fellow soldiers. To my great relief, the regiment's commanding officer came to my rescue. After learning about my education, he arranged for me to be transferred to the Sukhumi Border Guards, stationed on the coast of the Black Sea in Abkhazia and Northern Caucasus region, where my medical training could be put to good use.

In 1942, when the Germans had overwhelmed Soviet troops in the Crimea and started to push toward Stalingrad, the units of the Sukhumi Border Guards engaged in combat in the Northern Caucasus. The battles were bloody, and an endless stream of sick (a malaria epidemic was raging in the area of the fighting, and I came down with it myself) and wounded passed through my hands. My doctoring was limited to rendering first aid. The mountainous location with no roads made it impossible to set up even basic field hospitals. We had to work in tents and to ship our wounded to the rear on horses and donkeys. Many did not make it to hospitals—they perished along the way. For the first time I began to feel dissatisfaction with the medical profession. I was depressed by how little help we could truly offer to the wounded. This feeling grew in me with time.

In 1943 I was assigned to accompany a trainload of paroled criminals recruited from Caucasian prisons for the Red Army. It was almost three thousand miles from Tbilisi to Kaluga, a city located to the Northwest of Moscow. There the recruits were to be assigned to disciplinary units and sent to the front. At times our route took us through the sites of recent battles. We saw destroyed buildings, blown-up bridges, burning tanks and cannons, and unburied corpses everywhere.

The train cars or *teplushki* we traveled in were meant for cattle not people. We had to sleep on the floor covered with a thin layer of straw. There was no heat, and food supplies were sporadic. Food shortages were solved by robbery. The recruits plundered everything they could—warehouses, stores, farms—leaving a trail of fear and hatred behind us. The unsanitary conditions of the trip, freezing temperatures, and lack of food caused numerous diseases and poisoning, and once again it was impossible to provide effective medical help. Occasionally, we had to take our sick to local hospitals. I saw so many of these hospitals during our trip! They were all the same—run-down, dirty, poorly ventilated, and crowded. What could a doctor do under these conditions? Could he cure humanity of the greatest madness of all—mass destruction of people with the help of weapons? These were the questions tormenting me during the long and sleepless nights on the train.

A Change of Heart

With these doubts and thoughts I arrived in Kaluga in December 1943. The first thing I did was take a bath. I hadn't bathed or changed my clothes for almost two months. I couldn't wait to strip everything off—boots, underwear, everything—and burn it all in the furnace. A few days later, while passing through Moscow, I found myself visiting the home of my father's acquaintance, Vladimir Dekanozov, deputy minister of foreign affairs. I knew he was a powerful man and could help me at this difficult time.

I want to say a few words about Dekanozov because he played a considerable role in my life. I first met Dekanozov in Tbilisi in the 1930s. My father treated the children of many influential and powerful people, Dekanozov's son and daughter among them. My father sometimes made house calls and sometimes the children were brought to our house for treatment. Because of this our families became friends. A native of Georgia, who worked in Tbilisi for many years, Dekanozov was close to Lavrenty Beria, the leader of the Georgian communists and one of the most sinister figures in Soviet history. When Beria was later transferred to Moscow and appointed peoples' commissar of internal affairs, he took a group of devoted and loyal followers with him. Dekanozov was among them. In 1939, after working for a few years in the KGB, Dekanozov was appointed deputy peoples' commissar of foreign affairs and, in 1940, Soviet ambassador in Germany. He participated in important negotiations between Molotov and Hitler in November 1940. On the night of June 22, 1941, when the German foreign minister,

Joachim von Ribbentrop, issued Hitler's declaration of war on the Soviet Union, he handed it to Dekanozov.

When Dekanozov returned to Moscow and was appointed deputy minister, his authority in the Ministry of Foreign Affairs (MFA) was indisputable. Nobody wanted to be on the bad side of Beria's man. There were rumors that even Molotov's other deputy, the ferocious Andrei Vyshinsky, fawned on Dekanozov. He was the only Soviet ambassador that Stalin invited to Lenin's Tomb to review the May Day military parade on Red Square—clear evidence of Dekanozov's standing with Stalin, who liked the ambassador's sharp mind. After the war, however, he fell from grace. Most probably because Stalin never forgave Dekanozov for disagreeing with him at the time of Hitler's attack. He was dismissed from the MFA and was without job for a long time. In 1953 Beria was executed along with his closest supporters. Dekanozov's family, his wife and his grown children, were exiled to a remote town in Soviet Asia, where they were humiliated and robbed.

When I visited Dekanozov in the winter of 1943, I started by telling him of my disappointment with the medical profession and then told him some stories from my military life. One of the stories made Dekanozov laugh, and this unexpectedly affected my own future. The story went as follows:

In late November 1943 our train was parked in a siding for several days at a godforsaken station north of Stalingrad. It was there that one night our train was surrounded by KGB troops. We were ordered out of the train, and told to leave all personal belongings behind. When the train commander asked for an explanation, the KGB officer barked at him to shut up and carry out the order. Then we, about a hundred sleepy, half-dressed people, were organized into columns and escorted deep into the steppe. We walked for a long time into the cold darkness, as the wind howled around us. I know I was not only one who thought we were going to be executed.

When we were far from the station, we were ordered to stop and to stand with our backs to the station. "Here ends a short and meaningless life," I thought to myself. With a sinking heart I waited for the end. Seconds went by, then minutes, but the shots did not ring out. In bewilderment and fear we looked back only to see the silhouettes of our escorts leaving toward the station. We stood in the cold and darkness for another few hours, chilled to the bone but afraid to move lest we be shot dead. We remained standing there until the break of day. We returned to the station as quickly as we could and discovered, to our relief, our train was still there. We quickly got on board and took our places. We were even more relived when the switchman was given the green light and we continued our journey.

"That is how I nearly lost my life for the sins of others," I concluded my story. "Funny man you are," Dekanozov said breaking into laughter, "it was Comrade Stalin in his special train on his way to the Tehran Conference. The KGB received orders to clear the whole route ahead of him. That's all. You can consider yourself a part of the conference now." He smiled and added, "You'll be a diplomat some day."

The idea of abandoning medicine and becoming a diplomat continued to nag me after that conversation. I was certain that diplomacy was the best way to prevent wars and forge peaceful relations between countries. My early disappointment as a doctor undoubtedly played a considerable role in my thinking, and I'm certain that the prestige and cosmopolitanism I associated with a diplomatic career factored into my decision. But what could I do to make it happen? At the time there were no open educational institutions, preparing experts in the field of international relations and diplomacy. The Department of International Relations of Moscow State University wasn't created until 1944. Practically no one was aware of the existence of closed courses preparing students for a diplomatic career. These courses were later to become the Higher School of Diplomacy, and yet later—the Diplomatic Academy.* Besides I was not a member of the Communist Party and was not involved in political activities or public affairs. Above all was the war, which made any change of profession practically impossible.

Dekanozov turned out to be most helpful in introducing me into the diplomatic field. I asked my father to write him a letter, and the deputy minister responded promptly. In June 1944 my office received a cable from him, requesting my immediate presence in Moscow to take the entrance examinations for the Diplomatic Academy. I was delighted. I was very proud to receive Dekanozov's cable, but afraid of the examinations. Unfortunately, I knew little about history and law. I immediately wound up my unfinished business and left for Moscow.

Over the years my connection to Dekanozov had both good and bad effects on my diplomatic career. I was told later by friends in personnel that the first document in my personal file was my father's letter to Dekanozov followed by Dekanozov's cable, which was responsible for my acceptance in the Diplomatic Academy. Later, when Dekanozov was executed in connection with Beria's trial, anyone connected with Dekanozov became potentially suspect. Therefore, my personal file was a source of concern to those

---

* [Although not its official name until 1974, henceforth this institution will be referred to as the Diplomatic Academy.]

around me. Every bureaucrat, regardless of rank, was frightened by Dekanozov's letter. At times I was passed over for promotion and sidetracked when new assignments were offered. Although I didn't realize it at the time, few wanted to support a person, who entered diplomacy on the recommendation of an "enemy of the people." Only in the late 1960s, after I had been lucky enough to meet Brezhnev, did my connection with Dekanozov cease to play a significant role in my diplomatic career.

By and large, though, my feelings for Dekanozov have been those of gratitude. Without passing judgment on his political activity, I can only attest to the fact that he was a brilliant and extraordinary person, despite his tragic fate.

A Student at the Diplomatic Academy

The entrance examinations for the Diplomatic Academy turned out to be a mere formality, though we prepared for them with all seriousness. Only those with backing were accepted. Fortunately, I had the necessary support. Nearly 150 students enrolled in 1944 in the school from all Soviet republics. The school itself consisted of two divisions—Western and Oriental. Each faculty was composed of different language groups, some fifteen to twenty altogether. Because I was from the Caucasus, it was suggested that I should enter the Arabic section within the Oriental unit. I did not want to do this so I was placed in the Hungarian group, which consisted of four first-year students. We were to become experts on Hungary.

I started my studies in the fall of 1944. The major subjects were the history of diplomacy, foreign policy of the Soviet Union, international law, and world economics; however, priority was given to foreign languages. Besides Hungarian I studied English and worked on improving my German, which I had known from childhood. My German language teacher was Sofia Liebknecht, widow of the founder of the German Communist Party, Karl Liebknecht, who had come to live in the Soviet Union.

We were also taught diplomatic protocol, etiquette, and even ballroom dancing. After the harsh life at the front in conditions of hardship and deprivation caused by the war, these skills seemed unreal and useless to us. The truth of the matter is that they added a certain luster to our training, and we (as a rule, being single young men) showed off these accomplishments to our girlfriends. Our teachers drew on their own diplomatic practice and experience in explaining the importance of these subjects.

The teaching of social studies was, of course, based on the standard orthodoxy, the unwavering principles of Marxism-Leninism and the works and speeches of Stalin. Every interview and speech, not to mention Stalin's articles and brochures, were the subject of extensive discussion among students and professors, all comments being unfailingly laudatory. Although at times done artistically and with imagination, this empty praise contributed virtually nothing to the educational process.

The Diplomatic Academy was a closed elite educational institution. It was impossible to find information about it in any directory. We were discouraged from mentioning our affiliation with it. We all received rather high stipends and additional food vouchers; the students from other cities were lodged in good hostels or hotels. All school activities and the life of the student body took place under the vigilant supervision of the Central Committee of the Communist Party of the Soviet Union (CPSU), the MFA, and of course, the KGB. Therefore, we avoided discussions of controversial political issues, and we were always cautious in expressing our opinions about the Soviet government and the actions of the Communist Party.

The ethnic structure of the student body was rather diverse. My class (1944–46) consisted of representatives from all Soviet republics. There were no Jews though. When one of the students was found to have concealed his Jewish origins, he was immediately expelled from the DA on some trumped-up pretext. Anti-Semitism in the USSR was supposedly forbidden by law. Nonetheless, it existed. There were several Jews among the professors, and they were kept for one simple reason—the absence of equally qualified replacements. But during numerous anti-Semitic campaigns conducted on various specious pretexts (the struggle against cosmopolitanism, worship of the foreign, and so on), they suffered their share of persecution. Among other things, they were subjected to "resolute condemnation" at humiliating gatherings, were forced to confess to all manner of deadly sins, and underwent administrative harassment and demotions.

The educational process at the Diplomatic Academy gave students the opportunity to become acquainted with the leaders of foreign communist parties who at various times had been compelled to emigrate to the Soviet Union. Along with my classmates from the Hungarian section I was able to meet with Matyas Rakosi, one of the leaders of the Hungarian Communist Party. Conversations with Rakosi left a troubling impression on my classmates and me. His appearance was most unattractive: he was short, round, and restless, his eyes were constantly watering, and could not win our confidence or trust. Most important, he could not tell us anything new about Hungary, its political situation, or its prospects for development. His judgments were derived from standard Soviet propaganda stereotypes. "The Bloody Regime of Horthy," "Hitler's Satellites," "Exploiters of the Hungarian people"—these were the clichés he used to characterize the ruling elite of Hungary. In his opinion only the Soviet Union together with Hungarian communists could rescue the state from complete collapse. Rakosi could not really teach us anything without drawing criticism from the apparatchiks who were supervising his instruction. On the other hand, he himself knew very little about Hungarian literature, culture, and art. He could not give an intelligible answer to many questions and thus left us with the impression that Rakosi didn't know the real situation in Hungary.

The fact is that the young Rakosi, was one of the leaders of the Hungarian Soviet Republic, which existed for 133 days in 1919, and was captured by the Horthyites before he could escape after it was overthrown and was sentenced to death. Later the sentence was commuted to life in prison. The leader of Soviet Hungary, Bela Kun, was less fortunate. He managed to escape the Horthyites and settle in the USSR where he held an important post in the Comintern, but in the late 1930s he was executed in a Soviet prison. The Horthyites turned out to be more magnanimous in their treatment of Rakosi. In 1940 they agreed to exchange Rakosi for the banners of the Hungarian revolution of 1848–49, which were kept in the Soviet Union. Thus Rakosi appeared in the USSR. As he himself once admitted, his greatest dream was to resemble Comrade Stalin in everything and to be his best student.

The two years of study at the Diplomatic Academy flew by quickly, although they were filled with hard work. Every student had already received higher education (a prerequisite for entry), but international relations and diplomacy were totally unknown and new areas to all of us. The majority of the students did not speak any foreign language, and many of them, especially those from Soviet Asia and the Baltic republics, could hardly speak any Russian. In the years at the Diplomatic Academy not only did we acquire actual knowledge, but even more important, our mentality and overall understanding of international relations and the problems of Soviet foreign policy underwent a change.

However, unfortunately neither my classmates nor I had a clear, complete picture of the craft of diplomacy. We were taught to fight for the high purposes of communist foreign policy and to oppose the imperialist states, and so forth. We weren't trained to negotiate with representatives of other countries, to collect information, conduct correspondence, and draft reports to our capital. Many years later I realized that we had not been taught the ABCs of diplomacy. I still remember my embarrassment after my graduation from the Diplomatic Academy when I could not answer a question about the specifics of diplomatic work.

I have no recollection of any specific Soviet definition of diplomacy offered by our professors at the Diplomatic Academy. One appeared later in the Soviet diplomatic dictionary, and in the works of Valerian Zorin, Anatoly Kovalev, and other authors. Essentially, they stated that the core of diplomacy and world politics was the class struggle. They taught that the diverse activities of Soviet diplomats should first of all be built around the class interests of the victorious Soviet proletariat and its advance guard—the CPSU. Therefore, the methods, style, and the goals of Soviet diplomats should be dictated by these interests. "Comrade Stalin's faithful follower" Vyacheslav Molotov and later the no less "faithful" Andrei Vyshinsky were recommended to us as model exponents of the art of diplomacy.

I do not know whether the names of the leading Soviet "cold warriors" who represented the Soviet Union in the first postwar years and became important players in world diplomacy will find their places in the Diplomatic Hall of Fame alongside those of Metternich, Talleyrand, Bismarck, Gorchakov, Jefferson, and others, but I hope that the following sketches will provide a better understanding of the Soviet-style diplomat. As a junior diplomat and a lecturer I had only a few encounters with Molotov and Vyshinsky, so my sketches are based on a mixture of personal recollection and the stories I have heard from others.

Molotov the "Nyet Negotiator"

There is no doubt in my mind that Molotov was the most significant of the Soviet cold warriors. His appointment to the post of people's commissar for foreign affairs in the spring of 1939 not only marked a change in the leadership of the Soviet foreign service, it signified a serious turn in Soviet foreign policy. This was a sure sign of Stalin's growing influence over the state's international activities, which resulted in a complete reshuffling of the Soviet diplomatic corps.

Stalin could not have found a better figure for implementing his foreign policy changes than Molotov. He was very critical of his predecessor,

Litvinov, and his policy of cooperation with France and Britain, which was designed to create a system of collective security in Europe against Hitler's aggression. The failure of Litvinov's efforts in the late 1930s gave Molotov cause to rejoice, for he considered Litvinov "rotten" and a threat to the goals of the Kremlin leadership. Stalin, for his part, knew that Litvinov, a Jew, was the wrong man for implementing a policy of rapprochement with Hitler; and therefore, he chose Molotov, with whom he was close. During a meeting with Litvinov in the summer of 1946 one of our fellow Diplomatic Academy graduates asked the former people's commissar for foreign affairs why he had resigned his post in the spring of 1939. Litvinov answered bitterly: "Do you really think that I was the right person to sign a treaty with Hitler?" It was clear to me that he had always opposed and despised the rapprochement with Nazi Germany. At that time we were much amazed at his courage in voicing such an opinion even though it contradicted the official Soviet policy pursued under the "wise guidance of the great leader."

"When Litvinov was discharged and I became the head of the foreign service," Molotov recalled, "Stalin told me 'Get the Jews out of the Narkomat [foreign ministry].'" Following Stalin's instructions, Molotov, with considerable relish and diligence, had many Jews dismissed and arrested, even though he himself was married to Polina Zhemchuzhina, who was Jewish and had occupied a ministerial post in the 1930s.

Molotov was minister of foreign affairs twice: from 1939 to 1949, and from 1953 to 1956. His influence on the new generation of Soviet diplomats was due not only to his long tenure as minister but also to his close relationship with Stalin. He was second in command in the Soviet Union for many years. Sometimes he had "friendly" disagreements with Stalin on secondary issues. Stalin tolerated these challenges for a while but eventually they led to his downfall. Nonetheless, despite Stalin's wrath, and the arrest of his wife on the "great leader's" orders, Molotov remained as faithful to Stalin as a dog.

In the history of diplomacy, Molotov first emerges in connection with the Soviet-German Pact of August 23, 1939, and the secret protocols that accompanied it (the pact is usually referred to as the Molotov-Ribbentrop Pact). The Soviet minister was always proud of the deal he made with Hitler on the eve of the war. At a meeting Molotov had with the faculty of the Diplomatic Academy in the mid-1950s I asked him a question that was also on the minds of other professors and students: Were any secret protocols signed in connection with the nonaggression pact? Molotov's response showed his irritation with the question: "These are not matters with which you and your students should concern yourselves." At that time I was not so much surprised by the answer as by the fact that he had not denied the existence of such protocols. Soviet propaganda persistently denied it until the end of the 1980s, and he sometimes confirmed this propaganda.

During negotiations, Molotov typically ignored the person he was talking to and, moreover, did not consider what had been said. When his counterpart represented a small state, Molotov would use threats and blackmail. The stubbornness with which he repeated his position often caused his partner to lose his temper. The classic example occurred during the talks between Molotov and Hitler in November 1940 in Berlin. Dekanozov, who participated in the talks, recalled that Molotov was quite satisfied with the talks even though Hitler and Ribbentrop emphasized one view while Molotov clung to the other, thus achieving nothing. Molotov stuck so stubbornly to his demands that the Führer lost his temper. When Dekanozov related this to Stalin and expressed surprise that a man with such a fine mind as Molotov could conduct negotiations in this way, Stalin responded: "Of course, Molotov has a fine mind, but it's a stupid mind."

After World War II the Soviet Union claimed the former Italian colony of Libya as a protectorate because Stalin wanted to create a Soviet military base near Tripoli. Of course, there was no legal basis for such a claim, but Molotov, during several conferences of foreign ministers of the Big Powers, tried to impose the Soviet position upon his colleagues. Ernest Bevin, the British foreign secretary, had a breakdown and had to be attended to immediately by a doctor in the conference room. Churchill, who negotiated with Molotov several times, wrote in his memoirs that he had never seen a human being who more perfectly represented the modern conception of a robot than did Molotov. He was notorious for the way he conducted negotiations with poise, single-mindedness of purpose, and fantastic stubbornness.

Molotov's negotiating style had another remarkable feature. He never excused his partner's diplomatic blunders or slips but instead used them to his own advantage. At the London session of the Council of Ministers of Foreign Affairs in September 1945, the president of the conference, Bevin allowed himself to make an insulting remark about Soviet foreign policy, saying that its methods reminded him of the fascists.' Molotov immediately sprang from his seat and started for the door. Afraid of an international scandal, Bevin, who had only recently taken the post of foreign secretary, went up to Molotov and apologized for the "bad comparison." Nevertheless, the atmosphere remained tense thereafter, undoubtedly contributing to the ultimate failure of the conference. Afterwards, several observers blamed Bevin for his poor chairmanship. Molotov was pleased with himself.

I happened to witness another episode at a later session of the Council of Ministers of Foreign Affairs of the USSR, the United States, France, and Britain. The session took place in Moscow in March 1947. George Bidault of France was to make a statement as part of a general discussion of the German problem. However, he put aside the text of his statement and spoke "off the cuff." It became clear later that he was confused and had come to the meeting under the influence of alcohol; this was not the first time this had happened. Molotov, who was presiding over the meeting, immediately took advantage of the situation and interpreted everything Bidault said as agreement with the Soviet position. Bidault's deputy, after asking his minister to yield the floor, then clearly voiced France's position, which differed considerably from that of the Soviet Union. Disappointed by the failure of his "diplomatic maneuver," Molotov abandoned his formerly friendly attitude toward the French minister. John Dulles, who participated in the Moscow Conference, recalled that at the farewell dinner given by Stalin at the Kremlin, Molotov, who acted as toastmaster at his host's request, toasted Bevin, Secretary of State Marshall, and various other persons, and then made a belated toast to Bidault, couched in language that was deliberately insulting.

Molotov's goal as foreign minister was to expand the confines of "our Motherland," the Soviet Union. In a lecture given at the Diplomatic Academy he emphasized that the concept of "Motherland" should not be regarded from the viewpoint of Soviet national interests but from a class-oriented perspective. "The greatest pride of the Russian nation," he said, "is that it not only leads the USSR but world progress as well." He believed that Russian communists could not be separated from the world revolution, they must fight for the world revolution. He claimed that the only way to achieve this was to wage an uncompromising struggle against "imperialism," that is, capitalist countries that were dedicated to harming the "Motherland of Socialism" and deceiving the Soviet Union. Therefore, Molotov appealed to students and diplomats to be always on guard and alert to prevent "trickery" against the Soviets.

Molotov lived to be ninety-six, and to the very end of his long life he remained incorrigible, dogmatic, and stubbornly orthodox, viewing life through the prism of simplified, sometimes even primitive, conclusions formed during the October Revolution of 1917 and never relinquished. He opposed Khrushchev's very modest steps toward democracy. Even in his old age his conscience was untroubled despite his participation in the terror and crimes of the 1930s. He never expressed any regret over his actions.

Molotov considered himself a politician rather than a diplomat. As a foreign minister he created a centralized type of diplomacy. "Stalin and I held everything in our fist," Molotov once confessed. "We controlled diplomacy by directing everything from the center, from Moscow. We never ran risks, knowing that we had reliable people who understood their roles." Molotov could afford to be proud because he had recruited most of these "reliable people" himself. After his appointment in 1939, many young people came to work in the foreign service: Communist Party nomenklatura, political scientists, journalists. Few spoke foreign languages or had been abroad. Their image of the USSR's neighbors as well as that of the rest of the "capitalist encirclement" was based on propaganda in the Soviet press about the "class struggle of the bourgeoisie," about "the increasingly acute economic crisis in the capitalist countries," and so on. This generation, which could rightly be called Stalin's generation, was at the same time very diligent, obedient, persistent, and fanatically devoted to the "general line of the Communist Party and the Soviet government."

Representatives of this generation who were selected by Molotov later became important figures the world Cold War diplomacy: Andrei Gromyko, Fedor Gusev, Yakov Malik, Georgy Pushkin, Valerian Zorin, Vladimir Semenov, Kiril Novikov, Aleksandr Lavrishchev, and others. I have known and worked with many of them. Gromyko was minister of foreign affairs for most of my diplomatic career; Malik was my boss in New York; and I succeeded Novikov as head of a department in the MFA.

Molotov's activity in the political and diplomatic arena was viewed in different and sometimes conflicting ways. Litvinov's claim that Molotov understood nothing at all about foreign policy and diplomacy was based on his observation of Molotov's stand during several international negotiations. "Had Molotov been in Stalin's place," noted Litvinov, "this breakup [of the anti-Hitlerite coalition] would have occurred a long time ago." On the other hand, Dulles called Molotov the best diplomat of the twentieth century, and Churchill ranked him with the great diplomats of the nineteenth century. "In the conduct of foreign affairs, Mazarini, Talleyrand, Metternich, would welcome him [Molotov] to their company," wrote Churchill, "if there be another world to which Bolsheviks allow themselves to go."

ON THE BATTLEFIELDS OF THE COLD WAR

The Prosecutor's Diplomacy of Vyshinsky

The reader who turns to page 540 of the ninth volume of the 1952 edition of the *Large Soviet Encyclopedia* (*Bol'shaya Sovetskaya Entsiklopediya*) will find himself transfixed by the piercing, hypnotic stare, through a pair of horn-rimmed spectacles, of a man of intellectual appearance wearing the uniform of an Ambassador Extraordinary and Plenipotentiary of the Soviet Union. The photograph is accompanied by a brief biography containing this passage: "He relentlessly exposes the predatory policy of the reactionary ruling circles of the USA and Britain, and in the name of the USSR and all of the progressive humanity demands the banning of the criminal propaganda of war conducted with impunity in the countries of the imperialist aggressors against the USSR and the countries of the people's democracy." The subject of this passage is Andrei Vyshinsky, the man whose name is inseparable from the blood-stained pages of the history of the Soviet Union in the 1930s. The above passage, however, relates not to his career in the sphere of "jurisprudence" but in an altogether different field, in the international arena. For about fifteen years Vyshinsky served the USSR in the area of foreign policy and affairs, first as a deputy minister, and from 1949 to 1953 as minister of foreign affairs. Vyshinsky served as minister between two stints by Molotov, who replaced Vyshinsky after Stalin's death. Vyshinsky was also a member of the Soviet Academy of Science, and as a political scientist he envisaged the speedy collapse of the capitalist world.

Vyshinsky was an odious figure primarily because of his record as the chief public prosecutor at practically all the big political trials, the trials that shattered the lives of thousands upon thousands of human beings. "Whenever I looked into those pale eyes [Vyshinsky's]," Charles Bohlen, U.S. ambassador in the Soviet Union, wrote in his memoirs, "I saw the horrible spectacle of the prosecutor browbeating the defendants of the Bukharin trial [one of the most notorious trials during Stalin's purges of the 1930s]." Indelibly imprinted on the memory of George Kennan, who also worked for many years in Moscow, for a time as U.S. ambassador, were the political trials of the 1930s when, in the Hall of Columns of the House of Unions, he heard Vyshinsky "sounding the cry of suspicious, secretive Russia against the fancied hostility of the outside world." U.S. secretary of state Dean Acheson, Vyshinsky's opposite number, with whom he had talks on more than one occasion, also had anything but a high opinion of him. "As a public prosecutor during Stalin's bloody purges of the Party, officialdom, and army in the 1930s," Acheson wrote, "he had hounded former friends and colleagues to breakdown and death."

Vyshinsky was at the zenith of his diplomatic career in the late 1940s. Few of us newcomers to the diplomatic service had occasion to work directly with him. But we had listened to his speeches, attended meetings he chaired, and of course, talked about him a great deal. His speeches, his sarcastic remarks and comments, and the dressings-down he administered regularly to subordinates guilty or not guilty of misdemeanors were the subject of lively discussion. He was feared by nearly everyone. To get on his bad side, especially when he was in an ill humor, was nothing short of disaster.

I remember one instance when I briefly felt Vyshinsky's wrath. It was the day I received a call from his assistant, Ivan Lobanov, who told me to report immediately to the chief's office with some documents. I was delighted at this honor and rushed to Vyshinsky's office with a pile of documents. Lobanov was not at the reception desk, so I told the secretary that Vyshinsky expected me and entered the boss's office. He was sitting at his desk, which was covered with papers, absorbed in his reading. "Andrei Yanuaryevich, Israelyan reporting as ordered!" I announced eagerly. Clearly annoyed, Vyshinsky set his reading aside and gave me a menacing look. Putting a finger to his temple, he barked: "Are you out of your mind? You are interrupting my work. Get out!" Dismayed by his reaction I retreated hastily and returned to my office, only to be met with laughter from my colleagues. It became clear that it wasn't Lobanov who had called me, but one of our friends, who had the extraordinary ability to mimic other people's voices. I was the victim of his latest joke, which could have cost me dearly. He explained that he had expected Lobanov to prevent me from entering the office and hadn't anticipated that he would be away from his desk at the time. Naturally, I was terrified that the prank would have dire consequences for me, but fortunately Vyshinsky was so busy at the time that he forgot all about it.

Vyshinsky's "relentless exposures" of external enemies, his public speeches crammed with historical allusions and analogies (often highly dubious); his juggling of aphorisms, proverbs, and Latin phrases; and finally, the crushing labels he attached to his political opponents evoked the approval and even the delight of some admirers of his talent. To be fair, it must be admitted that he did possess this "gift" as well. It made him popular not only among "fighters against imperialism" but among some intelligent people too.

Vyshinsky's role in foreign affairs commanded particular attention in the years when he headed the MFA. I do not think one should overrate his importance in developing foreign policy concepts and in determining the key positions of the Soviet Union, partly because, unlike some of his predecessors and successors in the post of foreign minister, he was never a member of the Political Bureau (Politburo) of the CPSU's Central Committee. He was not one of Stalin's inner circle. However, in terms of putting these policies into effect, in other words, the diplomatic style, Vyshinsky's hand was immediately discernible. His style and passion for "exposures" only exacerbated the conflicting and confrontational elements in world diplomacy that fueled the Cold War.

Vyshinsky liked "public" diplomacy and was particularly partial to addressing international conferences. At the fourth UN General Assembly in 1949 he delivered twenty-nine speeches, at the fifth—twenty-six, and at the sixth—twenty-two. The speeches, as a rule, were lengthy, some of them lasting from two to two and a half hours, and sometimes more. In fact, to this day no foreign minister throughout the entire history of the United Nations has delivered as many speeches as Vyshinsky.

What is more remarkable is the nature of these orations. Vyshinsky's speeches were marked by an unusual mix of solemn, sonorous Latin, a cascade of Russian proverbs, and primitive, vulgar invective, which very often provoked ripostes from his opponents. The polemics he indulged in were deliberately confrontational, as he branded, pilloried, humiliated, and ridiculed other delegates. He was less concerned with finding mutually acceptable compromises than with disarming his opponent so that he could gain the negotiating advantage.

Vyshinsky, impatient, rude, and quick-tempered by nature, was never a real diplomat. François De Calliers once observed that "a man who by nature is strange, inconstant, and ruled by his own humors and passions should not enter the profession of diplomacy, but should go to the wars." Vyshinsky, unfortunately, was ill-equipped for the diplomatic profession.

Vyshinsky had a rather unusual custom, which distinguished him from other Soviet diplomats. Following standard procedure, he usually submitted to the Kremlin drafts of his statements in advance for their clearance. However, he always departed from the approved text and delivered a different version of the statement. On the level of substance the two versions weren't all that different, but it was risky nonetheless to veer from the approved text. Therefore, to be on the safe side, Vyshinsky always sent back to Moscow a version of his speech that was already in the Kremlin, not the one he had actually made. Later, when I started to work in the archives of the Ministry of Foreign Affairs,

I discovered these differences and reported it to my superior, but he advised me to keep my mouth shut about my discovery.

A tendency to indulge in denunciatory diatribes bordering on downright rudeness and to use "shocking language" was in Vyshinsky's very nature. In the choice of startling yet essentially meaningless epithets, his imagination knew no bounds. True, such epithets as "mad dog," "stinking offal," "accursed scoundrel," "despicable cur," and the like which he liberally used at political trials in the Soviet Union were not indulged in at international forums. However, expressions like "rabbit warmonger," "crude falsifier," "a gentleman run amok," "a mad man" or "semi-mad man," and "foul slanderer" abounded in his speeches even there.

Malik, who worked for many years with Vyshinsky and admired him, told me how, after one of Vyshinsky's insulting tirades, one of the foreign diplomats he had attacked challenged him to a duel. Vyshinsky, however, did not accept the challenge, instead voicing his "contempt" for the person. The use of offensive expressions by Vyshinsky evoked displeasure even in the Kremlin. He was told to curb his zeal. The former prosecutor's courtroom rhetoric was accompanied by the issuing of "wrathful protests" and the "contemptuous dismissal of brazen statements." At the same time Vyshinsky lied and misinformed his partners. On the issue of repatriation of Soviet POWs and displaced persons, violation of human rights and purges, the drive against "cosmopolitanism," and so forth, he had told outright lies without blushing.

The end result of Vyshinsky's behavior was that he was not trusted. People were reluctant to have with him the kind of unofficial, friendly contacts that are so important in diplomacy. However, the impression Vyshinsky made on Western politicians and diplomats was not entirely negative. President Roosevelt was fascinated when he met Vyshinsky in Yalta. Others considered him to be "courtly and aristocratic," to have "faultless manners," to be "a fine dancer despite his age," and so on. Edgar Snow maintained that Vyshinsky's distinctive talent would have won him recognition under any system, and he portrayed him as a handsome and clever, if somewhat egocentric, man. But the main result of Vyshinsky's "prosecutor diplomacy," alongside other manifestations of the confrontational policy, was that it helped to create the "image of the enemy."

Hartley Shawcross, British delegate to the UN, once speaking of Vyshinsky's style, said that when the Soviet delegation offered the olive branch it did so in such an aggressive manner that such actions seemed designed to kill any desire to accept it. Another diplomat observed that the meaning of Vyshinsky's speeches could be summed up in a German saying: "You better be my brother or I'll crack your skull." During a visit to Denmark in the late 1980s I had a talk with the well-known Danish champion of European security, Hermod Lannung, who worked for many years in the UN. I asked him whether he remembered Vyshinsky. Of course he did. "Every speech Vyshinsky delivered was an exciting show," he said. "Would you ever like to see his show repeated?" I asked. "God forbid, absolutely not!" was the answer, and I believed him.

Molotov and Vyshinsky were held up as the perfect models for us young diplomats to follow. Despite Molotov's downfall and expulsion from the Communist Party and Vyshinsky's condemnation for his role in the purges of the 1930s, both of them made a lasting impact on a generation of Soviet diplomats.

Graduation from the Academy

The international situation had a tremendous impact on the teaching process. And it was a very special time—the last year of the war. During the war the Kremlin was clearly concentrating its energies on getting the absolute maximum advantage from its cooperation with the United States and England. Thus, at least for the short term, Stalin and the Soviet propaganda machine chose to avoid such ideological matters as the role of the class struggle in the international arena and the final global victory of communism. It was in this light that we discussed with our teachers and among ourselves many Soviet political actions early in the war, such as the dissolution of the Comintern in 1943, the Moscow Conferences between the USSR, the United States, and Great Britain in 1941 and 1943, and the meetings of the Big Three in Teheran, Yalta, and Potsdam.

Stalin's 1944 speech to commemorate the October Revolution became a subject of considerable discussion. We were told that Stalin's statement about close cooperation among the leading states of the anti-Hitler coalition as a vital condition of the UN's effectiveness was a historic declaration. It should be interpreted as the determination of the Soviet leadership to continue cooperation between the USSR, the United States, and Britain.

The results of the 1945 Yalta Conference were widely discussed in the Soviet Union. Mass meetings were held in many Soviet cities—Moscow, Leningrad, Kiev, Minsk, among others—with most people expressing satisfaction with the results of the conference. The students of the Diplomatic Academy were sent to give lectures on the subject. I delivered a speech at a Moscow factory. Referring to the declaration by Stalin, Roosevelt, and Churchill, "Unity in Peace, and in War," which was adopted at the conference; I emphasized the general agreement among the three leaders to maintain and to expand the wartime cooperation in the ensuing period of peace. We knew very little about the disagreements among the allies. Nothing was ever mentioned about the heated arguments at the meetings of the Big Three and in the correspondence between Stalin, Roosevelt, and Churchill. All that was stressed was consent and the ability of the allies to agree. When I asked one of those who had participated in the conference, Boris Podtserob (subsequently deputy minister of foreign affairs), if there had been any disagreements at the conference, he said, "There were, but they were overcome."

From my point of view the height of these good feelings toward our allies was reached on the last day of the war in Europe. The news that Germany had signed the Act of Unconditional Surrender was announced on Moscow Radio on the night of May 9, 1945. As soon as I heard the news I called my Diplomatic Academy classmate and suggested we go to the center of Moscow to celebrate. Despite the late hour Gorky Street was full of people. A huge crowd had gathered at the American embassy on Manezhnaya Square not far from the Kremlin. The people were cheering for victory, peace, the Soviet Union, and America. Several Americans appeared and were immediately warmly welcomed by the crowd and carried shoulder high through the streets. We happily joined the jubilant crowd. We met several students from our academy among them. Never before (and unfortunately again never since that memorable day) had Soviet-American friendship been so rousingly celebrated as it was then right in front of the American embassy.

The Soviet people had warm feelings toward their other ally, the United Kingdom, as well, but the outpouring of goodwill was principally directed at the United States. There were a number of reasons for this, but certainly one of the key reasons was President Roosevelt, whose popularity was based on the fact that he was the American president who recognized the Soviet Union and established diplomatic relations between the two countries in 1933. Churchill on the other hand was remembered as one of the organizers and leaders of the military intervention of Britain and other countries against Soviet Russia after the October Revolution. Besides, every Soviet citizen had personally experienced American assistance in the form of food, vehicles, and other goods, which left a lasting impression on the Soviet people. And last, those who were involved in politics to any degree knew that the United States was more favorable to the USSR on certain key issues than was Britain.

Briefly, by the end of the war it was not only the Soviet public, but also the MFA that saw the prospects for cooperation among countries of the anti-Hitler coalition as incandescently bright. This impression arose from conversations and meetings with ministry officials. Furthermore, students were encouraged to study English and take extracurricular courses on American and English literature and history, which began to be offered at the Diplomatic Academy.

I took my graduation exams in June of 1946 and was awarded the highest marks in international law and diplomatic history. The examination commission consisted of ten or twelve leading Soviet professors. Maxim Litvinov, who was then deputy minister of foreign affairs, chaired the commission. However, his behavior during the exams showed that his involvement in Soviet foreign policy decision-making was minimal and that time had passed him by. Throughout the exams Litvinov was mostly passive, rarely asking the students any questions or offering comments. Only once during my English language oral test did he offer a comment. He spoke English with a strong accent, though he had lived in England for many years and was married to an Englishwoman.

With the Diplomatic Academy diploma we were awarded the lowest diplomatic rank, that of an attaché. But perhaps we were most excited by the fact that all graduates received the uniform of a Soviet diplomat. It was a usual three-piece suit with gold-plated buttons. The everyday uniform was gray, and the dress uniform black. The shoulder straps with their insignia were particularly prized. The uniform included a coat, a raincoat, a hat, an ornate cap bearing the diplomatic insignia—palm leaves, and a dagger to be worn with the dress uniform. Immediately after it was issued, we dressed up and paraded around Moscow drawing the attention and envy of children.

I am reminded of an amusing story involving my new uniform. I was on vacation and put it on and went for a walk in the streets of a small Georgian town, where German POWs were working. Passing by a group of prisoners, I was stopped by one of them. He shouted "Heil Hitler!" and gave me a Nazi salute. I was indignant and demanded an explanation from the guard commander. After talking to the prisoner, the officer told me with embarrassment, that the German had mistaken me for an SS officer and thought that there had been a turn in Soviet-German relations.

It is true that the Soviet diplomatic uniform was similar in some respects to the Nazi one, so the reasoning of the German POW was perhaps not surprising. I do not think, however, that this similarity was why the Soviet Union later discontinued the diplomatic uniform. Most likely the decision was based on the fact that the military, prosecutors, railroad workers, and employees of many other institutions also had service uniforms with shoulder straps. This made the whole country, and Moscow in particular, look like a military camp. The dress uniform without the dagger was eventually kept only for special occasions—presentation of credentials, receptions to celebrate national holidays, and so on. In the many years of my diplomatic service I, as well as the majority of my colleagues, hardly ever wore the uniform.

The reception in honor of the graduation was held in a magnificent private ministry residence, where important international negotiations and hospitality events were held. About a hundred and fifty people graduated from the Diplomatic Academy in 1946—the largest class in the school's history. Among the graduates there were four or five representatives from every one of the sixteen republics (at the time, the USSR included the Karelo-Finnish SSR). They were expected to return to their home republics and form the nuclei of their local ministries of foreign affairs. These ministries were established in March 1946 by a decree of the Presidium of the Supreme Soviet of the USSR. Many of us had joyful visions of becoming the trailblazers in the foreign policy and diplomacy of the republics of the Soviet Union. Some even dreamed of being appointed ambassadors of their republics to some wondrous land beyond the ocean. "Dreams, dreams, where are your sweetness?" a great poet said.

Any illusions about independent activity on the part of the union republics were shattered immediately. At the time of my graduation from the Diplomatic Academy, it was made clear to us that in the republics young diplomats such as ourselves would have no say. I had the alternative to either stay at the Diplomatic Academy postgraduate school to write my dissertation or seek a position with the Hungarian Department of the Foreign Ministry. Finally, after a discussion within the ministry, three of the graduates—Anatoly Dobrynin, Vladimir Meshera, and I—were informed that we would stay with the Diplomatic Academy as postdoctoral students and continue our careers as lecturers. We could not hide our disappointment, since our dream was to join the Foreign Service immediately. When we asked why we had been selected, we were told that Comrade Molotov himself had made the choice. This answer made it clear to us that we had to obey the minister's decision.

Molotov was expected to make an appearance at our graduation party that day. However, one of his assistants, Solomon Lozovsky, came in his place. A participant in the October Revolution, Lozovsky supervised the Soviet Information Bureau and maintained contacts with the press during the war. He was an educated person and sharp-witted. From his speech at the graduation party I particularly remember his comments regarding our future. Lozovsky compared our large class to a wagon filled with passengers that was setting off on a distant and arduous journey to the high goals of communism. "During this difficult trip," he continued, "not all of you will overcome the difficulties of the diplomatic job and will be thrown out of the wagon. Only the strongest of you with the most steadfast principles will successfully finish this trip and contribute to new victories for Soviet foreign policy and diplomacy." This was Lozovsky's prophecy. I am afraid, that he was wrong. The "wagon" never reached the destination he spoke of. Ironically, Lozovsky himself was the first to "fall out of the wagon." Soon after the meeting with the students at the Diplomatic Academy he was arrested, together with several prominent Jewish cultural and artistic figures, on charges of anti-Soviet activity.

Upon graduation I was assigned to the Department of the History of International Relations and Soviet Foreign Policy. On the strength of my special subject, I chose "Hungarian Foreign Policy on the Eve of World War II" as the title of my dissertation. This choice was determined in part by the fact that some archives, including personal archives of the Hungarian head of state Regent Horthy, were seized by Soviet troops and were delivered to Moscow as trophies. The appeal of the thesis for me was that it might shed some light on all the complexities of international relations in southeastern and central Europe, a region notorious for the variety of its conflicts. I familiarized myself with some of the archival materials. To my great surprise Horthy had written his personal notes in gothic German.

In the spring of 1947 I defended my thesis and was awarded an advanced degree in history—roughly equivalent to a master's degree. Thus my diplomatic education—a degree from the Diplomatic Academy and a postgraduate degree—was completed. Three years at the Diplomatic Academy, introductions to senior Soviet diplomats, daily contacts with alumni, working at the Foreign Ministry, and finally, deteriorating relations with our former allies—all of these factors made me begin to question my prospects in a diplomatic career and postwar international developments. Once again I was facing the question: What next?

2
THE FIRST COLLISIONS OF THE COLD WAR

The Cold War Breeze

After the war the atmosphere began to change rapidly. The death of President Roosevelt was to some extent a turning point in the relations between the two great powers. The Soviet people responded to Roosevelt's death with genuine grief. The Kremlin's attitude to this sad event also showed that the Soviet leadership was unprepared for a change of team in the White House. On the one hand, the Kremlin emphasized the continuation of Roosevelt's policy by the new president, but on the other hand, the Kremlin was clearly disturbed by President Truman's anti-Soviet attitude.

A sharp shift in the relations between the USSR and the United States became obvious during Molotov's trip to Washington in April 1945 and at the conference in San Francisco on the establishment of the UN (May–June 1945). As Kiril Novikov, who accompanied Molotov to Washington told me, Molotov was shocked and dismayed by the conversation with the new American president. Unlike the friendly and open Roosevelt, who received Molotov in the White House in 1942, Truman was very guarded while talking to Molotov. The Kremlin was very displeased with the discontinuance of U.S. shipments to the Soviet Union under Lend-Lease in early May of

1945 as well. The Kremlin placed the responsibility for the deterioration of Soviet-American relations on President Truman.

The future of the postwar world did not seem too bright at this time. Almost everyone, including future Soviet diplomats, shared the opinion that there was more likely to be rivalry than cooperation with our former military allies. This point of view was reaffirmed by Churchill's Iron Curtain speech in Fulton and Stalin's response to it. The Soviet people were encouraged to criticize Americans and British alike, our politicians and teachers labeled the leaders of the United States and Britain as "warmongers" and "imperialists enriching themselves on blood." We did not like these first icy gusts of the Cold War. We frequently discussed the conditions we would have to work under. How will the relations with our former military allies develop? The optimists among us said that the difficulties were only temporary. According to this view, the new and inexperienced people who had come to power (Truman and Burns in America, Attlee and Bevin in Britain) did not understand that a stable peace was only possible through cooperation with the Soviet Union. The orthodox Marxists saw the coming rupture in the relations between the allies as inevitable because of differences in social system between the socialist USSR and the capitalist United States and Britain.

Despite the differences in how we assessed the prospects for international relations, and the prevailing feeling of disappointment at the worsening relations among the allies, no one from my class changed his mind about becoming a diplomat. There were many reasons for such single-mindedness, the main one probably being the desire to learn firsthand about the outside world, which we understood was being untruthfully represented by the powerful Soviet propaganda machine. Throughout the prewar years Soviet leaders, bureaucrats, and the mass media had been convincing people that the USSR was surrounded by hostile capitalist countries. They claimed that the capitalist world was torn by deep internal "contradictions" between a small group of "millionaire-exploiters" and the vast majority of workers, who lived in poverty and deprivation. According to this scenario, the workers under the leadership of its "vanguard"—the Communist Party—were waging a resolute struggle against the capitalist elite. Strikes and revolts were part of everyday life. Such was the picture presented to the Soviet people of life abroad. Internal "contradictions" and the struggle between the classes went hand in hand with external confrontations between capitalist countries. These disputes were impossible to settle in a peaceful way and would inevitably result in the crash of the capitalist system. These concepts were foisted on

Soviet people from an early age and formed the basis of teaching in all educational institutions.

World War II brought about basic changes in the primitive and distorted images that many Soviet people had about life abroad, and this ultimately helped, at least partially, to promote better relations among the allies. Exchanges between governmental and public organizations, far greater in number than in former years, now became possible. But the radical turn in our thinking about the West took place when an avalanche of Soviet people, peasants, workers, intelligentsia, mostly dressed in military uniforms, poured into Europe in the years of the war. They came as POWs and deportees and later as soldiers bringing freedom from fascist domination. Millions of Soviet people came to understand that they had been deceived for decades. Life in European capitalist countries did not appear as bad as it had been painted in the Soviet Union. The fact that ordinary workers and peasants, not just "millionaire exploiters," had higher living standards than in the USSR left the strongest impression. Soviet peasants dared not dream of owning the farms that many European farmers owned. The representatives of the "most progressive political system" were amazed to discover that in the countries of "rotting capitalism" communal apartments shared by several families where an entire family lived in a single room were virtually unknown. And finally, the majority of Soviet people who did not act as conquerors while abroad were not treated with animosity and hostility. Indeed, many POWs and displaced persons who ended up in the countries of the "hostile capitalist world" found help and sympathy. Soviet soldiers were often greeted as liberators from the fascist yoke with joy, open hearts, and hospitality.

Consequently, one major result of the war was the simple fact that it stirred an awakening among the Soviet people. Returning home after the war, POWs, repatriated persons, and soldiers openly and often eagerly told the truth about life in the West. Later, when they were severely punished for "worshiping the foreign," they could only whisper the truth.

The situation was somewhat different for those of us who were students at the Diplomatic Academy. As young people starting out in life, we had been brainwashed with Marxist-Leninist dogmas and did not want to believe that life could be better "over there" than it was in our socialist motherland. A few were content with the old dogmas. They preferred to treat the truthful testimony about life in other countries as fantasy and fiction. There was one thing, however, we all agreed on—we all wanted to see for ourselves what life was like "over there," what was good about it and what was bad.

Working on Stalin's Assignment

After I had completed my doctoral work in 1947, I expected a job offer from the ministry, most likely to work in the Hungarian section of the Balkan Countries' Department. Time passed but there were no offers. The head of the department, Lavrishchev, avoided me. My friends in the department shrugged their shoulders, saying that there was nothing they could do to help. There was no point in calling Dekanozov because by this time he was already having problems with the leadership, and his dismissal from the ministry was imminent. Help came from Vladimir Khvostov, who headed the Archive Department of the MFA at that time. He was appointed to this post shortly before I finished my dissertation, and had many ideas on how to reorganize the work and structure of the Archive by transforming it into one of the important departments of the ministry. With this in mind he sought out young staff, in particular people whom he knew personally. I was among them. Before working in the MFA, Khvostov had headed the Diplomatic Academy for a brief time and was dean of the department where I was a postgraduate student.

Frankly speaking, the prospect of working in the Archive Department did not please me at all. The archive was considered as one of the least prestigious divisions of the MFA, far from the real operative diplomatic work. Traditionally only pre-retirees, suspended diplomats, and women (who were few in number at the ministry) worked in the archive. But I didn't have any other choice, so I spent two and a half years working there. In the late 1940s the Archive Department was transformed into the Historical-Diplomatic Department, which, along with the usual work of preserving documents, had to prepare various historical reviews for the management of the ministry and the Kremlin. I found the scholarly and research activity of the new department much more interesting and challenging than my previous work. Not only were we given the opportunity to familiarize ourselves with many important diplomatic documents but we were also required to evaluate them. The result of our work was that the department began to publish thematic collections of documents for both public and internal use. Meanwhile, the structure and staffing changed so that more young people were hired as researchers. Many of my colleagues from those years have subsequently made good careers: Igor Zemskov later became Deputy Minister of Foreign Affairs of the USSR; Leonid Kutakov, UN undersecretary-general. David Lashkaradze and Willi Sippols became outstanding philologists and historians. Khvostov himself after heading the department for a couple of years became member of the Collegium, an honor never before granted to an employee of the Archive. Naturally his advancement increased the authority of the Historical–Diplomatic Department and allowed him to obtain senior diplomatic rank for his staff, including myself.

The archival documents, those of the Soviet period in particular, were especially revealing to me—both for what they contained and what they didn't. On the one hand, there were some fascinating reports from Soviet ambassadors and key correspondence from delegations. On the other hand, some of the most important documents of Soviet foreign policy were not represented—decisions of the Politburo, notes from Molotov and Vyshinsky to Stalin and Stalin's replies, records of Stalin's conversations with foreign leaders. In general all documents containing Stalin's comments or decisions were unavailable. Thus it was simply impossible to get a clear picture of the dynamics and mechanism of foreign policy decision-making based on the documents stored at the MFA. Many key documents on Soviet foreign policy were kept in the special archives of the Central Committee of the CPSU, while the others undoubtedly went to the KGB. And I am sure that many important records were never filed anywhere, but disappeared as completely as the individuals they named.

The job Khvostov gave to me was to create an archive for the 1946 Paris Peace Conference. This proved to be instructive, both from the historical point of view and for understanding Stalin's mentality. Most of the archives of the German ministry of foreign affairs were seized by our Western allies with only a small part ending up in the hands of the Red Army. Soon after the war the governments of the United States, Britain, and France approached Moscow with an offer to undertake a joint publication of wartime documents. Knowing that the allies had documents related to Soviet-German relations of 1939–41, including various top secret agreements, Stalin firmly refused to cooperate and tried to prevent the allies from proceeding with publication on their own. When Western governments began publishing a series of documents of the former German ministry of foreign affairs, especially the collection titled "Soviet-Nazi relations, 1939–1941," Moscow took this as an act of hostility toward the Soviet Union and, as such, contrary to the principles governing relations between allies. Stalin gave instructions to "refute" the originators of the action. The MFA was entrusted with the job of preparing a publication showing the Western powers inciting Hitler to start a war against the Soviet Union. It was supposed to be based on archival documents. Vyshinsky headed this work and regularly provided Stalin with progress reports. Khvostov was responsible for the selection and the preparation of documents. Naturally, he made this the centerpiece project of the Historical–Diplomatic Department. Our staff had to put aside all other work for many months and seek out all relevant documents. In the German documents seized by the Red Army we managed to find something that confirmed the existence of confidential contacts between the British, the Americans, and the Germans on the eve of and during the war. However, our findings were hardly impressive, since at times they dealt with unofficial persons.

Therefore, when Vyshinsky summoned us and asked about our progress, we explained our difficulties and frustrations with the lack of Soviet documents, in particular those concerning Soviet-German relations. Vyshinsky was furious and rebuked us for our stupidity and lack of resourcefulness. We could guess that the aim of the publication was to deny Soviet-German cooperation and believed that the Soviet archives could prove that. Nevertheless, after having seen the documents Stalin decided that the publication would probably not achieve the desired effect and therefore ordered us to prepare a brochure. This order was carried out by a group of MFA staff and journalists, who under Stalin's careful scrutiny, produced a report titled "History's Falsifiers."

Once the brochure was printed, however, Stalin reviewed a pilot copy before official distribution. While checking the text he discovered a passage claiming that the Soviet government had moved the Soviet borders twenty to thirty kilometers further to the west in 1939–41. In reality the new borders were two to three *hundred* kilometers west of the old ones. Stalin was furious with Khvostov for permitting the book to be printed with this error so he punished him by making him pay for reprinting the brochure. It cost Khvostov 40,000 rubles, which was a significant amount in 1949.

"History's Falsifiers" certainly did nothing to disprove the existence of Soviet-German cooperation in the first years of World War II, a cooperation that to a certain degree assisted Hitler's plans. But it undoubtedly became a guidebook, so to speak, for an army of Soviet propagandists of the Cold War era in their attempts to prove that Hitler had unleashed the war aided and abetted by the Western states.

When Did the Cold War Start?

One can usually trace the beginning of a war to the year, month, day, and even hour. It is impossible, however, to establish the time when the Cold War started. Historians, politicians, and journalists all have their own opinions on the subject. Some associate its beginning with the Yalta Conference (February 1945) and the intervention of Soviet troops in Eastern Europe, others with the atomic bombing of Hiroshima and Nagasaki in August 1945, and yet others associate it with Churchill's Iron Curtain speech in 1946. One thing is clear: the Cold War did not start overnight. The second half of the 1940s represented a transition from equivocal and generally successful cooperation between the USSR, the United States, and Britain, to a confrontational roller coaster, interrupted from time to time by periods of détente.

The transition to a cold war required certain transformations in the mentality of the Soviet people, who were accustomed to regarding the Americans and British as allies and friends during World War II. Suddenly the Russians were told that the United States and Britain (their "ruling circles," of course) were pursuing policies that were hostile to the Soviet Union. Such a shift in viewpoint was especially difficult for diplomats, who had worked for four years to develop and strengthen allied relations. Now they were expected to do an about-face and oppose their former allies. Ivan Maisky, Gromyko, Gusev, Novikov, and others, who, during the war, within the framework of various bilateral and trilateral negotiations succeeded in producing mutually acceptable solutions to many complex problems with the representatives of the United States and Britain, now had to steer away from agreement. To be honest, I never heard any complaints about the new diplomacy of confrontation from my senior colleagues, either at meetings or in private conversations, but I could sense a certain nostalgia for the "good old days" of friendship and cooperation.

To be sure, there were some fruitful efforts at cooperation in the early postwar years. Among them was the development of peace treaties with the former German allies—Italy, Romania, Hungary, Bulgaria, and Finland (Paris Peace Conference in 1946). In a year and a half it had been possible to achieve a compromise on particularly intricate territorial, political, economic, and reparation issues involving the five countries located in various European regions, including the potentially explosive Balkans. The resolution of issues affecting the fate of Trieste, the future of the Italian colonies, and the demarcation of the border between Bulgaria and Greece was an invaluable accomplishment. It would be wrong to say, therefore, that none of the negotiating parties made any concessions. However, one cannot deny that confrontation and disruption came to dominate the relations of the Soviet Union with its wartime allies. Calls to "rebuff the aggressive policy of the imperialist states" were heard again and again in the speeches of Soviet leaders. Senior diplomats acted accordingly.

And at the same time I cannot say that the Kremlin's decision to break with its allies was a hasty one. Even the Marshall Plan of 1948, which the United States proposed as a means of helping to rebuild the economies of wartime Europe, was a subject of debate inside the Kremlin. The principal agenda item at one of the meetings of the MFA in April 1947 was the Marshall Plan. Many speakers mentioned certain positive features of the American plan. They emphasized that the U.S. offer to all European countries to participate in the plan was attractive in some ways, although it was felt that the exclusion of the USSR, the state that had suffered most from the war, was a clear sign that the plan was anti-Soviet in intent.

At first in May–June 1947 it seemed that the Soviet Union still had an opportunity to participate in the American project, as was demonstrated by the very fact that it was agreed to discuss this plan at the meeting of the Soviet, British, and French ministers of foreign affairs in Paris, as well as, some elements of Molotov's speech at this meeting. However, when Molotov reported on the Marshall Plan to the Politburo, Stalin resolutely opposed it. Toward the end of the Paris meeting Molotov declared that the USSR would not take any part in the American program of assistance to Europe. Later Molotov admitted to having doubts about this decision: "At first," he recalled, "we, in the MFA wanted to propose that all socialist countries should participate in it [Marshall Plan], but soon realized that this would be a bad thing. They [the capitalist states] were trying to bring us into their family, one in which we would, however, be the poor relations; we would become their dependents, but without anything to show for it."

The basis of the Soviet Union's decision was that "domestic measures and national efforts of every country rather than expectations of foreign aid" were crucial to the revival of European countries. The Paris meeting of the three foreign ministers was one of many that would end on the strident note of Molotov's resounding "nyet." The refusal of Moscow to participate in the Marshall Plan was followed by an extensive propaganda campaign in the Soviet Union in which the plan was referred to as "the American plan to enslave Europe." The Soviet response to the Marshall Plan was one of the turning points in the Cold War.

German troops had left terrible devastation behind them. Many towns and villages of the Soviet Union lay in ruins. Scarce supplies were rationed. The restoration of the destroyed economy meant a tremendous draining of human and material resources. "Labor Sundays" were held in all institutions, including the MFA. Large numbers of the ministry's staff went out to surrounding towns and villages, where we participated in construction projects.

At the same time, the return to peacetime life and the opening up of vast opportunities for constructive activity were accompanied by a revival of Stalin's old methods of governing the country. The Communist Party's resolutions on philosophy, biology, physiology, linguistics, political economy, the magazines *Zvezda* and *Leningrad*, and the movie *The Big Life* not only did serious internal damage but also had a negative effect on the Soviet Union internationally.

Diplomats were afraid of being accused of every deadly sin, including friendly relations with foreigners, especially the Americans and British. These fears revived memories of the 1930s, the dark times of the struggle against the "enemies of the people." The trumped-up "Leningrad Affair," which lead to the execution of prominent Soviet political leaders; the "Doctors Affair," which targeted a large group of eminent, predominantly Jewish, physicians; the harsh measures against persons deported by the Nazis during the war; and finally, the arrests in the Ministry of Foreign Affairs of Deputy Ministers Lozovsky and Maisky were all signs of a return to the bad old days.

Although the arrests in the ministry involved the older generation, none of us young diplomats felt immune to reprisals. I remember how frightened I was when a friend called from Tbilisi and told me that my parents had been arrested and exiled. I frantically dialed the number of my parents and was immensely relieved to hear the voice of my mother, who explained to me that they were safe but that our neighbors (also called Israelyan) had been exiled.

These new ideological purges and reprisals worried those of us who were starting out on our diplomatic careers. None of us worked directly with Maisky, Lozovsky, or other disgraced diplomats; some of us had never even met them. Nevertheless, in private we condemned their arrests. We couldn't believe that the people who had contributed to the victory over fascism, who had been participants in key diplomatic events during the war that had done so much to enhance Soviet international authority, could be traitors and spies. The issue of contacts with foreigners especially worried us. We frequently asked how we could successfully work in the diplomatic field if any encounter with a foreigner might be considered a criminal offense. We were not at all happy at the prospect of staying in an embassy and not associating with those around us. As the situation inside the country deteriorated, frank conversation at the MFA became rare, and then died out altogether. We continued meeting and socializing but avoided "dangerous issues." We recognized that sometimes even the walls had ears.

Thus both the international standing and the internal affairs of the Soviet Union deteriorated badly in the early postwar years. This was the exact opposite of what most of us had looked forward to and dreamed of during the war years. All the same, my work in the Historical–Diplomatic Department went on quite normally, even successfully. In the autumn of 1949 Khvostov offered me the position of head of management of the Scientific-Publishing Department and proposed me for promotion to the diplomatic rank of first secretary, second degree. I received the promotion, but Deputy Minister Fedor Gusev, in charge of personnel, refused to approve it. Khvostov was upset, and so was I. Again, I surmised that my father's letter to Dekanozov, who by this time had been purged from the MFA, had played its part.

The grim atmosphere in Moscow, dissatisfaction with my job, and Gusev's refusal to grant my promotion, as well as a succession of personal problems, prompted me to make a change. In 1950 I moved to Yerevan, the capital of Armenia.

Home in Armenia

One of the main considerations behind my decision to move to Armenia was the ethnic situation within the Soviet Union. I do not intend to give an in-depth analysis of the problem here, but I do want to give a few examples, drawn from my own experience.

As I have already mentioned, I was born in Tbilisi. This wonderful city, which in the days of my childhood was called Tiflis (many called it the Paris of the Caucasus), was ethnically diverse. It had an Armenian district called Avlabar, an Azeri district (Maidan), and a German district (Didubey). In the 1920s and early 1930s Tbilisi was the capital not only of Georgia but of the whole Caucasian Federation. This explained the friendly relations among the different communities both in the capital and in Georgia as a whole.

I attended a German primary school in Tbilisi. Most of the pupils were German, but we also had Georgian, Armenian, Russian, Jewish, Polish, Lithuanian, and Greek children. The same was true for the secondary school, where I continued my education. In all my years in school I do not remember one fight or argument caused by ethnic differences. My best friends were Vladislav Urbanovich, a Lithuanian, and Surchai Gadzhiev, an Azeri. We remained very close friends throughout their lives. The foundations of our friendship were laid in our childhood. I am sorry and embarrassed because today such relationships between Armenians and Azeris have now become impossible because of the events in Nagorno-Karabakh.

There were also many ethnic groups represented in the Moscow Medical Institute, where I continued my education, yet I did not detect any ethnic tensions among the students. We, the representatives of the soviet and autonomous republics, who were known as "national minorities," enjoyed certain privileges at universities. We were given priority in dormitories, stipends, and so on. Any discrimination against the "national minorities" was regarded as a crime.

However, this situation began to change during World War II and its aftermath. The war had different consequences for different peoples of the Soviet Union. The bloodiest battles took place on Russian soil (the battles of Moscow, Stalingrad, Kursk, and Orel), and Russia suffered the greatest destruction and casualties. The Caucasian and Asian republics, however, were not exposed to the full horror of war. This led to certain claims that it was Russia and the Russians that the Germans were fighting. Hitlerite propaganda also asserted that Germany differentiated among the Soviet peoples. Stalin's establishment of the Orders of Suvorov, Kutuzov, and Nakhimov (famous Russian generals and admirals) was regarded by many as also suggesting that the war was being fought against the Russians. All of this prompted some people, principally from the non-Slavic nations, to question the very involvement of their people in the war. Why should they sacrifice their lives if it was the Russians who were the Germans' enemies? Why should they sacrifice their lives if the war was targeted at the Russians? Such an attitude took various forms. I would like to share one episode from my experience.

In 1942 our unit was reinforced with recruits from Kazakhstan. They were teenagers, mainly from peasant families, who naturally had no clue about warfare. Many of them didn't even speak Russian. It was difficult for them to adjust to the hardships of military life, to a new climate, and to unfamiliar military duties. Soon after their arrival our unit was sent to fight a German mountain division in the area of Klukhor Mountain in the Caucasus.

Once two of the Kazakh rookies were sent on a reconnaissance mission. After some time one of them came running back. Terrified he said that his comrade was killed in a skirmish with the Germans. The commanding officer sent a group of experienced soldiers to the spot. When they returned, they reported that there was no sign of Germans in the designated area, that the landscape could not allow for the soldier to have been killed by a sniper, and that they had found a casing of a bullet shot from the gun of the survivor. The latter, when interrogated, confessed that he and his comrade had faked a skirmish. The idea was to inflict light wounds on each other so that they might be sent to a hospital and then home. Tragically, however, the inexperienced warrior killed his friend with the first shot. The soldier was immediately court-martialed and sentenced to death. As a military doctor I had to certify the death after the firing squad, which included Kazakhs as well as other nationalities, had executed the so-called murderer. His body was then buried. Ever since the two young Kazakhs from a faraway village have rested on the slopes of Klukhor Mountain.

Stalin's 1945 speech in which he praised the Russians for their contribution to the victory and underlined their special role in the war only made matters worse. After this speech the Russian Federation received the nickname of "Big Brother." The rest of the "brotherly family of nations" was supposed to follow its lead. Russians were given preference when it came to promotions and raises. During one of my meetings with Deputy Minister Dekanozov, he suddenly asked me if the Caucasians were being mistreated at the MFA. I couldn't think of any incidents or examples, so I avoided a straight answer. However, the very question showed that the problem existed and that the leadership was aware of it.

So in 1950, I felt the need to live again among Armenians in my motherland. I spoke with my parents, who were living in Tbilisi, and they were eager for me to come home. My father was able to land a position as head of the pediatric department of the Yerevan Medical Institute, and I was invited to teach at the Yerevan University. Our move was difficult in all respects. I, for one, was not fluent in Armenian. My parents, who were Armenians, spoke Russian at home and belonged to the group known as Russian-speaking Armenians. My mother was born in a Georgian town of Gori, which was famous as Stalin's birthplace. When she was older, I once heard her say, "It's a pity that we didn't make friends with Soso [Stalin's nickname], the son of our drunken neighbor Dzhugashvili." "Thank God, that you didn't," I replied. "The young Soso might have later remembered his rich neighbor's daughter, and we might now be in prison!"

Life in Armenia remains a vivid memory. Yerevan was under major construction. Houses and even whole districts were being built overnight. Old clay huts, so typical of the city, were being replaced with modern buildings. That period of Armenian history was marked by a wave of Armenians returning to their homeland. Tens of thousands of Armenians came from all over the world, including the United States. However, the leadership was not prepared to receive and accommodate so many people, so they cut off the influx, and this in turn led to a later exodus. For us, however, in those years, it was a joyful reunion with our homeland.

Our neighbors were a renowned poet and classic of Armenian literature Avetik Isaakian and the great artist Martiros Sarian. Their company and our association with many other outstanding people filled me with a feeling of pride in the people, who had succeeded in preserving our cultural heritage. I soon made new friends with histories like my own. Robert Khachatrian and Levon Manasarian were from Baku, Sergei Gasparian was from Nagorno-Karabakh. They were all well-educated and civilized young people who had decided to devote themselves to serving Armenia. In time all three of them made highly successful careers and reached ministerial positions.

A closer look at the work of the Armenian foreign ministry confirmed the dismal state of this institution. The minister, who at the same time was Armenia's prime minister, never visited his foreign ministry. Nor did he ever have anything to do with foreign relations for the simple reason that Armenia did not have any. I taught the history of Soviet foreign policy at the university's Department of International Relations but the department was dying because young people in Armenia realized there was no future in a career in international affairs in Armenia and would not enroll in the department.

In 1952 I received a letter from Moscow offering me a transfer to the Diplomatic Academy as deputy dean. I asked for time to think it over. My family in Yerevan thought that I should take the job; my friends told me to refuse the offer. They believed that my place was in Armenia and said that they would consider my departure as an act of treason that I would regret for the rest of my life. Having considered all the pros and cons I decided to return to Moscow. My main reason for leaving the warm and sunny land of my ancestors was the realization that I was of no use in Armenia—either as an international relations expert or as a diplomat. To stay in Yerevan meant that I would have to acquire a new profession or go back to medicine after an eight-year hiatus. I was not ready for this. And so, after a two-year stay in Yerevan, we returned to Moscow, which was to be my home for many years to come.

3
STALIN IS DEAD. WHAT NEXT?

The Training of Cold Warriors

In 1950, after two years of teaching at Yerevan University, I returned to Moscow, where I spent the next seventeen years at the Diplomatic Academy training Soviet diplomats, the next generation of cold warriors. I was senior lecturer, professor, and deputy dean of the Department of Historical and Diplomatic Sciences—the leading department within the Diplomatic Academy For the last six years I headed the department.

The teaching was based purely on Marxist-Leninist dogma, and every effort was made to ensure that orthodoxy was maintained. For instance, teachers would visit each other's classes, often without prior notice, in order to monitor the teaching. After the lectures, lengthy discussions were held, often focusing on ideological issues. The goal, of course, was to maintain a consistent level of ideological purity, but the ultimate effect was to unnerve professors, thereby reducing the value of their teaching and the overall learning experience of the students. In his turn the "inspector" had to give an evaluation of the lecture from the point of view of its ideological content. Frankly, the whole process was painful to observe. According to instructions the inspector's report had to contain critical remarks, but each of us understood that any criticism of ideological content could have dire consequences for the lecturer, and, for that matter, any one of us in the room at that time. Unfortunately, even the students participated in this process, for they were encouraged to critique the teaching methodology of their professors. Consequently, the untutored judgments of junior students frequently influenced the fate of a teacher.

Further contributing to the general air of suspicion and dogmatism was the fact that the provost had radio equipment with which he could listen secretly to any lecture in any classroom of the academy. Ultimately this reduced the level of teaching, making it dry and boring. Later in life I was exposed to the educational systems of many countries, including the United States, where I myself taught, and nowhere did I encounter a practice so demeaning and ultimately so detrimental to the learning process.

While teaching I started to write articles and reviews on international issues for various newspapers, magazines, and broadcasts of the Soviet Radio Committee and TASS. These were purely propagandistic pieces and had no scholarly or literary value. Nevertheless, everyone was pleased. The print and radio media were happy because they knew that the author, as an official of the Ministry of Foreign Affairs, would not deviate from the "guidelines of the CPSU Central Committee and the Soviet government." Meanwhile, the author was happy because he received a decent honorarium. In the end, the only ones who went away unhappy were the consumers, that is, the readers and listeners, who knew that they were reading or listening to obvious rubbish. No one, of course, was willing to blow the whistle, so the practice went on unchallenged.

I also started to write scholarly articles on Hungarian history. In the late 1940s and early 1950s the Kremlin was looking to make Hungary into an ally, so Moscow was in need of scholars who could write knowledgeably about Hungary. Consequently, the few of us who were Hungarian specialists were swamped with offers to write articles and books. I authored and coauthored a number of books, including the textbook *Recent Hungarian History*, which I coauthored with my former postgraduate student Leonid Nezhinsky.

From the mid-1950s on, however, my scholarly interests began to change. Because of my work at the academy, I became preoccupied with problems of foreign policy and international relations. Already holding the equivalent of a master's degree in history, I decided to take the next step—to write and defend a doctoral dissertation in history, knowing that this was a good move for my career. So, when it came time to choose a topic for my dissertation I chose the Paris Peace Conference of 1946. I trace my interest in this topic back to my work in the archives of the Ministry of Foreign Affairs, where I found a substantial set of documents from the conference. The Diplomatic Academy Research Council unanimously approved my topic, and I had five years to complete my work and produce a manuscript. However, during my work an event occurred that appeared to have nothing to do with my research but ultimately prevented me from completing it.

The event involved Molotov, who had headed the Soviet delegation at the Paris Peace Conference. Naturally, when describing the Soviet position at the conference I referred to and quoted Molotov as needed. However, when it came time for me to defend my dissertation before the Research Council, Molotov had just been purged from the Communist Party in 1957. On the eve of my defense the Diplomatic Academy director Mikhail Silin invited me in. He said, that he had serious doubts about my dissertation. He explained that my frequent references to Molotov, who had been expelled from the Party along with Vyshinsky, who had been tried and convicted (and was already dead), would cause, as he put it, "public surprise and misunderstanding." All my attempts to convince Silin that the subject of my dissertation was a historical event and that therefore I couldn't possibly change the names of the people involved, were unavailing. "Call the Central Committee," he said, refusing to allow me to defend the dissertation without special instructions from the communist leadership.

I followed Silin's advice and called one of the "instructors" from the Central Committee's Department of Propaganda. Before I could explain my problem he interrupted me and said that he was well aware of the situation, so that I knew that Silin had spoken with him. "Comrade Israelyan," he continued, "I have a question for you. Couldn't you find a theme for your dissertation somewhere in the entire history of international relations, where you wouldn't have to mention people who have compromised themselves in the eyes of the Soviet people and the Communist Party? Or can it be that you are in sympathy with the disgraced members of this anticommunist group?" What could I say? Certainly I could find another theme, but I had already spent years researching and writing a voluminous dissertation on a topic for which I had been given approval from the start. Understanding, of course, that there was no point in continuing this conversation, I could only agree with him and say good-bye. I did just that.

Colleagues with whom I shared my thoughts sympathized with me and advised me to keep the manuscript until "better times." I managed to publish two articles based on the research, but I was careful to choose topics where I could avoid mentioning Molotov and Vyshinsky. Later I stored the manuscript in the attic of my summer residence and awaited those "better times," but unfortunately they never came. Many years later I sold the summer house, without having time to remove the contents of the attic. The new owner of the house, assuming that I didn't need any of those things, threw them all out, including the manuscript.

World War II in the Distorting Mirror of the Cold War

In the early 1950s I taught a special course at the Diplomatic Academy titled "The Diplomatic History of World War II." The more I read on the subject to prepare for my lectures, the more interested I grew. For one thing, I had taken part in the war so I could appreciate at first hand many of the issues involved, but I also became intrigued by the fact that never before had there been such extensive and effective cooperation between the United States, the Soviet Union, and Great Britain. Never before had the vital interests of these three countries been so closely aligned, as in the war years. After the war, however, the relationships among these former allies, the leading countries of the anti-Hitler coalition, had grown increasingly acrimonious, and the Cold War was now at its height. So I came to realize how important it was to remind people of past cooperation in the hope that we might find opportunities in the future to revive the policy of cooperation, which clearly had justified itself during the war. Consequently, much of the work I have published over the years in the Soviet Union and abroad has been devoted to the subject of Soviet-British-American cooperation during World War II, beginning with my new doctoral dissertation, which I started after dropping the old one, and successfully defended in 1960. To this day I am deeply convinced that the diplomacy of World War II remains one of the most interesting and important chapters in the history of world diplomacy. And although I have reconsidered many of my judgments and conclusions over the years, the main conclusion I draw remains the same. If cooperation between countries with differing systems was possible in World War II, when the world was on the brink of total devastation, then cooperation was still possible, especially in the face of nuclear war and global conflicts that could result in the unprecedented destruction of human life. What is needed is for all peaceful states, regardless of race, ethnicity, or political regime, to unite in the interests of peace and humanity.

Unfortunately, I think there was a tendency during the Cold War for the West to diminish the importance of cooperation among the "Big Three." I have seen many books filled with references to the "strange" or "unnatural" union, about the "back-stabbing" Soviets, about "the Yalta arrangement," about Roosevelt's "capitulation," and so on. Certainly, the Soviet-Anglo-American Union was unusual in that it embraced countries with different social regimes, and certainly there were problems in the relationship, but has there ever been an instance of international cooperation where the parties did not have agendas of their own? What is most significant is not the differences among the allies but the sheer fact that the coalition achieved its main goal—victory in the most bloody and divisive war in the history of humanity. Therefore, as someone who fought in the war and a historian I have always been dismayed by those who choose to see only the bad side of the anti-Hitler coalition.

Most recently, in 1994, when I was living in the United States and nearly twenty monarchs, heads of state, and prime ministers representing the anti-Hitler coalition joined thirty thousand veterans of the Second World War in commemorating the fiftieth anniversary of the D-Day landing, I felt proud for the American veterans and happy that their heroism was being recognized, although I could not understand why there were no representatives of Russia, or even any Soviet veterans. After all, the decision to launch Operation Overlord marked the opening of the Second Front against the Nazis. Stalin, believing that the Germans would transfer their divisions from the Eastern Front, announced that the Soviet Army would launch a large-scale offensive simultaneously with the allied landing. The decision was approved by the Big Three at the Tehran Conference in 1943.

On the tenth of June—four days after D-Day—Soviet forces began their offensive against the Nazi troops north of Leningrad. A total of 130 divisions took part in this offensive, which caught the Nazis in a pincer movement. I did not participate in this offensive, but many of my schoolmates and friends did. Some of them lost their lives, and their names are now listed among the 27 million Soviets—Russians and Ukrainians, Armenians and Georgians, Kazakhs and Jews—killed fighting our common enemy: fascism.

President Roosevelt was impressed by the Soviet offensive. "The speed of the thrust of your armies," he wrote in July 1944 to Stalin, "is amazing and I wish that I could visit you to see how you are able to maintain your communications and supplies to the advancing troops." Soviet advances cheered and encouraged those engaged in the cross-Channel operation. Their feeling was echoed by General Eisenhower in a letter to Averell Harriman, the ambassador to Moscow: "I have been tracing Red Army progress on my map," he wrote. "Naturally I got a tremendous thrill out of the rate at which they are demolishing the enemy's fighting power."

Nevertheless, the Soviet veterans who, according to Eisenhower, had demolished the enemy's fighting power, were not invited to Normandy in the summer of 1994. Once again, I fear that the specter of the Cold War has clouded the memory of Soviet-American cooperation. The dwindling number of World War II veterans deserves greater respect and consideration, regardless of nationality.

Fruitless Theoretical Exercises

In 1960 I was appointed dean of the historical and diplomatic sciences department of the Diplomatic Academy. It was perhaps the most pretentious departmental titles in the entire Soviet Union. No one could explain what the label "historical and diplomatic sciences" really meant. But since my predecessor and scholarly mentor, Khvostov, had devised the title, I saw no reason to change it. At the same time I decided to make one significant change—to establish a specialty within the department, focusing on the theoretical foundations of Soviet foreign policy. It seemed to me that not only did we have to teach future diplomats the history of Soviet politics, we also had to provide them with a true understanding of foreign relations. Some of my colleagues were skeptical, but on the whole they accepted this new approach.

During my years as a diplomat, Soviet foreign policy as a rule was called "Lenin's foreign policy" in official documents and in learned journals. This was not only a tribute to the founder of the Soviet State; it also served as a constant reminder that Lenin had developed the basics and methods of Soviet foreign policy. Therefore, I made a point of carefully studying his numerous publications, articles, and speeches on foreign policy matters. (Thankfully, it was easy to find publications devoted to Lenin and questions of "external policy.") Nonetheless, I failed to find in Lenin's works a precisely formulated concept of Soviet foreign policy. What I did find was a set of varying, at times contradictory, statements about the inevitability of the near collapse of capitalism, about the necessity of rendering assistance to the "world proletariat" in its struggle to overthrow "global bourgeoisie," and about the value of developing trade with the same bourgeoisie. Lenin helped Hungarian and German communists in the proclamation of Soviet Hungary and Soviet Bavaria while, at the same time, recognizing the bourgeois governments of Poland, Finland, Estonia, and other countries, formed from fragments of the Russian empire. In other words, he came to agreements with them all, something which indicated to me the clear need for pragmatism in foreign policy. Lenin knew as well as anyone the complexity of internal and external conditions when devising a foreign policy that could work in the real world.

In my opinion, therefore, the department needed some sort of theoretical underpinnings in order to develop a workable Soviet foreign policy. Some in the department disagreed with me, believing that the basics of foreign policy were clearly elaborated and formulated at congresses of the CPSU and that students could learn all they needed to know from a comprehensive study of their documents. I, too, studied these documents and learned much from them. I even published a few articles about them. In these articles, I contended that Soviet foreign policy was based on three main principles. The first was the principle of proletarian or socialist internationalism, according to which the USSR should render extensive help to those states that were following the path of socialism and to all communist parties that were struggling against bourgeois governments. The second principle was that of anti-imperialist solidarity, by which the Soviet Union should band together with national liberation movements acting against the capitalist West; namely, those in colonies and in independent countries in Asia, Africa, and Latin America. And, finally, the third principle was that of peaceful coexistence, which called for the development of mutually beneficial relations between the Soviet Union and the capitalist states in the interests of preventing nuclear war.

I also tried to avoid certain of Lenin's principles, which he had proclaimed in the early years of the Revolution, because they no longer seemed to apply. Among these were his refusal to conduct secret diplomacy and conclude secret agreements and his rejection of annexations and reparations from the peoples who are compelled to pay for the "crimes of the bourgeoisie." It was clear to me that these principles had been violated a number of times since then, most notably in the confidential protocols of the 1939 Molotov-Ribbentrop pact, the secret agreements on the Far East (signed by Stalin, Roosevelt, and Churchill in 1945), and the Soviet annexation of significant territories during World War II, including lands that had never belonged to Russia. To stand by these principles was to deny the reality of current Soviet foreign policy.

My "theoretical" articles did not attract any special attention, even though some were published in socialist countries. The reason, frankly, was that the ideas I was putting forward were hardly new to me. In most cases I was repeating, at best systematizing, statements and positions I had gleaned from Soviet officials and documents. Everything looked fine on paper, my own articles included, and at times it even sounded convincing. Only years later did I learn from experience how inconsistent and contradictory the Soviet foreign policy principles were in practice.

The 1950s and 1960s were eventful decades in the history of the Soviet state and of the lives of all Soviet citizens, including my own. Stalin's death was, undoubtedly, one of the most significant events, in that it changed the course of the future. Early in March 1953, when the Soviet press officially announced that Stalin had fallen ill, most people understood that we were about to lose the leader who had ruled our country for almost thirty years. Never before had reports of his state of health been published. During Stalin's illness Moscow became strangely quiet. Theaters, movies, restaurants, and other gathering places were suddenly empty as people stayed late at work, listening to the radio with colleagues and speaking in hushed voices about what would happen when Stalin died. The Diplomatic Academy was no exception. I remember teachers and students gathering in the main auditorium, looking at the loudspeaker as if expecting an announcement at any moment. After work, we all hurried home to listen to the radio. Like everyone else, I was at a loss, unable to guess what might come next.

Stalin's death was announced on March 5. A letter from the Central Committee of the CPSU, the Soviet government, and the Presidium of the Supreme Council was addressed to every Soviet citizen. It read: "The heart of Joseph Vissarionovich Stalin, Lenin's brother-in-arms, brilliant upholder of his cause, and wise leader and teacher of the Communist Party and of the Soviet people, has beaten for the last time. . . . The immortal name of Stalin will live forever in the hearts of the Soviet people and of all progressive humanity." I rushed to work and went to see Viktor Popov, the deputy director of the academy, who was a close friend. Without saying a word, we embraced and wept. After a long silence I asked him: "What will happen?" but he only shrugged his shoulders in response.

A few days later we went to a mass meeting called in connection with

Stalin's funeral in Red Square, and I remember the scene around me: people were crying and shouting "What a tragedy! What a great tragedy." It was hard to imagine anyone not sharing this feeling. Khrushchev opened the meeting, and Beria was one of the speakers. "The enemies of the Soviet state," Beria said, "hope and expect that the terrible loss we have suffered will lead to conflict and panic in our ranks. But their hopes are in vain, and they are in for a cruel disappointment. Our unity is unshakable." (Ironically, four months later Beria was arrested and eventually executed, while Malenkov, Molotov, and others were ousted from the Communist Party.)

The following episode well conveys the atmosphere of the time. A Diplomatic Academy student from the Moscow suburbs was playing cards with a group of young people on the train home one day. Although they were not actually disturbing anyone, under the circumstances their harmless game of cards seemed blasphemous. Someone informed the secretary of the Diplomatic Academy communist committee that "while the Soviet people were mourning the Great Leader, a certain student of the academy was playing cards." Many students and professors were outraged at such behavior, and a special assembly was called, where he was subjected to public condemnation. I am ashamed to admit that I was one of the accusers. "If your father had died, would you be playing cards?" I asked indignantly.

In Moscow the mourning was widespread and seemingly heartfelt. Today many of my contemporaries would like to forget that they too shed tears over the death of the greatest dictator and tyrant in the history of humanity, someone who had ordered the extermination of millions of people. As for myself, I am ashamed of my tears. I suppose I could claim that I did not know at the time the full extent of his crimes, and to a degree this is true, but this is really poor consolation for me. I may not have known everything about Stalin but I certainly knew of his cruelty and inhumanity to his own family long before his death. But I chose to view him in the light of false glory, a glory created by his colleagues and entourage, and unfortunately also by the outstanding political leaders of the world, including Roosevelt, Churchill, Hopkins, and De Gaulle.

Stalin's Unfortunate Descendants

During my early days as a medical student, and then as a student of the academy, I lived in Moscow with the family of an engineer named Mikhail Guzikov, whose wife, Rosalia, was the sister of Yuliya Dzhugashvili, née

Meltser. Yuliya's husband, Yakov, was Stalin's older son from his first wife, Katerina (Keke) Svanidze. The sisters, Rosalia and Yuliya, were very close. Both were beautiful Jewish girls, cheerful, full of energy, and wonderful conversationalists. Yuliya frequently visited Rosalia, sometimes with Yakov. Being extremely sociable and open, Rosalia would tell us stories about the life of the Dzhugashvilis. Moreover, I attended some family celebrations of the Guzikovs and the Dzhugashvilis, thus becoming an accidental witness to the life of Stalin's older son.

When I first time met Yakov I was amazed by the fact that he shared with his father not only certain distinct facial features but also an uncanny likeness of voice, intonation, and manner of speaking. Though Stalin had spent a great part of his life in Russia and among Russians, he nevertheless spoke with a strong Georgian accent. His accent, however, was not typically Georgian; it was original and peculiar only to him, often referred to as the "Stalin accent." Especially characteristic was the style of speaking: slow, emotionless, and marked by brief statements, questions, and answers—absolutely nothing like the temperamental, fast speech of the Georgians. In many ways, his style was so distinctive that it was easy to imitate. I remember once, long after Stalin's death, doing my own imitation while reading a lecture. The students thought I sounded exactly like him. Yakov, however, did not imitate his father's voice: he inherited it. But every time I heard Yakov speak, I would get goose bumps for it seemed that Stalin was in the room.

In most other ways, Yakov was nothing like his father. He was a soft, kind, and sympathetic man, and he never took advantage of his name (unlike his younger brother, Vasily), for he was modest, even a little bit shy. His relations with his father had been strained ever since childhood. Stalin was dissatisfied with his son's academic achievements and openly voiced his disapproval of his personal life. Feeling his father's hostility and increasingly overwhelmed by personal difficulties, Yakov attempted suicide. Fortunately he was unsuccessful, but even in this failed attempt his father was merciless. Matters grew worse until eventually Stalin drove Yakov from home and forbade him to live in Moscow. Yakov then moved to Leningrad.

In the early 1930s Stalin permitted Yakov to return to Moscow. Why he did so is not entirely clear, but it was then that Yakov decided to marry Yuliya. Stalin received the news calmly but he refused to see the bride. He also set one condition, that his daughter-in-law must give up her career as a ballerina. Once Yakov told me that his father, when he learned that Yuliya was a dancer, expressed his displeasure at the fact that his daughter-in-law, who bore the name of Dzhugashvili should be "dangling her legs in front of the public." When the newlyweds had their daughter Gulya, the grandfather asked that she be brought to the Kremlin. Yakov said that Stalin was very pleased with the new, third generation. Later Stalin had many grandchildren from his other children, but, according to Yuliya, as a rule he did not wish to see them. Gulya was the exception. Only many years after Stalin's death did I learn that Yakov had a son by his first wife. Yevgeny Dzhugashvili, heir to the dynasty, tried to play a role in the political life of new Russia.

When Yakov returned to Moscow, he worked as an engineer at a Moscow factory, but soon, on Stalin's orders, he entered the Artillery Academy. Yakov explained that with war just around the corner, his father wanted his sons to be in the military. Yakov dared not disobey his father, though neither he nor Yuliya was happy about it.

Stalin's true attitude toward his son was displayed during the war. Yakov was among the first to find himself in the front lines after Germany's attack on the Soviet Union. He certainly could have used his name to get himself transferred to the rear or to a safe sinecure at headquarters but that was not in Yakov's nature. As the commanding officer of a howitzer battery he was in the thick of the fighting from the very start of the war, but for him and many other Soviet soldiers the war lasted only a few days. His entire unit was surrounded and captured by the Germans in July 1941. One can only imagine Hitler's joy when he found out that Stalin's son had been taken prisoner. We learned about it from leaflets, which the Germans dropped from airplanes. I do not remember the exact wording used in the leaflets, but they were clearly meant to convince us that Yakov had voluntarily surrendered to German troops and cooperated with them. (Knowing Yakov as I did, I knew this wasn't true, and I turned out to be right.) When Stalin heard the news, his reaction was one of sheer anger toward his son. He took his anger out on Yakov's family. Yuliya was arrested and spent about two years in an NKVD prison in the Lubyanka in Moscow, while little Gulya together with a nurse lived in one of the governmental summer residences. All communication with her mother was forbidden.

Yuliya was released from prison in April 1943. When I saw her for the first time after her release, I was surprised to see how the time in jail had taken its toll on her; I was struck by how withdrawn, cautious, and timid she had become. No longer was she cheerful and full of energy.

Yuliya explained how she had learned of Yakov's fate. She said that in the first days of the war she had made several attempts to learn about Yakov. She had called the academy, his colleagues, and the Defense Ministry, but she knew that everyone was hiding something from her. Then she decided to call Stalin, but was kept from getting through to him. Svetlana his daughter called him instead. When Stalin told her that Yakov had been captured, he warned Svetlana to say nothing to Yuliya. It was in late August of 1941. Svetlana did as she was told and lied to Yuliya, saying that her father knew nothing. Yuliya felt that Svetlana was hiding the truth and that Yakov had probably been killed in battle. She only found out what had really happened to him after her arrest. Yuliya thought that she had been arrested because Stalin believed that someone had deliberately betrayed Yakov to the Germans and that Yuliya must have been involved in some way.

In prison Yuliya was told that Yakov was being kept in a special camp for high-ranking POWs and had been invited to visit the German High Command—Goering, Himmler, Rosenberg, and others. When I heard this story I wondered if perhaps Yuliya was being fed all these lies to see if she would admit to a "conspiracy," but I have no way of knowing if this was the case. Was there any chance of freeing him from the Germans? Yuliya was convinced that there was. She maintained that the Germans had made several offers to exchange POWs, including Yakov. She did not know the details of these proposals, but she was confident that such offers had been made to Stalin. As for Stalin, he categorically rejected these offers. I can only guess how much truth there was to Yuliya's stories, but when I heard them, I remember thinking what a monster Stalin would have to be not to attempt to rescue his son. I am sure that the same thought must have occurred to Yuliya, but neither of us dared speak our minds.

Yuliya claimed that toward the end of the war Yakov had been liberated by the Red Army and sent to a concentration camp in Siberia on Stalin's orders. I do not know where she heard this story, and my guess is that she chose to accept it because it allowed her to hope that she might eventually be reunited with him. Most likely the sad truth is that after being subjected to torture, interrogations, threats, and blackmail, and afraid that the Nazis would do everything possible to force him to make disloyal statements, Yakov decided to kill himself. On April 14, 1943, he rushed a high-voltage barbed-wire fence and was shot dead by a sentry.

After prison Yuliya was forced to vacate her home on Granovsky Street, so she moved with her daughter into a small apartment in a building that belonged to the KGB. I had left for Armenia, and lost touch with her and Rosalia for some time. In the early 1960s, when the campaign against the "Stalin cult" was in full swing, and I had already returned to the Diplomatic

Academy, I received a call from Yuliya. She needed help. The problem concerned her daughter, Gulya, who by then was a very attractive young woman who had learned French and graduated from the university. Nevertheless, she had become a pariah because of her grandfather. No one wanted to be associated with her, old acquaintances turned away, and she could not make new ones. Yuliya, therefore, was hoping that I would introduce Gulya to some of my friends. She knew that I taught in an exclusively male educational institution, and she thought that, through me, her daughter might get to meet eligible young men. This was something I had never been asked to do, but what could I say? I agreed.

For a long time I thought about the possible candidates and, eventually, came up with one of my colleagues. We had graduated from the Diplomatic Academy together, and he had mastered several foreign languages, including French, was interesting, single, and wanted to marry. Altogether, I couldn't have wished for a better prospect. I remember describing Gulya to him, even though I hadn't seen her for a long time. Maybe I should have said something about her family background and thus prevented a potential embarrassment? I was inexperienced in the matchmaking business so I kept silent.

I told Yuliya about the candidate and boosted him as a potential match. Both mother and daughter approved of my choice. We agreed that Yuliya would invite us to supper, where the introduction would take place. My friend and I arrived on time and with a bouquet of flowers and a box of chocolates. My friend was actually pleased to find that she lived in a KGB house. "Serious people," he muttered at the door to the apartment. They were introduced, and I thought that they liked each other. They started to chat in French, and Yuliya and I went to the kitchen to give them some privacy after supper. In the kitchen we started reminiscing about Yakov and common acquaintances and friends. We could hear laughter and sounds of a lively conversation coming from the next room. We were happy. But suddenly there was total silence, and neither conversation nor laughter could be heard. Having known my friend for many years, I dismissed any "unsavory thoughts" from my mind, certain that he would never try anything untoward. Yuliya, too was getting worried.

We decided to peek into the room. My God! It was the last thing we expected. My friend was in a cold sweat and gave me a baleful look, while Gulya, visibly pale, was looking reproachfully at both of us. "It's time to go," my friend declared firmly and, saying a general good-bye, let himself out. Not knowing what had happened, I wished the ladies goodnight and caught up with my friend. In the street, he called me every name in the book. "Where the hell did you take me? You tricked me!" he yelled. "To a decent, cultured family," I answered. "Oh yes! Really decent," he complained sarcastically. What had happened was that during his conversation with Gulya my friend had noticed a small portrait of Stalin in a bookcase. "Gulya, why do you keep a photo of that criminal?" he asked. "How dare you speak about my grandfather like that! He was a great man and did a lot of good for the people." That was when he broke out in a cold sweat, and the evening was at an end. Needless to say, I never acted as matchmaker again, and my friend never married. As for Gulya I never heard from her again.

Diplomats of the Stalin School and the "Struggle Against the Cult"

The Soviet people did not mourn Stalin's death for very long. They weren't permitted to. A series of actions by the leadership indicated that a serious reappraisal of the Stalin years was under way. In 1956 Nikita Khrushchev, in his confidential report to the Twentieth Congress of the CPSU, undertook a detailed exposure of Stalin's crimes and his methods of governing the country. This was an unusual, although, from my point of view, inevitable move by the new leader. Sooner or later the Soviet people would have to learn about the crimes of Stalin and his associates, including Khrushchev himself. "The Struggle Against the Cult of Stalin" had become an ideological credo of the Communist Party and remained its principal rallying cry for a long time after Khrushchev's "confidential report."

I belonged to that generation of Soviet diplomats who embarked on their careers only after the Cold War had already started and because of their junior rank never came into contact with Stalin himself. We only learned of his methods and manner of conducting foreign policy from stories told by senior diplomats and official reports. Gromyko, Gusev, Boris Podtserob, Vladimir Semenov, Malik, Novikov, and other Soviet diplomats who had participated in various conferences and negotiations with Stalin over the years loved to share their impressions of the Soviet leader's diplomatic skills. They remembered every meeting with him. Gromyko, for example, used to talk about his first meeting with Stalin on the eve of his trip to the United States, when Stalin, an arch-atheist, advised the young diplomat to go to church while in America because, he said, it would help him understand the

American mentality. Gromyko enjoyed telling how he, as ambassador in Washington during World War II, answered Stalin's questions about President Roosevelt, his life and methods of government. He always emphasized that Stalin had a deep respect for the American president.

Malik in turn recollected with pride how during the war when he was the Soviet ambassador in Tokyo, he personally reported to Stalin on the situation in Japan. According to Malik, at one of the meetings in the summer of 1945 Stalin unexpectedly asked him: "And what should we do about Japan, comrade ambassador?" Malik responded without hesitation: "Fight them, Yosif Vissarionovich, fight them." "Correct, good thinking," replied Stalin. Viktor Lebedev, the first Soviet ambassador to postwar Poland, claimed that Stalin always had a special interest in Poland. According to Lebedev, Stalin repeatedly emphasized that Poland would have paramount importance in the international policy of the USSR, and that the Soviet role in world affairs would largely depend on the state of Soviet-Polish relations.

Diplomats who worked directly with Stalin all agreed that the most characteristic feature of his style was his firmness in making decisions and his rigidity once he had made them. They could hardly remember any real debate when international questions were raised at the highest level of the Soviet leadership. If there was debate, Stalin ended it as soon as he had come to a decision, which he would present as the conclusion of the discussion. Questions and further comments were completely inadmissible. Such an absolutist style was rather unique even for a totalitarian state such as the USSR.

For the most part, diplomats of the "Stalin school" chose not to criticize Stalin even during the fierce struggle against the "cult of Stalin." I do not recall any particular statements by Gromyko or his colleagues condemning Stalin of mass repression in the 1930s, or even criticizing his foreign policy. For example, when Gromyko addressed the Twenty-Second Congress of the CPSU in 1961, which was mainly devoted to the "struggle against the cult of Stalin," the minister of foreign affairs chose not to speak against Stalin's actions, even in the foreign policy area. As a matter of fact he also declined to criticize Molotov, who at one time had actively promoted Gromyko's brilliant diplomatic career, and who also came in for fierce criticism at the congress, and this illustrates something important about the anti-Stalin campaign. When the anti-Stalin propaganda campaign started to level off in the mid-1960s, the high-ranking "Stalin diplomats" started, at times openly through mass media, to pledge loyalty to Stalin and his "headstrong diplomacy." Semenov's article in the ministry publication *International Affairs*, for example, caused quite a stir in the perestroika years by its pro-Stalin slant.

Will There Be an End to the Cold War?

The majority of Soviet diplomats of my generation and our successors understood that the campaign "against the cult of Stalin" was a deliberate attempt by the new leadership to distance itself from the xenophobia and terror of the Stalin era. We welcomed the attempt. In fact, my friends from the MFA and the Diplomatic Academy dreamed that Stalin's death would be followed by an end to his isolationism in the international arena and that the doors would now be opened to dialogue with other countries. We welcomed the practice of regular meetings between Khrushchev and his colleagues with foreign ambassadors and government and political leaders. There are stories circulating about a reception arranged by the Soviet leadership for the diplomatic corps in Moscow in the summer of 1956. The normal conversations, boat rides (the reception took place at one of the governmental summer residences), jokes, and laughter at this reception were so untypical of the methods of "class diplomacy" that it all seemed to be a scene from a fairy tale.

Contacts between Soviet leaders and representatives of the foreign press underwent striking changes. Under Stalin they were rare and perfunctory. As a rule Stalin personally answered questions on matters of foreign policy. This gave the interview a special importance. Frequently he prepared the questions by himself or at meetings of the Central Committee of the CPSU. Correspondents were usually not permitted to put questions of their own. The best way of learning Stalin's answers was from the pages of newspapers. Any personal meeting, even a telephone interview, was out of the question.

Khrushchev discontinued this practice, for he was not afraid of open conversations with foreigners. In fact, he loved to get into arguments with them. The "kitchen debate" between Khrushchev and Nixon at the American exhibition in Moscow in 1958 represented one of the new trends and caused quite a stir in the Soviet Union. For diplomats who were in constant, working dialogue with foreigners, Khrushchev's open, live conversations with foreign representatives were an inspiring example. We were confident that the new approach to world politics would result in the dismantling of the old, nondemocratic forms of government. We expected, in particular, that a truly representative legislative authority, elected on the basis of free elections would replace the puppet Supreme Soviet—the Soviet parliament. I remember the excitement caused by the statement made by the new Central Committee secretary Dmitry Shepilov at the Academy of Social Sciences of the Central Committee of the CPSU after the Twentieth Congress of the

Communist Party. He said that it was time to put forward several candidates for seats in the Supreme Soviet. And at one of the party meetings of the Diplomatic Academy I remember that one of the students spoke in favor of a multiparty system, provided that all parties are Marxist-Leninist. We all thought this to be an extremely bold and original proposal and congratulated the speaker!

The Soviet people also expected serious economic reforms, which would give broad freedoms to the private sector. In a small village near Moscow, where I lived in the summer, a farm woman, who brought us milk, commented on "the struggle against the cult of Stalin" by saying: "Nikita Sergeyevich is a very good man. Soon they will start returning the land to us peasants!" In a word, everyone had his own interpretation of the "struggle against the cult" but it seemed that everyone agreed that life would now be better and that there would be more freedom.

There was in fact a new approach to foreign policy that surfaced after Stalin's death, and it could be seen in a certain dynamism and flexibility in our relations with the West. Vyshinsky's removal from the post of minister and Molotov's reinstatement in 1953 played a part. Vyshinsky had been cruel, vindictive, and irascible. He also occupied a rather low position in the party hierarchy (he was not a Politburo member). Thus, he was both feared and looked down on by the staff of the ministry. It was different with Molotov. The report on the reshuffling in the Soviet leadership after Stalin's death said that Molotov's assignment to the post of first vice prime minister and minister of foreign affairs would allow foreign policy to enjoy an honorable status in the Soviet state. We applauded this declaration in the belief that under such an authoritative minister as Molotov the making and implementation of foreign policy would become the basic prerogative of the ministry. We expected the new CPSU leader Khrushchev, who was not experienced in the area of diplomatic activity, not to interfere in this delicate area, but to rely instead on his more experienced colleagues.

Reality did not live up to our expectations. Khrushchev was greatly interested in matters of foreign policy and in many instances he imposed his own decisions on key issues even when they openly contradicted Molotov's view. News of these disagreements leaked from the Kremlin, and we diplomats faced a dilemma: which of the two was right? Which political line would prevail, the old Stalinist one, geared toward an uncompromising confrontation with the West, or the new one, which allowed for the possibility of agreement with the West?

4
SOWING THE SEEDS OF HATRED IN HUNGARY

A Central Committee Assignment

In early November of 1956 Mikhail Silin, director of the Diplomatic Academy, summoned me to his office. He told me, rather mysteriously, that I was to go to the Communist Party's headquarters on Old Square, where I was to be given an important mission. He gave me no further details so I left immediately, not quite knowing what to expect.

This was my first visit to the headquarters, the high altar of communists all over the world. I have visited that building many times since, but I have never forgotten how it felt the first time I crossed its threshold—the atmosphere and spirit of the place. I felt significance and anxiety, importance and diffidence, pride and fear, at the same time. Remarkably, there were very few people around. I remember passing through long corridors without seeing anyone except guards. The closer I came to the offices of the powerful, the more people I saw, but I was struck by the quiet of the place. People spoke in hushed tones as though they were in a holy sanctum. I still remember being struck by the size of the desks in the offices and how that size increased with the importance of the functionary seated at it.

I met with an official of the Propaganda Department of the Central Committee. He was very polite and told that he had read my articles on

Hungary and found them interesting. He asked my opinion about the latest developments in Hungary, and without a moment's hesitation I gave him an answer fully in keeping with the official Soviet line. He was obviously pleased with my response and added that the international imperialists, and above all the American imperialists, had suffered a devastating defeat in Hungary. But now, in the wake of their defeat, they were trying to misrepresent what had really happened in there. Our task, he stated emphatically, was to rebuff these slanders.

He then told me that the Central Committee had decided to entrust a group of political scientists and journalists with the task of writing articles and pamphlets that would present a "true picture" of the events in and around Hungary. You, he said, as an expert on international policy have been chosen to write the pamphlet describing the key role of the Americans and other imperialists in Hungary. You know, of course, that they masterminded and organized the counterrevolution. You must expose the truth. Then he explained that the task was an urgent one. The manuscript had to be submitted to the publishing house in three to four weeks. The pamphlet was to be printed in several foreign languages—English, French, German, and Spanish.

I expressed my deep gratitude for the honor and the Central Committee's confidence in me. Naturally, as a historian, I was curious about the documents and records I would be using but when I asked him about this he told me that I would need no special sources, for I could find all I needed in Soviet press accounts and in TASS bulletins. I was told that I was to be freed from all my teaching and other duties at the academy so that I could get down to work at once.

I started with a careful study of the Soviet media—*Pravda, Izvestiya*, and transcripts from Moscow radio accounts. However, I soon found that I was having a difficult time learning what had actually happened. In the first days of the dramatic events in Hungary Soviet media had published stories stressing the failure of the "antipopular venture in Budapest." Almost every day the media had claimed that order had been restored and that the government was in complete control of the situation. However, I also found reports from correspondents in Budapest that the "antipopular venture" was continuing. A couple of days later the Soviet press acknowledged that there had been an uprising in Hungary but that it was now over.

It was not until October 27 that the Soviet media addressed the role of the Western powers in Hungary. The leading Soviet newspapers charged

Western countries, especially the United States, with inciting an underground counterrevolutionary uprising. As evidence of these charges the papers cited the appropriation by the U.S. Congress of $100,000,000 annually for what was called "subversion against the Socialist states." *Pravda* wrote that the money was used by "spies and diversionists" in the socialist states of Eastern Europe to stir up trouble. It even recalled President Eisenhower's 1955 Christmas address in which he supported the democratic aspirations of people living under communism. This was called "an open appeal" to the people of socialist states to rebel against their "freely elected" governments. The Soviet papers also mentioned that balloons carrying anti-Soviet propaganda were being released over Eastern Europe. Moscow radio charged that Western intelligence services, especially the CIA, were "the initiators" of the counterrevolution. It was reported that the Hungarian insurgents were well armed and well trained, implying that they were receiving underground supplies through direct foreign connections.

The official Soviet attacks on the United States and the other Western powers grew increasingly vehement, but unfortunately I could find very little evidence to support the charges so I had little to go on in writing my pamphlet, which meant, as I soon realized, that I would have to turn to my colleagues in the Hungarian Division of the Foreign Ministry. The Hungarian Division was a relative newcomer to the Foreign Ministry because official contact between the Soviet Union and Hungary had been very limited before World War II. Diplomatic relations had been established only in 1934 and then suspended in 1939. In 1941 Hungary joined Germany in attacking the Soviet Union, and this resulted in a complete breakdown in diplomatic relations. However, from the time the Red Army entered Hungary in 1944, Hungary assumed an important role in the overall Soviet strategy in Eastern Europe. The Politburo appointed Klim Voroshilov, one of Stalin's closest associates, as coordinator of the Soviet Union's policy in Hungary and Georgy Pushkin, an experienced diplomat, as the first Soviet ambassador to Hungary.

In keeping with the growing Soviet presence in Eastern Europe, a Hungarian Division was set up in the Foreign Ministry. The head of the division was Boris Geiger, a real expert on Hungary. An ethnic Hungarian himself, he was born in Hungary and had grown up in the Soviet Union, so he knew both countries well—their culture, languages, and traditions. Although he was a Soviet citizen and a member of the CPSU, he was always considered an alien, so he was advised to change his name from Geiger to a Russian-sounding one. He chose the name Grigorev but unfortunately this did not save him. He had a keen sense of humor and liked to tell jokes and anecdotes, but eventually he went too far and was discharged from the ministry for being too free with his unguarded, spontaneous comments, which were labeled as anti-Soviet slanders.

During the war the Diplomatic Academy, and later the Institute of International Relations, began offering specialized courses in Hungarian language, culture, and history. This meant that there was no lack of Hungarian experts in the Foreign Ministry in Moscow or in the Soviet embassy in Budapest. The Hungarian Division of the Foreign Ministry usually employed four to five diplomats, while the embassy in Budapest became one of the largest Soviet embassies in any of the socialist countries. As a rule all diplomats spoke Hungarian, were well versed in Hungarian affairs, and were competent professionals. This could not be said of all Soviet ambassadors to Budapest. With a few exceptions, they were mostly former party bosses who considered any stay in Hungary as exile. Consequently, they did not know and did not want to know Hungary, its people, or its traditions.

Therefore, when I needed help with my writing assignment, I knew whom to look for. Vladimir Brykin and Nikolai Sikachev, both of whom had been my classmates at the Diplomatic Academy, had been the pillars of the Hungarian Division when the Hungarian crisis broke in 1956. Brykin was called to Budapest by Yury Andropov, who was then the Soviet ambassador in Hungary, while Sikachev remained in Moscow throughout the crisis, drafting many of the key documents. Naturally I expected Brykin and Sikachev to have plenty of useful information that would help me to write my pamphlet, so I was quite surprised when I approached them and they explained that they too were searching for evidence to implicate the West in the events in Hungary but were having very little luck. All they could do was advise me to resort to the Voice of America and Radio Free Europe. I concluded, therefore, that they were outside the decision-making process. Even Dmitry Shepilov, the new foreign minister, as a candidate member of the Politburo, was obviously aware of the decisions, but was not playing an important role in the process. The main players—Khrushchev himself, and Politburo members Anastas Mikoyan and Mikhail Suslov.

I knew nothing at the time of the secret visits of Mikoyan and Suslov to Hungary in October 1956. Perhaps my friends knew about these visits and didn't tell me, but if they did they hid it well. I was informed only later that after the formation of a new Hungarian government headed by Imre Nagy on October 23 Khrushchev decided to send Mikoyan and Suslov to establish friendly relations and close cooperation with the new government. Nagy did not see any reason for Soviet military intervention in Hungary. The Soviet emissaries' report caused a heated discussion in the Politburo. Some of the Kremlin bosses were in favor of a hard line on Hungary. Subsequently, the Politburo decided to issue a special declaration, which appeared to sound a note of accommodation and rapprochement. The basic intent of the document, however, was to save the situation and avoid a total Soviet commitment in Hungary. On the other hand, the conciliatory tone of the document and the readiness to make certain concessions did not exclude harsh measures, including the ruthless suppression of the uprising.

The drafting of the document and its clearance took several days, and the declaration was approved on October 30. The cumbersome machine that was the Soviet bureaucracy could not keep up with the rapid pace of events in Hungary. Andropov was instructed to set up an urgent meeting with Hungarian prime minister Nagy so that he could personally deliver the declaration. However, Andropov's subsequent report to Moscow made it clear that Nagy was unimpressed by the document, not even referring to it in his public statements. This, of course, made the Kremlin furious, so they immediately dispatched Mikoyan and Suslov to Hungary once more to induce Nagy to accept a negotiated settlement on the basis of the Soviet declaration. However, an agreement could not be worked out. The situation became even more complicated when on November 1, Imre Nagy sent an urgent communication to the secretary-general of the UN, informing him of Hungary's repudiation of the Warsaw Pact and the declaration of Hungary's neutrality. The Soviet mass media were given strict instructions by the Politburo to keep silent about Nagy's letter.

To improve the Soviet position in the United Nations the Politburo appointed First Deputy Foreign Minister Vasily Kuznetsov head of the Soviet delegation to the emergency session of the General Assembly. One of his aides, a former student of mine, who knew that I was having difficulty writing my pamphlet, showed me the draft of Kuznetsov's speech and assured me that it contained ample evidence that the Western powers were aiding the Hungarian "counterrevolutionaries." When I read the speech, however, I found nothing new.

Sadly, I was beginning to realize that I wasn't going to find any evidence to prove that the Hungarian uprising had been organized and orchestrated by the Western powers. However, I did begin to detect an evolution in the

Soviet position toward Hungary. In particular, I noticed two important changes. First, at the beginning of the crisis Soviet representatives called it an "antipopular venture" and then a "counterrevolution," but by the time of Kuznetsov's speech in the UN it was being described as a "fascist putsch." Second, it seemed that the Kremlin was beginning to see a connection between the events in Hungary and the other great crisis of that time—in the Middle East. At first, I believe that the Kremlin viewed the two situations in different terms. Hungary was seen as a domestic crisis and the act by Britain, France, and Israel against Egypt was seen as an international one. Later, after Kadar's government was formed, these crises were seen as links in the same chain.

Time was slipping away, and soon I would have to submit my manuscript to the Central Committee. I called the official with whom I had spoken earlier and shared with him the problems I was having. Don't worry, he said. If you utilize all the facts available in the Soviet press and in the speeches of Comrades Shepilov, Kuznetsov, and others, there won't be any problem. Relieved, I followed his advice and concluded my work in early December 1956, when I sent the manuscript to the Foreign Languages Publishing House.

Andropov Tells the Story of the Hungarian Uprising

A few days later I learned that Ambassador Andropov was in Moscow and that he had agreed to meet the students and faculty of the Diplomatic Academy. What a great piece of luck, I thought, for surely he would be able to answer all my questions!

I had heard much about Andropov's unusual style. Unlike other Soviet ambassadors, who preferred to learn about their assigned countries mainly from the reports of their subordinates, Andropov traveled a great deal throughout Hungary, talking to workers, peasants, and intellectuals. He even took lessons in Hungarian and earned a reputation for treating Hungarian officials with respect. Instead of issuing orders, as his predecessors had done, he always "advised" and "recommended." He was also a cultured man, enjoying a range of interests from sports to music and the arts. Under Andropov the Soviet embassy in Budapest was known for its social events. Andropov was an expert dancer, and it was not unusual for the ambassador to ask the wives of his guests to dance.

His lecture in the academy was a success. Frankly, I was surprised by his knowledge of Hungarian history and literature; he quoted Sandor Petöfi's verses, told Hungarian stories, and spoke at length about the tragic events in Hungary in the fall of 1956. He explained the uprising mainly as a result of the mistakes and blunders of the former Hungarian communist leadership, primarily Rakosi and Gero. As he explained it, the demonstration of October 23 began because the people, both communists and noncommunists, had become deeply embittered. The resulting events were unfortunately necessary to correct these mistakes and blunders.

Subsequently, the demands of the demonstrators had been met: a new government was formed, the leadership of the communist party was changed, all members of the new leadership had been in prison under Rakosi, and they promised to right the wrongs of the Rakosi regime. In spite of this, Andropov stated, the insurgents continued the bloodshed. He claimed that on October 25, Soviet tanks were stationed at the center of a square in Budapest when fire was opened on the crowd from the neighboring rooftops. Members of the Soviet crews were also wounded or killed. It was only after being attacked that they had returned the fire. The Soviet forces suffered only minimal losses, and their fighting capacity was unimpaired. According to Andropov, the generally friendly attitude of the Hungarians toward the Soviet Army remained unchanged.

Andropov further claimed that Nagy had been concentrating his energies not on solving domestic problems but almost entirely on challenging "traditional Soviet-Hungarian friendship." In late October and early November, Andropov had met with Nagy every day, sometimes several times a day. (He did not, however, mention the two visits of Mikoyan and Suslov, which had played an important role in the developing crisis.) Despite this, the Nagy government had moved further and further to the right; and therefore, the installation of Janos Kadar's government on November 4 was the only way to "save socialism in Hungary."

I chatted with Andropov after the lecture. I asked him about the decisive role of "American imperialism" in organizing the Hungarian "counterrevolution"—the subject of my pamphlet. "That's nonsense," he laughed. "The events in Hungary took the Americans by surprise. They came to the Soviet embassy and asked us to explain what was happening in Budapest. They played no role in the events." Taken aback, I then asked him to explain what had been the turning point in the Soviet attitude toward Nagy's government. Without any hesitation he told me that Nagy's decision to repudiate the Warsaw Treaty and declare Hungarian neutrality was totally unacceptable to us, and Moscow had no intention of even discussing such issues. He assured me, however, that the Kremlin had wanted to avoid any direct military involvement in Hungary, and had been ready to cooperate with Nagy, but when Nagy had stated his intentions to Andropov on November 1, it became crystal clear that Nagy could no longer be trusted. But how could that have happened? I wondered. Nagy had lived many years in the Soviet Union and was considered by some to be an "old Moscow hand." To this, Andropov responded that perhaps Nagy had became arrogant—familiarity breeds contempt. And, with a smile, Andropov added that he had never liked Nagy.

I was astonished by such frankness from the young ambassador, but I must confess that I liked him—his openness and his candor. Tall and distinguished looking, there was no question that he had a forceful and compelling presence. But his smile could be disarming. It seemed sincere, and yet it was strangely enigmatic. At times I could feel the cold in his eyes. Little did I know at the time that I was speaking to the future head of the mighty KGB, the general secretary of the CPSU, and the leader of the Soviet Union!

One footnote to this story. Many years after our chat I learned that Andropov had delivered a secret report to the Central Committee soon after the Hungarian uprising. In the report he alluded to a "counterrevolution" in Hungary that had resulted from certain connections between the "treacherous group of Imre Nagy," the leader of the uprising, and the "imperialists." That was Andropov! He knew better than any other Soviet leader the real situation within the Soviet Union and abroad. But if the truth did not fit the political or ideological perception of the Communist leadership, Andropov did not hesitate to ignore it. This ability to charm people and adapt effortlessly to a particular situation showed itself in my later encounters with him. When I was working in the Foreign Ministry in Moscow, I remember that he phoned me several times asking for information about the activities of international organizations. He addressed me not as "Comrade Israelyan," but as "Victor Levonovich," which was very unusual for communications between Soviet officials of such different ranks.

To be frank, some of his actions puzzled me. Once his son Igor,' whom I came to know in the 1970s when he worked at the Diplomatic Academy, informed me that he wanted to take a master's degree in history. He was thinking of writing his thesis on Soviet-German relations from 1939 to 1941 so he asked me for my advice. This made me nervous because I knew about the Soviet Union's close political and economic cooperation with Hitler during the first years of the war, but I didn't know if he or his father knew about it, so I asked Igor if his father knew of his chosen thesis topic, to which he said yes. Did this mean that his father knew of the secret deals with Hitler and perhaps wanted his son to uncover the truth? I told Igor that he should follow his father's advice.

Vladimir Brykin, who was assigned to the Soviet embassy in November 1956, confirmed Andropov's assertion that Moscow had tried in vain to induce Nagy to accept a negotiated settlement and that therefore Nagy was no longer considered to be a "reliable comrade." According to Brykin, this did not necessarily exclude the possibility of a negotiated settlement in Hungary. In fact, the Soviet government actually suggested setting up two commissions—one political, to discuss questions of Soviet-Hungarian relations, the other military, to consider technical and military questions pertaining to a Soviet troop withdrawal. Brykin was appointed to the Soviet delegation at the bilateral political commission. The core issue, however, of the future of Soviet-Hungarian relations was, most certainly, the position and activity of the "reliable Hungarian comrades." On this point, unfortunately, none of my friends—Soviet experts on Hungary and later my Hungarian colleagues—could give me any details on the formation of Janos Kadar's government, and I didn't dare ask Andropov such a delicate question! At the same time everybody acknowledged that Kadar and Andropov had maintained mutual respect and friendship throughout their long careers. I can only add that Kadar was one of the few leaders of the Eastern European socialist states who was highly respected in the Soviet Union.

Not surprisingly, Andropov's lecture and our subsequent talk made me think again about what I had written in my pamphlet. I tried to make certain amendments to the manuscript but the publishing house categorically turned down my request, stating that it was too late to make changes. The only concession they allowed me was to publish the pamphlet under a pen name because I did not want my name on something I knew to be flawed. In early 1957, a fifty-page brochure titled "The Events in Hungary" was published under the name V. Leonov. It was issued in four foreign languages and disseminated abroad. I never saw any reviews, although I do know that some authors referred to it as the Soviet interpretation of the 1956 uprising in Hungary.

Imre Nagy's Great Love

My story of the Hungarian uprising of 1956 would be incomplete were I to fail to mention the lively discussions I later had with my colleagues from the Foreign Ministry and the Diplomatic Academy. For us the most important thing was to identify the causes of the uprising and to judge the wisdom of the Soviet response. Did the Soviet Union react properly to the events in Hungary? All of us acknowledged that the Kremlin had every reason to believe that the Hungarian communist leadership under Rakosi was reliable and faithful to the Soviet Union. Budapest had been receptive to Moscow's instructions, so the Kremlin had come to see the Hungarians as friendly to the Soviet Union—even to the Soviet Army, which had liberated Hungary from German occupation.

My colleagues from the ministry showed me the files containing reports from the Soviet embassy in Budapest describing the reaction to Stalin's death in 1953. Tens of thousands of Hungarians had assembled in Budapest's Stalin Square at the foot of the giant statue of the dead Soviet leader to show their respect and sorrow. At a session of the Hungarian Parliament a unanimous resolution was passed in reverent commemoration of Stalin. Imre Nagy, then the deputy prime minister, submitting the motion, stated: "My heart is heavy as I mount this podium in order to express the great love of our deeply grieving people for our greatest friend, liberator, and teacher. At this solemn hour the Hungarian people are rallying around the Party, the Government, and our beloved Comrade Rakosi, and they are devoting all their energies to bringing about the triumph of Stalin's great cause in our country." And these were the words of a man who would be breaking off the Soviet-Hungarian relationship in just a few years!

At the same time, one must also remember that perhaps nowhere were the effects of Khrushchev's anti-Stalin campaign felt more powerfully than in Hungary. Many of my colleagues accounted for this fact by noting that nowhere else was Stalinism still as firmly entrenched as in Hungary. Even after the Twentieth Congress of the CPSU Rakosi and his supporters never took full responsibility for their mistakes and crimes. Consequently, the belated renunciation of Stalin and his policies touched off a chain reaction of unexpected proportions in Hungary. My colleagues and I agreed that the principal blame for the tragic events in Hungary must rest with the extremist policies of the Hungarian communist leaders. "The Hungarians want to be more Catholic than the pope," someone noted.

More interesting was our discussion of the Soviet response to the events in Hungary. Could the Soviet Union risk further demonstrations and public opposition to the socialist system and perhaps full-scale civil war involving Soviet troops, or would the Soviet Union essentially restructure its relations with Eastern Europe, thus running another (albeit lesser) imminent risk? Why did the Soviet Union fail to detect and contain the situation before it had exploded out of control? All of these questions became the subject of heated discussion among us, especially because we knew that within the walls of the Kremlin the Foreign Ministry was being scrutinized to see if a share of the blame might rest there. We knew that Molotov had categorically rejected these charges and claimed that Khrushchev's "secret anti-Stalin report" had been the cause of the anti-Soviet demonstrations in the socialist states. The majority of diplomats shared Molotov's view. This major conflict between Khrushchev and Molotov resulted in the Foreign Ministry's being virtually stripped of its responsibility for dealing with the socialist countries. Mikoyan became the main trouble-shooter in Hungary. As a result of his visit to Hungary Rakosi was dismissed in July 1956, and the role of the Foreign Ministry in Soviet-Hungarian relations gradually declined. In addition there were deep differences between Khrushchev and Molotov on the Soviet stand on Tito of Yugoslavia. Khrushchev wanted to revise the hostile policy to the Yugoslav leader, while Molotov opposed a new approach. For this reason, among others, Molotov resigned from his post as minister of foreign affairs, and this cleared the way for Khrushchev's complete control over Soviet Union's foreign policy.

A consensus emerged in our discussion on the assessment of the Hungarian uprising or "counterrevolution." The participants sensed that it was the first serious challenge to vital Soviet security interests in East Europe, tantamount to an attempt to revise the Yalta agreements. Therefore, the decisions of the Soviet leaders on such fundamental issues had to be dictated by the decisions of the leaders of the Big Three. The supporters of this view justified the Kremlin's action in 1956. Others believed that the Soviet leaders should have been more sensitive to the potential international consequences of the military intervention in Hungary and tried to have avoided bloodshed there. Such general and vague views expressed by some of the participants cloaked mild disapproval of the Central Committee's actions. How frank were our discussions? Some people were speaking their minds; some were guarded in the expression of their views. However, the common view was not particularly startling or radical: the Soviet Union should unhesitatingly support the communist regimes in Hungary and in other Eastern European countries.

I have to confess that I shared these views. What I did not and could not take into account was the actual attitude of the Hungarians—the Hungarian workers and peasants—toward the regime, toward their communist leaders, and above all toward the Soviet Union. Our only source of information was the Soviet mass media. We believed that history would never forgive us if twelve years after the defeat of Hitler's hordes in World War II, the Soviet people and the Hungarians had retreated in the face of "a counterrevolutionary putsch" and permitted Hungary to become once again a breeding ground for fascism. My first doubts began to surface when I learned from Andropov that the uprising was not orchestrated from abroad, but by the Hungarians themselves. That meant that something was wrong with the character of the people's democracy in Hungary and with our policy toward Hungary. At the time, however, my doubts were only latent. I don't know if I even realized or acknowledged them.

Of course, this does not mean that I concluded that the Western powers had played no role in the events in Hungary. They had certainly encouraged resistance and supported opposition to the pro-Soviet regimes in Eastern Europe, but this was not decisive for the political transformation of Hungary. The cause of the malady was inside Hungary and the "socialist camp." However, I did not have a clear picture of the whole situation, nor did I know the right treatment for the malady.

Postscript: I visited Budapest for the first time in the middle of the 1960s. Later I returned to Hungary several times as a historian, attending various conferences, as a diplomat conducting consultations and negotiations with my Hungarian partners, and as a tourist and guest vacationing at Lake Balaton. I already knew much about Hungarian history from textbooks and research in archives but now I had the good fortune to see the country and people with my own eyes. To understand Hungarian character, pride, and dignity one has to be in Hungary. To feel the beauty of its ancient cities, palaces, and castles one has to see them. Budapest is undoubtedly one of the most beautiful and charming cities in the world.

While in Hungary I delivered occasional lectures and conducted seminars at Budapest University. My two books on the diplomatic history of World War II were published in Hungary, and in 1975 I was awarded an honorary doctorate by Budapest University. Thanks to my "Hungarian background," I always had a special relationship with my Hungarian diplomatic colleagues. They were not only representatives of an allied state but personal friends as well. On the international scene, Hungarian diplomats were highly respected for their diligence, erudition, and thorough knowledge of problems. The names of ambassadors Karoly Chatorday, Matyas Domokos, Imre Hollai, Imre Komives, and Karoly Szarka were very well known in the multilateral diplomatic circles of the period of the 1960s, 1970s, and 1980s.

Chatorday, for example, had unparalleled linguistic ability. In addition to his native Hungarian, he knew English, French, Russian, Spanish, Italian, Chinese, Japanese, Dutch, and Finnish. In March 1969 Chatorday presided over the UN Security Council and conducted the council's meetings in all the official languages of the United Nations. This was a singular event. Once, when he was chairman of the First Committee of the General Assembly he offered some comments on the speech of the Taiwanese representative in Chinese. Since at that time there was no simultaneous translation from Chinese into English, and the Taiwanese diplomat did not speak Chinese, he asked the chairman to repeat his comments in English. The members of the committee broke out in laughter.

Imre Hollai, as president of the UN General Assembly from 1980 to 1981, conducted the business of the General Assembly with brisk efficiency. Karoly Szarka conducted consultations in many international bodies in truly masterly fashion. All of the Hungarian diplomats were liked for their courtesy and fairness.

During my stays in Hungary I visited many famous places, including historic sites where the Hungarians had fought foreign invaders. Once, I went to see some buildings in Budapest with their walls pitted with bullet holes from the shooting during the fall of 1956. I stood beside my Hungarian hosts, silent and ashamed. I was wishing that none of it had ever happened, and I am sure they felt the same.

5
THE KHRUSHCHEV STYLE OF DIPLOMACY

Smoke Without Fire

After Stalin's death in 1953 foreign policy became increasingly important to Soviet leaders, and especially to Nikita Khrushchev. Under Stalin the handling of international affairs had been shrouded in great secrecy. All decisions of the Politburo were in one form or another Stalin's own, and any rival or dissident views were summarily crushed and their adherents liquidated. This was in stark contrast to the early years of the Soviet Union, when Lenin encouraged public discussion of key foreign policy issues. Thus, when Stalin died and the Kremlin declared that foreign policy was to be truly Leninist, we understood that Khrushchev was implicitly criticizing Stalin's foreign policy and that the winds of change would be blowing through the halls of the Ministry of Foreign Affairs.

The turning point for Khrushchev came in June 1957 with the plenary meeting of the CPSU Central Committee. It was at this meeting that his most vocal critics were removed from the Politburo and exiled from Moscow: namely, Molotov, Malenkov, Kaganovich, and a few others who were still identified with Stalin. In March of the following year Khrushchev, while still remaining party leader, took the post of prime minister. Reacting against what he considered to be Stalin's outmoded dogmas, he aspired to renew the communist concept of world development—the notion that the balance of world power was shifting inevitably in favor of the communist world. The transformation of the Castro regime in Cuba, from an anti-imperialist, national liberation regime into a socialist regime was viewed as a prototype of this process. This is why Khrushchev became an adamant propagandist of the principle of peaceful coexistence of two social systems—communist and capitalist. As the balance of power shifted to the communist world, the communist regime would be established without bloodshed. However, with coexistence would come a time of permanent conflict and change, in which institutions would arise and decay in accordance with the dialectic that would lead inexorably to the preordained future—world communism. Hence, Khrushchev's famous statement, "We will bury you [i.e., the capitalist world]," was not so much a threat but a statement of the inevitable.

This in part explains why Khrushchev traveled so much outside the Soviet Union during his years in power. Upon returning from his trips, he would often go directly from his plane to a stadium or arena, where he would speak to large audiences that had gathered to hear news of his trip. Such large gatherings were supposed to demonstrate the unity of the Soviet people with "dear Nikita Sergeyevich," who spoke for hours about the advantages of socialism and the futility of "that, other, rotting world."

My colleagues and I often went to these events, encouraged by the party officials at the MFA. From time to time it was interesting to listen to Khrushchev because he spoke with great passion and emotion, but his speeches were usually long and repetitive, and this became tedious after a while to his audience. He also spoke in a crude manner, lacing his speeches with colloquial, even vulgar language. This was particularly striking to those of us in the MFA, for whom diplomatic etiquette and protocol were very important. One of his interpreters, Viktor Sukhodrev, told me that while translating Khrushchev into English he frequently had to change his wording to eliminate crude expressions and clumsy phrases that would have been embarrassing if translated directly. Also contrary to everything we had been taught at the Diplomatic Academy was the fact that Khrushchev gave free rein to his feelings. Such tactics as the infamous beating of a shoe on the table at a session of the General Assembly or shaking his fist at interlocutors was Khrushchev's style of diplomacy. The Soviet public liked this and applauded him, something which in turn was interpreted by the outside world as a sign of his populism and simplicity. He loved to "play to the crowd," and he could not restrain himself even when his outbursts rebounded against him. But this did not last long. In time it became clear that Khrushchev was not so much a populist as an uneducated and ill-mannered boor.

The "Stalin Tribe" Under a New Banner

What did these changes mean to those of us in the diplomatic corps? Khrushchev made it very clear to the Foreign Ministry that Soviet diplomacy should be more assertive and aggressive, that it would not give the imperialists a minute's respite in the struggle for the victory of communism. Following this order, Soviet diplomats worked hard drafting proposals, memoranda, and declarations in accordance with this new spirit. At the same time, the Kremlin took a more active role in high-profile issues of international importance. This became readily apparent when, in the middle of the 1950s, the Kremlin released a whole salvo of détente-related proposals. These included memoranda on the creation of a nuclear-free zone in Central Europe, on the liquidation of foreign military bases, on preventing sudden military attacks, and on prohibiting the use of space for military purposes. In the following years many more proposals were produced, at the instigation of Khrushchev, on a whole range of matters.

In some cases, the ideas behind these proposals were noble but unrealistic or impractical. For example, in one proposal Khrushchev recommended that the UN executive body be divided into three parts to reflect the division of the world into socialist, capitalist, and nonaligned states. He also called for dividing up the secretariat so that there would be three UN secretaries-general instead of one. As a result, the Russian word *troika* (threesome) became a buzzword around the UN, but it was all smoke and no fire because such a radical reorganization would have been disastrous for the UN. At best it would have resulted in three competing organizations, but most likely it would have brought down the entire organization. When I asked Kiril Novikov, then director of the International Organizations Department of the MFA (IOD), what he thought about the so-called troika, he waved his hand and called it nonsense. Nevertheless, acting on instructions from the top leadership, he worked hard for this "historic" initiative.

Another example comes to mind. In 1960, at the fifteenth session of the UN General Assembly, Khrushchev submitted the basic rules for the treaty on general and complete disarmament. The Soviet offer was a radical one, calling for the destruction of nuclear arsenals and the abolition of military units and national defense universities. However, according to the Soviet proposal, disarmament was to be completed in only four years, an obviously unrealistic time frame for such a drastic change. When British prime minister Harold Macmillan made a counterproposal of five to ten years, Khrushchev ridiculed the offer, even though the Soviet proposal allowed for some negotiation on an "agreed-upon period." Khrushchev knew that the Soviet proposal was not viable but this was a clear example of the way he used diplomacy as a weapon in the propaganda war.

It is difficult to say for sure how those of us within the MFA, the so-called warriors against international imperialism, reacted to Khrushchev's innovations because we were not all of the same mind. Most of the diplomats of that time were brought up in the Stalin era. They were known within the MFA as the "Stalin Tribe," a label they wore with pride, and therefore they were more skeptical of the new developments. On the other hand, many diplomats were attracted to Khrushchev's increasingly proactive line because it opened up new opportunities for diplomatic service. For instance, there was much enthusiasm within the MFA for Khrushchev's initiatives in Asia, Africa, and Latin America, regions once considered off-limits to Soviet diplomats because they were considered to be under Western influence. Increasingly these places seemed not so much fallow land but fertile soil, ready for tilling by eager Soviet diplomats. Even Khrushchev's innumerable trips abroad opened up prospects for scores of diplomats longing to display their knowledge of foreign countries. As one might expect, all these developments raised the profile of the MFA within the state apparatus and helped to revive a sagging diplomatic service. Frankly, many a Soviet diplomat made his career during these years.

Nonetheless, with every passing year Khrushchev's dictatorial habits became more and more obvious to everyone and led to a growing sense of uneasiness throughout the MFA. His outrageous behavior (e.g., his so-called shoe diplomacy), which had initially been laughed off, began to cause us shame and embarrassment as it became clear that it was damaging Soviet external relations. For example, following the notorious U-2 incident in May 1960, when an American spy plane was shot down over the Soviet Union, Khrushchev issued an ultimatum demanding a public apology from Eisenhower. At the time, the leaders of the four major nations were in Paris for an important meeting to discuss the German problem. Khrushchev, however, insisted that Eisenhower should not be allowed to attend the meeting until he apologized. Later I learned from Andrei Gromyko's assistant, Boris

Makashev, that the ministry had in fact prepared an alternative offer, requiring assurances from the American government that it would end spy flights over Soviet territory. The point of such an offer was to avoid a public scandal and allow Eisenhower to save face, but unfortunately Gromyko, knowing Khrushchev's style, did not actually make the offer, and Khrushchev ultimately called off the Paris meeting. This was a shame because the meeting could have been an important stepping-stone in the settlement of the German problem and the ending of the Cold War. Such policy zigzagging displeased many diplomats on Smolenskaya Square, and thus the initial goodwill and support that Khrushchev had enjoyed among the diplomats in his early years gradually seeped away.

Gromyko: "An Unpromising Diplomat"

In February 1957 Molotov's successor Aleksandr Shepilov lost his post as minister of foreign affairs after only eight months in office. Shepilov was tall, handsome, and a passionate lover of the "fine things" in life, especially opera, Cuban cigars, and romancing women. His time at the ministry was no less notable for being brief. He spoke out on behalf of civilized relations with the West, created the basis for future Soviet policy toward the Middle East, and made a number of important trips to third world countries, which helped to establish friendly relations between the Soviet Union and several nonaligned countries. Especially important was Shepilov's personal friendship with the Egyptian president Nasser, which resulted in close Soviet-Egyptian cooperation. Unfortunately Shepilov's gift—he was an affable man, blessed with great self-confidence—was also his undoing. He said about Khrushchev, "An illiterate person cannot govern a country," and with this Shepilov's political career was over. When Khrushchev learned of the quip, he immediately fired him.

There were two likely candidates to succeed Shepilov, Kuznetsov and Gromyko, both of whom were first deputy ministers. Kuznetsov seemed to have the better chance of getting the post because of his impressive political background. He had already held a number of important offices in the Soviet bureaucratic apparatus. He was the chairman of the Soviet trade unions, and briefly a member of the Presidium of the Central Committee. He was also well traveled. As the trade-union leader he made frequent trips to Britain and the United States, where in his early years he had trained to be an engineer at an American factory.

Gromyko's record was more modest by comparison. With a background in economics, he joined the MFA in 1939 as part of "Molotov's draft." That same year he received his first assignment abroad as counselor of the Soviet embassy in Washington, where Maxim Litvinov was the ambassador. Relations between the two men (who together were to supervise Soviet foreign affairs for a total of about forty years) were never very good. According to various people assigned to the Soviet embassy in Washington, Litvinov considered Gromyko to be a mediocre, unpromising diplomat. And when, in 1943, Gromyko was given the American ambassadorship, Litvinov was understandably resentful. He regarded himself as the Soviet Union's best diplomat, which was why Stalin had appointed him ambassador at the beginning of World War II. As Litvinov saw it, Stalin wanted Roosevelt to be more responsive to Soviet needs (especially regarding the need to open the second front), but when this did not happen, Litvinov took the blame. Stalin decided to replace the experienced and renowned diplomat with the weak and inexperienced Gromyko. It is hard to be sure, but the simultaneous replacement of Litvinov in Washington and of Ambassador Maisky in London certainly suggested political considerations.

Gromyko, for his part, was known to regard Litvinov as an arrogant politician who had lost contact with the Kremlin leadership. I witnessed firsthand Gromyko's distaste for Litvinov when in the 1960s I organized an evening in memory of Litvinov at the Moscow House of Scientists. I was informed in no uncertain terms that my initiative did not meet with the minister's approval and that he would not come. Nevertheless, I have to say that in his last years Gromyko sometimes spoke well of his former chief and even found kind words for him.

I do not know for sure what happened at the 1957 session of the Politburo where the candidacies of Kuznetsov and Gromyko were discussed. The secrets of this discussion are kept in the archives. One thing, however, is clear: without Khrushchev's support Gromyko would not have been appointed minister. Therefore, I am sure that Khrushchev gave considerable weight to Gromyko's professionalism, self-control, and discipline—features that always impressed me about Gromyko over the years. To be perfectly honest, however, I think the main reason for Gromyko's appointment was Khrushchev's need for a faithful and obedient minister of foreign affairs. Once I was told of an offhand remark that Khrushchev made about Gromyko, which sums up rather nicely well his estimate of the man: "If you told Gromyko to take his pants off on a winter day and sit his naked ass on the ice, he would do it." No doubt this is a crude and tactless way to characterize a man, but knowing what I know of Khrushchev, it rings true, and I've always thought it went to the heart of the Khrushchev-Gromyko relationship.

So, the man whom Litvinov called an "unpromising" diplomat held the office of minister of foreign affairs of one of the superpowers for twenty-eight years! Despite Gromyko's obedience, however, he was, remarkably enough, not part of Khrushchev's inner circle of trusted advisers when it came time to make important decisions on international matters. Khrushchev's son-in-law and chief editor of *Izvestiya* Aleksei Adzhubei, not only became an influential adviser but also his personal representative at sensitive diplomatic negotiations, some of which Gromyko was not even aware of. In the early 1960s, rumors persistently circulated throughout the MFA that Khrushchev was going to replace Gromyko with Adzhubei as foreign minister. Naturally, Gromyko was aware of such rumors, which unnerved him and made his situation unstable. Once in a conversation in late 1964 he expressed his unreserved satisfaction at Adzhubei's dismissal after Khrushchev had been ousted.

The Continuing Ugly Struggle Against the Stalin Cult

Once Khrushchev had solidified his standing within the party apparatus by eliminating his political opponents, he decided it was time to give his own interpretation of the country's history. The Stalin cult was replaced by the endless lauding of "dear Nikita Sergeyevich" and his achievements. History, including its foreign policy, was rewritten before our very eyes. To even mention Stalin's name was practically forbidden, unless of course it was in the context of a discussion of his crimes. Meanwhile, Khrushchev became one of the main heroes of the war.

I too once suffered from these ugly forms of falsification of history which masqueraded as "struggle against the cult." In a way reminiscent of my earlier run-in with the censors over my thesis on the Paris Peace Conference, I ran into trouble again when in 1960 the Moscow publishing house, International Relations, signed a contract with me to publish my dissertation "The Anti-Hitler Coalition" (see Chapter 3). As the subject of my dissertation was diplomatic cooperation between the Soviet Union, the United

States, and the United Kingdom during World War II, it was naturally full of references to Stalin, Roosevelt, and Churchill. Stalin's name was mentioned the most, though probably not much more than those of Churchill and Roosevelt, and in no way could the study be viewed as a panegyric to Stalin. It had passed the scrutiny of several official organizations, the MFA, and four official reviewers. It also passed the final hurdle, the Supreme Attestation Commission of the Ministry of Higher Education. After such thorough scrutiny, it seemed impossible to me that anyone could criticize the work for containing materials that conflicted with the struggle against the cult.

I have always believed, and continue to believe, that Soviet diplomacy during the war years was made not by the government or by the Communist Party and Politburo but by Stalin himself. As opposed to military matters, where he consulted (and occasionally listened to) Zhukov, Vasylevsky, and other commanders, in the area of diplomacy Stalin was the only decision-maker. He did not really need the advice of Molotov or of any of his professional diplomats, even though he had many talented people he could call upon. The way I see it, and the way I explained it in the dissertation, Stalin's diplomacy depended mostly on his ability to exploit to the full the military successes of the Red Army.

The publishing house planned to print my book around the time of the Twenty-Second Congress of the CPSU, which was scheduled for mid-October 1961. At that congress Khrushchev would deliver a report attacking, with even greater vigor, Stalin and the "antiparty group" of Molotov, Kaganovich, Malenkov, and others. (Khrushchev's report to the Twentieth Congress in 1956 was a secret one but the 1961 congress was public.) Khrushchev's directive—to put an end to the Stalin cult and the antiparty opposition—would be supported enthusiastically by the congress. Almost immediately thereafter, nearly everyone in Khrushchev's entourage did their best to outdo each other in maligning Stalin, and the whole country would be swept up in a campaign to destroy all monuments to Stalin and rename all cities, settlements, factories, or collective farms that bore his name.

Soon after the closing of the congress, when my book was nearing publication, the chief editor of the International Relations publishing house called me into his office for a chat. He asked me if I had been watching the work of the CPSU congress, which unnerved me a little because, of course, I had been following the congress. I then became guarded in my responses, as I sensed something was wrong. At last, he asked me, "So what shall we do about your book?" "Publish it," I said resolutely. "But Victor Levonovich don't you see that we can't publish your book, since it would contradict the line of the Communist Party?" Taken aback, I asked him just how my book contradicted the party line, and he answered by explaining that Stalin's name appeared frequently throughout the book. Perplexed, I explained that writing a book about Soviet-American-British relations during World War II would be impossible without mentioning Stalin's name. It would be making a farce of history, and readers would be naturally and rightly outraged.

At this point I was beginning to get excited but the chief editor was unperturbed. He launched into a lengthy litany on the positive importance of the "struggle against the Stalin cult" for the Soviet people and for all of progressive humanity." He emphasized the consistent party orientation of the Soviet press. Finally, losing patience, I interrupted him in the middle of his discourse and asked him, "What do you suggest?" "It is very simple," he replied, "whenever Stalin's name appears, replace it with 'the Soviet government' or 'Soviet delegation' for conferences, or the 'Soviet Supreme Command,' or even just, 'Moscow.'" I failed to understand why this was necessary but he explained to me that the hated name of Stalin would be an "eyesore" to my readers. Then I pointed out to him that the name of anticommunist no. 1, Winston Churchill, was mentioned many hundreds of times in my book, not to mention the name of Nazi no. 1, Adolf Hitler. Why won't these names be an eyesore to the readers? Perhaps I should replace all names in the book with geographical ones. In such a scenario, the description of the Crimea meeting of Stalin, Roosevelt, and Churchill would look something like: "Moscow speaking at the Yalta Conference, addressed Washington and reminded him of the offer of London at the Teheran meeting, expressing concern about the San Francisco Conference." Not surprisingly, the chief editor did not appreciate my humor. He simply said that it was not up to him but to me to fix the problem. He ended by stating that the publishing house would only print the book if I agreed to reduce the number of times Stalin's name appeared to ten. He never explained why he chose the number ten but I knew that the conversation was over.

After this meeting, I had one last idea of how I might save the book from such wholesale editing. I decided to appeal to the CPSU Central Committee. I had clearly failed to learn my lesson from the fate of my earlier Paris Peace Conference manuscript. I called the CPSU secretary for ideology, Leonid Ilyichev, who had worked for some time in the Press Department of the MFA. Many spoke of him as an educated and cultured person, so I thought he might understand my plight and help me. Happily, as I realized later, it was impossible to get an appointment with him. His assistant was kind enough to tell me on the phone that the secretary was busy and asked me to call back another time. In the meantime, the publisher canceled my book, settling the matter once and for all. Naturally, I was disappointed, but on the other hand, I was relieved because there were no repercussions for me either from the Party or from the learned societies.

A postscript: A few years later, in 1964, when the atmosphere was more conducive, International Relations finally published *The Anti-Hitler Coalition*. Although Stalin's name appeared many more than ten times, his title was frequently substituted instead. Perhaps I felt a certain degree of vindication, but there was no real satisfaction because the book was indelibly marred by what was known as the rectification of history so favored by Soviet historiography.

Disputes About the Cuban Missile Crisis

Of all the international conflicts that erupted during the decade of Khrushchev's rule, the Cuban missile crisis of 1962 damaged his authority the most. Despite its brevity and happy ending, it remains one of the most disturbing episodes of the Cold War, for it nearly sucked the two superpowers and with them the whole world down into a deadly quicksand.

I remember that in the autumn of 1962, Moscow was basking in an Indian summer, and the international climate was similarly balmy. Khrushchev had decided not to inform any of the leading diplomats, except for the ambassador to Cuba Aleksandr Alekseyev—that Soviet missiles were going to be deployed in Cuba. Not even the Soviet ambassador in Washington Anatoly Dobrynin or the Soviet representative to the UN Valerian Zorin were informed. Needless to say, the lower-ranking diplomats did not know what was coming. I myself first learned of the crisis from the Soviet newspapers, which pinned responsibility for it on "reactionary U.S. circles." And yet, even from the newspaper reports, one could see the inconsistency and questionable nature of the Soviet position. My colleagues and I at the MFA questioned, for example, how the deployment of Soviet missiles in Cuba could possibly improve the international situation and Soviet-American relations. How could it possibly promote the principles of peaceful coexistence?

After the United States announced its plans to blockade Cuba, the Soviet government issued its own declaration on October 23, containing "a resolute warning" to the U.S. government that it was "taking serious responsibility for the fate of the world" and that it "carelessly plays with fire." As expected, the Soviet public response to this statement was the right one—of outrage that Washington should claim the right to search vessels headed for Cuba. This was seen as unprecedented arrogance and an attempt to humiliate the Soviet Union. Meanwhile, inside the MFA and the Diplomatic Academy there was much discussion as well. While approving the firmness and determination not to give in to American threats, we all wondered what would happen if the Americans stood by their threats. Some, especially those who were experts on the United States, did not believe this would happen. "The Yanks won't dare touch us," they declared, "because their arms are too short." Most, however, were not so confident that the United States would lift the blockade. Nevertheless, no one expressed any enthusiasm for a military confrontation that might trigger a full-scale war—which would be a big mistake.

Many different "winning" scenarios were imagined that had the Soviet Union emerging victorious from the crisis. Frankly, I do not remember a single one of them. Those of us involved in these discussions were really no better informed than the Russian population at large, and our judgments were probably no more reliable. I was under the impression at the time that it was Fidel Castro who had drawn the Soviet Union into the Caribbean. I remember saying as much to a diplomat from the Latin American Department of the MFA, who was soon to become ambassador to a South American country. I said to him, "Well, the Beard (our nickname for Castro) really got us into a mess this time." "On the contrary," he answered, "it isn't the Beard who dragged us into this mess. We dragged him in, and now we're trying to get ourselves out regardless of what happens to the Beard." I was stunned by this comment; I was unaware at that time that Khrushchev had been the one demanding that Castro permit the deployment of Soviet missiles in Cuba. Soviet propaganda tried to create the impression that the fatal decision was made at the request of Cuba and that responsibility for the potential consequences of the crisis could not be attributed to the Soviets.

Anxiety and tension mounted with each passing day. The public in Moscow knew nothing about the daily intensive communications between Khrushchev and Kennedy. It was, therefore, with great relief and satisfaction that the city heard Khrushchev's announcement on October 27. Unlike the October 23 declaration, this one was free of propagandist considerations.

Instead, it seemed to us to be an honorable and mutually acceptable way out of the crisis. The Soviet side agreed to remove the missiles from Cuba, and the Americans declared that they would remove their own missiles from Turkey, missiles that had been targeting the Soviet Union for years. Everything seemed fair. This deal was called "the exchange variant."

On the following morning, October 28, I received a call from a friend who urged me to turn on the radio because they were broadcasting Khrushchev's message. When I tuned in, I heard the voice of an announcer solemnly reading out a message from Khrushchev, assuring the Soviet people that their nation was on the rise and that they were enjoying the fruits of peaceful labor on their march toward global social progress—and so on and so forth. I listened to the rest of the address but could not figure out what he was driving at, so I called my friend and asked him about Turkey, assuming that Khrushchev must have talked about the American withdrawal of missiles from Turkey in a part of his speech I had missed. "You haven't missed a thing," my friend said. "Khrushchev sidestepped the issue and simply accepted the American conditions. So, with our tails between our legs we shall remove our missiles while we can," my friend concluded. I could not believe this, and decided that something must have gone wrong with the radio broadcast. To my dismay, however, once I had read the text of Khrushchev's October 28 message to Kennedy I understood that my friend was right. In exchange for actual disarmament steps by the Soviet Union, the removal of Soviet missiles from Cuba, the Americans stated only their readiness to give a general sort of promise. This was the interpretation of the diplomatic and military establishments, especially those members of them who were involved in the Caribbean crisis to any degree.

After Khrushchev's statement the Soviet media tried to put the right "spin" on it by repeating over and over again that Khrushchev had received a "major concession" from Kennedy—an assurance that the United States would not attack Cuba—thus averting the threat of global thermonuclear war. In fact, however, Khrushchev had caved in, betraying the principle of the "exchange variant." To be honest, many people I know believed that Khrushchev had simply gotten scared and taken the easy way out. In Armenia, for instance, according to my long-time friend Robert Khachatrian, who was secretary of the Communist Party of Armenia, Khrushchev's actions were publicly criticized. American military bases in Turkey were so close to the Soviet border that they could be seen through binoculars from Armenia. One could, therefore, easily understand the desire of the Armenians to get rid of such dangerous neighbors. The unwillingness of Moscow to take this opportunity was undisguised disappointment to them.

At the Ministry of Foreign Affairs the Cuban missile crisis was a demoralizing episode, first and foremost because many of the diplomats whom Khrushchev could have and should have consulted, were simply left in the dark. This was humiliating to these diplomats because it signaled to everyone in the diplomatic corps that they did not have the trust or the confidence of their leader. Over and above the personal slight, however, this incident aroused widespread dissatisfaction among diplomats who had serious questions about the Kremlin's judgment during the crisis. The fact that Khrushchev had secretly put missiles in Cuba and then, under American pressure, openly agreed to remove them, was obviously a humiliation for the Soviet Union and one of Khrushchev's gravest miscalculations. I don't know of a single diplomat who would have defended the decision.

Boris Poklad, an experienced diplomat and assistant of Kuznetsov for many years, accompanied Kuznetsov to the negotiating sessions, which were held several times a month and began in New York on October 29. He testified, that Kuznetsov's American opposite numbers, John MacCloy, chairman of the American Coordination Committee on Cuba, and Adlai Stevenson, permanent representative of the United States to the UN, had adopted a highly inflexible negotiating posture, offering no concessions and constantly imposing new conditions. Poklad said that the frequent briefings of the American negotiators by the White House resulted in a hardening of their position at the talks. It took great patience and effort on the part of Kuznetsov, a true artist in the field of diplomacy, to keep the Soviet-American dialogue constructive. In spite of the good personal relations he established with his negotiating partners, he nevertheless failed to win acceptance of any formal commitments by the United States in connection with the crisis.

Many diplomats felt that Khrushchev never fully understood or took into account U.S. interests in Cuba. Frightened at the prospect of a military collision, Khrushchev sought to end the crisis as soon as possible. Under these conditions the Americans used every device in their diplomatic arsenal to secure decisions favorable to them. I heard from many Soviet diplomats, including those who had participated in the New York negotiations, that it was Khrushchev's style to begin with confrontational tactics, which simply had the effect of escalating the situation. Then, when the other side reacted, he would be intimidated. After that it was up to the Ministry of Foreign Affairs to find a way out of the impasse. It was at the time of the Caribbean crisis that Kuznetsov earned his nickname "troubleshooter," a nickname I believe was well earned.

Perhaps some of these perceptions of Khrushchev and the Cuban missile crisis were mistaken, but there is no doubt that these events strengthened the general discontent with Khrushchev on Smolenskaya Square. Diplomats considered the crisis a diplomatic failure on the part of the Soviet Union. Not surprisingly, therefore, neither the official *History of the Foreign Policy of the USSR*, nor the *Diplomatic Dictionary*, both publications of the MFA, devoted as much as a page to the Cuban missile crisis. The incident was rarely mentioned until after Khrushchev's removal at the plenary meeting of the CPSU Central Committee in October 1964. Only then was the subject of the Cuban missile crisis discussed, and then only to criticize Khrushchev's handling of it.

The Dawn of the "Great Decade"

The year 1963 marked the tenth anniversary of Stalin's death. All the ideological resources of the state bureaucracy were marshaled for the celebration of what the Kremlin was now calling "The Great Decade." I became involved in these activities when the CPSU Department of Propaganda charged the professors and teachers of my department at the Diplomatic Academy with the task of preparing a textbook on Soviet foreign policy during the decade. My editor from the Central Committee emphasized that the main theme of the book should be the role of Soviet diplomacy in promoting the communist concept of world development. The textbook was intended for a variety of courses to be offered in schools throughout the Soviet Union, and therefore it was important to correctly set forth the official version of events together, of course, with basic information about Marxist-Leninist philosophy.

My colleagues readily agreed to coauthor the textbook, knowing that Gospolitizdat, the most authoritative and prestigious publishing house, would publish it. We were given very little time, since the book was to be ready by the 1964 school year. Fortunately, our faculty were efficient and responsible so that the textbook was ready in time. The result was a typical example of Soviet political literature. Everything was depicted in black and white, all the characters either "good guys" or "bad guys," and the plot led inexorably to the inevitable triumph of communism. Khrushchev, of course, appeared everywhere in the book. Though never called "Leader," "Father of the people," or "the ingenious teacher" as Stalin had been, Khrushchev was awarded such epithets as "ardent peace champion," "fighter for friendship and happiness of the people," "progressive follower of Lenin," "the outstanding organizer and chief," and so forth.

For a title we chose *Soviet Foreign Policy in a New Era*. We did not incorporate "a great decade" in the title because the term had not yet received formal recognition. Published in 1964, the book quickly sold out and was reprinted in the following year with certain amendments and additions (with one, truly essential amendment, which I shall talk about later). It continued to be reprinted over the years and remained in print in a second edition throughout the last years of the Soviet Union. In 1981 my colleagues and I received the USSR State Award for the book, which by then was simply titled *Soviet Foreign Policy*.

The appearance of our textbook was one example of the fast-growing phenomenon of the glorification of Khrushchev, to which we were all witnesses, if not actual participants. I became even more deeply involved in this process of glorification when, in 1962, I was asked to write an article on Khrushchev for the three-volume *Diplomatic Dictionary*, for which Gromyko served as chief editor. I was flattered but also daunted, fearing that I would have to cover the whole range of Khrushchev's diverse activities. Fortunately, however, I was assured that I should focus exclusively on Khrushchev's diplomatic activities, which of course I had supposedly witnessed firsthand. Accordingly, I wrote the piece depicting Khrushchev's glorious achievements in only the most glowing colors. Even so, when the book was finally published, I could not recognize my article, for it had been rewritten completely. First of all, it was five times as long as the text I had submitted, coming in at over ten pages of fine print, far longer than the standard for a concise dictionary. Furthermore, the substance of the article was entirely different from what I had written, from the basic structure to the nature of the prose. Under the circumstances I did not feel that I could claim authorship of the article, but the publisher insisted on it and paid me a decent fee.

No Time-outs in the Struggle for Peace

The Cuban missile crisis dealt a severe blow to Khrushchev and the image he was cultivating of a peace-loving leader, which meant that there was much to do in the area of foreign policy after 1962. I remember a meeting late in

1963 at the MFA, where Gromyko spoke about the threat of war and the need for new, more radical measures if we were to achieve détente. Gromyko's talk was meant to prepare us for a major speech that Khrushchev was planning to give on international territorial disputes. I was included in a small working group, "a think tank," charged with formulating a proposal that would be given to Khrushchev in advance of his initiative.

That territorial disputes have always been an urgent matter is clear from even a cursory look at the history of international relations. The problems of establishing borders and settling territorial claims are often the source of dangerous friction between states, sometimes ending in wars. In one of his speeches Khrushchev had blamed territorial disputes on the bourgeoisie. "The question of borders," he said, "is one of the most serious and complex problems we have inherited from the old, capitalist world." Who could imagine then the terrible socialist heritage of territorial disputes that would arise from the dissolution of the Soviet Union in 1991, when in 1963 it had seemed that the problems of territorial demarcation and borders between the nations of the Soviet Union had been solved once and for all. We were convinced that such issues were problems only for nonsocialist countries. Therefore, our initiative provided for the signing of an international agreement that would require a solemn undertaking from countries not to resort to force in order to change their established state borders.

This offer was included in Khrushchev's December 31, 1963, message to the heads of state and governments of all countries of the world. It was intended as the centerpiece of an international dialogue. All embassies and missions were instructed to consider Khrushchev's proposal on territorial issues as a guideline in all of their diplomatic activities. To this end instructions were issued to all institutions and organs with propaganda functions. Together with Leonid Zamyatin, head of the press department, and Lev Mendelevich, a distinguished diplomat, I coauthored a brochure on this subject. I can't even remember how many lectures my colleagues and I gave in 1964 on territorial problems. Now that I had become an expert I was included in the Soviet delegation to the nineteenth session of the UN General Assembly. This was especially significant for me because there were rumors circulating around the MFA that Khrushchev was planning to attend the General Assembly in order to present his proposal in person. That would have given me a chance to join his entourage and see him up close, but it did not happen. First, the opening of the session was postponed because of the presidential elections in the United States and the financial crisis in the UN. Then, by December 1964 when the elections in the United States were over and the financial crisis had eased, Khrushchev's participation was no longer possible for the simple reason that in mid-October he had been removed from all his posts and had gone into retirement. To ordinary Soviet citizens like myself it came as a great surprise; I had to read about it in the newspaper.

Enough Energy But Not Enough Time

I had an opportunity to see Khrushchev shortly before his dismissal. On September 19, 1964, a reception was held in Moscow at the Palace of Congresses honoring the participants in the World Youth Forum attended by Khrushchev and other Kremlin leaders. He gave an emotional speech in which he predicted the eventual victory of communism. He was repeatedly interrupted by applause, but strangely enough he began to lose the interest of his audience. Many of the young people, tired and hungry after a long day of meetings, began drifting over to the tables, which were laden with hors d'oeuvres and drinks, including vodka and wine. The hall became noisy as the alcohol began to have its effect on the guests. Khrushchev, meanwhile, continued to speak, but he became nervous when he realized that he was losing his audience, so he started to shout and to repeat himself. Feeling the awkwardness of the situation, Mikoyan approached Khrushchev and whispered something in his ear, presumably advising him to cut short his speech, but Khrushchev, looking irritated, waved him off and continued. I remember him repeatedly mentioning his age, energy, and potential. "I have enough energy but not enough time," he said, obviously having in mind the time limits of the speech. However, unwittingly he had predicted his own fate. In less than in a month his political career had come to an end.

The Ministry of Foreign Affairs took Khrushchev's ouster in its stride. "Good riddance, we are tired of him," were the words I heard one diplomat utter when he heard the news. We were optimistic that the period of unpredictable initiatives and diplomatic missteps was over and that under the new "collective leadership" of Brezhnev, Podgorny, and Kosygin the MFA would play a more independent role and that the interference of Khrushchev's son-in-law in diplomatic affairs would finally end.

Khrushchev's ouster changed the Kremlin's approach to many political issues. The territorial issue, for instance, which had been occupying center stage for months, suddenly became peripheral, a minor matter. "Old Square" was now telling us that it had been unrealistic to pursue an international agreement on territorial disputes and that it had simply been a propaganda tool. The instructions to the Soviet delegation at the nineteenth session of the UN General Assembly were urgently revised in the changed circumstances. In his speech at the opening session, Gromyko hardly mentioned the international agreement on territorial disputes, even though we had spent the whole year campaigning for it in every UN body. Now that the issue was dead, I expected to be removed from the delegation, but for whatever reason, bureaucratic oversight or to spare my feelings, I spent December 1964 in New York. I was of no use, since my subject was not discussed in any UN body, but I took away many impressions from my stay, and the best news of all was that in Moscow my wife had given birth to my son. At the time, however, I could not have imagined what an important role this great city would come to play in my life. I will have more to say about New York in later chapters.

There is one final loose end still to be tied up regarding the territorial issue—the brochure that Zamyatin, Mendelevich, and I had written for publication. After Khrushchev's dismissal, we all decided that it would be best to cancel publication rather than be publicly associated with an issue that was now virtually discredited. However, the brochure was already in the works, and the publishing house had incurred considerable expenses, so it insisted on going ahead with publication. To cut our losses, Zamyatin, Mendelevich, and I agreed to the following: any and all mention of Khrushchev's name was to be removed from the text, and the publishing house would issue it under a pseudonym. Accordingly, in 1965 International Relations published a brochure on the territorial question under the name P. Smolensky. Khrushchev's name was never mentioned in the text, and the reader never would have guessed that this was an issue of great interest to Khrushchev.

A different situation developed with the article about Khrushchev in the *Diplomatic Dictionary*. The publication of the volume, which contained "monumental" research on Khrushchev, was dated April 1964 in honor of his seventieth birthday. However, when Khrushchev was dismissed a few months later, it was decided to publish a new and revised edition from which the "corrupt" article had been removed.

Naturally, the same problem arose with the textbook, *Soviet Foreign Policy in the New Era*, which was devoted to Khrushchev's "Great Decade." Almost as soon as the book was published and circulated to students, the "hero" of the book had been disavowed. This put teachers in an awkward situation because the school year had already begun and the students no longer had a textbook. I was called to the Central Committee and urgently directed to "revise and amend" the book. "You understand," said the Central Committee "instructor," "that in its present form the textbook is antiparty in nature." As the leader of the authors' group I took offense at this interpretation and snapped back that the book was a good one and had been approved by the Party. The "instructor" backed down, insisting only that all references to Khrushchev be removed. This surgical operation—dare I call it a Khrushchevectomy?—was not difficult, and by the end of the year the second "revised and supplemented" edition was published.

The struggle against the Stalin cult, which Khrushchev had initiated, had clearly backfired on him. It frequently happened during the years of the Soviet Union that such propaganda campaigns were taken to ugly extremes. The ultimate thrust of such campaigns was the message that everything good in the life of the country was to the credit of the Communist Party, and everything bad was the doing of Stalin and Khrushchev. This created a convenient alibi for the Party.

What had really happened during "The Great Decade"? The struggle against the Stalin cult did not make any meaningful change in the structure or nature of power in the Soviet Union. The supreme body remained the same puppet that it had been under Stalin. There was still no possibility of a multiparty system, and all power and authority remained the monopoly of the Communist Party. Moreover, Khrushchev followed his predecessor's methods and style in many areas. The Politburo's decision-making process remained essentially unchanged. All major decisions on domestic and foreign policy issues were made without consulting the legislative bodies, trade unions, or public organizations. Only the mass repressions of Stalin's time were terminated. The persecution of dissidents, however, continued.

Khrushchev's foreign policy was supposed to bring about an easing of tension in international relations, but his sudden and reckless initiatives aimed at knocking opponents off balance only served to discredit these very initiatives. In fact his tactics, far from contributing to peaceful solutions, caused several international crises. Khrushchev was personally responsible for provoking the Cuban and the Berlin crises, two of the most serious incidents in Cold War history. He was furious over the continuation of the U.S.

U-2 spy flights, which resulted in an abrupt suspension of Soviet-American summit contacts. At the same time he ordered the proliferation of Soviet spy activities in the late 1950s and early 1960s. Was this activity not of the same nature as the American spy missions?

6
THAWS AND FROSTS

Foreign Policy Should Not Be Planned by Diplomats

The political and cultural life of the Soviet Union in the 1950s and 1960s was marked by alternating "thaws" and "frosts." This was hardly surprising. De-Stalinization, accompanied by the mass rehabilitation of political criminals and their release from prisons and camps, opened a window on the truth about Soviet reality. Freedom of speech had been severely suppressed in the years of Stalin's dictatorship, but the need for free expression was so great that the authorities had to permit it at least to some degree. On the other hand, Soviet leaders knew that to allow people their civil rights would mean loosening the grip of communist ideological dictatorship, and they certainly had no intention of going that far.

The Cuban missile crisis provoked considerable criticism of Khrushchev's policy in the Caribbean, and much of it appeared in print. In fact the sheer volume of criticism reached such proportions that it threatened to damage the Soviet system itself. Novels about the Gulag by Solzhenitsyn and other liberal authors became popular. Afraid of this, the Kremlin decided to crack down by persecuting writers and artists whose work was considered dangerous.

Brezhnev and his colleagues, who came to power in 1964, appreciably downplayed the anti-Stalin campaign. An example of the truly restrictive measures that were introduced was the formula that began to be widely used against those convicted of political crimes, namely the "dissemination of anti-Soviet, falsified views." Two of the first victims of this weapon used to crush dissent were the writers Andrei Sinyavsky and Yuly Daniel, who were prosecuted in 1965.

It is hard to think of a sector of Soviet society that was not affected by the ideological currents of the day, for everyone was exposed to literature, art, and cinema. Diplomats were no exception. There was always a line in the MFA library to read the bestsellers, and we all went to the movies and art exhibitions. At my seminars at the Diplomatic Academy some students tried to discuss the works of new authors, but I stopped them. I was afraid of being accused of organizing "unnecessary" or provocative discussions. Khrushchev's meetings with writers and artists where he demonstrated his total ignorance in these areas were discussed in the corridors. From numerous conversations, I came to the conclusion that the majority of diplomats liked the new cultural options open to them and continued to read books labeled "erroneous" by the Kremlin leadership. They read them, but kept their opinions to themselves. and adopted the attitude that "whatever the authorities decide is 'erroneous' is 'erroneous'; that's not our business, we are diplomats and do not want to get involved." Soviet functionaries, as servants of their government, had little opportunity to express themselves, but the creative impulse, present in each person, required some sort of outlet. For example, in the early 1960s there was a popular proposal to create a new office within the MFA for drafting national foreign policy projections on a continuing basis. This reflected an appetite for some professional independence, and its advocates invoked in its support the experience of diplomatic colleagues in other countries, particularly in the United States.

Vladimir Khvostov was one of the authors of the proposal and involved me in the project. Minister Gromyko supported the general idea and promised to circulate the idea within the Kremlin. However, as one might have expected, the proposal was firmly rejected. The functionaries from the Old Square treated the idea of planning and projecting Soviet foreign policy outside the CPSU Central Committee as blasphemous. At a meeting of the MFA working group on the creation of a foreign policy planning structure, a representative from the Central Committee showed his undisguised contempt for the MFA proposal. He gave us to understand in no uncertain terms that Soviet foreign policy is determined and planned by the Politburo and that no academics or career diplomats will be allowed to usurp its functions. Two influential members of the Central Committee, Boris Ponomarev and Aleksandr Panyushkin said much the same thing at a session of the Central Committee Secretariat. After a long discussion a compromise was reached whereby an External Planning Department was created within the MFA with the task of sifting through decisions made by the Politburo, the congresses, and plenary meetings of the CPSU Central Committee on global policy issues. It was clear, however, that the party leadership had no intention of investing this body with any real power or influence. As the first head of the department, the Central Committee nominated Aleksandr Soldatov, a career diplomat and experienced bureaucrat, rather than Professor Khvostov, an academic who would have been a natural choice for the position.

The creation of the External Planning Department did not make any appreciable change in the way foreign policy decisions were made in the Soviet Union. Nevertheless, it must be said that this division, which changed its name over the years, did play a useful role as a think tank within the MFA, a bureaucratic dinosaur not known for the freshness of its thinking. The unremitting vigilance of the CPSU Central Committee would never permit free and creative discussions of world politics.

The Soviet Academy of Science's Council on the History of Soviet Foreign Policy and International Relations, which was created in the early 1960s, could have been a forum for the wide discussion of international problems. Like other councils, it brought together experts in the appropriate areas for open discussions of the most urgent issues of the day. Initially this body showed great interest in foreign affairs. Maisky, Khvostov, Aleksei Narochnitsky, and Vladimir Trukhanovsky were among the well-known historians and diplomats who joined the council. I was also one of its members. It was agreed at the founders' meeting that the council would not shy away from discussing tough questions, would fill in the "black holes" in the history of Soviet foreign policy, develop a theory of foreign affairs, and entertain the possibility of reasonable, scientifically based projections, and so on. However, this turned out to be only wishful thinking. I remember during one session that the proposal of a certain member to start a discussion of Soviet-German relations in 1939–41 was greeted with a stunned silence, since everyone in the room knew that it was impossible to gain access to the archival documents, and that in any case there was no way that the Central Committee leadership would permit such an initiative. "What is there to discuss? It is clear as it is," was the response of another board member, and we moved on to another topic. Attempts to discuss other controversial issues usually had the same outcome, and this supposedly expert body spent its time mainly organizing anniversaries.

As an enthusiastic supporter of the council, I was especially discouraged by its failure. I understood that its work should be based on the Marxist-Leninist concept of historical process, but this ultimately excluded any opportunity for serious discussion or disagreement on basic issues. The incompatibility between obedience to Marxist-Leninist dogma and a free, unbiased approach to historical processes eventually became clear to me. After Aleksandr Nekrich, one of its active members had run into trouble for his attempts to state unorthodox views, the futility of the work of the council became chronic.

The Aleksandr Nekrich Case

I got to know Aleksandr Nekrich in the early 1960s at the Institute of History. A field officer during World War II, he had earned a master's degree in history at the Institute. Despite this rather modest position, he was a renowned historian, regularly called upon to participate in scholarly conferences and forums on foreign affairs. He had authored several books, mainly on the history of British foreign policy and international relations, as well as numerous articles on the history of diplomacy and Soviet foreign policy. I had read a number of his works over the years and liked his fresh approach and lively writing style. (It is no surprise that he was a popular young man, known for being both affable and a gifted conversationalist. Together with Ponomarev, secretary of the CPSU Central Committee, Nekrich coauthored the highly regarded book, *The History of Soviet Foreign Policy*. Ponomarev, Gromyko, and Khvostov were chief editors of this official two-volume work, which was reprinted five times and only went out of print in Gorbachev's era of perestroika.

In early 1966 Nekrich approached me with a request to participate in a discussion of his new book *June 22, 1941*. In this book he blamed Stalin for the military disaster that befell the Soviet Union on the day Germany attacked the USSR. Although he used a full range of sources, he had not produced any new or previously unknown facts because he did not have access to the archives. His only sources were the former head of military intelligence, General Filipp Golikov, and eyewitness accounts of important prewar and wartime events. I read the book and found his brilliant account of the pernicious effects of Stalin's policy on the start of the war fascinating. Nevertheless, the book had grave consequences for Nekrich's career in a way that is symptomatic of the Cold War Soviet system. The story has been told before by Nekrich himself, among others, so I will confine myself to describing the reactions of my colleagues from the MFA.

First of all I have to say that although he didn't work at the MFA, Nekrich nonetheless enjoyed authority as an expert in diplomatic history, and many of us considered him to be one of our own. He was involved in various MFA publications, participated in some meetings, and lectured at MFA educational functions. Diplomats greeted *June 22, 1941* with interest, but with definite reservations. This was because the book came out in late 1965, when Stalin's reputation was undergoing a very subtle shift. This became evident in May 1965 when Brezhnev in his report marking the twentieth anniversary of V-Day made no reference to Stalin's miscalculations in the war. He merely said that a State Defense Committee headed by general secretary of the CPSU, Yosif Vissarionovich Stalin, had been set up to coordinate all operations to prosecute the war against the enemy. This phrase was met with applause, a sign that the "struggle against the Stalin cult" was coming to an end.

In these circumstances many diplomats regarded the timing of the publication of Nekrich's book as unfortunate. A key part of his text cited comments by former political prisoners who had spent decades in the gulags, which were highly critical of Stalin. Some of them demanded the prosecution of Stalin's closest colleagues, who were viewed as being responsible for Soviet losses in the beginning of the war. These sentiments in particular were not in line with the position of the communist leadership.

Having heard so many positive comments about the book, I could not have imagined that it would lead to negative consequences for the author, but I was wrong. Fueling the controversy about Stalin at a time when the new Soviet leadership was obviously trying to muffle it could only cause alarm in the Kremlin. The leadership was further enraged when the German weekly *Der Spiegel* used Nekrich's book to contradict Brezhnev's evaluation of Stalin's role in the war. It was soon clear that Nekrich was in trouble. He was purged from the Party, after which the oppressions and persecutions began, and his name disappeared from the list of authors in the second edition of *The History of Soviet Foreign Policy*.

One of Nekrich's enemies wrote to the Supreme Attestation Commission demanding that his doctoral degree be revoked. The sole reason for this demand was Nekrich's expulsion from the Communist Party. Otherwise it was absolutely unjustified because Nekrich's dissertation was on British foreign policy and had nothing to do with the subject of his heretical book. Nevertheless, the Attestation Commission, presided over by Minister Vyacheslav Yelutin, approved a shameful resolution to reconsider its former decision. The commission requested official opponents of the dissertation to present new reviews. Academician Maisky and I confirmed our original positive judgments and recommendations. According to Nekrich, a Professor Meryagheye from Estonia refused to repeat his positive evaluation, obviously fearing possible difficulties.

Many Soviet scholars protested against the actions of the Attestation Commission, threatening to cause a scandal in world academic circles. Subsequently, Nekrich kept his degree but was prevented from engaging in academic research. Most of his subsequent work could not be published in the Soviet Union. Eventually he was compelled to emigrate in the early 1970s to the United States, where he was quickly recognized as an outstanding Sovietologist.

Remember, Truth Is on Our Side

The Nekrich case showed that the authorities were not going to tolerate political discussion that went beyond the ideological limits set by the CPSU. Here is another example. In the 1960s I joined Professor Yury Borisov in creating an international section within the Moscow Club of Scholars. It was supposed to acquaint young scholars with life abroad—the distinctive traditions and customs of different peoples throughout the world. Renowned scholars, who had seen life in many countries, willingly shared their impressions through lectures and presentations. Within the framework of the section we organized so-called diplomatic chats, which turned into open discussions of various political issues. Meetings devoted to veterans of the Soviet diplomatic service were especially popular and were attended by relatives, former colleagues, and eyewitnesses to the events of the 1920s and 1930s. Their memories, naturally, revived tragic episodes from the lives of the pioneers of Soviet diplomacy. The theme of Stalin's bloody and despotic rule was the usual leitmotif.

I was not surprised, therefore, when the director of the Club advised me "as a friend" to discontinue these "gatherings of the elderly," which she said might mean serious trouble for all of us. Invoking "the directives of the comrades," obviously meaning the high-ranking party functionaries, she asked me to organize a cycle of lectures titled "The Leninist Foreign Policy of the USSR." She wanted me to invite "reliable comrades" to lecture. Not knowing whom she meant I invited my former Diplomatic Academy classmates, who by that time had become quite successful in their careers. Their lectures were pure boilerplate. They opened with a panegyric to the peaceful foreign policy of the Soviet Union and the growing support it was receiving from the Soviet people and "all progressive humanity." The next part of the lecture was devoted "to condemning the militarist and aggressive" nature of the imperialists' policy, which was inevitably "doomed to failure." These philippics were generally followed by a few anecdotes, which were harmless enough to guarantee approval from the propaganda bureaucracy. Despite the simplistic nature of these talks they enjoyed considerable success in the Soviet Union, something which can only be explained by the indefatigable curiosity of the Soviet people about life in the capitalist world. They wanted to be reassured that their daily hardships were truly justified by the "interests of the world."

Once in the mid-1960s social science teachers of Moscow universities and institutes, including lecturers from the Diplomatic Academy, were invited to a meeting at the Old Square. We were informed that the Central Committee had decided to send lecturers abroad in order to promote Soviet propaganda outside the Soviet Union. The Central Committee official who chaired the meeting assured us that the lecturers should not fear argument or free and frank discussions of the most difficult issues. He urged us to deliver the "truth about our party" to the workers in other countries, who in his opinion, were in "ideological captivity" to bourgeois propaganda.

Soon thereafter Lev Bashkin, who worked in the Central Committee and was my former classmate, told me that I had been chosen to lecture about Soviet foreign policy in the Netherlands, Britain, and Germany. Having known me for years, he knew that he did not have to instruct me about the "hostility surrounding the Soviet Union" or "the intrigues of class enemies." Instead we spoke about the substance of my lectures. His advice was to avoid ideas about world revolution and instead to structure my lectures around the idea of peaceful coexistence and the Soviet aspiration to cooperate with all countries. He further recommended avoiding arguments unless the audience was especially aggressive. Bashkin's words were a great relief to me because, frankly, I was not prepared to promote world revolution and was not about to threaten to bury capitalism.

In the Lecture Halls of the World

I remember my 1965–67 trips abroad quite well. My schedule of lectures was coordinated by Soviet embassies with appropriate local authorities, and I was told not to deviate from this schedule without their express consent. Nor was I to make contact with any local communist organizations unless I had the approval of the local authorities.

These years were special in the history of the Cold War. Khrushchev had left the political stage. The audiences I lectured to were quite diverse. At a meeting in Bonn, for example, there were officials from the federal chancellor's office, the Ministry for Foreign Affairs, the Defense Ministry, and other departments. In the Hague I spoke at the West-East Institute to young Dutch diplomats and held a press conference for journalists from the major Dutch newspapers. In Hamburg and Birmingham I met with business people. However, university students remained my core audience. I visited the universities of Bonn and Hamburg and a number of Dutch schools, one of which was in Groningen. I had a very interesting discussion in Imperial College in London with students and teachers from a wide range of countries, including the developing ones. I also visited Cambridge, namely Peterhouse College, where I had spent more than six months working on my doctoral dissertation in the 1950s.

My lectures dealt mainly with issues of Soviet foreign policy, though on occasion I spoke on special themes such as the fiftieth anniversary of the October Revolution, which was celebrated in 1967. Questions from students and the discussions that followed them were certainly the most interesting part of my presentations. The favorite method of Soviet lecturers was to deliver long lectures with little or no time for discussion but a diplomat from the Soviet embassy in Holland Ivan Gozochov warned me on my arrival in the Hague not to speak too long lest my listeners get up and leave. I followed his advice.

I cannot recall all the questions I was asked, but I do remember that audiences were concerned above all with Soviet policy in Europe. Everyone remembered the events in Hungary and especially in East Germany. The tense situation in Berlin with the erection of the Wall and the continuing defections of Germans and citizens from other socialist countries to the West gave sufficient grounds for fears of new complications. Many asked about the possibility of a reunified Germany or, more cautiously, about the prospects of relations between the Federal Republic of Germany (FRG) and the German Democratic Republic (GDR). The name of the East German leader Ulbricht was mentioned only in a negative context during our discussions. There were also worries that the maverick policy of the Romanian dictator Nicolae Ceauçescu could create a dangerous center of tension in Europe. Naturally, I was asked about Brezhnev and other new Soviet leaders.

I, certainly, could not provide complete answers to all of these questions, the last one in particular. I would beat around the bush as much as I could, using our propaganda clichés as a basis for my replies. I depicted the future in bright colors. I tried to convince my listeners that peace, friendship, and international cooperation were vital to the Soviet Union, and therefore it was in the interest of the Soviet leadership to build good relations with all countries on the basis of goodwill and mutual understanding. I spoke with passion and conviction, and I believe I won over at least some of my audience. In responding to specific questions about Germany I invoked the troubled history of Russian-German relations, and these references usually evoked a sympathetic response, especially in Britain and Holland.

The most difficult questions to answer were the ones dealing with human rights violations in the Soviet Union, the lack of freedom to leave and return to the USSR, and the growing numbers of refugees from socialist countries. "If as you insist socialist countries enjoy free public health services and education, inexpensive housing and transportation, and no unemployment, why so many of your citizens prefer not to return home from abroad?" I was asked this question a multitude of time. I certainly could not use the arguments the Soviet ambassador to the GDR Peter Abrasimov used once when responding to the same question about why East Germans were fleeing to West Germany. He said: "only to tell their Western brothers how good it is to live in the GDR." His reply was invariably followed by a new question "Why, then, don't they go back home after having told their brothers how good life is in the GDR"? The ambassador would calmly say that in the West there are so many who want to hear about life in the GDR that the East Germans don't have time return home.

I answered differently. I acknowledged that the standard of living in the West was higher than in the USSR and other socialist countries. I then pointed out that this could be explained by the fact that the East had sustained much greater destruction and devastation than the West in World War II. Errors and miscalculations in the course of postwar economic recovery also played their part. All this, I argued, induced some citizens of socialist countries to seek better lives in the West. There was certainly some truth in what I was telling my audiences but it was not the whole truth. Most

Soviet citizens defected for political reasons, but I would never say this.

Some people asked practical questions about the experience of being a diplomat in the USSR, and about the educational institutions in which they were trained. I was most vague when speaking about the Diplomatic Academy, where I was a professor, because the Diplomatic Academy was a classified establishment. I shared my experience of work in the Soviet archives. In this connection, there was the issue of the Secret Protocols of the August 23, 1939, Soviet-German pact. I was asked this question in the German foreign ministry after being shown a German copy of the protocols, signed by Molotov and Ribbentrop. I admitted to participating in the preparation of the sensational "Falsifiers of History" note, connected with the 1939 agreement. I also acknowledged that neither my fellow diplomats nor I had ever seen the confidential protocols, something that astonished my listeners.

My lectures were not without their humorous moments. In Hamburg the organizers of my visit told me that I was to perform in front of a pro-Soviet audience where local communists were to be present. I certainly did not object. The speech was delivered in an overcrowded bar where the organizers had a hard time controlling the unruly audience. As soon as I began to speak, I felt hostility. People interrupted, shouted, whistled, and kept up a constant barrage of noise. In a word, their attitude to the Soviet Union was anything but friendly. When in the course of the lecture I remarked that the Soviet people never had any hostility toward the German people, but only to the Nazis, the audience exploded. Someone climbed onto the stage and told me: "Mister lecturer we do not believe a single word you're saying. Everything you just said is nothing but cheap communist propaganda. By listening we were only paying tribute to your courage. Coming here and saying the things you said takes guts. Now we want you to leave." I was forced to leave to the sounds of shouting and singing. It turned out that the organizers had mistakenly taken me to the wrong place, where some neo-Nazi organization happened to be meeting. I flatly refused to go to the other, "friendly" bar. The organizers must take the blame for this lost opportunity to strengthen Soviet-German cooperation.

Not all the surprises were unpleasant. Speaking to a rather small group of German businessmen and bankers in Hamburg, my attention was attracted by a pleasant-looking member of the audience who did not pose a single question or participate in the discussion. After the lecture he approached me and said that he had no interest in the Soviet Union whatsoever. The only reason he had come to my lecture was because he thought that I was an ethnic Armenian like himself. We went to a restaurant, where he told me he had been taken to Syria by his parents, who barely survived the Turkish Genocide during World War I. He was brought up there and then left in search of work and education in the West. Ibrahim Cutujian, my new acquaintance, settled down in West Germany and became a businessman and a respectable German citizen. He married a German woman and had three daughters with Armenian names. To his credit, he had made it his goal to help people in Armenia, where he had never actually been. He asked me to tell him about life in Soviet Armenia, about its problems, about the Armenian presence in the Moscow power structure, and so on. We talked for several hours and remained lifelong friends until the day of his untimely death. A routine lecture in Hamburg about Soviet foreign policy had won me the invaluable acquaintance of a wonderful, talented (apart from his business abilities Ibrahim knew about ten languages), and kind person.

As a rule someone from the Soviet embassy would be present at my lectures. Apart from any interest there might be in the lectures of a professor at the Diplomatic Academy, Moscow wanted to keep track of me. Fortunately we had no problems or disagreements. I always behaved cautiously, and any levity I permitted myself was generally perceived by the audiences as a sign of sincerity and contributed to the success of my lectures, and this also satisfied the embassy.

The majority of the people I met during my lectures and talks were friendly. Some of course, like the neo-Nazis in Hamburg, were hostile, but for every hostile person it seemed that there was a corresponding radical or procommunist. Many university teachers and lecturers expressed their belief that the mingling of socialist and capitalist systems would ultimately benefit human society. These people liked my lectures. Those who were most unsympathetic to lectures by Soviet speakers tended to be refugees from the Soviet Union and other socialist countries. They had absolutely no interest in hearing standard Soviet boilerplate from a Soviet career diplomat. During the Cold War the public was interested in peace and true international cooperation

My lecture tour acquainted me with the work of Soviet embassies and other Soviet establishments abroad. I met many of my Diplomatic Academy classmates and former students who were working at the embassies in Britain, the Netherlands, West Germany, Hungary, and other countries I visited. They told me what it was like working and living in the particular country and about relations with its government and the work of diplomacy in that specific context. Conversations about the internal life of the embassy, about relations among the diplomats, and communications with Moscow were equally interesting. I was privy to much gossip, including tales about ambassadors and the financial situation of the embassy staff. I was also advised on where to shop and find the best deals.

It seemed that the rigid compliance and total obedience to Moscow had eased somewhat. Contacts with public figures, activists, politicians, and nongovernmental organizations had broadened. My classmates told me about the interesting people, including eminent artists and writers, whom they had the opportunity to meet. According to the diplomats, the authority and influence of the Soviet Union abroad was growing steadily, largely because of Soviet success in space exploration.

As I learned more about work of the embassies a thought began to disturb me. It was the discrepancy between the nature of the training of Soviet diplomats and their practical work in the field. This was something that had actually been worrying my colleagues and myself for many years. We came to the conclusion that all the principal professors at the academy should have to work, at least temporarily, at one of the embassies. Former Diplomatic Academy students, some of whom had already held high diplomatic posts in the past, supported the idea. "You're supposed to be able to do it yourself before you teach others," one of them said.

A group of teachers managed to meet Panyushkin, a Central Committee member who headed the CPSU's Department of Personnel. He was very understanding and sympathetic.

My First Meetings with Gromyko

The turning point in my life was linked to my relations with Gromyko's family. I had known Andrei Andreyevich Gromyko for more than twenty years. I had had many opportunities to see him at work—at conferences, in conversations with state leaders and diplomats, both Soviet and foreign. I had also spent a lot of time with him in social settings outside the office. I saw him in both good and bad moods. In general he was very quiet, a little slow, and unemotional. My diplomatic career largely depended on him. At the same time it would be wrong to say that I belonged to his inner circle, but I do believe that he trusted and relied on me.

I met Gromyko in New York at the nineteenth session of the UN General Assembly in 1964 when he had already been serving for several years as the foreign minister of the Soviet Union. As a professor at the Diplomatic Academy, I was with the Soviet delegation as an expert. In a free moment between meetings, Gromyko engaged me in conversation. He was curious about my impressions of the work of the General Assembly. He advised me, while in New York, to establish contacts with American experts in the area of Soviet-American relations. He suggested I visit Columbia University and the offices of *Foreign Affairs* magazine. Following his advice I met with Philip Mosley and Hans Morgenthau at Columbia and George Campbell at *Foreign Affairs*.

My second meeting with Gromyko took place in the summer of 1967, at his summer residence in Vnukovo. I was invited by his son, Anatoly, who worked in the Diplomatic Academy and lived in the residence with his wife and parents. We spent that summer day in conversation with Andrei Andreyevich. We talked about history and the Second World War in particular. He was familiar with my book, *The Anti-Hitler Coalition*, which he said he liked. He commented on diplomatic events of the war, and gave interesting insight into the characters of the wartime leaders. He especially enjoyed talking about his meetings with President Roosevelt, whom he called "a great man." "He will never have an equal in the capitalist world," Gromyko was fond of saying.

The day passed in pleasant conversations and jokes. Gromyko was relaxed—absolutely different from the mean, grumbling functionary so often described by his colleagues. Only one episode marred the peaceful family atmosphere of that day. It was getting dark as we were sitting at the table finishing our meal when the telephone rang. It was a call for Andrei Andreyevich. As soon as he took the call he jumped to his feet and briefly answered the caller: "Yes," "Absolutely," "Certainly," "I'll be right over." As soon as he had hung up, he got up from the table and left without saying a word to any of us. My wife Alla and I looked at each other, afraid that something terrible had happened. Could it be war? we wondered. Meanwhile, everyone else at the dinner table continued eating and talking as if nothing had happened. Noticing our embarrassment, our hostess Lidya Dmitriyevna, Gromyko's wife, said with a smile: "Don't worry, it was Leonid Ilyich [Brezhnev] who called. He probably invited Andryusha hunting, just to have a good time." Such a reaction to a call from the general secretary was, obviously, natural but it was the first time I had witnessed such subservience at the highest level. Not at all an agreeable spectacle!

In mid-October 1967 I was suddenly called away from a meeting and told that Minister Gromyko wanted to talk with me. I had no idea what it might be about, but remembering the friendly chats in the summer I hoped for good news. When I entered Gromyko's office, he told me that I had worked in the teaching field long enough, and it seemed to him that the time had come to try something else. He asked me how I would like to work as a deputy permanent representative to the UN. He also made me another offer. He said that the CPSU Central Committee had decided to create a United States Institute. Georgy Arbatov, who had worked in the Central Committee, had been nominated as director but the MFA and the KGB could each nominate one candidate for the posts of deputy director. So Gromyko asked me if I would prefer instead to continue my academic career and take the position of deputy director of the Institute. Of course, I was very happy with my academic work. I had become very comfortable with teaching and research. Having been a career diplomat for several decades, I always tried to lecture and write articles and books on the history of international relations. Nevertheless, I thought it would be good to have an opportunity to work, at least temporarily, as a diplomat. I shared with Gromyko the view of many of us in the Diplomatic Academy that a teacher of diplomacy ought to be required to work as a diplomat before teaching others.

I therefore told Gromyko that I would like to work in the diplomatic field for two to three years and then return to my pedagogical and scholarly work possibly at the United States Institute. Gromyko suggested that I not look so far ahead. Smiling at me, he said, "Only time will tell." At that, the conversation ended, and I left the room. All in all, our talk probably lasted no more than twenty minutes, but it had changed my life forever. Gromyko decided to appoint me deputy permanent representative to the UN.

A Meeting with Brezhnev

On December 2, 1967, I came back late from work and was surprised when my wife Alla told me that Brezhnev was expecting me at his office the following morning at nine o'clock. At first I thought she was joking, so I smiled and asked when I was scheduled to meet with President Johnson, but after she gave me the name of the person in Gromyko's secretariat who had confirmed the appointment, I knew she was serious. I spent the rest of the evening speculating about the possible reasons for such an unusual summons.

Needless to say, I arrived at the party building on Old Square long before my scheduled appointment and went directly to Brezhnev's reception area, where I waited nervously for my appointment. I asked Brezhnev's senior assistant, Andrei Aleksandrov-Agentov (whom I had known for many years) why I was there, but he refused to tell me. "Leonid Ilyich will inform you," he answered. Although he was kind enough to add in a reassuring voice: "Nothing bad is going to happen." Party-bureaucratic etiquette did not allow him to inform a subordinate about personnel issues. Also waiting in the reception area was head of the MFA Foreign Planning Department, Aleksandr Soldatov. He too had been called in to meet with the general secretary and was also in the dark as to the reason for the meeting. He had brought along with him a thick file containing papers having to do with his work in the department. As it turned out, this was unnecessary because he was being called in connection with his assignment as ambassador to Cuba. This was the only subject of his meeting with Brezhnev. And Soldatov was duly appointed Soviet ambassador to Havana.

When I was finally called into Brezhnev's office, the conversation began in a most unexpected way. He told me that during a recent Politburo session Gromyko had recommended me for the post of deputy permanent representative to the UN, but nobody in the Politburo had known who I was. Brezhnev looked me in the eye and asked, "Why is this so?" Of course, I didn't know what to say. How could I answer such a question? And how could it be that at age forty-eight I was completely unknown in the Politburo? This made me all the more nervous and confused, but seeing my confusion Brezhnev backed off a bit and explained that it was precisely for this reason that he had decided to meet with me. I then tried to tell him about my pedagogical work, but he interrupted me and told me that he was familiar with my personal file. At that point, the conversation was over, and the monologue had begun. Brezhnev went on to explain that the United Nations was very important to Soviet foreign policy and that the Soviet leadership had decided to strengthen the Soviet delegation in the UN. He made some vague mention of past mistakes we had made in the UN, but I couldn't tell for certain if he was referring to the Cuban missile crisis or some other incident that had turned out badly for us.

As an inexperienced diplomat, I didn't quite know how to interpret the news of my new assignment. I suppose that deep inside I was flattered at the thought of being promoted to such a responsible post, and perhaps I thought for a fleeting moment that the Soviet leadership considered my appointment as part of its efforts to "strengthen" the delegation. At that moment I was not aware that a decision had been made to expand the managerial body of the UN mission from three deputies to five. Nor did I know that Nikolai Fedorenko had been removed as permanent representative, and Yakov Malik appointed in his place. Fortunately, therefore, I kept my mouth closed and didn't speculate out loud about the reasons for my appointment.

Brezhnev did not touch upon the specifics of work in the UN. He only mentioned the disarmament issue and the Middle East settlement. He attached great importance to maintaining good relations with the UN secretary-general, U Thant, of whom he spoke very warmly. U Thant had met with Brezhnev during a visit to the Soviet Union; and therefore, he was of the opinion that U Thant was friendly to the Soviet Union and shared its views on many issues. Brezhnev also told me to bear in mind that the UN was located in the United States and warned me that I should "give this fact serious thought." "The United States is our main rival, and they dream of destroying us," he said, "but we have to live together side by side." From this I understood that Soviet-American relations would be an important part of my work in New York, but beyond this I was given no real specifics concerning the nature of my assignment.

In conclusion Brezhnev asked me to convey to Gromyko that he supported my appointment and that I was to work in New York. Then he surprised me with an unexpected question. "Do you know what politics are?" he asked. Without waiting for my reply he told me an anecdote about Ukrainian peasants arguing about the nature of politics. After a long discussion the peasants came to the conclusion that it was a delicate matter but how delicate no one could say. Then the elder resolved the arguments by drawing a line and stating that "politics are as delicate as grandpa's member." We both laughed at this, although I didn't quite understand why he had made this off-color joke or exactly what he meant by it. I wanted to respond with a joke of my own but I didn't dare. I simply thanked him for his confidence, expressed readiness to apply all my knowledge and skills, and left his office happy.

Upon my return to the academy, I told the rector Mikhail Yakovlev of my meeting with Brezhnev. He advised me to write down the details of our conversation so that I would have a permanent record of it. "You don't have meetings like this every day," he joked. I did, in fact, try to write down what we had said, but I found it very difficult because there was nothing very specific to record: Brezhnev's general speculations on some international problems, a few jokes, and one obscene anecdote. That was all there was to our meeting. In fact, the more I thought about it the harder it was for me to discern the real purpose of our conversation. Why had Brezhnev really called me into his office? I knew perfectly well that it wasn't routine for an ambassador to meet with the general secretary prior to an appointment. Usually they met with the prime minister or other high-ranking party or government officials. This time the general secretary had spent about half an hour of his time speaking to the future deputy permanent representative to the UN—a rare occurrence! My experienced colleagues could not remember anything like it.

I still do not know for sure why Brezhnev took the time to meet with me that day, but later on I did learn a few facts that certainly must have had something to do with it. At one Politburo meeting Gromyko had spoken about the necessity to broaden Soviet policy in the UN and to strengthen the mission of the USSR. He had in mind in particular nominating Malik as well as a few new deputies. My name appeared on the list and drew objections from the party head of the CPSU personnel department Panyushkin. I can only guess why he was against me. He might have been afraid of the 1944 letter from my father to Dekanozov, which I described in an earlier chapter. Later I learned that he had tried to find out from the Diplomatic Academy if I was Jewish. Also the tense relations between Panyushkin and Gromyko may have played a role. Generally speaking, no one in the Politburo wished to ignore an objection from a member of the Central Committee, especially considering the fact that no one from the Politburo knew me. Under the circumstances, it is entirely possible that Brezhnev decided that he would settle the matter by meeting with me directly. Why, however, he didn't ask me more detailed questions is hard to explain. Certainly he had no interest in my personality. Rather, he probably needed to demonstrate his skill at settling disputes, even small ones, within the Politburo. He supported Gromyko's nominee when Gromyko's position in the Kremlin was growing, but he needed to show that he could listen to everyone and not take sides. Furthermore, as party leader he was demonstrating, for all to see, his serious interest in foreign affairs and in the selection of diplomatic staff.

At any rate, shortly after my meeting with Brezhnev, the bureaucratic machinery began to move. I filled out questionnaires, gathered information, and underwent medical examinations in anticipation of my move to New York. Meanwhile, no public announcement of my appointment was made within the MFA, so naturally, rumors began to spread that I had been entrusted with a special mission for which I would report directly to Brezhnev. The Soviet bureaucracy did not consider it necessary to make any official announcement of such appointments. About the same time I was also awarded the Order of the Red Labor Banner for my pedagogical work, which further fueled speculations about my mystery mission. Of course, I knew that all of this was pure nonsense, but frankly speaking, I didn't try to scotch the rumors because I enjoyed the attention and the air of mystery it lent me at this momentous time in my life.

The Elite Department of the Ministry

Before my departure for New York I was given an internship at the International Organizations Department of the MFA (IOD). This was quite natural because I had no practice in diplomatic work, especially in international organizations and multilateral diplomacy. Having no office of my own, I moved around from room to room, thus expanding the circle of my acquaintances. I could listen to conversations and hear my colleagues give their assessments of events and their feelings about the work of other departments. From these conversations I gradually began to realize that I had landed in one of the leading departments of the ministry. The department participated in drafting important political documents, for it was directly involved in disarmament issues—one of the major international problems of the day and a favorite subject for Soviet foreign initiatives during the Cold War. The IOD was also responsible for many of the international political issues discussed at international forums. The staff of the department informed me, not without pride, that not a day passed without Gromyko or his first deputy Kuznetsov giving assignments to Kiril Novikov, the head of the department, or one of his deputies.

Novikov was an important figure, undoubtedly one of the leading Soviet diplomats during World War II and the early postwar years. I frequently worked with him during my academic years, preparing articles and participating in academic conferences, usually on UN matters. He understood the work of international organizations very well, and was frequently called upon to attend sessions of the UN General Assembly. He joined the MFA in 1940, soon after Molotov became minister. Although for the most part he worked in post-Stalin times, he unquestionably belonged to the "Stalin generation" of Soviet diplomats. He was orthodox and rigid in the best tradition of Stalin's diplomats. He was also a good speaker and able to command the attention of large audiences.

When I asked Novikov what I should concentrate on during my internship at the IOD, he answered without hesitation: "Take the rules and procedures of the General Assembly and the Security Council. Read them and learn them by heart. You will always need these whatever you do at the UN." Throughout my career I had many occasions to recognize the wisdom of this advice. As for my assignment, Novikov believed that I would be involved to a certain degree in the question of a Middle East settlement because he was convinced that the Middle East would remain on the agenda of world diplomacy for many years to come. He was certainly right.

Novikov enjoyed nearly unlimited authority at the IOD. The young staff members attempted to imitate him in everything, some even copying his bad habits. For instance, he was a heavy drinker, something that sometimes interfered with his career. He once had to stay in bed at the hotel throughout a whole session of the General Assembly in the early 1960s. After this incident Gromyko dropped him from the delegation.

One of the most important topics of our discussions was the role of bilateral and multilateral diplomacy in global politics. The majority of us understood the special opportunities the UN offered in the Cold War years. The General Assembly was more than a place to launch propaganda campaigns and fight ideological duels; it also served as a convenient place for any and every possible kind of bilateral and multilateral meeting, public and private. Experienced diplomats, including veterans, understood that the various inter-allied, Soviet-American-British mechanisms, effective in the years of the Second World War, were now a thing of the past. Interminable arguments among diplomats have made it abundantly clear that bilateral and multilateral diplomacy should supplement each other.

My MFA training had shown me that the questions I would be working on were crucial, urgent, and subject to close scrutiny by the leadership. Some of my Diplomatic Academy classmates who worked in other MFA departments agreed with my assessment of the situation and warmly congratulated me on my appointment to the IOD.

In the spring of 1968 I began a new life. For decades I had been training future Soviet diplomats—hundreds of them, in fact—in the art of Cold War diplomacy. Now I was destined to become one of the combatants myself. I was venturing into the unknown with my new wife and two young sons. I did not know how we would adjust to the new conditions, and deep inside I wondered if perhaps it was too late for someone approaching fifty to make such a drastic change of course.

7
ON THE DIPLOMATIC SIDELINES

The Changing of the Guard

In 1968 there was significant "changing of the guard" in the Soviet mission to the UN. Malik was appointed the new permanent representative. His predecessor Fedorenko after a thirty-year career in diplomacy, five of which were spent in New York, left the MFA and devoted himself to scholarly and literary endeavors. His voluntary resignation from the ministry was an exception to the established rules and practices of the Soviet diplomatic service. The famous diplomat Maisky switched careers to work at the Academy of Science, but this transition took place in Stalin's times via a prison cell. Nothing nearly as tragic happened to Fedorenko, though it was well known that he did not get along with Gromyko. Moscow did not like Fedorenko's independence.

Malik arrived in New York in early March of 1968. Upon arrival he gave an interview in which, along with the customary propaganda clichés, he made a true prophecy. "The Cold War," he said, "will bring neither glory nor honor to anyone." Many saw in this statement a foreshadowing of the readiness of the Soviet Union to put an end to the Cold War, but alas, the events of the spring and summer of that year in Czechoslovakia and their international ramifications laid those speculations to rest.

Malik began his work in the UN by paying protocol visits. His first was to the UN secretary-general U Thant, followed by calls on the representatives of the permanent members of the Security Council—Arthur Goldberg (United States), Lord Caradon (United Kingdom), Armand Berar (France), and other ambassadors. (The Soviet Union did not recognize the Kuomintang government as representing China.)

Since I had arrived practically at the same time as Malik, he took me along with him on these visits. Sometimes he introduced me, and sometimes not, and I had to keep silent. These visits reminded me of a scene from Gogol's *Dead Souls*, when happy-go-lucky Nozdrev always brought along a relative on his social calls but always forgot to introduce him, until he was just about to leave. My situation wasn't quite that bad, but I often thought of Gogol.

Malik's appointment was greeted with mixed feelings at the UN. On the one hand, he was known in diplomatic circles as an experienced professional, who was familiar with the inner workings of the UN. On the other hand, aware of the hard line he had taken at the UN when he was the permanent representative from 1948 to 1952, many feared a recurrence of acrimonious verbal confrontations. The British representative, Lord Caradon, well expressed these ambivalent feelings about Malik, when he welcomed him at the first meeting of the Security Council attended by the new Soviet representative. Caradon pointed out that Malik had shown himself an outstanding performer "in the ritual dance of argument" so characteristic of the Cold War, and added that he had no doubt that Malik would live up to that reputation both in public discussions and in private negotiations. Caradon's words were prophetic. Only a couple of weeks later, speaking on the situation in the Middle East at the Security Council, Malik attacked the Israeli government with the withering criticism typical of confrontational diplomacy. And yet Malik also showed his usual courtesy, grace, and wit, for which he was equally well known. His sociability and professionalism made him one of the most popular ambassadors.

An Inverted Pyramid

Five new deputy permanent representative were also appointed along with Malik. Hitherto there had only been one or two. This Soviet tendency toward "post inflation" emerged in the late 1960s. While in Moscow I had no idea that this was happening and was unacquainted with some of my future colleagues. Malik was fond of saying that the structure of the mission reminded him of an inverted pyramid. He was right: the mission was top-heavy.

At the beginning, our work suffered from the confusion and disarray caused by overmanagement. It was not always possible for functions to be organized and distributed efficiently, and the bureaucratic machine became clogged. Previously, mission staff had had to report directly to the permanent representative, but now reports had to pass through a series of intermediaries. The diplomatic staff, who had enjoyed considerable freedom under Fedorenko, did not take kindly to this innovation.

Of all the new deputies, Aleksei Zakharov had the greatest experience in government service. Before coming to New York he had held the posts of deputy minister of foreign trade, deputy minister of foreign affairs, and ambassador to Finland. In spite of being a protégé of Mikoyan, he had had to relinquish the post of Gromyko's deputy. Consequently, his appointment to New York was undoubtedly viewed as a career setback. He was clearly disgruntled and tried to behave as Malik's equal. I remember that once Malik, who had inherited from the Stalin era the habit of staying at work until two or three o'clock in the morning, decided to call a meeting well after midnight. He telephoned Zakharov and asked him to come to the meeting. We could not hear Zakharov's reply, but Malik hung up in frustration and announced, "Zakharov says that the night is for fulfilling one's marital duties, and that is what he is doing now." We laughed to ourselves, but Malik was indignant.

Because of his long experience in international trade, Zakharov was the representative in ECOSOC and dealt with economic issues at the UN. Malik, however, was absorbed in Security Council matters, so they tried to stay out of each other's way as much as possible.

Zakharov's long and varied diplomatic career came to an unusual end. After New York he was appointed ambassador to Uganda, where he managed to establish close relations with Field Marshal Idi Amin. This relationship began to assume the form of bouts of heavy drinking. One of these parties ended in a serious quarrel and as a result the "field marshal" pronounced Zakharov persona non grata, and he was compelled to leave the country.

Malik's other deputy, Lev Mendelevich, was quite an anomaly in Soviet diplomacy. He was believed to be the sole ethnic Jew in the MFA diplomatic structure during the years of the Cold War. Actually it was far from true, as many Soviet diplomats concealed their true ethnic backgrounds. To his credit Mendelevich did not follow this path. Although he spent his whole diplomatic career in the Cold War era, he was anything but a "cold warrior." He, of course, had to do his share of debating and arguing, but he did so in a gentlemanly manner, eschewing acrimony and abuse. Mendelevich was without doubt a talented person, a consummate speechwriter (he wrote a great many of Gromyko's speeches), a good journalist, and the author of a number of important diplomatic documents.

In New York Malik put Mendelevich in charge of political affairs. Their styles and approaches to the Cold War were very different, and I was therefore not surprised to learn that Mendelevich had had to return to Moscow after less than two years in New York. According to one version, he was withdrawn from the UN at the request of our "Arab friends," who emphatically voiced their dissatisfaction at seeing a Jew representing the Soviet Union in the negotiations on the Middle East. I have no doubt that such dissatisfaction was indeed voiced by the Arabs, but I think that the true reason for his recall was Mendelevich's differences with Malik.

Nikolai Tarasov, an MFA department head, was another deputy permanent representative. He had a degree in jurisprudence and was very knowledgeable in matters of international law. These were the issues entrusted to him in New York. He was an extremely responsible official and a quiet and balanced personality. His election, after having served in a number of ambassadorial posts, to the International Court in the Hague in 1985 was in my opinion quite natural and deserved. Tarasov was a well-known philatelist and numismatist. His collections were the most extensive in Moscow. He was a person of broad interests and knowledge, and it was always a pleasure talking with him.

One of the posts of deputy permanent representative belonged to the KGB. During my time in New York the KGB *rezidenty* were Vikenty Sobolev and Boris Solomatin. Sobolev, a veteran of the intelligence service who had worked in the East for many years, never seemed to be interested in America, nor did he seem to like it. I do not know anything about his professional competence, but as a personality he was uncommunicative, closed, and colorless. He knew nothing about UN matters and was entirely uninterested in them. I never managed to develop a relationship with him. As for Solomatin, he was an equally experienced intelligence agent, but understood America well and involved himself in UN problems.

My own situation at the mission was rather difficult at first. Although I had several years at the MFA and the Diplomatic Academy behind me, the members of the New York mission, including Malik, saw me as an alien, as an outsider. Malik frequently stated that I had been appointed without his consent. Soon after our arrival in New York he told me that he did not object to my scholarly activities such as writing books and articles and so on as long as it didn't "hinder the work of the mission." I was annoyed and retorted that I was sent to New York as a diplomat and that if he objected he should raise the matter with Moscow. Naturally Malik did not go that far, and we agreed that I would be working on colonial problems in the Trusteeship Council, as well as propaganda. I was also to maintain contacts between the mission and American political scientists

Some of the career diplomats were not happy about working under me and often complained about it to Malik, who missed no opportunity to deliver a sarcastic reprimand: "Comrade professor, this is different from lecturing your students, this is diplomacy, you have to think here."

How Many of Us Are There?

The structure of the Soviet mission corresponded basically with the requirements of UN business. There were the political, economic, legal, colonial, budgetary, and personnel areas. Of these, it was the political area that was deemed the most important, since it embraced the Security Council. Each area was handled by a few diplomats who later earned wider recognition in diplomatic circles—Arkady Shevchenko, Roland Timerbayev, Vladimir Shustov, Vsevolod Oleandrov, Evgeny Makeyev, Vasily Safronchyuk, Valentin Lozinsky, Gennady Stashevsky, and others.

When I arrived in New York, the diplomatic staff of the mission numbered sixty-five, more than the mission of any other member state. This was partially explained by the Soviet enthusiasm for top-heavy staffing. The Soviet mission to the UN also performed functions that had nothing to do with UN business. For instance, it did the work of the Soviet consulate in New York, which had long since been defunct. At the same time, since New York was the only American city that had direct flights to the Soviet Union, it was the point of arrival for numerous governmental and nongovernmental delegations visiting the United States. Meeting them, arranging accommodations, rendering diverse assistance—all were unwritten duties of the mission.

As a rule, all Soviet delegations tried to schedule their stay in the United States so as to leave the most time possible for New York City—not only because of the museums, shows, and other sights in the "Capital of the World," but also because of New York's downtown discount stores, which were particularly popular with Soviet visitors. All this, of course, distracted the mission staff from their real work, especially when "big shots" from Moscow—ministers, members of the Central Committee, and other high-ranking Kremlin leaders flew into New York. Even Malik had to put off his UN business and busy himself with these visitors. His deputies and other diplomatic staff also had their work cut out, acting as factotums for the distinguished visitors. For example, once two party administrators arrived in New York with instructions to buy dresses for the wives of the Politburo members, and our wives had to assist the visitors from Moscow in this delicate mission.

Under such circumstances, it should come as no surprise that the size of the mission was constantly increasing, but fewer than half of the Soviet diplomats officially accredited to the UN were actually busy performing diplomatic functions. Even Communist officials engaged exclusively in party work were registered as diplomats. Their powers were considerable. Their job was to enforce the party line among the staff of the mission, the other Soviet establishments in New York, as well as among Soviet nationals on the staff of the UN Secretariat. They knew next to nothing about the work or goals of international organizations. Their focus of interest lay in relations between people. Who met whom? Who were whose enemies? What were people talking about among themselves? Who bought what? Who abused alcohol, and so on. They collected all the gossip that was going around and reported it to Moscow as evidence of the "moral-political atmosphere in the collective."

Since the days of Stalin local party officials had posed as "independent" trade-union leaders ostensibly elected by the employees. During my time in New York this function was performed first by German Kondakov and later by Yury Khilchevsky. Both were generally reasonable people and enjoyed the respect of the staff. Neither of them seemed to relish disputes; as a rule they steered clear of confrontation, but whether they liked it or not, they were obliged by their positions to keep an eye on the "moral-political atmosphere." This watchdog role clearly did not appeal to Khilchevsky, and he soon became the Soviet representative to UNESCO in Paris, and later the Soviet deputy minister of culture.

Most of the mission staff, however, were agents of the KGB and the Central Intelligence Department of the Defense Ministry (GRU). The diplomats on the staff naturally knew very little about their work in New York.

Everyone in the mission, of course, knew who was who, but we could only guess what some of our people actually did. The rooms occupied by the agents (almost the entire eighth floor) were out of bounds to all diplomatic staff, including the permanent representative, while the KGB agents, who were formally assigned to different departments of the mission, had access to all offices. On the grounds that they needed to acquaint themselves with the work of the UN, they often rummaged through the bookcases and desks of the diplomats—to their quite natural annoyance. The diplomats also resented the fact that these operatives obviously enjoyed higher pay and allowances. Almost all of them, for example, had official cars, whereas many diplomats had difficulties with transportation. That said, I do not remember any serious conflicts between the intelligence agents and the diplomats. The latter were afraid of the former, preferring to avoid them and, so to speak, live as one "big happy family."

Nobody Is Interested in Your Personal Opinion

At first in New York I had trouble determining my role in the mission and the nature of my work at the UN. It was very hard to understand the complex structure of the United Nations, the secretariat with its innumerable divisions, the mechanism of decision-making, and the competence of various UN bodies. It was even harder to get used to the kaleidoscope of problems arising in the organization almost every day. Just as you had begun to grasp the essence of one contentious issue, you were faced with the next one. Overlapping problems just piled up on one another—all compounded by the intricate mosaic of the endlessly differing opinions and positions of almost a hundred UN member states. It became apparent that if you wanted to establish good working relations with representatives of other countries, you had to know and reckon with the whole gamut of opinion and position.

Imprecise or fuzzy comments, even in an informal conversation with representatives from other countries, could be misinterpreted. In this regard my diplomatic debut was rather instructive. I frequented the delegate's lounge of the General Assembly where I would get into conversation with new diplomatic acquaintances from other missions over a cup of coffee. In my first year at the UN I was not so busy with meetings of UN committees, so I had plenty of time for such conversations. In these conversations I was open to any topic, including some I did not know very much about.

My openness and sociability made me quite popular, and there was no lack of conversational partners. In fact, I always found someone waiting for me in the delegate's lounge. However, my companions soon noticed that my opinions did not always correspond with the official view being purveyed by my Soviet colleagues. Not surprisingly, people lost interest in talking to me and actually started avoiding me.

At first, I couldn't understand the reason for this change of attitude. Only later did it become clear that people were disturbed by the discrepancies between some of my opinions and the official Soviet position, and they started wondering whether I was deliberately misinforming them, or simply did not know the official Soviet position. The ambassador from Czechoslovakia Milan Klusak once said to me, "Listen, Victor, you are the deputy permanent representative of a superpower and your interlocutors usually report conversations with you to their capitals. And then they find out that you have misled them. You understand the situation this puts them in with their bosses. That's why they don't want anything to do with you." I tried to justify myself. "But you see, all I'm trying to do is to express my opinion, which is hardly any different from the official one." The ambassador explained: "You have to realize that nobody is interested in your personal opinion in diplomacy. Your fellow diplomats are only interested in getting a precise and accurate statement of the Soviet position, and not the personal opinion of a former professor." My friend was perfectly right. It was a bitter pill to swallow, but I took his advice to heart, and from then on I made a point of hewing strictly to the official line. A diplomat has to do his best to explain his government's policy to his fellow diplomats as cogently, as fully, and as accurately as possible. This simple rule now became obvious to me; and if a diplomat cannot bring himself to respect this rule, he should find some other, more palatable occupation.

I sometimes heard Western colleagues saying that they intended to leave the diplomatic service because of differences with their capitals. I remember my American partner at the Geneva negotiations on disarmament, one of the most highly qualified professionals in the field, once telling me, that he was going back to Washington and would no longer agree to represent his government in the negotiations. When I asked him why, the ambassador answered without hesitation: "I am not happy about the line of our new president. I would rather resign and do something else." True to his word, he ended his long diplomatic career and opened a successful law practice.

I do not recall anything like this ever happening in the Soviet diplomatic service—it would have been impossible. Soviet diplomatic careers were only ended by dismissal from the MFA or transfer to other jobs, sometimes even with a raise—something that actually happened quite frequently. This does not, of course, take into account the toll taken on the Soviet diplomatic service by the epidemics of reprisals, arrests, and executions that swept the Soviet Union in the 1930s and 1940s. There were the very rare occasions, when some diplomats had to look for other jobs for health or family reasons, but the idea that someone would quit the diplomatic service because he disagreed with Soviet foreign policy was unthinkable—and certainly unsayable.

Personally Offended

The mark of the typical Soviet diplomat was demonstrative, unswerving, and unconditional loyalty to the Communist Party line, in both domestic and foreign policy matters. During the Cold War every Soviet diplomat strove to outdo his colleagues in demonstrating his loyalty to the Kremlin. Hypocrisy and false patriotism were the hallmarks of our profession. I do not know whether Khrushchev led the way in this by banging his shoe on his desktop at a meeting of the General Assembly in a blustering attempt to demonstrate to the whole world how grievously and personally he had been insulted and offended by what he saw as an attempt to distort the policy of the Soviet government.

I believe, however, that Vyshinsky was the best example of hypocrisy in Soviet diplomacy during the Cold War. Well educated, with perfect self-control, and without stooping to "shoe" antics, he made his ideological opponents the butt of his scorn and ridicule. By appearing to take disagreement with the Soviet position personally, he left the impression that the personal opinions of Soviet diplomats unfailingly coincided with official government positions on each and every subject.

You only had to observe my more experienced colleagues to realize the truth of this. For example, one sophisticated member of the Soviet delegation once had occasion to make an impromptu statement in one of the main committees of the General Assembly in response to the attempts of a number of delegations to interpret the Soviet policy on the Middle East settlement in their own way. Our representative was well versed in the subject and a competent and experienced diplomat. His statement was well argued and emotional. Everyone stopped their usual private conversations to listen to the speaker.

After the meeting several colleagues and other delegates congratulated him on a successful speech. The same evening at a reception, talking with the ambassador from one of the friendly nonaligned countries, I asked what he thought of the statement of the Soviet representative. To my amazement, he told me that he didn't care for it all. When I asked him why, he said that he didn't object to the substance of the speech, just to the way it was delivered. Why invest it with so much emotion and passion, he asked? This is absolutely out of place. "We diplomats are paid for our work., which is to deliver precisely and clearly the official position of our government. That's all."

I thought that such a pragmatic approach to our crucial duties didn't reflect well on anyone, least of all a diplomat, who has the privilege of representing his country. Soviet diplomats felt that just going through the motions in a dispassionate manner did not reflect the required level of patriotism and commitment to a cause, which the CPSU Central Committee and the Soviet government have charged the diplomat to defend, and many of us, including myself, thought and acted accordingly.

As I mentioned earlier, my work in the UN was limited to colonial matters. I was the Soviet representative in the Committee on Decolonization, the Trusteeship Council, and the Fourth Committee of the General Assembly, which dealt with problems of colonial territories. These issues were simple for me, since the Soviet Union had no direct interests in them and possessed no colonies or territories, although after the war Stalin had tried to persuade the United States and England to give him Libya, the former Italian colony. It is worth recalling that it was the redoubtable U.S. Secretary of State James Byrnes who rejected the Soviet bid. However, although it never became a Soviet satellite, Libya turned out to be one of the fiercest opponents of the United States in the years of the Cold War.

At meetings of these committees I would always observe Moscow's instructions to support the position of the colonial nations of Africa and Asia, thus exposing myself to regular criticism from Western colonial powers. Sometimes I would deliver emotional speeches, but frankly, I was more comfortable using a more even-tempered approach. My style was to draw on my knowledge of the history of international relations, trying to place my statements on a sound, sober, academic footing. I wasn't always successful in making my case persuasively, but Malik and my other colleagues recognized the value of the rational approach.

On occasion I made statements that were sharply critical of the United States. My statement in one of committees of General Assembly in 1968 provoked strong reactions. I stated that the United States was using military bases in Puerto Rico and Guam to exert pressure on small countries and peoples. I demanded the liquidation of these bases. As a result I was flooded with mail. Some of it, such as the letter from the Movement for the Independence of Puerto Rico, agreed with the demands of the Soviet delegation. Other writers vehemently denounced our demands. One Puerto Rican wrote that he strongly objected to the Soviet ultimatums and suggested that "the Soviet ambassador would do better to focus his attention on Hungary, Romania, Yugoslavia, Poland, Bulgaria, Latvia, Estonia, Czechoslovakia and other countries seized by the Soviet Union," and to leave free peoples alone.

Propaganda Activities Outside the UN

Sadly, I can't recall anything useful coming out of the Committee on Decolonization during my tenure, and as a result my interest in colonial issues waned. I began asking my colleagues to make the speeches in my place, which left me more time for the activities assigned to me outside the UN, mainly "foreign propaganda." Every day our mission received invitations from American universities, colleges, and various organizations to give lectures, conduct seminars, and participate in conferences. Malik accepted some of them himself, but he passed most of them on to the other diplomatic staff, including me.

I had an especially close relationship with Columbia University. Soon after my arrival in New York, Marshall Schulman, director of the university's Russian Institute, invited me to speak to the students. I gladly accepted the invitation. Schulman and I kept in touch for several decades, even after the collapse of the Soviet Union. He frequently visited Moscow, and I always had the impression that he had a soft spot for the Russian people. He and his wife did some work with my daughter, who was on the staff of the Moscow U.S. and Canada Institute.

At that time the director of the Institute for Communist Research Zbigniew Brzezinski approached me with a request to conduct a seminar. In the late 1960s he had already become one of the leading American Soviet specialists and was well known in Moscow. There he was known as "virulently anti-Soviet." Gromyko's deputy, Semenov, a well-known diplomat, once told me that he wanted to write a book called "Anti-Brzezinski," but as far as I know he never wrote it. To those of us in the Soviet mission, it seemed that Brzezinski was hostile to everything having to do with the Soviet Union, and I'm afraid that my impressions have only been strengthened over the years. I felt this hostility the moment we met and even during that one seminar at his institute. Brzezinski did not want me present at the discussion following my own lecture on Soviet foreign policy. This seemed unethical to me, but I did not insist. I was told about Brzezinski's reaction to my presentation by someone who had attended the discussion and whom I happened to run into afterwards. Of course, if I had been present I could have buttressed my case with supporting arguments and have provided a more complete picture of the Soviet position. Obviously Brzezinski wished to avoid that.

More successful, from my perspective, were the seminars organized by Charles Yost, who had resigned from the diplomatic service to teach at Columbia. Yost invited me to conduct some seminars on Soviet-American relations and Soviet policy in Europe, and I found the general atmosphere at these seminars considerably more cordial and conducive to the exchange of ideas. Likewise, in December 1972 I had the honor of serving as the guest speaker at Columbia's annual history department dinner. At that time the head of the department was Eugene Rice. Although I was a doctor of historical sciences and had been a professor in the USSR, I actually had very little experience in Soviet universities and was not very familiar with how our historians were trained. Although this was precisely the subject that most interested the audience, my speech to about a hundred guests turned out to be a success, thanks largely to the festive mood created by the end of the fall semester and the approaching Christmas holiday.

I must say that I was surprised and pleased to see how much interest Americans showed in the Soviet Union. This was partly explained by the fact that the new Soviet leadership, which had ousted Khrushchev, had not yet shown its hand, so that judgments were temporarily suspended. Four years passed before Brezhnev, Kosygin, and others rose to the top of the Kremlin leadership, but in 1968 they were mostly unknown quantities in the international arena.

People were most interested in learning about Soviet domestic and foreign policy. UN issues as a rule were only of secondary interest. The most frequently asked questions had to do with the Soviet power structure—Who were the leaders and what were they like? People also wanted to know about Soviet attitudes toward the United States and the future of Soviet-American relations. Our answers to such questions were usually quite vague. We would emphasize that the Kremlin attached great importance to good relations with the United States. I frequently mentioned my meetings with Brezhnev and Gromyko, giving my general impressions of them, but I really couldn't go much further than that, in large part because we simply didn't know our leaders well enough.

Apart from certain official contacts such as speeches, lectures, and seminars with American political scientists, there were also many more informal contacts: breakfasts, dinners, and receptions. Istvan Deak, William Fox, Richard Gardner, Philip Mosley, and Ruth Russell were just a few of the other colleagues from Columbia whom I met and with whom I exchanged views and argued about international politics. With some of them I developed useful working relations.

Another person with whom I established friendly working relations was Hans Morgenthau. Although Morgenthau taught at the University of Chicago, he was frequently at Columbia, and we would meet there occasionally. I first met Morgenthau in Moscow in 1965 at a conference on the twentieth anniversary of the end of World War II, an event that was marked by a rather curious incident. Morgenthau was one of the main foreign participants, and during his speech he spoke favorably of Roosevelt's policy and of Soviet-American military cooperation. In the ensuing discussion, the well-known Soviet historian Grigory Deborin, who clearly had taken offense at Morgenthau's presentation, criticized him, saying that he was impressing no one with his praise of Roosevelt. After all, he had been a close friend of the president and a member of his cabinet for many years. Someone in the audience started to laugh, realizing that the Soviet professor had mistaken Hans Morgenthau for Henry Morgenthau, the former secretary of the treasury, who had no connection whatsoever with the conference. When I, as chairman of the meeting, gently drew Deborin's attention to this fact, he was quite unabashed and sharply retorted, "Hans or Henry. It makes no difference." This remark was greeted by a burst of laughter.

Visits to Miami and Dallas

We received many invitations to participate in events outside the New York area, and this afforded me numerous opportunities to travel to places in the United States that otherwise I might never have seen. By this time I had acquired a lot of public-speaking experience during my trips to England and other countries, so I was quite comfortable speaking in front of audiences. In the majority of cases, the meetings passed without controversy, although in the Cold War years conflict could arise quite unexpectedly, as it did during a trip to Florida.

In March 1970 Malik and I were invited to participate in a model UN forum organized by the University of Miami. The organizers of the event asked us to speak about the Soviet position in the UN, especially focusing on our role in the Security Council. Both Malik and I wanted to see Florida so we accepted the invitation. We agreed that Malik would be the speaker, with additions from me if necessary. Surprises lay in store for us.

On arrival in Miami we were taken to a different hotel than the one we had expected to stay in. When we asked why the organizers had switched hotels, we were told that it was for security reasons: the local authorities had been informed that Cuban immigrants were planning a big anti-Castro demonstration to coincide with the arrival of Fidel's "Soviet bosses." The second surprise came when we were notified that the U.S. State Department would not permit us to enter the university campus. I don't completely understand the reasons behind this decision, but I can definitely say that we were extremely upset and considered packing up and returning to New York. However, we decided to avoid a row, especially when the president of the university, Henry Stanford, let us know how very displeased he was by the decision of the State Department. Arrangements were made to move the site for Malik's speech to an off-campus location in the city.

But this was only the beginning, for it was not until the next day, when we were setting off for the forum, that the trouble really started. In the morning we noticed a large crowd behind a police line outside our hotel. People were shouting things at us in Spanish—things that did not sound at all complimentary. Police cars escorted us to a hall filled with students and professors. Malik's speech was received with interest, and a few people asked questions afterward. The audience behaved quite well and applauded us at the end.

Later in the day as we prepared to do some sightseeing, we received word that Cuban immigrants were planning to confront us and block our way, so following the advice of our hosts we canceled our sightseeing plans and left directly for the airport. The journey turned out to be quite difficult, since crowds of demonstrators had blocked the roads leading to the airport. It was only the resolute action and crowd control experience of the large number of police that enabled us to get through and reach the airport safely. Our car was the target of angry shouts and was pelted by the crowd. Needless to say, we never had the chance to see much of Florida.

Soon after our return from Miami we received a letter of apology from the organizers of the meeting. Malik held a special meeting about our trip to Florida at which people talked about the tense international situation and the need to increase our vigilance, and condemned the Cuban protesters and the State Department. What it all amounted to was that in the Cold War we should learn to expect the unexpected.

My trip to Dallas in March 1972 was no less busy or interesting. Besides the two or three lectures and seminars for the professors and students of several universities, I had a number of business meetings, which were far outside my scope. I was invited to meet Fred Zeder, chairman of the board of a company called Hydrometals, which manufactured pipe, machine tools, and various other kinds of equipment. Zeder was interested in developing economic and trade contacts with the Soviet Union as a way of trading his company's products for various raw materials and goods from Russia. I welcomed his interest in establishing business relations with my country and gave him names of useful contacts in Moscow and Leningrad, but I was not in a position to discuss the substance of his proposals. Later I was happy to learn, that he had taken my advice and visited the Soviet Union.

I also had the opportunity of meeting George Allen, Ross Perot, Clint Marchison, and other leading Texan financiers and industrialists. At receptions in my honor I was showered with questions about the political and particularly the economic stability of the Soviet Union. Naturally, in my replies I struck an optimistic note, even though the economic development of the USSR did not give any grounds for enthusiasm.

I do not think that I managed to change anyone's perceptions of the Soviet Union to any appreciable extent, and I'm afraid that Fred Zeder, whom I subsequently lost track of, never became a supporter of American-Soviet economic cooperation. The time for that had not yet come. Nevertheless, my trip to Dallas did at least give Texan businessmen a chance to catch a glimpse of a "live Soviet"—quite an exotic phenomenon at the time. Before my return to New York City, the mayor of Dallas, Wes Wise, organized a reception in my honor, where he declared me an honorary citizen of Dallas and gave me the keys to the city. This was the only time in my life when I was granted honorary citizenship of any kind. I have kept the letter and the keys as a precious memory of some of the warmer days of the Cold War.

ON THE DIPLOMATIC SIDELINES

The Future World Order

In 1972 I was asked to participate in an ambitious research project titled "The Future International Order." The leading forces behind this project were Cyril Black and Richard Falk of Princeton University. Their idea was to bring together well-known American and foreign experts on international relations to participate in a series of conferences to be held at Princeton with support from the Council on Foreign Relations in New York. The best papers would be collected and published in five volumes corresponding to the themes of the conferences. My task was to write about the Soviet vision of a global order, and the article would eventually appear in the fifth volume.

In my article I argued that the socialist system would continue to expand, as would international cooperation between the socialist and capitalist orders. By the end of the twentieth century, there would be peaceful coexistence between the two orders, and the global community would move toward world integration. I predicted an end to the Cold War, the advent of a stable era of international détente, and the application of new and radical measures in the areas of disarmament and security. Essentially, my article reflected the Soviet, communist vision of the evolution of society, which I had borrowed from party documents.

For reasons unknown to me, the fifth volume of the project was never published, so my article never saw the light of day. This is probably for the better because a number of years ago, not long after the fall of the Soviet Union, I found the article and decided to reread it. How dated it seemed! A work of pure fantasy and totally out of touch with reality. My only consolation was to tell myself that the other contributors, many of them quite eminent, were probably just as far off the mark in their visions for a future world order as I was.

Another visit took me to Boston in 1969 together with Georgy Arbatov, the director of the newly created Moscow U.S. Institute (later it was renamed the U.S. and Canada Institute). We had conversations with American experts who in many respects determined Washington's position on arms control—Jerome Wiesner, George Kistyakovsky, Paul Doty, Robert Bowie, Max Millikan, and others. Everyone confirmed a need for a new approach to disarmament and set their hopes on bilateral negotiations between the United States and the USSR on strategic, assault, and defensive weapons limitation.

The same ideas were expressed at the meeting of American and Soviet experts in Moscow in 1968 attended by Jerome Wiesner, Henry Kissinger, Paul Doty, and others. The conversations at Harvard took place in an atmosphere of optimism, and no one mentioned Czechoslovakia or Vietnam. Arbatov seemed to have made a good impression. This was very important to him, as it was one of his first visits to America.

I remember meeting with Kistyakovsky in an informal setting. We did not talk politics; instead he asked me about Russia, about Moscow, and about rural Russia. He spoke Russian, but with a noticeable accent. Although he had had a successful career in the United States (he was at one time an adviser to President Eisenhower), I sensed in him a certain wistfulness and nostalgia for Russia.

Kistyakovsky recalled his participation in the negotiations between Eisenhower and Khrushchev in 1959 in the United States. The latter astounded him with his rudeness and tactlessness. He was outraged: "How could such an ignorant peasant as Khrushchev ever come to rule such a great country as Russia?"

A Diplomat Should Display His Wares

At first glance my academic connections might not have appeared to have anything to do with my diplomatic work at the UN, but that was only at first glance. Discussions of Soviet foreign policy in an informal setting, even when the audience was not particularly sophisticated, were always useful from my point of view.

It has to be understood that Soviet foreign policy in international organizations, particularly the UN, was overtly propagandistic in nature. Soviet proposals were designed for public consumption, and their message was simple, even simplistic, but clear to the average person. Often they could be distilled down to a sentiment as trite as "Down with war!" or "Long live peace!" Whether these proposals were genuine, or had the slightest chance of being implemented, was a matter of little interest to those who formulated them.

During public lectures and open discussions I usually found that the more sophisticated the audience, the more difficult it was to explain the seemingly simple proposals. I remember speaking, together with Yuly Vorontsov, the number two of the Soviet embassy in Washington, to a group of American professionals in the field of arms control. We were delivering the Soviet proposal for a short-term program for complete and general disarmament. After we had spoken, we had to face a lot of difficult questions.

As a general rule, the more enthusiastic and unreserved the response to a Soviet proposal, the less sophisticated the audience.

There were many questions about life in the Soviet Union that were difficult to field. One could always sidestep what we thought of as provocative questions by pleading ignorance, but this approach only confirmed the weakness of the Soviet position, so we had to be creative. The most provocative questions I faced during my years in New York usually pertained to anti-Semitism in the Soviet Union and the fate of prominent Soviet dissidents such as Solzhenitsyn and Sakharov. In these cases, I had little choice but to respond with half-truths. For example, the question about anti-Semitism I answered by telling the audience that many leading artists, scientists, doctors, and writers in the USSR were Jews, and I would mention them by name. I also said that among the relatively small group of Soviet diplomats in New York, the deputy permanent representative was a Jew. I mentioned my conversation with Yaguda Leub Levinì, the chief rabbi of Moscow, who had visited New York and the attention and consideration with which he had been treated by the Soviet mission. All this was true and yet it obviously sidestepped the real issue—the general treatment of Jews in the Soviet Union. Access to many Soviet establishments was practically denied to Jews, and there was hidden anti-Semitism. I refrained from mentioning that most Jews were prohibited from going to Israel.

As to the treatment of Solzhenitsyn, I argued that since the writer was becoming increasingly disenchanted with the Soviet system, the Kremlin's decision to expel him from the USSR only served to accommodate his ambition to go and live in some other country with a different, nonsocialist system. Since this was entirely in accordance with his own wishes, what on earth could be wrong with that? In reality Solzhenitsyn's expulsion from the Soviet Union was a flagrant violation of basic human rights.

Some of my listeners were convinced by my explanations and arguments. They trusted me because I spoke confidently, did not avoid argument, and frequently believed in what I was saying. I received many letters expressing gratitude for my "frank," "candid," and "convincing" performance. I derived considerable satisfaction from these letters, and Malik, to whom most of these letters were delivered, read them aloud to my colleagues, setting me up as an example to be followed. However, I can't deny the fact that I was left feeling uneasy. The seasoned diplomats among my colleagues simply thought that I had been skillful enough to pull the wool over the eyes of my student audiences and gave me an amiable grin. This disappointed me, knowing as I did that there was a certain degree of truth in their view. However, I consoled myself with the thought that it was a diplomat's job to cast his country in the best possible light and win as much sympathy as possible for it. And this was precisely what I had been doing my best to achieve.

An Embarrassment at a Reception

My activities outside the UN helped me learn much about Americans and America. Most of all I was interested in a dialogue with Americans and, of course, in learning their attitudes toward the Soviet Union. I was surprised at how little Americans knew about Russia. Of course, this was not true of academics or the intelligentsia, whom I could count on to know such names as Pushkin, Dostoyevsky, Tolstoy, and Tchaikovsky, but among average Americans, even university students, one encountered amazing ignorance and cultural limitations. The names of such Russian cultural giants meant nothing to the average American. I was frequently amazed to learn how few people knew whose side Russia fought on in World War II. Some actually believed that Russia fought on Hitler's side against America. This was all the more surprising when you consider how recently these historic events had occurred.

The widespread belief that anything Russian or Soviet was automatically "bad" was always disappointing to me, undoubtedly a by-product of an ingrained fear of the USSR. "The Russians are coming" was the grim specter continuously being conjured up by the media to strike terror into the heart of the average American. At the same time, I did not sense implacable or overt hostility to Russians or the Soviet Union. Usually it was not very difficult to convince individual Americans that Russia was not actually "evil." It even seemed that many Americans were willing to discard their negative attitude in favor of a positive one when presented with a living and breathing representative of the Soviet Union who spoke to them on their own terms. This undoubtedly explains why lectures by Soviet diplomats often ended in a much more cordial and upbeat atmosphere than they had started.

I did, of course, encounter people in the course of my activities who for various reasons hated the Soviet Union and all that it stood for. As the representative of the Soviet Union, I unfortunately was the target of that hate. Such encounters were deeply depressing for me, and I could not forget them for a long time. As an example of this type of encounter, I was once invited with my wife to dinner by a New York professor. At the table I sat next to Mrs. Brzezinski; my wife was at the other table next to Zbigniew Brzezinski himself. The conversation at the table was the usual social chit-chat, far removed from politics. We learned that our children were about the same age and even talked about our families spending a weekend together.

After dinner I invited the lady to dance and happened to mention that I was a Soviet diplomat. As soon as she heard this Mrs. Brzezinski abruptly stopped dancing, turned on her heel, and left the room. An awkward silence ensued. I even wondered if my partner wasn't feeling well. However, our host, in some embarrassment, assured me, that the lady's action had nothing to do with her health. Her motives became obvious, when our host invited the guests to take their places at the table to continue the meal. The chair next to me was left unoccupied. Mrs. Brzezinski moved to another seat, avoided conversation with me, and left without saying good-bye. The evening was spoiled for me as well as for the host and the other guests. I learned later that Mrs. Brzezinski's closest relatives, who had been prominent political leaders in Czechoslovakia, had been victims of the pro-Soviet, "people's" regime in that country.

As Soviet representatives we all reacted differently to such manifestations of hostility and animosity to the Soviet Union. Some, including myself, took them to heart and were troubled by them. Others shrugged them off and simply viewed them as manifestations of the "class struggle." While such confrontations did not contribute to the policy of coexistence, they were facts of Cold War life and, as such, had to be endured.

8
THE BATTLEFIELD, THE UN

A Litmus Test for International Relations

During the Cold War the UN played an extremely important role in the complex world of international relations. It was the principal arena where disagreements between the two superpowers emerged and were played out before the world. At times there were as many as two-hundred items on the agenda of General Assembly sessions, ranging from minor matters to urgent ones and from local to universal; and although not every issue demanded general participation, as a rule both the USSR and the United States voiced their points of view. Not surprisingly, the Americans and Soviets opposed each other in the majority of cases, not necessarily because of any substantive disagreement but because the two sides were drawing upon incompatible concepts and approaches to problems of international security. It was clear, therefore, that the UN had become a litmus test for establishing the positions of the two superpowers.

Hundreds of resolutions were passed at each session of the General Assembly. Not surprisingly, the Soviet Union and the United States often lined up on opposite sides—a situation that seemed natural, even preferable, to most Soviet diplomats. For many years I saw this firsthand because I was responsible for reporting to the MFA board, and sometimes to the CPSU

Politburo, on the results of the General Assembly sessions. Opposing the American position was a way of accentuating the differences between our two countries on the basic issues on the UN agenda. In fact, it may have even helped us to define our position more clearly in our own minds. We all implicitly understood this, and nobody expressed any regrets. I do not know if the same was always true for the American diplomats but I suspect that it was at least some of the time.

The members of the Soviet mission recognized that the UN was the main stage for playing out the political and ideological confrontation between the Soviet Union and the United States. This was how we perceived the work of every UN body—the Security Council, all committees of the General Assembly, conferences, the UN Secretariat. How will the Americans react, how will they vote, whom will they support? These questions were always on our minds. We closely watched the work of the U.S. delegation, always careful to meet and establish good working relations with its members. Meanwhile, we kept abreast of their activities through regular intelligence reports, which also identified the ones who supposedly worked for the CIA. I doubt whether this information was always accurate, but we could not ignore it, and we always regarded every American diplomat as a potential CIA agent.

The Kremlin's approach to the UN and its role in Soviet-American relations clearly had its roots in Stalin's time. Some of the older diplomats would bring up Stalin and Stalin's opinions whenever the opportunity arose. One of the main points that often came up was Stalin's view that the world would always be ruled by superpowers who would need bilateral channels to agree between themselves. However, he was not enthusiastic about Roosevelt's ideas, discussed in Teheran in 1943, of creating a new postwar international organization. He told Roosevelt that it would be more desirable to create two centers, one in Europe and the other in the Far East, where the Big Three (the USSR, the United States, and Britain) could station their troops and deploy them at any moment to preserve world order.

In the first years of the Cold War, when forty of the fifty-one UN member states supported the U.S. and British positions, Stalin became increasingly, and understandably, negative toward the new organization. During the Korean War he began calling the UN an "American organization" that had to be destroyed. Veterans of the diplomatic service told me that shortly before his death, Stalin spoke with the Chinese prime minister Jou Enlai in 1952, and advised him to create an "Asian UN" in response to the Americans' refusal to admit the People's Republic of China into the United Nations.

Likewise, he believed that the Soviet Union could found a "European UN" and other regional international organizations as well—anything to put an end to American domination in the UN.

A Time of Hopes and Dreams

My years of service in New York coincided with a general period of optimism during the Cold War. There was genuine hope for equal, stable, and mutually advantageous relations between the United States and the Soviet Union. From my conversations with Soviet officials at various levels I knew that Moscow was interested in normalizing relations with Washington. The need for improved relations became imperative after the instability and the emotional and unpredictable events of the Khrushchev era, when the world was on the verge of a nuclear war during the Cuban crisis. The 1967 meeting of Prime Minister Kosygin with President Johnson in Glassboro convinced me that the desire for improved relations was not unique to the Soviets. It was shared by both sides. When President Nixon continued the policy of rapprochement, pledging in 1972 that an era of confrontation had to be followed by an era of negotiations, Moscow responded with undisguised enthusiasm. I remember a meeting of the MFA board on Soviet-American relations during which Gromyko explained that if the United States demonstrated good will, "we will not remain in debt."

Certain positive steps were taken. In the summer of 1968 the Soviet-American Convention on Consular Issues finally took effect, and a small number of consulates in both countries were set up. The United States and the USSR began to cooperate, on a limited basis, on international security, arms limitation, and disarmament. Arms control negotiations began with the diplomatic contacts of late 1969 in Helsinki and continued in subsequent years in Vienna, again in Helsinki, and then in Geneva. These negotiations signaled the start of a special dialogue between the superpowers, involving the participation of their leaders. Meanwhile, the good will could be felt in other areas as well. Aeroflot and Pan-American signed an agreement establishing a direct line between Moscow and New York. And although it was small in scope, an exchange program was set up for students, teachers, and athletes from the two countries.

Nevertheless, the key years for Soviet-American relations came in 1972–73 with the Nixon-Brezhnev meetings—the beginning of détente. In those years more bilateral Soviet-American agreements were signed than in all the previous forty years of diplomatic relations between the USSR and the United States. It seemed to many of us that détente was a warm breeze, blowing away the frigid air of the Cold War.

This was one side of the coin—the détente side, so to speak. The other side of the coin was much less pleasant but no less distinctive. In those days it was defined mainly by the war in Vietnam. Throughout the war the Soviet Union aided North Vietnam in every possible way, by supplying the most modern weapons, ammunitions, and whatever material resources Vietnam needed to fight the United States. There were also other arenas for the superpower conflict. In the Middle East, both sides showed their political cards during the June war of 1967. In Czechoslovakia, the entry of Soviet troops in 1968 had a negative effect on the international climate and on bilateral relations as well. All this occurred simultaneously with important steps toward détente. On certain issues it was possible to come to an agreement, whereas on others there were difficulties, tensions, and sometimes completely unexpected complications.

The following episode in New York was characteristic of these relations. In the spring of 1968, work on the Treaty on the Non-proliferation of Nuclear Weapons was about to be completed. The initiators of the agreement—the USSR, the United States, and Britain—intended to make the final push at the UN General Assembly, which was expected to recommend the treaty for signature by the member states. Cooperation between the two superpowers in this complex and rather delicate undertaking had been mostly effective. When they managed to coordinate positions between themselves, they jointly exerted pressure on their allies and on other countries. The initiators decided to send their most experienced disarmament experts and negotiators to the General Assembly. Kuznetsov headed the Soviet delegation. His participation in the final work on the treaty was widely welcomed, in particular by the Americans.

At the end of April 1968 Kuznetsov arrived at Kennedy airport in New York. Soon after the landing he and his entourage were detained in a separate room for documents inspection. We were frankly shocked that an official of Kuznetsov's standing should be treated in this way, but there was nothing we could do so we waited and watched as the other Aeroflot passengers passed the checkpoint. Kuznetsov, meanwhile, remained seated behind a glass partition, looking over at us smiling and shrugging his shoulders to show that he did not know what was going on. Other members of the Soviet delegation joined us, as perplexed as we were. We grew increasingly indignant, thinking that an international conflict was brewing—and on the eve of important nuclear arms negotiations no less! Malik, outraged, went to the airport administration, which informed him that they were acting under instructions from Washington. This answer only increased our bafflement. Ambassador Dobrynin, who had arrived from Washington to meet Kuznetsov, called Secretary of State Dean Rusk, but Rusk was out of his office. The ambassador had to search for the secretary in other places. We were losing precious time.

Finally Dobrynin managed to get through to Rusk, who was aware of the situation. He calmly explained to Dobrynin that Kuznetsov would be released very soon—as soon as he had waited the same amount of time an American ambassador had recently waited for his luggage in Moscow's Sheremetyevo airport. Sure enough Kuznetsov emerged a few minutes later. We berated the American authorities for their insolence, even threatening to relocate the final treaty negotiations to Geneva. Kuznetsov, however, strictly forbade any retaliatory measures, saying that he would personally inform Moscow about the incident.

Upon his arrival in the city, Kuznetsov established contact with the head of the American delegation, Arthur Goldberg. Their effective cooperation was essential if there was to be any hope of a successful conclusion to the negotiations. At a Security Council meeting in June 1968, Kuznetsov, Goldberg, and Britain's Lord Caradon all read similar statements offering guarantees to non-nuclear parties to the Non-proliferation Treaty. Thus the long story came to an end, and the agreement was open for signing. The main participants in the negotiations could not praise each other too highly at the final meeting of the Security Council. Goldberg declared that he was deeply supportive of détente, as it was vital to world peace and security. Kuznetsov in turn noted that, despite the fundamental differences between the two countries, he nevertheless was impressed by the American delegation's desire to cooperate. Naturally nobody mentioned the incident at Kennedy airport, which could have scuttled the negotiations.

We Swing Our Fists, Then Hug and Kiss

I offer the following episode as a vivid example of the inconsistent, unstable relations between the superpowers in the years of hopes and dreams. It happened in the spring of 1972. The international situation was then complicated by the protracted war in Vietnam. All the attempts of the Nixon administration to extricate itself had failed. Furthermore, the situation was becoming even worse for the United States as the North Vietnamese were advancing southward in April and May of that year, occupying important locations in the South. Despite the obvious tensions in the international arena, the situation in the UN was surprisingly calm. Not a single session of the Security Council was held in March, April, or May, and successive presidents of the Council did not even find it necessary to conduct informal consultations.

If calm prevailed within the walls of the UN, the same could not be said for the outside world. Antiwar demonstrations were frequent in New York. On one rainy Saturday in April 1972 I observed a huge demonstration in New York as antiwar protesters were voicing their disagreement with Washington's Vietnam policy. Despite the rain, tens of thousands of people came to Times Square, Central Park, and other places throughout the city. In my many years of living in New York I have never seen anything like it. In these volatile days, petitioners even came to the Soviet mission, calling upon the Soviet Union to take more resolute action within the UN to end the war in Vietnam.

The mission naturally reported to Moscow on the developing situation, giving detailed accounts of the meetings and demonstrations that were occurring throughout the city. For the most part, we simply reported the events because analysis of the U.S. domestic situation was not seen as being within our competence. Nonetheless, the question arose of whether the Soviet Union should bring the situation in Vietnam up for discussion in the UN. We discussed this idea with Malik and agreed that such an initiative could bring propaganda dividends. At the same time there was some concern that it might backfire and have a counterproductive or negative impact on the military campaign of the North Vietnamese.

Besides there were many signs, including indications from the Soviet embassy in Washington, that our "top brass" were preparing for a Soviet-American high-level meeting. We in New York, of course, did not know that Kissinger was planning a secret trip to Moscow at that time, but we suspected from some of our American contacts in the UN that Washington was preparing for a major event in relations between the superpowers. In these conditions of uncertainty we came to the conclusion that Moscow should not come forward with any initiative on Vietnam.

On the other hand, the situation in Vietnam was deteriorating rapidly. On May 8 Nixon gave orders to intensify the bombing of Vietnam and to mine all entrances to South Vietnamese ports to deny access to ships. The escalated bombing of Vietnam and the mining, which created a direct threat to Soviet vessels, would mean harsh retaliatory measures from the Soviet Union. This was the conclusion of almost all the diplomats of the mission. The information we received from Moscow indicated that the Kremlin was becoming ever more alarmed. Numerous meetings in support of "the heroic Vietnamese people in its courageous war against American imperialism" held in the Soviet Union were symptomatic. Soviet mass media reported anti-American attitudes all over the world. We expected that the Kremlin would take further decisive measures.

After Nixon's order to intensify the bombing, Malik said that it was time to put the unacceptable actions of the United States, which were threatening peace and international security, up for discussion at the UN. He charged me with the task of preparing our case for the Security Council. My first step was to contact the Vietnamese representatives to the UN and to find out if they would consider a discussion of the U.S. aggression against North Vietnam in the Security Council. The Vietnamese responded evasively. They unequivocally confirmed the necessity of "a resolute condemnation of the bandit policy of the American imperialism" but they refused to comment on the usefulness of a Security Council meeting. After discussing the matter with Malik, we decided not to consult with other delegations. It was too risky to start discussions on this delicate issue without explicit instructions from Moscow.

At last, on May 12 the Soviet government issued a declaration on the situation in Vietnam. The language employed in the declaration was characteristically harsh, condemning the "predatory nature of the war launched by the United States against the Vietnamese people," about "the barbarous acts" of the American military, about "the unacceptable actions that threatened the freedom of navigation and safety of ships," and so on. The declaration also demanded the immediate lifting of the U.S. blockade of the coast of Vietnam. Nevertheless, the statement stopped short of threats or ultimatums. Nor did it recommend any UN action. When one of Malik's assistants pointed out that Moscow had failed to point out that the United States had violated the 1958 Geneva convention on maritime law, the ambassador smiled, "Don't you see that Moscow does not want a fight in the Security Council?"

The Soviet declaration ended with assurances that the Soviet people, "faithful to the principles of socialist internationalism, express their continued solidarity with the heroic struggle of the Vietnamese people" and will continue to render necessary support. At the same time the propaganda campaign was temporarily cut back. From mid-May the flow of reports from Vietnam was sharply reduced. The newspapers only published brief reports of military operations. The flow of letters and declarations "from the mass of Soviet workers" expressing solidarity with their "Vietnamese class brothers " came to an end. The Solidarity Committee with the peoples of Asia and Africa, the Peace Committee, and other organizations, who had demonstrated such enthusiastic activism over the Vietnam War, fell silent. Moscow was preparing for the arrival of its eminent American guest.

In anticipation of Nixon's arrival in the Soviet Union on May 22, the powerful Soviet propaganda machine had to be remodeled. A few days before the arrival of the American president, the Politburo approved the policy of rapprochement with the United States at a plenary meeting of the CPSU Central Committee. The mass media began promoting a new line to the Soviet consumer; a policy of peaceful coexistence, the necessity of maintaining good relations with the United States, and the special responsibilities of the two superpowers for the fate of humanity, and so on. Party organizations all over the country and at all levels, armed with the decisions of the Central Committee, praised "the soundness and consistency" of Lenin's foreign policy.

Up until the last minute, we in New York were preparing ourselves for another round of battles with the Americans in the UN. There was always the chance that a Soviet vessel, even a naval vessel, could strike an American mine near one of the Vietnamese ports. Such a situation, of course, could lead to immediate and direct military confrontation. I participated in the preparations for handling such a contingency in the Security Council. We drafted appropriate documents and statements, while developing scenarios, including the worst case scenario, to cover all possible outcomes. It seemed that we were well equipped for a possible confrontation in the Security Council.

Were the Americans prepared for such a fight in the Council? I do not know for sure, but I guess that they allowed for the possibility. In any case, we never discussed this with them, but at meetings we eyed each other with suspicion and anxiety. However, all our preparations, fears and apprehensions were in vain. Sometime in mid-May we learned the date of Nixon's visit to Moscow, and it became perfectly obvious, that this time the UN would not become the cockpit for an Soviet-American confrontation.

Did I regret that all our work had been for nothing? Not at all. No doubt some of our colleagues were laughing at us, but I think that the majority of diplomats were happy at this turn in Soviet-American relations. Any discontent was due only to the see-sawing in our diplomacy, which only served to throw into sharp relief the abrupt replacement of our earlier harsh declarations by the language of conciliation and rapprochement. When we heard the news of Nixon's visit to Moscow, the senior adviser of the mission, Gennady Lisov, showed his disapproval most expressively by swinging his fists at, and then miming hugs and kisses for, an imaginary American president. We in New York, although we did not exactly start hugging or kissing our American colleagues, when we did meet them, we certainly were all smiles and affability.

Such was the inconsistent and bumpy course of superpower relations in the years of hopes and dreams.

Some Ambassadors Should Speak Out, Some Should Keep Quiet

The two superpowers took many strides in the late 1960s and early 1970s toward good working relations. Nothing, however, could overcome completely the traditions of confrontational diplomacy and the fundamental ideological differences that existed between our two countries. Frequently Soviet and American representatives fought over insignificant details. When, for instance, the U.S. representative asked the Security Council to move the voting on a resolution (for legitimate reasons) to one o'clock, his Soviet colleague mischievously remarked that it appeared that no one, apart from the American delegation, had difficulties understanding the document, which was submitted in English: "Do the Americans have problems with the language?" he asked. Or, when the American ambassador objected to the screening of a documentary about Namibia as part of an official Security Council meeting, the Soviet ambassador advised him to leave, if he were not interested, and to go see a detective movie while the Council dealt with Namibia.

During one lengthy discussion on another escalation of the Middle East situation Malik spoke about ten times. As usual, his main point of attack was to sharply criticize the American policy of supporting Israel. The American representative, Charles Yost, kept silent during many of these meetings. This silence provoked Malik into mocking the American for his silence. Yost then retorted that the two ambassadors should trade places, since Malik was speaking for both of them.

Ambassadors were not the only ones to play this game. Other diplomats rarely missed a chance for some cut and thrust or public wrangling with their American counterparts. They were never at a loss for words, but I must admit that they usually not as skillful or zealous as their superiors. I should also point out that during my years in New York First Secretaries Valentin Lozinsky, Vsevolod Oleandrov, Gennady Stashevsky, and many other diplomats from our mission did resist the temptation to resort to confrontational polemics. As consummate professionals, they understood the destructive nature of confrontational diplomacy and tried to avoid it. None of this, of course changed the essence of relations between the superpowers, or between the Soviet and American delegations but their efforts helped to mitigate an otherwise hostile climate.

Charles Yost: A Master of His Craft

As a rule Malik was the only one to deal directly with the U.S. permanent representative. As his deputies, we dealt with our American counterparts in the different UN bodies. For instance, when I was working on the decolonization issues my colleague was Ambassador Max Fisher. Later on, when I was dealing with political matters, my counterparts were Christopher Phillips and Tapley Bennett. Nonetheless, I did have opportunities to get to know a few of the American permanent representatives during my years in New York, 1968–73. I was most impressed by Yost and Bush. I did not get to know the others—Arthur Goldberg, George Ball, James Wilkins, and John Scali—very well, since I overlapped with them only for a short period.

In my opinion, Charles Yost was one of the best and most effective U.S. representatives to the United Nations, and I know that my opinion was shared by many of my colleagues. A career diplomat, Yost was an obvious exception to the general American practice of appointing amateurs to the responsible post of UN representative. I could never understand why the United States maintained this practice because it seemed to me that it almost always hurt them in the international arena. Once I asked Yost about the practice, and he explained that Washington as a rule underestimated and underappreciated the role of the United Nations in the world arena. He much preferred the Soviet practice of appointing experienced diplomats.

During his rather short term as U.S. permanent representative—about two years—Yost often found himself in situations where American policy was being sharply criticized—for example, in Vietnam, the Middle East, and

South Africa, to name a few. Many of his predecessors and successors became nervous and flustered in such situations, but Yost was usually able to keep his emotions and temper under control and do whatever it took to "save face and minimize the damage"—exactly as a diplomat should.

Yost was interested in Soviet-American relations, although he did not have many opportunities to deal with them directly. Unless it was absolutely necessary Yost tried to avoid "hot" issues. Although he was appointed soon after the Soviet invasion of Czechoslovakia in 1968, he never touched on the issue in his speeches. In a private conversation Yost told me that he was not satisfied with my arguments explaining the Soviet action. He said with sincere disappointment: "Why do you do such things? They will not do any good to our cooperation." Perhaps it was his lack of aggressiveness, his tact, and his modesty that led to his unexpected and unprecedented dismissal in 1971. Yost publicly admitted that he had learned about his removal from the morning papers.

After leaving the diplomatic service, Yost remained active, writing articles, giving lectures, and participating in symposia and seminars. He also visited the Soviet Union several times and participated in various Soviet-American discussions on international politics. In his book, *The Insecurity of Nations*, he emphasized that peace in Europe and in the entire world could not be safeguarded while the two superpowers were in a state of hostile confrontation. From his point of view, Europe was the place where the superpower confrontation was at its most critical, tense, and chronic. He wrote: "Anything that promotes détente has a favorable effect on European security, as well as on the security of the superpowers. Therefore any measures promoting conciliation between the U.S. and the USSR, such as arms control and arms reduction, even if seemingly in contradiction with the immediate needs of European security, meets the vital interests of Europe." A quarter of a century after Yost wrote these words, the world has changed dramatically, but at the time his ideas were progressive and, I believe, correct. Even today, Europe continues to feel the effects of the superpower conflict.

A Tough Guy from Texas

In March 1971, the representatives of UN Security Council members—France, Great Britain, the Soviet Union, and the United States—held one of their regular meetings at the Waldorf Astoria residence of the U.S. ambassador. This particular meeting was devoted to finding a peaceful settlement in the Middle East in accordance with Security Council Resolution 242.

These meetings were convened regularly by each representative in turn and were held once or twice a month. Great stress was always laid on the closed, confidential nature of the meetings. Neither the public nor the press were admitted. As a rule, two diplomats from each delegation attended each meeting: the permanent representative and his deputy. Yost chaired the March 1971 meeting. Malik represented the Soviet Union, and I accompanied him as his deputy. Sir Colin Crowe represented the United Kingdom and Jacques Kosciusko-Morizet was the French diplomat. The meeting was typical of the Cold War period. Malik, true to form, let loose his standard barrage of anti-imperialist, anti-Zionist fulminations, while his partners, with somewhat less zeal, rebutted them. Like all such meetings, this one too ended in deadlock, and Yost adjourned it. The sole result of the meeting was agreement on the date of the next meeting.

After the meeting had been officially adjourned, an American whom I did not know and who was sitting next to Yost shouted out heatedly: "Hey, guys! Why are you shouting at each other? Let's get down to business." This outburst shocked the other participants. I had arrived late and that was why I did not know who the American was. To my query Malik replied: "That's the new American representative, he's called Bush. George Bush."

Much later the new American representative became the forty-first president of the United States, and I think it is worth describing his work as permanent representative to the UN in some detail. Bush's amazement and frustration with the futility of the proceedings was quite genuine. He had acquired considerable experience as a politician, a member of the U.S. House of Representatives, and also as a prominent businessman and had learned over the years how to conduct successful negotiations. Now that he had embarked on a career as a diplomat, he had come up against a process that struck him as pointless and counterproductive. He discovered representatives of a profession whose essence was explained in all international relations textbooks as the art of reaching mutually acceptable resolutions, rending the air with propaganda speeches unlikely to sway even a nonprofessional audience. I doubt whether Bush was favorably impressed by this first encounter his colleagues-to-be.

It is worth noting that Bush met with a chilly response when he first appeared at the UN headquarters. First of all, he was practically unknown in diplomatic circles, and there were rumors in the UN that his appointment was a payment for services rendered to Nixon during the presidential campaign. Second, many delegations were openly disappointed at Yost's dismissal. "Another moth attracted by the UN light" was Malik's comment on Bush's appointment. However, the general UN attitude toward Bush changed rather quickly. His openness, accessibility, and straightforwardness were refreshingly different from the standard ambassadorial approach. He was often to be seen at the UN surrounded by diplomats of less than ambassadorial rank, engaged in animated conversation. For some, this behavior went beyond the bounds of accepted protocol; Malik referred to it as "cheap populism," while others were charmed by the American, and his popularity grew.

No significant international events occurred during the first months of Bush's stay at the UN. In fact, during the spring of 1971 the Security Council was rarely in session, so it was not until late May that Bush delivered his first speech in the Council, three months after his appointment. Consequently, many of his colleagues took that opportunity to congratulate him on his new appointment. Because U.S. ambassadors to the UN usually served very brief terms, however, some joked that Bush should combine his opening and farewell speeches into one.

Bush is probably best remembered at the UN for his broad view of the UN as a means for solving international problems. He understood the great opportunity the UN offered not only for dialogue between countries but also as a means for the United States to influence other countries in favor of its own national interests. He promoted improved relationships between the UN and its delegations, the American public, business circles, and the mass media. Bush encouraged foreign diplomats to lecture to American groups and in particular to military academies. "I personally believe that it is very important," he wrote after my lecture to the students and teachers of the Engineering College of the armed forces, "that groups such as these are exposed to senior representatives of the Soviet government."

I had another experience with Bush that shows his general openness toward rapprochement. Having learned that I had never visited his native Texas, Bush invited me to Dallas to give a series of lectures about the Soviet Union (which I mentioned in an earlier chapter). I soon received an official invitation from the University of Texas in Arlington. While I was preparing the lectures, an official of the American mission to the UN informed me that Dallas was in a zone restricted to Soviet diplomats and, therefore, in accordance with existing Cold War practice, I would have to address an official request for permission to the State Department.

I called Bush to inform him of the problem. He was aware of it and said that it was a formality that had to be observed. After consulting with Malik we decided to report the situation to Moscow, hoping to receive the necessary instructions for addressing a note to the State Department. The response, however, was negative. The problem was not my lectures; rather, they explained that the Americans, by way of reciprocity for my Texas trip, might request permission for a U.S. diplomat to visit a restricted Soviet area where he would undoubtedly "engage in espionage." With regret I informed Bush that I could not accept his offer and that my trip would have to be canceled. In a few days Bush called me and said that the problem could be resolved if the request were made orally instead of in writing. I knew, of course, that the form of my request would not change Moscow's attitude so I again had to tell Bush that I could not make the trip to Texas.

I had began to forget about the whole matter when I received a call from the American mission explaining that Washington had cleared my trip to Dallas, unprompted by me or by anyone in the Soviet mission. Malik and I were delighted with this news but decided not to approach Moscow again. We had concluded that, because the American side had voluntarily invited me to Dallas, we had avoided a situation in which we would have to provide an American diplomat with a reciprocal travel opportunity in the Soviet Union, hence avoiding any possible threat of "espionage."

At the first opportunity I asked Bush how he had managed to resolve the problem. He said that it had not been easy but that he had called Secretary of State William Rogers himself—something of which Bush was noticeably proud. I understood that my lecture at the University of Texas had become a matter of principle for him, a matter of keeping his word. Furthermore, the trip would generate good publicity in Texas, which was important to him. In general this episode demonstrated to me that Bush was a capable and strong-willed person, one who was very reluctant to go back on something he had decided on. It was not without reason that he was known as the "tough guy from Texas."

While head of the U.S. mission to the UN, Bush made U.S. official diplomatic hospitality less formal, frequently inviting guests for lunches and dinners not at prestigious restaurants but at small intimate places, known for their cuisine and traditions. At such gatherings seating protocol according to rank and position was disregarded. This, I felt, promoted more comfortable, relaxed, and spontaneous exchanges.

The Soviet Mission Is Fired On

No doubt, the high priority of Bush and the Americans was promoting close relations with their allies. However, Bush paid a good deal of attention to contacts with the Soviet Union. I never felt that he was anti-Soviet, as I had felt of some of his predecessors and successors. He always reiterated his loyalty to the ideals of Western democracy and the American way of life, and he certainly criticized communism and the Soviet system, but he was never openly hostile to the Soviet people or their diplomatic representatives.

One illuminating episode occurred on the evening of October 20, 1971, during a diplomatic reception at the Soviet mission on Sixty-seventh Street in Manhattan. The dinner party was for delegates to the General Assembly session. In the middle of the reception a security officer hurried up to me and reported that the Soviet mission had been fired upon. The shots had been fired from a roof of a neighboring Hunter College building and had hit the windows of the apartment of Yury Khilchevsky, the representative of the Central Committee of the CPSU. I do not know whether Khilchevsky had been deliberately chosen as the target, but the windows and the walls of his apartment, where his children were playing at that time, were sprayed with bullets. Fortunately, nobody was hurt.

I immediately reported the incident to the police and to the American mission and sent a note of protest to local authorities. The media soon arrived on the scene asking to see the premises that had been attacked. We declined their requests in keeping with security procedures, which forbade the presence of foreigners in offices and living quarters of the mission. Suddenly Bush showed up at the mission. He had been informed of the incident while at another reception and had rushed to the Soviet mission. He wanted to see the apartment; and feeling that I could not refuse him (Malik was away at the time), I showed him in. He was shocked by what he saw and offered his apologies to the family and the mission. He condemned the attack, calling it a "disgrace to America," and openly expressed concern that it would complicate relations between our two countries.

His concern proved justified. The following morning Bush called a press conference at the U.S. mission where he condemned the shooting as "the outrageous and cowardly hostile action of fanatics and barbarians." He said that the New York police were taking all possible steps to apprehend and punish the criminals and to ensure the security of the Soviet mission. He pointed out that the "incident works against everything that we are doing to improve our relations with the Soviet Union." He also offered Malik his formal regrets, although Malik had no intention of settling for a formal statement and a press conference. He was preparing to dramatize the event in the plenary of the General Assembly. At the opening of this meeting Bush made a statement in the spirit of his press conference. However, as soon as the discussion moved beyond the issue of the attack itself, he started rebut what he considered to be the groundless accusations leveled against the U.S. authorities. It is hard to say if this dispute, triggered by Malik, contributed at all to the security of the missions. Probably not, but this was definitely a setback, even if temporary, for relations between the U.S. and Soviet missions.

I had worked at the MFA at the time of Molotov and Vyshinsky, the Soviet champions of confrontational diplomacy. I knew about their American counterpart John Foster Dulles only by hearsay, but had to deal with many Americans who espoused Dulles's approach to diplomacy. George Bush was certainly not one of them. It seemed that he detested argument and confrontational invective, and he was never one to fire the opening shot. We once sat next to one another during a meeting of a General Committee of the General Assembly. The question under discussion was the agenda and the order of items. Many diplomats, including myself, I am afraid, were trying their best to outdo one another in taunting and ridiculing their opponents and accusing them of every crime in the book. Bush, however, took no part in all this. Toward the end of this futile wrangling he smiled and handed me a card with a picture of a dog. The card read: "Why bark when you have a dog?" I laughed and realized that Bush had not said a word throughout the acrimonious exchange.

Bush did not like wrangling over procedure. Only once did I see him allow himself to be drawn into this snare. In the summer of 1972 Syria and Lebanon (on the one hand) and Israel (on the other) submitted requests to the Security Council to convene an urgent meeting to examine their respective complaints regarding the aggressive acts of the other. Some members of the Council suggested that all the complaints should be considered jointly, others wanted them considered separately. The United States was in the first group, the Soviet Union in the second. The supporters of separate consideration (and they were the majority) contended that it was impossible to put victims of aggression (Syria and Lebanon) on the same level as the aggressor (Israel).

Bush was committed to the idea of joint consideration of the complaints. In the discussion he declared that, though he hated arguments over procedure, he was compelled to weigh in on the matter. He took the floor more than ten times. Several hours of fruitless discussion ensued, to which I, as the Soviet representative, unfortunately made my own contribution. All we did was to muddy the waters and complicate an otherwise clear issue. After the meeting Bush remarked with disappointment that the public had every reason to be dissatisfied with the work of the UN.

This was one of Bush's last statements at the UN. In mid-December of 1972 American newspapers announced that George Bush had been elected chairman of the Republican Party. Within New York diplomatic circles this move was seen as inevitable. Bush was clearly a high-flier. Despite its prestige, the post of permanent representative to the UN was far from the center of Washington politics, which was where Bush wanted to be. He publicly announced his regret at leaving the United Nations, but readily accepted his new job as a step forward in his political career.

The farewell to Bush in the UN was unusual. A significant part of the 1972 closing meeting of the Security Council was taken up by speeches of farewell and congratulations to Bush on his new appointment. Everyone spoke of his outstanding diplomatic qualities and expressed the hope that his UN experience would prove useful in his new job. I believe Malik was most objective when he said: "It is possible to have differences on very important issues, it is possible to disagree on fundamentals, but one has to respect a decent person." Diplomats who worked with him, myself included, always remember George Bush as a good and decent person.

9
THE SOVIET UNION'S 105TH VETO

Events in Czechoslovakia Are None of Your Business

In the spring of 1968 one of the most burning issues discussed in the Delegate's Lounge of the East River Headquarters of the United Nations was the state of affairs inside Czechoslovakia and around it. Everybody was talking about the "Prague Spring." Most diplomats welcomed the liberalization in Czechoslovakia, which had been initiated by the country's new leadership headed by Alexander Dubček, first secretary of the Czechoslovak Communist Party. Our colleagues from other UN member states were naturally very keen to know how the Soviet Union viewed these developments. During informal meetings, conversations, receptions, and consultations, as well as in encounters with the American public, we were constantly questioned.

The situation in Czechoslovakia became the main subject of our talks and lectures organized by the Soviet mission's Council for Foreign Policy. As the official in charge of the council I had to advise my junior colleagues on how to respond when fielding questions from the audience, although I myself knew very little. No specific information on the issue was forthcoming from Moscow, so we were left to draw our own conclusions from official Soviet documents and press reports. At the meeting of the council we decided that, when asked, we would emphasize that the communist party of Czechoslovakia, conscious of its responsibility, would naturally take the necessary steps to safeguard the gains of socialism. When asked to give the Soviet position on the matter, we decided that we would answer in a very general way, saying that in "the Czechoslovak communists' struggle for peace and socialism, they can count on the solidarity and assistance of the Soviet Union and other fraternal socialist countries." We all knew, of course, that such replies would please no one, but we had no other choice.

In mid-July we were instructed by Moscow to make public and give the widest dissemination to what was known as the Five States' Letter from the leaders of the Soviet Union, Bulgaria, East Germany, Hungary, and Poland to the leaders of Czechoslovakia. This letter had been adopted at the summit of the five states in Warsaw on July 14–15 and published in the *New York Times*. In addition we received from Moscow a set of articles published in the Soviet press concerning the events in Czechoslovakia. Reading the letter and these articles one could not help but notice that the Kremlin had hardened its line and that its political demands on Prague were becoming increasingly uncompromising. The Czechoslovak media was coming under especially harsh criticism. The statement of a group of liberals bearing the title "The 2,000 Words" was alleged to contain an outright call for struggle against the constitutional order in the country. The Five States' Letter declared that the developments in Czechoslovakia "opened the door to counterrevolution and exposed the socialist camp to imperialist military threat." Particularly strange was a *Pravda* article that alleged that American agents, in cooperation with "insurgent elements" in Eastern Europe, were using subversive tactics especially in Czechoslovakia. The article reminded me of the events in Hungary in 1956 when Soviet commentators, including myself, blamed the Hungarian uprising on "international imperialism," especially American imperialism.

The most important novelty in the Five States' Letter, however, was the claim that any threat of severing Czechoslovakia from the socialist community was not only Czechoslovakia's cause, but a common cause of all Warsaw Treaty member states. The leaders of the five states declared that the task of conclusively defeating the anticommunist forces and preserving the socialist system in Czechoslovakia belonged not to Czechoslovakia alone but to the whole socialist community. That was definitely a new twist in relations between the states of the socialist community and an innovation in international law in general. Later this became known as the "Brezhnev Doctrine," although I doubt that the Soviet leader was its true author.

Heated Debates on the "Prague Spring"

Malik was embarrassed when he learned that a Czech newsman Carel Kral had asked Secretary-General U Thant at a UN briefing if he could reconcile the pressure being exerted by the Soviet Union on Czechoslovakia with the Soviet-sponsored United Nations resolution barring intervention in the internal affairs of other states. Although Thant did not respond to the question, Malik asked me to talk to the Czechoslovak mission about Kral's "provocative behavior." I spoke to Ilya Hulinsky of the Czechoslovak mission, who shared our disapproval and assured us that the newsman was speaking on his own initiative and not on instructions from the mission. In my frustration, I pointed out bitterly, "Our Soviet correspondents would never dare to make such irresponsible statements."

Whenever the subject of Czechoslovakia was raised officially, members of the Soviet mission fell back on statements borrowed from the Five States' Letter and the leading Soviet media, but at private parties, and in confidential conversations, quite different views were voiced. These views varied from sympathy for to outright condemnation of the "Prague Spring," but were never aired publicly.

Everybody agreed that there could be no withdrawal from the Warsaw Treaty or any declaration of neutrality by Czechoslovakia, although many of us welcomed the liberalizing trends in Czechoslovakia, especially freedom of press. After my own troubles in publishing my books under Khrushchev I was an outspoken opponent of press censorship. And I was not alone. Many members of our mission, especially the younger members, supported a socialist order different from the old, Stalinist model—the rule of democracy, socialism with human face.

On the other hand, some diplomats believed that the political trend in Czechoslovakia was dangerous because it might lead to a weakened communist leadership. They favored any steps that would uphold the traditional socialist system and defeat antisocialist, bourgeois elements. I cannot say what the prevailing view within the mission was, particularly since many of its members preferred to remain silent on such obviously sensitive political issues.

The different views within our mission can partly be explained by the lack of information we received from Moscow and the discordant stories and reports published in the press. Nor did our contacts with the Czechoslovak mission help much to make the picture clearer. Our relations with Czechoslovak diplomats in New York were certainly cordial, in keeping with the official Soviet-Czechoslovak cooperation of the postwar period. The permanent representative of Czechoslovakia to the UN at that time was Ambassador Milan Klusak, an experienced politician close to the nation's leadership (he was son-in-law of President Ludvik Svoboda). He was not in New York, however, when the Czechoslovak crisis was at its peak. He had completed his term as permanent representative to the UN and returned to Prague in the summer of 1968, soon afterward to be appointed minister of culture. His deputy was J. Muzic, who dealt mostly with economic and social matters. I. Hulinsky, a very active diplomat, represented Czechoslovakia in several political bodies of the UN. Soviet diplomats were in constant contact, both in the course of their work and unofficially, with practically all members of the Czechoslovak mission. Most of them were fluent in Russian, so communication was easy.

After talking with our Czechoslovak colleagues, members of the Soviet mission, including myself, had the impression that within the Czechoslovak mission and among the Czechoslovakian nationals in the UN Secretariat there had been heated debate about the "Prague Spring." Some were ardent supporters, and others implacable opponents. We were told of heated debates that had taken place in the Czechoslovak mission on Madison Avenue. This worried us, and we were relieved to hear of reports of a meeting between Soviet and Czechoslovak leaders in Cerny on the Tissa (a small city on the border between the Soviet Union and Czechoslovakia) and later of a conference of leaders of the Soviet Union, Czechoslovakia, Bulgaria, Hungary, Poland, and the GDR in Bratislava in late July/early August 1968. I learned from my contacts with Czechoslovak colleagues that despite differences of view the overwhelming majority of diplomats preferred a peaceful, "friendly" solution to the dispute. Everybody to whom I talked emphasized the need to avoid a conflict between Czechoslovakia and the Soviet Union.

The ten-page document adopted at the conference in Bratislava was a reiteration of all the recent international statements made by the socialist states, ranging from the need to safeguard the achievements of socialism to condemnations of imperialism and colonialism, especially American actions in Vietnam, West German "revenge-seeking," and the Israeli aggression in the Middle East. Some diplomats in the Delegates' Lounge believed that the meetings in Cerny and Bratislava had led to Prague's acceptance of the basic Soviet demands, while others saw them as a face-saving device for Moscow, which had staked much prestige on its campaign to turn Prague back from the path toward democratic socialism with a human face.

The meetings in Cerny and Bratislava, however, did not lead to any practical solutions for resolving disagreements within the "socialist camp," so we in the Soviet mission in New York hoped to keep the events in Czechoslovakia off the table at the UN.

The Prague Spring and Soviet-American Relations

We in the mission were concerned that the image of Soviet foreign policy would suffer and that Soviet-American relations would be severely jeopardized by a possible Soviet military intervention in Czechoslovakia. While the Soviet embassy in Washington maintained contacts with American high officials in the capital, we in New York had our own informal meetings with Americans—diplomats at the UN, businessmen, public figures, and political scientists. Almost all of the Americans were of the view that the United States would support the attempt of the Czechoslovak people to reassert elements of their humanist and democratic tradition. Some expressed the concern that Soviet intervention in Czechoslovakia would imperil President Johnson's effort to improve U.S.-Soviet relations and negate the positive effects of recent progress in negotiations on the treaty on nonproliferation of nuclear weapons.

In a conversation with me in the summer of 1968, Hans Morgenthau stated that if the Soviet Union used force to impose its preferred political system on Czechoslovakia, it would inevitably raise the most serious doubts throughout the world as to the sincerity of the Soviet Union's policy of détente, and it would certainly be a blow to Soviet prestige and authority. I remember one meeting of senior Soviet diplomats and intelligence officers in New York in July 1968 when the stand of the American government on the Czechoslovak question was on the agenda. Some participants expressed the view that Czechoslovakia's "Prague Spring" had been instigated by the CIA, which naturally would do all in its power to destroy the socialist system in Czechoslovakia. Therefore, they expected even more drastic anti-Soviet steps from the White House, including demonstrative moves of some kind by the American military (partial mobilization, movement of troops, and so forth). One senior diplomat said that Washington would use the crisis in Czechoslovakia to explain away deteriorating Soviet-American relations.

The majority of my colleagues did not share this view. Most believed that even though the Americans sympathized with the "Prague Spring," they would not do anything to jeopardize Johnson's efforts to improve U.S.-Soviet relations. One colleague said that as the Vietnam War seemed to be moving into its final phase, and the White House was hoping for a post-Vietnam understanding with the Soviet Union, an American overreaction to the crisis in Czechoslovakia would only interfere with these plans. Many also believed that the Americans would respect the agreement reached by Stalin, Roosevelt, and Churchill concerning the spheres of influence, which established the postwar political and territorial status quo. In the end we concluded that the American reaction would most probably be mild, mainly propagandist in character, and this is what we reported to Moscow.

An Anthill Disturbed

Up until August 20, 1968, the UN took no formal cognizance of the turbulent situation in Czechoslovakia. However, late that afternoon the situation changed drastically. Toward the end of the working day just as we were all set to leave, Malik called together his senior aides. He told us that he had received very important information from Moscow concerning Czechoslovakia. Moscow believed that the developing situation in Czechoslovakia threatened the vital interests of the Soviet Union and the security of the entire socialist community. Therefore, the Soviet government, together with the governments of Bulgaria, Hungary, the GDR, and Poland, "proceeding from the principle of inseparable friendship and cooperation," had decided to send troops into Czechoslovakia. Moscow claimed that this decision was made in accordance with the request of government of Czechoslovakia. Prague had allegedly appealed to Moscow for help in the face of the threat to the socialist system and constitutional statehood of Czechoslovakia from both domestic and foreign reactionaries.

Moscow then issued urgent instructions that members of the permanent mission in New York were immediately to contact UN delegates from countries having no diplomatic relations with the Soviet Union, and pass on oral information from the Soviet government concerning the latest developments. (I should mention that on many occasions in the past we had resorted to this practice as a way of conveying information to countries with which we did not maintain diplomatic relations.) Ambassador Mendelevich suggested that we immediately contact the Czechoslovak mission and report to our colleagues there the instructions we had received so that we could coordinate our actions. Malik, the permanent representative, rejected the idea in no uncertain terms, saying that Moscow had given no instructions to that effect. This itself put me, and no doubt my colleagues too, on our guard, for if the assertions in the Moscow document were to be believed, all of our diplomatic moves would have been closely coordinated with Czechoslovakia. Something was definitely amiss.

Next morning, August 21, I paid visits to the missions of Spain and Saudi Arabia. The mission heads, Ambassadors Haim Pinhez and Jamil Barudi listened to my news, asking for some details and confirmation that the foreign troops had been brought in at the request of the Czechoslovak government and on a temporary basis. With no additional information to draw on, I simply confirmed everything contained in the Moscow message. "Well, since it's all being done amicably by agreement of the governments, then there is no problem," was Ambassador Barudi's conclusion.

Early that afternoon Malik went to see Secretary-General U Thant, informing him "objectively" of the situation in Prague. The Soviet ambassador was satisfied that he had presented the Soviet position in a "convincing" fashion, but I doubt the secretary-general agreed.

Back in the mission I learned that the Security Council president, J. Castro of Brazil, was expecting the Soviet representatives in his office. He told us when we met that a group of the Security Council members, the delegates of the United States, Britain, France, Canada, Denmark, and Paraguay had approached Castro with a request to convene an urgent meeting of the Council to discuss the developments in Czechoslovakia. Malik tried to prevent the meeting, claiming the matter was "an internal affair of the socialist nations" and that the troops had been brought in with the consent of the governments concerned and under the UN Charter, but the Security Council president was unrelenting. He said he intended to call a council meeting within a couple of hours.

As Malik and a group of his aides were leaving the Soviet mission for the UN, across the street, on the north side of Sixty-seventh Street, a small group of people were clustered around a speaker, who was criticizing the

Soviet actions in Czechoslovakia. The police moved in quickly, blocking off the street with wooden sawhorse barricades and sealing off the access to the mission by the demonstrators—a scene that had become only too familiar during major political crises.

On August 21 the UN Headquarters on the East River was much like a disturbed anthill. On our way to the Security Council Room we were besieged by colleagues, asking us to clarify the latest events in Czechoslovakia. A stream of reports of varying truthfulness was coming out of the media all over the world. What did we have to tell our importunate colleagues to offset that media avalanche? Practically nothing. All we had was the minimal information given us by Moscow. As a matter of fact, our briefcases were practically empty as we entered the Council session. Instead of arming ourselves with documents related to Czechoslovakia, as Malik had instructed, we took along articles and notes on the aggressive nature of American imperialism, West German revenge-seekers and Israeli occupiers, and so on.

On that day at 5:30 P.M. the Council meeting was called to order. The Council chamber was filled with representatives of the UN member states, and every seat was taken in the sections reserved for the press and the public. When the president of the Council proposed a vote on the approval of the agenda, Malik stalled, hoping to delay the item on Czechoslovakia as long as possible. Having nothing new to add to what he had already said, he simply repeated that the events in Czechoslovakia were the internal affair of the socialist nations and of no concern to anyone else. After more than two hours the agenda was finally approved by a vote at the insistence of the U.S. delegation, thereby enabling Council members to state their views on the crisis in Czechoslovakia.

The Security Council discussion was acrimonious in the extreme. Never before or since have I witnessed a debate as polemical, bitter, vituperative, or offensive. The protagonists were the delegations of the United States and the Soviet Union. The U.S. delegation was headed by Permanent Representative George Ball, a well-known statesman, politician, and former undersecretary of state. Ball had only had a few months experience in the UN, so the debate on Czechoslovakia was a kind of baptism of fire for him. He proved to be a hard-hitting, pugnacious, and combative debater. Another active participant in the debate was Lord Caradon of the United Kingdom, an entirely different sort of personality, calm and well-mannered, and with a sharp edge to his tongue, which he used to excellent effect in support of

Ball. Time after time he would stump his political opponents, elegantly and without once ever raising his voice or losing his composure. Joining the chorus against the Soviet Union and its allies were the Western states and the majority of nonaligned countries.

As one might expect, our delegation found it extremely difficult to defend Moscow's version of events. And the more we were questioned, the more entangled we became in our own dubious arguments. At first, for example, we claimed that the troops had been sent in in response to a request from the Czechoslovak government and leadership, but soon this was replaced by a different version. While the Council's first meeting was in progress, we received instructions from Moscow to the effect that the action had been undertaken to meet not the request of the government, but of some "party and state figures of Czechoslovakia." These party and government figures were not named and who they were, what authority they had, and what stand was taken by the legitimate leaders of Czechoslovakia all remained a mystery.

The increasingly bitter wrangling between Malik and Ball dominated the session of the Security Council. "Mr. President, I think the loss of equanimity, the irritation, and the tone in which the American representative delivered his speech, with the trite anti-Soviet and antisocialist tirades, speak for themselves," Malik berated his opponents. "Here at the Security Council," he went on, "these slanderous fabrications were dreamed up by the American, British, and other delegates of the NATO countries."

Ambassador Ball riposted: "Never have I heard such an impossible, tawdry case stated with such diligence, if not with effectiveness, but as regards the attitude which the Soviet representative displays." Ball continued, "Toward the people of Czechoslovakia and their reactions, I can only recall an anecdote told by a very famous English writer, Dean Swift. What he said is this: 'This dog, Sir, is vicious and dangerous and should be destroyed. When attacked he defends himself.'"

At the beginning of the meeting it seemed to us that those of our colleagues who had expected a harsh response from the Americans, including ringing denunciations of the Soviet Union, were proved right, but the public duel between the two permanent representatives was certainly more than Moscow had bargained for. On the other hand, the Soviet diplomats in New York derived some encouragement from a news conference following a cabinet meeting at the White House. Although Secretary of State Rusk denounced the Soviet action, he acknowledged that "we have no bilateral commitments to Czechoslovakia." Likewise Senator Richard B. Russell, chairman of the Senate Armed Services Committee, told newsmen that the United States had not been called upon to respond militarily or by NATO action to the Soviet-led invasion of Czechoslovakia. He made it clear that the denunciation of the Soviet Union in the UN was the only response the world should expect. After reading the news reports, Malik remarked in his usual cocksure manner, "the Americans won't get even that."

Czechoslovakia's Representatives Respond

Czechoslovakia was represented in the Security Council, first by the acting permanent representative, Jan Muzic, and later by the foreign minister, Jiri Gaek. Muzic was given the floor at the first meeting of the Security Council on the situation in Czechoslovakia. During the Cold War, representatives of socialist countries almost invariably echoed what was said by the representatives of the Soviet Union. So everybody—the diplomats, the media, the public—was anxious to see what would happen this time. Would the Czechoslovaks endorse the Soviet version of events? Muzic's speech was to provide the answer.

We had no knowledge of what the Czechoslovak representative was going to say, although delegates of allied nations, not just socialist nations, usually shared with one another the texts of statements before they were delivered. It was a routine practice. In this case, however, our traditional contacts with the Czechoslovak delegation had been interrupted. Neither we, the Soviet diplomats, nor the Czechoslovaks sought contacts. We were avoiding each other. This in itself was not a good sign.

Muzic was obviously nervous as he addressed the Security Council at such a dramatic moment. I remember that he frequently stopped to sip water while he was reading his statement. Muzic stressed that he was speaking on behalf of his minister, and mostly he quoted documents received by the mission from Prague after the troops of the Soviet Union and other socialist countries had entered Czechoslovakia. These were statements by the leadership of the Communist Party, members of the government, and members of the Presidium of the National Assembly of Czechoslovakia and also President Svoboda's address broadcast from Prague late in the evening of August 21.

These documents stated unambiguously that the Soviet, Bulgarian, Hungarian, East German and Polish troops had been sent in without knowledge of the president, the chairman of the National Assembly, the prime minister, the first secretary of the communist party, or of the members of these state and government bodies. According to one of the documents, on August 21 the Czechoslovak foreign ministry issued the strongest possible protest to the ambassadors of the Soviet Union, Bulgaria, the GDR, Hungary, and Poland in Prague, demanding an immediate end to the illegal occupation of Czechoslovakia and withdrawal of all troops from Czechoslovakia. The protest was to be transmitted to each of the governments in question. Another document alleged that Czechoslovak leaders—President Ludvik Svoboda, Prime Minister O. Cernic, National Assembly Chairman J. Smrkovsky, First Secretary of the Czechoslovak Communist Party A. Dubček, and others—had been detained by the troops and were unable to carry out their constitutional duties. "Now we know where the Czech leaders are," Lord Caradon whispered to Malik, his immediate neighbor at the Security Council table.

The members of the Council listened to Muzic with rapt attention. I was particularly impressed by his concluding remarks in which he reiterated the position of the Czechoslovak government, stated many times in previous weeks, that the changes in Czechoslovakia since January of that year were aimed only at improving the socialist system. Czechoslovakia, he stated, was seeking the "cherished goals of freer socialism and the realization of all human rights and freedoms which must be an indispensable part of any socialist system." When Muzic stated that the unity of the Czechoslovak people and their loyalty to socialism would enable them to reach the goals to which all progressive humanity aspires, I whispered to Mendelevich: "Sounds very reasonable." Mendelevich was about to agree with me, but was stopped in his tracks by the look that Malik was giving us.

A few days later, the Czechoslovak foreign minister, Gaek, echoed Muzic's comments. He was well known in international circles from his years of service as his country's representative in the UN. In his statement he reflected on the serious damage inflicted on the ideas of socialism by sending foreign troops into Czechoslovakia, for the Czechoslovak Communist Party had initiated a process that was essential and aimed, as he put it, at the elimination of bureaucratism and the implementation of humane and democratic principles of socialism.

At times Gaek became emotional. "We are profoundly disappointed, offended and humiliated," he confessed, "and particularly so because this is an occupation by countries from who we least expected such a thing and from which we have least deserved it." He expressed his conviction that the "fatal act" of sending in troops was the result of a wrong approach, wrong information, and wrong analysis of the situation.

The Voice of America broadcast Gaek's speech around the world. While the discussion in the Council was continuing, a member of the Soviet mission brought us the news that a large group of demonstrators was marching through the streets of midtown Manhattan protesting both the Soviet bloc occupation of Czechoslovakia and U.S. involvement in the war in Vietnam. "Not a bad partner to be condemned with," smiled Malik when he got the news.

Cain's Help to Abel

For the Soviet diplomats, listening to our Czechoslovak allies turned adversaries was a bitter pill to swallow. Was it really a "fatal" move? How did it happen, and who was responsible for it? History would supply the answers, that much was clear. However, we the official representatives had no choice but to reply immediately in defense of the Soviet position.

Malik could only fall back on the so-called Brezhnev doctrine. He described it in the following words in one of his tiresome speeches: "We are stating here most definitely that no one will ever be allowed to tear away a single link of the community of socialist nations, which has been and remains a bulwark against every kind of imperialist attack." Once in the heat of argument Malik grumbled that "the imperialists should not put their noses into socialist and communist affairs, otherwise they may be left without noses."

Ball, for his part, stated that the world was disgusted by the pious claim that this invasion and occupation amounted to merely "fraternal assistance." "It is a very curious kind of fraternal assistance," the American went on, "and, if the Soviet representative will not be offended by my reference to the Holy Bible, I can point out to him one famous precedent that may illustrate the answer to the question of what he means by fraternal assistance. The kind of fraternal assistance that the Soviet Union is according to Czechoslovakia is exactly the same kind that Cain gave to Abel."

In a word, the atmosphere in the Security Council was extremely fraught and belligerent for everyone involved. I remember Malik rebuking me for talking to my American colleague William Buffum, who was Ambassador Ball's deputy, during a break in the meeting. "Don't you realize what the international situation is?" Outwardly Malik was confident and imperturbable. He was in what he liked to call his "attacking mode," though I doubt whether he was as calm as he pretended to be. Moscow meanwhile seemed to show no interest whatsoever in the Security Council proceedings. We received no instructions, no advice, and no reactions to Malik's performance in New York. Most frustrating of all was the lack of any information about negotiations between the Soviet and Czechoslovak leaders. All we could do was wait, stall, and play for time.

Meanwhile, on the second day of the debate, August 22, representatives of seven members of the Security Council (the United Kingdom, Brazil, Denmark, Canada, Paraguay, the United States, and France) introduced a draft resolution, that, among other things, denounced the armed intervention of the Soviet Union and other members of the Warsaw Treaty in Czechoslovakia's domestic affairs, and called for immediate withdrawal of their troops from the country, and for an end to all other interference in Czechoslovakia's domestic affairs.

A new round of lengthy discussion ensued, but of course, it led nowhere. The president consulted with the Security Council members, but to no effect because positions were irreconcilable. The night meeting of August 22 began at 9.00 P.M. Hard as we tried to delay the voting in the hope that the situation might change, we failed. At about 4.00 A.M. on August 23 the draft resolution was put to the vote. Ten Council members voted in favor (the sponsors were backed by China, Senegal, and Ethiopia); Algeria, India, and Pakistan abstained; and the Soviet Union and Hungary voted against. The resolution did not pass because of the Soviet veto. It was the 105th veto cast by the Soviet Union in the Security Council.

A Harbinger of the Socialist Collapse

After the vote a number of delegates indicated that they wished to speak. Despite the late hour (it was long after midnight) and the extreme fatigue of the participants, the meeting continued. Some of the speeches and comments of the delegates were striking and memorable. Ball stated: "History will unquestionably demonstrate that the most wretched victims of the veto you [Malik] have cast tonight will not be the government or the people of Czechoslovakia but rather those frightened and rattled leaders of the Soviet Union who launched the invasion and brutal occupation of Czechoslovakia, for their action has called into question not only their judgment, not only their perception, it has also called into question their humanity. And let there be no doubt, Ambassador Malik, what they have done, what your government has done is self-destructive. Their repressive action will some day be repudiated by their successors with the same violence, with the same vehemence that the cruel and repressive acts of Stalin were repudiated by his successors."

Malik, naturally, was grossly offended by Ball's remarks. The original draft of his speech, which he showed to me, contained a long paragraph devoted to the "criminal actions" of Washington's rulers. When he spoke, however, he restrained himself, characterizing Ball's comments as a "malice, slander, insinuation, pathological animosity and hatred toward the socialist countries, socialism, the lofty ideals of communism." At the same time Malik clearly valued the Soviet veto, which, according to him, "had enabled, is enabling, and will continue to enable the Soviet Union to defend the just cause and interests of many, many peoples of its own and other countries against the threat of imperialist aggression, subversion, invasion, slander, as well as the cause of that fight which was mounted against the first socialist state in the world, the Soviet Union, from the very first days of the great and glorious, 1917 October Revolution."

At daybreak, on August, 23, I was returning to the mission, driving through the empty streets of New York, with my aide, a junior diplomat. Suddenly my young colleague broke our silence by asking my opinion of Ball's prophecy. "I don't believe that our leaders will ever repudiate their policy and actions in Czechoslovakia, at least in my lifetime," was my answer. I was, however, wrong. Many years later, in December 1989, I had the good fortune to witness the top political leadership of the Soviet Union, Bulgaria, the GDR, Hungary, and Poland admitting that the action against Czechoslovakia undertaken in the summer of 1968 had been "an error." This was the harbinger of the collapse of the socialist regime in all these countries.

The Deep Scar Remains

It was another week or so before the Security Council gave up the fruitless effort to debate the situation in Czechoslovakia. Meanwhile, the Czechoslovak political leaders were brought to Moscow, where under pressure from their Kremlin hosts they agreed to Soviet demands to restore the "classical," Soviet style of socialism in Czechoslovakia. New leaders were appointed in Prague, and slogans proclaiming indestructible fraternal friendship among the socialist states were once again being churned out by the propaganda machine of Moscow and its allies. The conflict seemed to be over, and we diplomats turned our attention to other matters.

Subsequently, from time to time we came back to the subject of the Prague Spring and its consequences. Sometimes with pride and self-respect, other times with bitterness and sorrow. Perhaps, we thought, it was inexperience and the lack of precedent for building socialism in that kind of country that explained what had happened, but if so, why then was the "Prague Spring" so popular, so strongly supported by the people of Czechoslovakia, why was the Soviet action denounced by the majority of nonaligned and even socialist states? The answers to these questions were clear to us but we rejected them, otherwise it would have meant accepting the unacceptable, that Soviet-style socialism was unpopular, even though the truth of this conclusion had been demonstrated to us, first in Hungary, and now in Czechoslovakia.

I think it was a mistake for us to overlook the similarities between Czechoslovakia in 1968 and Hungary in 1956 in spite of the differences in the style and methods used by the protagonists in the two cases. History, traditions, and, certainly, the temper of the people played a very significant role. To consider what happened in Hungary as a counterrevolution, and the events in Czechoslovakia as a mistake committed by its leadership is to miss the point. Both situations were manifestations of the deep frustration of the peoples of those countries at having the Soviet social and economic system imposed on them. In both cases, forthright public protest against Soviet-style socialism was crushed by the Soviet Army.

It was with some surprise, therefore, that I heard Muzic tell this story in the Security Council. He said that a long time ago his family, which lived in Prague very close to a soccer stadium, told him upon what had happened on Sunday, November 4, 1956, while he had been away, when the soccer stadium, packed with fans, broke into applause when it learned of the Soviet victory over the "counterrevolution" in Hungary. I could not help wondering why the reaction of those same soccer fans to another victory, twelve years later, by the Soviet Army on the streets of Prague, had been so different.

And one last point. The events in Czechoslovakia in 1968, especially the Soviet Union's attitude toward these events, poisoned relations between the two countries. This was a wound so deep that even time could not heal it. Signs and banners bearing the popular slogan "Together with the Soviet Union for ever!" disappeared; the friendly feelings the Czechs had once had for the Soviets evaporated. What was even more disturbing, but understandable, was the growing disdain and contempt of many in the Soviet Union toward the new Czechoslovak leadership, and the Czechs themselves. "These 'Schweiks' [a name for Czechs taken from the title of Hasek's novel, as the Soviet man in the street liked to put it] cannot even defend themselves." In such circumstances, how could we expect to build relations with our allies based on equality, trust, and respect, and prevent the further downgrading of the role of the Warsaw Treaty Organization? These were questions that bothered many Soviet diplomats.

10
THE COLD WAR ON THE MIDDLE EAST FRONT

The Middle East in Ferment

My colleagues in Moscow predicted that the principal problem I would have to deal with at the UN in the next few years would be the Middle East. They were absolutely correct. Although the "Six-Day" War of 1967 was over, there was no peace in the Middle East. The problem continued to fester in the form of an endless series of armed conflicts, skirmishes, ambushes, and terrorist acts. The Middle East issue became a constant on the agenda of all UN General Assembly meetings. Meetings of the Security Council to deal with outbreaks of hostilities in the region became an unwelcome tradition.

When I first arrived in New York, the Middle East issue was not part of my duties, although it soon became clear to me that Malik and his deputy Mendelevich (as well as the whole political department) were completely wrapped up in it. As a result, to be involved in the Middle East issue was increasingly seen as a mark of prestige. Generally speaking, the Middle East had been growing in importance in Soviet strategic global planning since the 1956 war between Egypt and the coalition of Britain, France, and Israel, and especially since the Six-Day War of 1967. As a teacher of international politics, I naturally followed these developments. There were even rumors at the MFA that the promotion of Shepilov, the editor-in-chief of *Pravda*, in 1956 to the post of minister of foreign affairs was in recognition of his successful trip to Egypt and the establishment of friendly relations with Nasser. Nevertheless, I had never displayed any particular interest in the region, even having refused to join the Arabic department of the Diplomatic Academy.

Therefore, I was surprised and delighted when, after Mendelevich's departure for Moscow in 1969, Malik put me in charge of Middle East issues. Not surprisingly, I quickly learned how extremely complex and thorny the problem was. The more I worked on it the more insoluble it seemed. The history of Arab-Jewish relations going back through the centuries was replete with tragedy and suffering. Israel's Declaration of Independence in 1948, which was actively backed by the Soviet Union, opened up a new chapter in these relations. Regrettably, however, mutual intolerance between these two neighboring peoples, who had so much in common, continued to dominate their relations.

Does the Resolution Contain a Definite Article?

Resolution 242 adopted on November 22, 1967, by the Security Council was the point of departure for UN negotiations on the Middle East in the 1970s. Perhaps no other Security Council resolution was ever as well known. It became a subject of special research and was referred to in many monographs and textbooks on the history of international relations and the question of a Middle East peace settlement in particular. Many years later the author of the resolution, Lord Caradon said: "Hardly anyone remembers Lord Caradon, but resolution 242 is still well known." He was right.

The resolution was a successful attempt at compromise. It appeared acceptable to the majority of Arabs and Israelis. The superpowers also supported it. However, as with any compromise, the resolution allowed for various interpretations, and as the rival parties—the Arabs and the Israelis —maintained their essentially divergent positions, these interpretations turned into an insuperable stumbling-block to a peaceful settlement, and the resolution never succeeded in becoming a basis for the establishment of peace in the Middle East.

Without going into great detail, the essence of the debate was this: the Arab countries claimed that the Security Council resolution provided for the withdrawal of Israeli troops from territories occupied during the Six-Day War. Once the troops had been removed, then discussion could begin to determine secure and recognized borders of all states in the region. Israel contended that withdrawal could begin only when secure and recognized state borders had been defined. Practically all nonaligned countries and the Soviet Union supported the Arabs. The United States along with some other Western countries supported Israel.

The American statement that paragraph 1 of the resolution provided for a withdrawal of Israeli armed forces "from territories occupied during the recent conflict," but not from *all* occupied territories only lent fuel to the fire of the disputes concerning the interpretation of the resolution. The Americans argued that the English text of the resolution did not contain a definite article, which it would need to have if in fact it meant *all* occupied territories.

This problem did not arise in other official languages: Russian, French, Spanish, or Chinese. When the Security Council discussed the situation following the Six-Day War, speakers argued that all territories occupied by Israel should be relinquished unconditionally. This condition was reflected in the various drafts of the resolution, including the Soviet version. When I reported to Moscow on our dispute with the Americans over this issue of the definite article, Gromyko said bitterly, "They're nothing but cheats."

General Disappointment

Nevertheless, Resolution 242 did yield some benefits within the United Nations. Pursuant to the resolution, U Thant appointed the Swedish diplomat Gunnar Jarring his special representative responsible for the establishment and maintenance of contacts between Arab countries and Israel for the purpose of implementing provisions specified in the resolution. Early in 1969, on the initiative of the French, an informal body, known as "The Big Four," was assigned the role of facilitating Jarring's difficult and delicate mission.

After the adoption of Resolution 242 there was renewed optimism that the UN would now be able to play an effective role in the Middle East. The Big Four held weekly meetings, and its working group, consisting of deputy permanent representatives, met even more frequently. Also, Jarring held briefings and discussions with interested delegations, which helped the parties to the negotiations narrow their differences on some minor issues. This work took up a great deal of the time of permanent representatives and their deputies.

As the Big Four embarked on their work, Malik, on the strength of the broad support enjoyed by the Arabs and the compromise in the Security Council, hoped that the United States would feel it necessary to pressure Israel to leave the Arab territories. He also thought that Charles Yost, who represented the United States in the "Big Four," would be more cooperative than his predecessor Goldberg, who had represented the United States in negotiating Resolution 242. Malik, therefore, adopted a businesslike approach and tried to avoid getting into arguments with Yost, with whom he held bilateral consultations. At one of the first meetings he submitted a working document that outlined a plan of action for Jarring. Other ambassadors submitted similar documents, and some fundamental principles were established on which the Swede could base his work.

Jarring, who formally retained his post as Swedish ambassador in Moscow, immersed himself completely in his new and difficult responsibilities. He visited the Middle East, where he negotiated with the leaders of the countries involved in the conflict. He also engaged in extensive correspondence, hoping to elicit enough common ground to constitute a possible agreement.

Time passed without any perceptible progress on the part of Jarring or the Big Four. Every meeting only seemed to accentuate the differences among the parties with the result that positions became even more entrenched. The Arabs demanded the unconditional withdrawal of Israeli troops from territories occupied in the Six-Day War, followed by the establishment of secure borders. Israel, on the other hand, first wanted the establishment of secure and recognized borders before withdrawing its troops behind these borders. Jarring failed to move these rigid and mutually exclusive positions even one inch closer. The work of "The Big Four" also proved to be ineffective. Neither the Soviet Union nor the United States was willing to exert pressure on its "clients," afraid that it would damage its superpower authority.

Sad to say, the truth is that both Jarring's mission and the Big Four mechanism created by Resolution 242 appeared to be stillborn offspring. Interest in them gradually waned. Jarring spent more and more time performing his ambassadorial duties in Moscow, and the meetings of the Big Four became pointless as all four ambassadors were reduced to making formal declarations that only repeated well-worn arguments.

I had helped to draft some of Malik's speeches, but by 1971 neither one of us believed any longer in the process. It was clear, that the mechanism for a Middle East settlement, created by Resolution 242, was dying a slow death.

The failure of Jarring's mission and the quadripartite negotiations had one rather important consequence. The number of those who believed in the possibility of resolving the Middle East conflict within the UN framework and with its assistance declined. The helplessness of the international organization was obvious. The Arab countries along with all nonaligned states were especially disappointed at Jarring's failure. They had thought that the General Assembly's condemnation of Israel's occupation of Arab territories and the unanimously approved November 1967 decision of the Security Council provided a basis for an honorable settlement in the Middle East. However, this did not happen.

Almost all Arab diplomats voiced to us, the Soviet representatives, their disappointment and dissatisfaction with the ineffectiveness of the UN. To some extent these complaints were addressed to the Soviet Union in its capacity as a founding member of the organization and as a permanent member of the Security Council. The inability of the UN to eliminate the consequences of the Six-Day War had a major impact on relations between the Arab countries and the Soviet Union, although we always supported the Arabs in word and deed.

Was Malik an Anti-Semite?

The Middle East became one of the major fronts of the Cold War, an arena of fierce Soviet-American confrontation in the 1960s and 1970s. Many Arab countries, including Egypt, broke off relations with the United States, which meant that American influence in the Arab world declined appreciably while Arab dependence on the Soviet Union increased. We all understood the consequences of this political transformation. Arab leaders made no secret of the fact that they needed military supplies from the Soviet Union, not only to replace their losses, but also to prepare for a new war against Israel. Moscow, as a rule, tried to satisfy their demands. It is difficult to overestimate the importance to the Arab countries of this cooperation with the Soviet Union.

On the other hand, the Soviet Union was extremely interested in good relations and even alliances with the Arab countries. The position of the

USSR on the Middle East question basically coincided with that of the Arabs. We frequently received instructions from Moscow to work together with Arab delegations on a variety of issues on the UN agenda, and relations between the Soviet and Arab missions at the UN reflected this policy.

Malik had never served in the Middle East, but as deputy minister of foreign affairs he supervised Soviet-Arab relations, which meant that he was well-informed on Middle East questions, and I believe he actively relished debating the subject. None of the representatives of the other countries directly involved in the conflict spoke so frequently and at such length as Malik. In preparation for his speeches he read widely about Israel, its domestic and foreign policy, and about Zionism.

Usually Malik's statements were bitterly anti-Israel. Besides the usual in-depth exposition of official Soviet policy, as a rule they contained attacks against Israeli leaders. Even those whom he knew personally were not immune to his attacks. After Malik's debut in the Security Council in March of 1968, the Israeli permanent representative Joseph Tekoah declared that the Soviet ambassador's speech reminded him of the Russian saying from imperial times: "Kill the Jews and save Russia." This part of his statement Tekoah made in Russian.

Was Malik an anti-Semite? He was, of course, accused of it often enough, but he repeatedly denied it in public. For my own part, I never heard him make any anti-Semitic remarks or jokes in private. On the other hand, I was astounded by the venom and aggressiveness of his speeches. Frequently he was provoked by Tekoah himself, who possessed a sharp tongue of his own, but Malik was only too eager to take the bait, joining the fray with great pleasure. Oddly enough, he always claimed that he and Tekoah were on friendly terms in the past.

I remember one incident involving Malik and Tekoah in which Malik almost went too far. One evening during a formal ball at the Waldorf Astoria I was approached by more than a few guests who stared at my face and started smiling. One of them remarked in mock amazement: "His nose is not that long." I failed to get the point, but then they explained the following story: A few hours before the diplomatic reception, Malik, in the midst of a heated exchange in the Security Council, retorted to Tekoah with a paraphrase of a Russian proverb: "Mister ambassador, do not stick your long nose in our Soviet garden." Everyone present gasped, for they took it as an anti-Semitic slur against Tekoah. In fact, Tekoah's nose actually was rather long but Malik's comment sounded too much like stereotypical insults made against Jews. In protest against this gratuitously offensive and tactless remark, the Israeli ambassador walked out of the room. Malik's colleagues, even those who shared his views and were his friends, expressed their distaste for his insulting and offensive personal attack. Even the president of the Council expressed his deep regrets about the incident.

Malik tried to defend himself by saying that the proverb he was using was only figurative and that surely he had not intended to imply anything about the length of Tekoah's nose, but his protestations were in vain. For, as another Russian proverb says, "A word is not a bird"—once it's out there's no way of taking it back. Rumors about the incident in the Security Council spread quickly through the UN, and Malik then decided to go to the plenary meeting of the General Assembly to explain the incident. He assured his colleagues again, that he had had no intention of offending Tekoah and was not referring to *his* nose in quoting the proverb. Malik went on to say that there were many people with long noses, even in the Soviet delegation. "For example, my deputy Israelyan. And I respect him despite the size of his nose." At any rate, it was this remark that explained all the attention my nose had received at the Waldorf Astoria ball. When Malik came to the ball after his speech, we had a good laugh at the whole episode, although he seemed to realize that he had gone too far this time.

The Arabs approved of Malik's inflexible hard line, but over time they began expressing concern that the jousting between Malik and Tekoah was becoming a sideshow that was diverting the attention of the Security Council from the essence of the Middle East problem. Naturally, the Arabs were not at all happy when the issue of Israel's withdrawal from the occupied Arab territories took a back seat to disputes over the plight of Jews in the Soviet Union. They hinted at this to Malik, but complained directly to me. Moreover, once they took their complaint to the ministerial level, which according to Malik resulted in a very unpleasant conversation on the subject between himself and Gromyko.

The Failed Confidential Mission

I am convinced that the Kremlin relished the fact that our mission in New York was taking a hard line toward Israel. When in Moscow, I frequently heard approving references to Malik's tough anti-Israel statements, and this approval was shared even by those who knew that such belligerence had little chance of success. The fact is that the more we alienated Israel, the closer Israel got to the United States, and the more remote became the prospects for a peace settlement.

This view was shared by quite a few of us in New York as well as in Moscow. Evgeny Pirlin, the deputy head of the MFA Middle East department, who frequently visited New York as a Middle East expert, told me that within both the MFA and the Central Committee there was support for establishing direct contacts with the Israeli leadership. This would have been much easier to do in New York, but nobody thought of entrusting Malik with such a delicate mission, so this task was assigned to Deputy Minister of Foreign Affairs Vladimir Semenov. Semenov, one of the leading Soviet diplomats of the "Stalin School," had an excellent professional reputation. During World War II he had been entrusted with crucial confidential missions, and this new assignment certainly was confidential. Very few members of the Soviet mission knew about it, and it was to be kept secret from the Arabs. As part of his cover he was to be seen attending some plenary meetings of the Assembly. Nevertheless, the permanent representative of Egypt, El Zayat, later told me with a smile: "So you are making friends with the Israelis now!" To mask my embarrassment I just shrugged my shoulders and feigned ignorance.

The meeting between Semenov and the Israeli representative took place in a private apartment in Manhattan. He had prepared thoroughly for this rendezvous. Whom he saw and exactly where they met, I never knew because everything was kept secret. When he talked to me after the meeting Semenov made no attempt to conceal his disappointment and frustration. He blamed the New York mission, and Malik in particular, for damaging relations with the Israelis so badly that they would be very difficult to repair. Up to a point he was right, but Malik was not the only problem, nor was he even the main problem. The real obstacle to restoring normal diplomatic relations with Israel lay in Moscow where the Kremlin made rapprochement impossible by insisting on unacceptable preliminary conditions for the Israelis.

Pirlin once told me, with obvious bitterness, that the failure of Semenov's mission secretly pleased some high-ranking officials in Moscow, who believed that bad relations between the Soviet Union and Israel only meant stronger, better relations with the Arabs. Unfortunately, there were some in our mission who shared this opinion.

Relations with Egypt

Malik attached a great deal of importance to personal contacts with Arab ambassadors. He himself spent quite a lot of time with them, and he encouraged me to do the same. Our closest contacts were with the Egyptians, whose mission was located only a stone's throw away from ours on the same street. This sort of coincidence sometimes makes a difference in New York, where traffic is often difficult.

Three distinguished diplomats represented Egypt at the UN at different times, El Kouni, El Zayat, and Megid. I barely knew El Kouni, but I had occasion to work closely with El Zayat and Megid. Both had successful careers and later served as foreign ministers of Egypt. Megid even rose to deputy premier. I remember El Zayat as a calm, self-possessed, and affable personality as well as a true gentleman. He also possessed a quality that was rather rare among diplomats, especially those from the East—sincerity. Quite often I visited him in his residence, where he would receive me in a dressing gown. Although he was bulky and overweight and suffered from high blood pressure, he was a gourmet and a chain-smoker. I think he was well disposed toward the Soviet Union, seeing us as a friendly country. He was also a realist, and I doubt very much that he believed in the possibility of implementing Resolution 242. He was skeptical of Jarring's mission, seeing it as a "diplomatic rat race" (as he called it) and only a waste of time. Malik kept him informed about the work of the Big Four, our contacts with Jarring, and Moscow's major decisions on the Middle East. Frankly, it was my impression that Zayat had little faith in the ability of the UN to successfully resolve the crisis in the Middle East.

El Zayat regarded the Soviet Union's endless propaganda initiatives in the UN as little more than a distractions designed to keep a child amused and prevent it from crying. Always he would listen closely to our arguments about the urgent need to implement the next in the series of "historic" Soviet proposals. Often, he would smile, promising his support. And he always kept his promise, but even during the hey-day of Soviet-Egyptian cooperation he would never agree to cosponsor any of these proposals, even when asked. Once, I remember being particularly persistent in my attempts to discover why this was so. He leaned over to me and whispered in my ear: "They are all too frivolous." I can't recall now whether I was actually offended or just looked as if I were. In any case our relations did not suffer, and we continued our regular conversations on various topics, including the Middle East.

El Zayat's successor, Abdel Ismat Megid, was quite a different type of person. A consummate professional and a highly educated intellectual, he was interested in a vast array of international problems. Megid frequently participated in academic seminars and conferences on subjects far removed from the Middle East. He quickly rose through the ranks to become one of the most authoritative ambassadors in the UN. He established equally good working relations with Malik and myself as well as with other Soviet diplomats. The focal point of our dealings with Megid was, naturally, the Middle East problem. We met often at academic gatherings both then and later, when he became minister of foreign affairs. As a rule, our views on disarmament, the UN role in world politics, and a number of other issues coincided.

Nevertheless, in New York we began to feel a certain frostiness settling into our relations with the Egyptians. At one time it had been their custom to keep us informed of their contacts with the Americans, but no longer. Moreover we noticed that these contacts were becoming more and more frequent. Both Malik and I attributed this to the "changing of the guard" in the Egyptian mission in New York. The new permanent representative appeared to be leaning toward the Americans. We did not know at the time that Anwar Sadat, having come into power, had begun a radical revision of Egyptian policy.

We at the New York mission were not informed that the Kremlin was increasingly anxious about this new tendency in Sadat's policy. Only later did we learn of the April 1971 Politburo meeting which featured a discussion of Soviet-Egyptian relations and their prospects. That meeting brought to the fore the disagreement between the MFA and the KGB on Sadat's policy. This information might have been sent to the KGB *rezident* in New York, but it is improbable because I believe that Malik would have notified me. At that time we were blissfully ignorant of the imminent radical change in the balance of forces in the Middle East.

These changes only really came home to us in July 1972. At the time I was acting permanent representative, and Megid urgently asked to see me. During the meeting, Megid observed strict formality. He informed me that on July 8 Sadat had summoned the Soviet ambassador in Cairo Vladimir Vinogradov and told him of the decision to terminate the Soviet military mission in Egypt and that it would be required to leave within the next few days. When I asked about Sadat's reasons for this decision, Megid told me that Sadat had explained everything to the Soviet ambassador.

I must say that this news was completely unexpected, and I was not authorized to react in any way. I just asked him if this step had been coordinated with the Soviet government beforehand and if the details had been worked out. What did it mean to require the withdrawal of ten thousand military personnel "within the next few days" and what was the connection between the removal of Soviet troops from Egypt and Sadat's intention to make 1972 "decisive" in the struggle with Israel? In response to my questions, Megid made it quite clear that all matters related to his president's decision were undoubtedly discussed in his conversation with the Soviet ambassador in Cairo and that he was not prepared to discuss them with me. No doubt feeling a certain embarrassment about the effect that this uncompromising statement might have on me, he hastened to assure me that Soviet-Egyptian relations would continue unimpaired and that he had every intention of continuing our mutually advantageous cooperation in the UN. On that note our conversation ended.

It is true that on the surface nothing changed in relations between our two missions; nevertheless, a certain frigidity seemed to have set in, as was clear from our contacts with other Egyptian diplomats, who were clearly anxious to tip-toe around the issue. Many of our colleagues from other missions, including the U.S., wanted to know our reaction to Sadat's decision. Some diplomats considered Sadat unfriendly, even hostile to the Soviet Union. The truth was that we were unable to say anything, since we had not received any instructions from Moscow and Malik did not want to ask the MFA.

Peopling Palestine

The Soviet mission had excellent contacts with practically all Arab ambassadors, even those from countries that did not have diplomatic relations with the USSR.

The permanent representative of Jordan, Mohammed El Farra, was one of the more prominent Arab diplomats. He knew the UN inside out, having served there for more than ten years. He had started in the Syrian mission and for the last seven years had been a member of the mission of Jordan. He was a Palestinian and shared his people's pain at the loss of their country. Born to a patrician Palestinian family, he received a first-class education in America and went on to become a diplomat in order to work for the return of his country to its people. It seemed to me that among Arab ambassadors El Farra was the most militant opponent of Israel and the policy of its leaders. He was convinced that Israel's aggressiveness sprang exclusively from U.S. support. He was always saying that were it not for the tremendous Zionist influence on American foreign policy Israel's arrogance would have disappeared without a trace.

The British too came in for their share of El Farra's criticism. He blamed them for the perpetuation of the Palestine problem and never tired of repeating this point. A curious episode once occurred at a dinner in honor of the British minister of foreign affairs George Brown at the British mission in New York. El Farra, who was present, reminded Brown during the dinner that at one time Britain had promised the Arabs and Jews an equitable solution to the Palestine problem. In reality, the ambassador continued, the Arabs had been deceived because the Palestinian State had never been created. At that point it was not clear whether the minister was deliberately ignoring the remark or whether he was simply totally absorbed in the task of eating fruit. By mistake Brown picked out an artificial replica of a berry and tried to chew it. "My God," he exclaimed realizing his blunder, "I can't imagine an Englishman deceiving anyone!" It was not clear whether the remark was addressed to his British host or referred to the British government and its failure to keep its promise. "That is precisely my point, mister minister," declared El Farra to the sounds of laughter.

El Farra and I often talked about the Soviet Union and its policy, but this subject never seemed to interest him. The subject that *did* provoke him, however, was the fact that Soviet Jews were being allowed to go to Israel. "What do you think you are doing?" he would ask me again and again. "You are helping Israel to populate Palestinian land with Jews. How does this help the Arabs?" My attempts to explain why Jews were leaving the USSR and how negative the Soviet government was about it failed to convince him. He had little faith in the effectiveness of Soviet Middle East policy. El Farra believed that a fair solution to the Middle East problem could be brought about only by the successful use of force by the Arabs, or by the United States exerting the necessary pressure on Israel. When I asked him what prevents the Arabs from uniting and exerting concerted, although not necessarily military, pressure, El Farra answered that in practice the Arabs could never muster sufficient unity and that Israel was perfectly well aware of the fact, exploiting it to their advantage. He said that although the Israelis might very well return the Sinai peninsula to Egypt, they would never voluntarily leave Western Jordan and Gaza. El Farra was proved right in many respects.

The permanent representative of Syria, George Tomeh, was one of the main protagonists in the Middle East political drama being played out in the UN. He had an academic background and had spent many years teaching in various universities. This showed in his statements, which were always detailed and well argued. He exhibited the same qualities in his conversations with me about the position of Syria. Tome was one of the most formidable opponents in debates with Israeli representatives. Joseph Tekoah, the Israeli permanent representative, is known to have prepared his statements with particular care when he knew that he was entering the ring against Tome. In order to rebut his arguments the Israeli had to research the sources drawn on by the Syrian. Tome told me about the time Zionists attacked his New York residence in 1966 when they stole a number of important documents and materials from which he frequently quoted. In his opinion, this attack was carried out with the knowledge and consent of the Israeli mission.

Tome confirmed what Farra had said about the lack of unity among Arabs on key Middle East questions. For example, Resolution 242, adopted unanimously by the Security Council, was not supported by Syria on the grounds that it completely bypassed the Palestinian problem. Accordingly, Syria did not recognize Jarring's mission and did not maintain any contact with the special representative of the UN secretary-general.

While boycotting the resolution and all that was connected with it, Syria at the same time wanted to be kept fully informed about the work of the Big Four and of Ambassador Jarring. Tome frequently invited me to his home. After dinner we would sit by ourselves, and he would quite straightforwardly ask me about all the developments in connection with Resolution 242. I readily shared any information available to me, although I avoided discussing the merits of the resolution. He shared El Farra's view that the Soviet Union was helping Israel to populate Palestinian lands with Jews.

I cannot conclude this section without mentioning another Arab diplomat, who was an unfailing participant in almost all debates on the Middle East. Saudi Arabia's representative to the UN Jamil Murad Barudi was widely known for his witty, combative speeches and retorts. Barudi once said that King Faisal of Saudi Arabia was a man of very few words and that it was to make up for this that he had appointed Barudi to the UN. It must be said that Barudi more than made up for his monarch's reserve. The king must have had a great deal of trust in Barudi to keep him as head of the Saudi mission to the UN for over fifteen years. At various times Barudi had also served in both the Syrian and Lebanese civil service. He took a great interest in literature and wrote poetry as well as political pamphlets. He was also independently wealthy, and there were rumors that he was a successful stock market player.

Short and balding, Barudi had sharp, darting eyes. He usually entered a meeting room very slowly with his hands behind his back, looking around as if he were checking to see who was present at the meeting, and only when he had satisfied himself did he take his seat. He never confined himself in his statements strictly to the Middle East problem. Barudi would show up periodically in all UN bodies and spoke on a wide variety of political, economic, humanitarian, and other issues. Not all his speeches were marked with in-depth knowledge of the subject. However, the form and manner with which he made them invariably attracted the attention of any audience. Barudi spoke easily, never had a prepared text, and was skillful at using any of his opponents' mistakes against them. No delegate wanted to become a target of his ridicule.

Here is one example of his original style. In April 1969 during one of the debates on the Middle East situation in the Security Council, the delegations of a number of nonaligned countries submitted a draft of a resolution. It contained a condemnation of Israeli actions against the Palestinians. The American delegation introduced an amendment to the draft, which changed the nature of the whole resolution submitted by the nonaligned countries.

In this connection Barudi told us the following Arabic story. The position of the United States, he began, reminded him of the Bedouin who loved his camel very much, not because it was his means of transportation but because he could drink her milk and also use her wool for clothes. In the same way that people become attached to their pets, so do Arabs become attached to their horses and camels, which are considered family members. The camel fell ill and was in such a bad way that the Bedouin was frightened for her life. So he made a pledge and said: "Almighty God! If you spare my camel, I shall sell it for just one *real* to prove to you, that I do not value her only for my own sake." Thanks to God the camel recovered, and the Bedouin was suddenly faced with a dilemma. What should he do to keep both his promise and the camel? After talking to one of the wise men, he took the camel to the market and began to shout: "Camel for sale! Only one real." Naturally, many people came running, and seeing a strong, healthy animal, they started making offers. "I shall sell it only together with a cat," said the Bedouin, taking a cat out of a bag and tying it to the camel's tail. The people agreed: "Very well. We shall buy it together with the cat." Then the Bedouin said "I am selling the camel for one real, but the cat will cost you nine hundred ninety nine, and I shall only sell them together." "The American representative," concluded Barudi, "wants to attach the cat to the draft of the resolution and will vote only if the cat is tied to the camel's tail."

Almost every speech of Barudi's, accompanied as it was by all sorts of historical digressions, anecdotes, jokes, and stories, helped to relieve the tedium and monotony of most meetings, but the manner and style of his statements did absolutely nothing to promote consensus. The roots of the confrontational diplomacy of the Cold War were too deep. Still, I always preferred an atmosphere of humor and laughter to arguments and insults. Sadly, the results were usually the same in any case.

Relations with Israeli Representatives

This picture of UN Middle East dueling would be incomplete if I did not say a few words about the Israeli permanent representative Joseph Tekoah. He was undoubtedly a staunch patriot and an experienced speaker who never missed an opportunity to enter a verbal fray, although, in so doing, he did not promote the peaceful resolution of conflict. In the meeting room Tekoah was tense and grim, keeping a close watch on his opponent and yielding only to the occasional smirk. I never saw him relaxed or cheerful, although, of course, my relations with Tekoah were limited to political confrontation, which usually involved mutual recrimination and harsh words.

Whether it was on the initiative of the mission itself, or on instructions from Moscow I do not know, but the Soviet mission in New York clearly practiced discrimination against Israel. The fact is that when the Soviet Union, for any reason, did not enjoy normal diplomatic relations with a given country, contacts with the ambassador of that country to the UN were maintained by our mission through meetings, exchanges of information, opinions, and documents on relevant issues. For example, from time to time I would meet Jaime Piñes, the ambassador of Franco's Spain. Not without reason did Barudi call Malik, with whom he had frequent conversations, "a good friend." The same applied in many other similar situations. The exception was Israel and its representatives. There was virtually no communication whatsoever between Soviet diplomats and their Israeli counterparts. I remember a friend of mine before his departure to New York being instructed at Central Committee headquarters: "Meet with American Jews as much as you wish, but not with the representatives of Israel."

When Soviet and Israeli diplomats bumped into each other, we pretended not to notice each other and did not exchange greetings. I remember once offering a seat to Tekoah's companion, who turned out to be his daughter. The ambassador was taken aback. The pattern of Soviet-Israeli relations established in New York left no room even for elementary courtesy. The reason for this political ugliness lay in our superpower ambitions, and the Soviet Union was the first to suffer from it. This overweening, high-handed, and dogmatic approach led to many errors and blunders in the diplomatic field. For all the apparent stability of the Soviet position in the Arab world, it was at about this time that the USSR clearly began to lose ground on the Middle East front of the Cold War.

11
CHINA—A NEW FRONT IN THE COLD WAR

How Many Angels Can Dance on the Head of a Pin?

Relations between the Soviet Union and the People's Republic of China occupy a special place in the history of the Cold War. These relations are hard to categorize when one considers that the Cold War was a standoff between two different socioeconomic systems—capitalism and socialism. As the two largest socialist countries, the USSR and China should perhaps have been allies, at least in theory, but relations between the two powers were often contentious, and this resulted from deep-seated problems that went far beyond their bilateral relations.

During the late 1940s and early 1950s the Soviet Union and China boasted a friendship that was "indestructible," "eternal," and "brotherly," but the tone of that friendship soon degenerated into an open, fierce conflict that even erupted in an armed confrontation. It is safe to say without fear of exaggeration that Sino-Soviet disagreements had global consequences. Any appreciable strengthening or weakening, let alone the total demise, of one of these countries would have had major consequences for the whole balance of international relations.

My generation well remembers the honeymoon of Sino-Soviet relations after the Chinese Revolution in 1949. The visit of Mao Zedong to the Soviet

Union, his participation in Stalin's seventieth birthday celebration, the rallies in Moscow celebrating the signing of the 1950 treaty of friendship all bespoke an era of cooperation and mutual assistance between the USSR and the People's Republic of China. I will never forget the rally where we sang a song called "Moscow—Peking" and generally proclaimed our support for the Chinese.

The first symptoms of disagreement between the leaders of the two countries surfaced soon after the Twentieth Congress of the CPSU in 1956. For those of us observing from outside the inner circle, the disagreement seemed superficial, subjective, and temporary in nature. What appeared to be a purely academic debate over the nature of true socialism was beginning to show sign of becoming a serious cleavage. It reminded me of disputes between medieval scholastic theologians over how many angels could dance on the head of a pin. After all, what did it really matter? Well, unfortunately, it came to matter a great deal as these academic debates turned quickly into very specific disputes including territorial claims. Mao Zedong stated openly that the main hindrance to China's development was the "Soviet social-imperialists." He proclaimed the need "to stage a war against Khrushchev."

The Kremlin applied no less opprobrious labels to the Chinese leaders. At that point, however, these were only verbal battles, which presented no actual threat to international security. When, however, arguments over the 1860 and 1861 Sino-Russian agreements resulted in an armed clash on Domansky Island on the Ussuri River in March 1969, the whole world was shocked and felt threatened by the possibility of a military conflict in the Far East between two nuclear countries.

In academic and diplomatic circles in Moscow we attributed the Sino-Soviet confrontation to two main causes. First, we blamed Mao for his overweening ambition in dubbing himself the leader of the world revolutionary movement after Stalin's death. Second, we blamed Khrushchev for his impatience and inconsistency and his deluded idea of himself as a great innovator in the theory and practice of Marxism-Leninism. Our only hope was that these artificial disagreements would pass and that friendly relations would return; but sad to say, as time passed and leaders changed, the differences only became more acute. Every disagreement had a new explanation, but the result was always the same, and we all understood perfectly well that the only ones who benefited from our disputes were our common political adversaries.

Does the Soviet Union Need China in the UN?

The nature of Soviet-Chinese relations had an impact on the work of our mission in New York. Because the Soviet Union's presence in China decreased dramatically in the 1960s, resulting in the reduction of sources of information, the Politburo decided to establish special posts for China experts in Soviet embassies and delegations abroad, including the Soviet embassy in Washington, D.C., and the UN mission in New York. In Washington this position was first held by Igor Rogachev, who subsequently became the leading Soviet expert on the Far East, deputy foreign minister, and then Russian ambassador to China for many years. In New York, Vyacheslav Kuzmin and later Felix Strock dealt with Chinese affairs. The principal duty of these experts was to collect information about the situation in China and to monitor its international relations.

For my work in New York I often had to read reports prepared by our China experts. They used whatever sources they had at their disposal—press reports, academic texts and articles, and conversations with American political analysts. Morton Halperin was one of the American experts I remember our diplomats resorting to most frequently. I occasionally had my own opportunities to talk with some of these people. Not surprisingly, they were interested in gleaning from me any information I might have on the prospects of Soviet-Chinese relations.

Conferences were held from time to time on issues of Chinese-American relations at the Soviet embassy in Washington and in our mission in New York. I remember one such conference in the late 1960s when we discussed China becoming a UN member. Opinion was divided on the question of whether Chinese participation in international organizations was favorable to the Soviet Union. Many thought that the Chinese would only complicate our position in the UN and other international organizations. The source of greatest anxiety was the prospect of a decrease in Soviet influence in third world countries as a result of the appearance of the People's Republic of China in the UN, an organization whose authority was growing with each passing year. Some thought we should support the Americans, who had for many years succeeded in blocking China's admission to international organizations. I even remember someone joking that the Americans were working on our behalf without even knowing it.

As a supporter of the normalization of Soviet-Chinese relations, I could not agree with this approach. To oppose China's taking its rightful seat in the UN would only complicate our relations with the Chinese, to say nothing of the fact that it would openly contradict the proclaimed Soviet policy of normalization. On the whole, it seemed that the majority of my colleagues supported normalization but as a group we failed to come to a common conclusion. Nonetheless, we drew up a report and delivered it to the MFA, which on the whole was pleased with the materials coming from Washington and New York that was used both for propaganda purposes and in the course of normal diplomatic activities.

Complex Negotiations

The absurdity of China's absence from the UN was apparent in 1970, when the UN celebrated its twenty-fifth anniversary. The most populous country in the world, one of the great centers of world civilization, and now a nuclear state—the People's Republic of China was not a UN member. And this in spite of the fact that more than twenty years before China had declared its desire to enter the organization and expressed its readiness to abide by the UN charter. On the eve of the Twenty-Sixth Meeting of the UN General Assembly in 1971 it became clear that it would be impossible to delay China's admission any further.

On the face of it, the Soviet position had not changed since 1949 when the People's Republic of China first sought admission to the UN. At that time the Soviet Union had established friendly relations with China and resolutely demanded China's admission to the international body. If this demand were to be rejected, the USSR threatened to boycott the work of the organization. The United States opposed the Soviet position, as did a number of other UN members, and consequently the Soviet Union took the unprecedented step, from mid-January to late July of 1950, of refusing to participate in the work of the Security Council. To date, after the UN has been in existence for more than a half-century, no other country has taken such a step.

Many inside the UN assumed that it was Jacob Malik who was responsible for our hard-line stance. It was his first term as the Soviet permanent representative, and I suppose it seemed like the sort of move Malik would make. However, years later when I worked with Malik I remember that he often brought up this particular incident so I once asked him why we had taken such a risky step when it was clear that our resolution would not be accepted. Malik answered that he personally opposed the ultimatum but that Moscow was behind it. He noted that it took six and half months of Soviet nonparticipation in the work of the Security Council for the Kremlin to realize what a terrible mistake it had made. During our boycott, not only did the Korean War break out (June 1950), but also several resolutions were adopted by Security Council that were unacceptable to the Soviet Union. Ironically, however, no one could be punished for such an obvious blunder, since it had been Stalin who had personally authorized the Soviet protest. I was hoping that Malik would confirm this blunder was Stalin's doing but, as a good Stalinist, he put the blame on "others" who had misled the great leader.

In the ensuing years the issue of China's admission came up regularly in the UN, but it was always defeated, usually after a brief but heated debate. The main opponent was, of course, the United States, and no amount of discussion or attempts at compromise could change the American position, not even the "Two Chinas" formula, whereby both China and Taiwan would be admitted to the UN. The White House was adamant in its belief that the Communist regime in China would collapse and that the Chinese Nationalists would return to the mainland. The "Two Chinas" formula was designed to emphasize the temporary character of the communist regime in China.

With the subsequent deterioration of Soviet-Chinese relations, the zeal and persistence of Soviet representatives in defending the interests of China in the UN appreciably diminished and other countries took their place as Peking's advocates. Among them was Albania, which enthusiastically supported the anti-Soviet orientation of the Chinese leadership. Nevertheless, Moscow always voted in favor of Peking's admission, knowing that it would have no effect.

Washington was beginning to realize the inevitability of China's admission into the UN, but it was determined to make that admission as palatable as possible. In 1971, the U.S. permanent representative George Bush once again proposed a plan that would give both Taiwan and the People's Republic of China seats in the UN. According to this plan the People's Republic would be granted a seat in the General Assembly and in the Security Council as a permanent member, while Taiwan (the "Republic of China") would get a seat in the General Assembly. Although, formally speaking, this plan was a step back from the previous "Two Chinas" formula with its insistence on "double representation," it did not change the core of the issue. If the new plan were accepted, Taiwan would receive international legal recognition as an independent, sovereign state, something which, of course, was totally unacceptable to China.

Bush brought to bear every possible kind of pressure to make the plan succeed. He held innumerable consultations with delegates from nearly all the member countries. One could see Bush or his aides discussing the "Chinese issue" all over the place—at meetings of committees of the General Assembly, in the corridor, and even at parties and receptions. No matter what you discussed with American diplomats, they only seemed to be interested in China being admitted to the UN on American terms. It was clearly one of their main concerns at that time.

The Soviet delegation to the General Assembly remained entirely passive in this matter. We were specifically instructed only to state the Soviet "position of principle" and the decisions of the Twenty-Sixth Congress of the CPSU. The proceedings of this congress, held in the spring of 1971, contained a special section dedicated to Soviet-Chinese relations. In this section, which was somewhat controversial, the Chinese leadership was accused of persistently pursuing a policy "directed against socialist countries, and aimed at creating a breach in the international communist and anti-imperialist movements." At the same time, it stated that improved relations between the USSR and the People's Republic of China would promote the "interests of world socialism and the interests of strengthening the struggle against imperialism." In short, the report criticized Mao's policy while simultaneously emphasizing the need for concerted action with Peking. Without giving the matter too much thought, we in the delegation decided to vote as we had in the past.

The Soviet Delegation in the Shadows

The debate on the admission of China to the UN lasted for about ten days in October of 1971. This was a major news item that attracted worldwide attention. The General Assembly hall was crowded with delegations, correspondents, and members of the public. Permanent representatives rarely missed any of the meetings, and even some of their spouses came along for fear of missing the opportunity of being eyewitnesses to this historic event.

The Albanian foreign minister, Neshti Nase, opened the first days of the debate on October 14. Never before, or since, has the Albanian delegation attracted so much attention. Everyone knew that Nase would support the position of Peking, and he was extremely forceful, stressing repeatedly and unremittingly that Peking would accept no compromise. At the same time, he was careful to pay tribute to the wisdom and foresight of the two "Great Leaders"—Enver Hoxha and Mao Zedong—who predicted the inevitable defeat of imperialism.

The Albanian representative introduced a draft resolution, on behalf of a large group of mostly nonaligned countries, providing for the restoration of all its rights to the People's Republic of China as a member of the UN and a permanent member of the Security Council. The resolution also called for the unconditional and immediate expulsion of Taiwan from the organization. On the first day the debate was dominated by those countries which had cosponsored the "Albanian resolution"—Algeria, Iraq, Mauritania, Somalia, Nigeria, and Guinea.

It so happened that George Bush was also one of the first day's speakers. In his statement he declared "the time has come to find a way to greet the People's Republic of China in the UN." At the same time Bush firmly objected to the expulsion of the "Republic of China" (Taiwan) from the UN. He explained the American plan contained in the draft of the resolution he had submitted, and then he adduced a number of arguments in support of the plan. For instance, he drew attention to the fact that the Soviet Union and two of its republics—the Ukrainian SSR and the Byelorussian SSR—were all UN members. Therefore, he asked, why could not the People's Republic of China and the Republic of China both be members of the UN?

The Ukrainian foreign minister Grigory Shevel, exercising his right of reply, rejected this analogy, invoking the pact establishing the Soviet Union in 1922, whereby Ukraine entered the new federation as an independent state. He also spoke of the contribution of Ukraine to the victory over fascism during the Second World War. Malik and I, after listening to Shevel, both strenuously urged the Byelorussian foreign minister not to follow his example. A discussion of the sovereignty of Soviet republics was not something we welcomed at this particular moment. In any case, the real reason why only two Soviet republics had been granted the special right of membership in international organizations was the deal arranged among Stalin, Roosevelt, and Churchill at the Yalta Conference. It would have been unwise to allow the debate to be sidetracked by this question.

Malik's turn to speak came only at the sixth meeting, after many of the important points had already been made by other delegates. His speech was unusually brief and, I have to admit, beside the point. He spent most of his time lauding the Soviet Union's decision in 1950 to withdraw from the Security Council over China's exclusion from the UN. Malik repeatedly quoted from his own countrymen in the Security Council from 1950 onward, as well as the speech of his idol Vyshinsky at the General Assembly and other Soviet documents from that period. It was a pompous speech, and of course, he never once admitted that the move failed to produce the intended results.

Many people were surprised by Malik's speech, failing as it did to address current Soviet-Chinese relations. One ambassador approached me after the meeting and quipped: "What does that Malik of yours think we're here for? To share memories?" However, Malik was in a difficult situation. After the resolutions of the CPSU congress, denouncing Peking for discrediting Soviet foreign policy at every turn, Malik could hardly come out in open support of China. Perhaps in his mind the only way around the problem was to dwell on the past.

Meanwhile, the diplomatic wheels were turning at the General Assembly. George Bush, working behind the scenes, had managed to recruit twenty countries to cosponsor the American draft resolution calling for "double representation of China." No European countries or NATO members had signed on, but Bush managed to get his resolution voted on before that of the nonaligned countries, even though he had submitted it later than theirs. Nevertheless, it was clear from the very beginning that the Americans were battling in a losing cause. The Chinese leadership had made it perfectly clear that under no conditions would it participate in UN activities until the "Kuomintang renegades" had been ousted from the organization. Thus the UN had a very clear choice to make, and the majority of countries were no longer willing to accept the old order. Neither the power and authority of the United States nor the tremendous efforts of Bush and his team could stem the irreversible tide.

I regret to have to say that the Soviet Union played almost no role in this momentous diplomatic battle. In that respect it was a most unusual event in the history of the Cold War—a major political conflict in which the Soviet delegation was little more than a spectator. Even the ambassadors of Soviet-bloc countries remained largely outside the fray—except, of course, the Romanian "mavericks" who had cosponsored the resolution of the non-aligned countries. We in the Soviet delegation, and Malik in particular, felt decidedly uncomfortable with this state of affairs. Then, suddenly, events confirmed the truth of the old Russian proverb: "There is no unhappiness that a little misfortune can't cure."

The Vote in the General Assembly

On the evening of October 21, 1971, in the heat of the debate on the China question, the Soviet mission in New York was attacked by terrorists (I recount this event in Chapter 10). The next day Malik took the floor of the General Assembly to report the barbarous attack. The tone and general indignation of Malik's statement were certainly understandable, but he obviously relished the opportunity to politicize the incident. Malik attacked the American authorities for, as he put it, "supporting" the terrorist activity of the Zionists.

Ambassadors from Arab countries were quick to support Malik's accusations, and some of them, at Malik's personal request, publicly joined the denunciations. Even Saudi Arabia, the Americans' most faithful ally on the China question, joined in, with Ambassador Jamil Barudi resorting to his familiar anti-Semitic rhetoric. The Syrian ambassador, George Tomeh, took the floor several times, as did the Israeli ambassador Joseph Tekoah. The latter even read out a long excerpt from Yevtushenko's "Babyi Yar" during his exchanges with Malik. The Cuban representative, Ricardo Alarcon, then unexpectedly asked for the floor and proceeded to attack the UN security service for allowing strangers to enter the General Assembly. The British representative, Sir Colin Crowe, took exception to some of Malik's remarks.

Malik succeeded in wreaking havoc at three or four meetings of the Plenary of the General Assembly by upstaging the question of the admission of China with the attack on the Soviet Mission. Malik was jubilant. From his position in the wings on the China question he had now taken center stage with this entirely new controversy. In my darker moments I sometimes wonder whether this had not been Malik's intention all along.

In the midst of the commotion, the cosponsors of the resolution of the nonaligned countries managed to persuade the president of the Assembly to resume the China debate and to bring the issue to a vote. The results were not unexpected. Despite the best efforts of George Bush the American draft was soundly defeated. Over fifty states voted in its favor but the significant majority—seventy-six states—approved the draft of the nonaligned countries. Thirty-seven voted against it. Especially unpleasant for the Americans was the fact that among the countries supporting this resolution were numerous U.S. allies, including Britain, France, Italy, the Netherlands, and Israel.

Immediately after the results of the voting were announced that evening, the delegates from Taiwan were escorted out of the General Assembly. It is difficult to describe the scene that followed. Delegations that had supported the People's Republic of China expressed their delight in every possible way. Some shouted out greetings to the People's Republic of China, others applauded, and some even sang songs and performed victory dances on their desks. Among them was the Tanzanian delegation, led by one of the fiercest opponents of the American resolution, Salim Salim, who sat next to the U.S. delegation.

Chagrined by the results of the voting, Bush could only sit and gloomily observed the celebrations taking place all around him. I am sure that he never forgot this episode for many years later, when he was vice president of the United States, the American delegation in the Security Council vetoed the nomination of Salim Salim as a candidate for the post of secretary-general of the UN sixteen times!

You Are No Comrades of Ours

When the time came to congratulate the Chinese delegation in the General Assembly, Malik took his place in line and enthusiastically congratulated China's deputy minister of foreign affairs, Jiao Huanhu. He also reminded him of their personal acquaintance, which dated back to the 1950s.

The following day Malik held a meeting of his deputies to determine which line the Soviet mission would take in dealing with our "worst friends," the mission of the People's Republic of China. Opinions differed. Some were adamant that we should offer no initiative whatsoever, leaving it to the Chinese to take the first step. They were, after all, the newcomers to the UN, and according to diplomatic protocol the newcomers should be the first to pay a courtesy call. Others insisted that if the Soviet Union was really interested in restoring good neighborly and friendly relations with the Chinese, we in the Soviet mission should take the initiative and reach out to the Chinese, without "standing on protocol." Malik supported the second point of view, and in the end it was decided that we should invite the Chinese to a working meeting. The agenda was to be determined jointly.

I was delegated to meet with the permanent representative of the People's Republic of China, Huang Hua, and on behalf of Malik to extend our offer. I decided to do it in the UN building. During a break between meetings I approached the ambassador and introduced myself. Not knowing who I was, Huang Hua smiled at first, but as soon as he realized that he was talking to a Soviet representative, his smile turned to a frown. I gave the ambassador our proposal and said that we would be looking forward to hearing from him. Huang Hua nodded, promising a reply.

After a few days had gone by without a response from the Chinese. I began wondering if I may have misunderstood something in our conversation or had not made myself clear. Once again, as I had on the previous occasion, I approached the ambassador during a break between meetings, greeting him as "Comrade Ambassador." I repeated Malik's proposal to hold a joint working meeting. The answer came swiftly, and this time there was no attempt at a smile: "Tell Mr. Malik [the word "Mr." was stressed] that we have nothing to discuss and that we are not your comrades." Naturally I was taken aback, and all I could do was to turn and leave. When the news spread among my colleagues at the Soviet mission, the supporters of the wait-and-see approach to establishing relations with China were triumphantly vindicated. They were convinced that there was no chance of establishing friendly relations between the two countries.

That was just the beginning. At the first meeting of the Security Council after China's admission in late November of 1971, Ambassador Huang Hua expressed gratitude for the congratulations he had received and then briefly proclaimed Peking's ideas of world order. Quoting Mao Zedong, he said, "Countries want independence and freedom. The peoples aspire to revolution." He then appealed to people around the world to fight against one or both superpowers (that is to say, against the USSR and the United States). Several of us were alarmed by this brazen call-to-arms, but I remember Bush's deputy, Christopher Phillips, joking with us that the Soviets and Americans were now "on the same team," which, he added, "wasn't such a bad thing."

Although we were disappointed by Huang's speech, we decided to suspend judgment for the moment. After all, this was his first speech, and he was certainly entitled to praise the "Great Helmsman." After that we thought everything would return to normal and business as usual; but the reality exceeded our worst expectations.

At about that time, the French ambassador, Jacques Kosciusko-Morizet arranged a working luncheon for the permanent members of the Security Council. He wanted to discuss the nominees for the post of secretary-general, since U Thant's term was due to expire at the end of the year. Such meetings were common when a new secretary-general was to be chosen, and they were usually helpful. Malik and I were the last to arrive at the luncheon so Malik moved around the room greeting each ambassador with a handshake.

However, as he approached Huang Hua he stopped short, noticing that the ambassador had put both of his hands behind his back so that he could not shake hands. Suddenly a dead silence fell on the room, and everyone became noticeably uncomfortable. To his credit, Malik did his best to ignore this snub but his face reddened with fury. Having known Malik for several decades, I had never seen him in such a state.

Fortunately, the silence was interrupted with a joke by the host, but no amount of joking could ease the tension in the air. On our way back from the lunch I remember thinking that Malik and Hua had just become personal as well as professional enemies. My fears were justified during the Security Council debate on the Indo-Pakistani war in December 1971.

The Explosive Subcontinent

The conflict between India and Pakistan had deep roots and was always liable to erupt. Today, of course, both countries have nuclear weapons. This was not the case in 1971, but they certainly possessed significant military potential and nuclear ambitions. Furthermore, both superpowers and all the permanent members of the Security Council had interests in the region that were in conflict. The Soviet Union had been developing close military and other types of cooperation with India, which was reaffirmed in the summer of 1971 in the Soviet-Indian treaty on peace, friendship, and cooperation. Gromyko considered this treaty to be one of the major achievements of his diplomatic career. China had tensions with India over many issues, including territorial matters, so geopolitical interests pushed it in the direction of cooperation with Pakistan. The same was true of the United States, which considered Pakistan its ally. Meanwhile, neither Britain nor France, two countries which had played important roles in the region for centuries, wished to take sides in the conflict, although objectively their position under normal circumstances would be closer to that of India.

A rather unusual line-up of political forces thus emerged in the Security Council—the United States and China on one side, the Soviet Union on the other, with Britain and France somewhere in between. This unusual alignment opened up a unique, if unenviable, role for Soviet diplomacy in the Security Council in the winter of 1971.

By way of background, I should mention that parliamentary elections in Pakistan in late 1970 had brought to power the Awami League of Sheik

Mujibur Rahman, which then called for the separation of East Pakistan from West Pakistan and the establishment of a new independent country of Bangladesh in the east. This demand was widely supported in the east but repressive measures on the part of the Pakistan authorities against the supporters of independence resulted in mass migrations from East Pakistan into India. According to Indian sources, nearly 10 million people crossed into India in a very short time.

The Indian government was sympathetic to the aspirations of East Pakistan to create its own state and pledged all-out (including military) support of Bangladesh. In late 1971 the military tension in the subcontinent was growing daily. After India had moved its troops into East Pakistan in November and started to play a decisive role in the conflict, UN intervention had become inevitable. The United States took the initiative in this matter. On December 4, George Bush with the support from the Italians, Belgians, and Somalia called for an urgent meeting of the Security Council. The position of the White House was clear—the United States did not favor the secession of East Pakistan and the establishment of Bangladesh. Washington strongly opposed the military intervention of India in the conflict and the Soviet Union's growing involvement in the region.

The Kremlin's position was also clear. The Soviet Union openly sympathized with Bangladesh and unequivocally supported India. That said, it was not entirely clear which tactical line the Soviet delegation should pursue in the Security Council. The instructions we received from Moscow did not give us much to go on. We were simply advised to follow the standard Soviet position on the Indo-Pakistani war (as set forth in a number of official Soviet documents) and to work closely with the Indian delegation in the Security Council. On the one hand, the instructions to coordinate all our steps with the Indians facilitated our work, but we soon learned that this also tied our hands.

On December 4 the Soviet and Indian missions began to maintain daily contact, which continued for more than two weeks, and Malik and I were meeting with the permanent representative of India, Samar Sen, and later with Foreign Minister Svaran Singh, who had flown to New York from Delhi.

The Soviet mission had always maintained good relations with the Indian permanent representative—Sen as well as his predecessors, and his successors. They were all extremely professional diplomats and understood the importance of cooperation with the Soviet Union, but even in that company Sen stood out for his exceptional hands-on diplomatic skills. One would often find Ambassador Sen in the meeting rooms and delegate's lounge of the UN conferring with his own people. I once asked why he did not hold these meetings at the Indian mission, rather than at the UN, and he told me that he hardly had time to go to the mission. In the mornings he went straight to the UN, where he not only attended meetings but also observed his diplomats at work in various UN bodies, helping and advising them. Sen frequently drafted and sent cables, and if necessary called Delhi directly from the UN. I found his own analogy between himself and the general who prefers to accompany his troops into battle to transmitting orders from behind the lines perfectly appropriate. In this, his approach differed markedly from that of many other permanent representatives, who rarely put in an appearance except to read the texts of their statements or to attend receptions. These ambassadors never truly acquire a feel for the international climate and were of very little real use as diplomats.

Sen was the consummate multilateral diplomat. He wielded significant authority in Delhi, enjoying the trust of Indira Gandhi, and soon after the successful end of the Indo-Pakistani war he was rewarded with the post of ambassador of India to Bangladesh—a post of particular importance to India at the time.

We met frequently with the Indians at that time in 1971, at both of our missions, at the UN, and even in the hotels where Singh was staying. Malik was very busy with other matters so frequently that I was the one who went to the minister's hotel, spoke with him in the UN, and coordinated our action in the Security Council. For obvious reasons neither of us wished to reveal all our cards but I had many opportunities to show the Indians drafts of Soviet resolutions and other documents.

Veto as Many Times as Necessary

Malik was at a definite disadvantage in representing the Soviet position. The information he was receiving from Moscow was too vague and as a rule outdated, and our Indian colleagues were not particularly helpful either, revealing to us little more than the gist of forthcoming statements in the Security Council. Singh and Sen knew that Malik had instructions from Moscow to work closely with the Indian delegation, and they interpreted these instructions as a sort of obligation on the part of the Soviet delegation to work in complete conformity with India's position. At times conversations with our Indian colleagues seemed more like briefings where they issued instructions to the Soviet delegation, something which we, and Malik in particular, were not at all used to and to which we did not take at all kindly.

In our conversations with Singh and Sen they explained that India would only agree to a cease-fire and to enter into negotiations with the Pakistani government after the unconditional surrender of Pakistani forces. They told us that such a surrender was only a matter of days away, so they asked the Soviet delegation to block any decision of the Security Council until that time. Days went by, however, and nothing happened, and this only increased everyone's dissatisfaction with the unyielding position of the Soviet Union.

Malik explained to the Indians that the longer the war dragged on, the more difficult it would be for the Soviet Union to continue vetoing any Security Council decision that might possibly end the war. Singh replied that in the history of the UN the Soviet Union had used the veto more than a hundred times; so would it really be so terrible if Malik were to use it a few times more. Once I visited Singh at his hotel to inform him of an impending Soviet veto in the Security Council, and the minister merely nodded his head and smiled as if to say, "Fine, let Malik veto as many times as is necessary." Naturally, Malik and I resented this attitude, because we felt that Singh was disregarding the effect on the Soviet Union's international standing of vetoing one cease-fire resolution after the other and thereby being perceived as perpetuating the bloodshed.

On the very first day of the debate in the Security Council, George Bush delivered a brief statement and then submitted a draft resolution providing for the immediate termination of hostilities and a reciprocal withdrawal of troops from each other's territory. He then insisted that the resolution should go to an immediate vote. Malik tried to delay the voting, but after all of his maneuvering had failed, he did as the Indians had requested and vetoed the American resolution. Eleven countries voted in favor of the resolution, two (Britain and France) abstained, and Poland joined the Soviet Union in voting against it. Malik explained his veto and the vote of our ally Poland by saying that he had not had enough time to receive instructions from Moscow.

The following day as Indian troops continued to advance in East Pakistan, a group of nonpermanent members led by Argentina demanded that the Security Council take measures to end the war. When a resolution was brought to the vote, Malik could not plead lack of time yet again, so he justified his veto by explaining that the resolution failed to tackle the question of a political settlement in East Pakistan. This second Soviet veto naturally met with India's entire approval, but it put us in a difficult situation, for now we were distancing ourselves even from the nonaligned countries. When we discussed this with Sen, he remarked that these countries will complain at first and then they will forget all about it.

To soften the negative impact of our repeated vetoes, we decided to submit our own draft resolution. It made any cease-fire conditional upon a political settlement in East Pakistan. Sen approved of our initiative because he understood that it was doomed to failure. He was right: only two delegations (the USSR and Poland) voted for the Soviet resolution. One (China) voted against it, and twelve (the remaining members of the Security Council) abstained. Our discomfiture was impossible to disguise, since practically no delegation was willing to support our resolution. When Soviet journalists asked me how they were to explain the result of the vote to their readers, I advised them to blame it all on China's negative vote even though, in reality, the draft failed because it did not receive the required majority of votes.

After Malik's second veto, the nonpermanent members of the Council, with Bush's support, asked that the item be referred to the General Assembly for consideration. On December 8 there was a meeting of the General Assembly, and despite the best efforts of Malik and Sen to prolong the discussion, it lasted only a day. The overwhelming majority of countries wanted an immediate cease-fire, and the resolution to this effect cosponsored by Argentina and a group of nonaligned countries received 104 votes in favor, with only 11 against.

Frankly many of us were surprised that India, one of the leaders of the nonaligned movement, had made almost no special effort to influence the votes of these countries in its favor, so we concluded that the Indians were prepared to ignore the resolution, despite the negative fallout, knowing, as they did, that decisions of the General Assembly were not binding. At this point, it became clear to all (if it had not been clear before) that India was trying to annihilate Pakistani forces in East Pakistan and was using the Soviet veto as a protective screen, but as the Russian proverb says, "You can't hide a knife in a bag."

During this whole conflict the Soviet Union was naturally guided by its own interests, but from my point of view, our cooperation with India could have been (and should have been) more effective and "cleaner." We certainly made many mistakes, but so did the Indians. In the end I was left with a distinctly unfavorable impression of Indian diplomatic strategy during this troubling time. At the very least, the Indians failed to see the larger picture and refused to acknowledge the complexity of the situation.

CHINA—A NEW FRONT IN THE COLD WAR

The Sino-American Duet

My most unpleasant memories of the Indo-Pakistani war come not from our dealings with the Indians but with the Chinese. From the very first meeting of the Security Council, Huang Hua took an openly pro-Pakistani position and was active in promoting their cause. He spoke frequently and even submitted a draft resolution [supporting Pakistan], which he later withdrew, but what really surprised many of us was the virulence of the anti-Soviet thrust of the Chinese delegation. Huang Hua's hostility was directed not so much against India as against the Soviet Union. For instance, he repeatedly used the inflammatory term "Soviet social-imperialism," frequently citing the Soviet incursion into Czechoslovakia in 1968 as an example. He accused the Soviet Union of creating "a puppet regime" in Bangladesh and compared the establishment of Bangladesh "by the Soviets" with the establishment of Manchukuo by the Japanese—yet one more instance of its blatant interference in the internal affairs of other countries. As further evidence of such interference, Huang Hua recalled Soviet efforts to "detach" one of China's northern provinces in 1962 and actually naming the "traitors to the Chinese people" recruited by the Soviet social-imperialists.

I was certainly not the only diplomat who found it difficult to understand the connection between the formation of the puppet state of Manchukuo in the 1930s and the bloodshed in East Pakistan. What did the fate of Emperor Pu Yi have to do with the war between India and Pakistan? It did not help matters that Huang Hua singled out Malik, calling him a "Soviet social-imperialist" and deriding him as "shorty Malik." This kind of opprobrium made it clear to all of us that cooperation with the Chinese in the Security Council would thereafter be impossible.

Malik did not back down. Early on he asked me if I thought he should respond to the verbal attacks, and I advised him against it, knowing of course that there was no way of restraining Malik. "Now," he declared in the heat of one debate, "it is clear why the People's Republic of China wanted to join the UN—so that it could spread monstrous lies about the first socialist country in the world." He accused Huang Hua of falsifying history and suggested that the Chinese ambassador deserved a special award from the imperialists. Malik then began making insinuations about the convergence of the American and Chinese positions and hammered away at the term "Sino-American duet" to make his point. He even reminded the Chinese that 1971 marked the thirtieth anniversary of the defeat of Hitler's forces in the battle for Moscow. Not content with that, Malik even went to the extreme of lumping together China's leaders with the likes of Hitler, Himmler, and Goebbels.

With this unfortunate tirade, the Chinese-Soviet relationship hit rock bottom. The virulence of the exchanges between these two senior diplomats reminded me of the duels between Malik and Tekoah, with the difference that Malik's attacks were always echoed by a chorus of Arab delegations while nobody wanted to join in the wangling between the Soviets and the Chinese. As a matter of fact I was quite disturbed—nor was I by any means alone in this to judge by some of the remarks that were passed—by the brawling between Malik and Huang Hua because there was absolutely nothing to be gained by it. The point of diplomacy is to create the opportunity for compromise in conflict situations and this was the very antithesis of diplomacy.

Would it have been possible to avoid these mutual recriminations in the UN? The differences were there, certainly, but they need not have been aired in that kind of language. Much depended on the temperament and style of the ambassadors themselves. I have already acknowledged that Malik was one of the arch-exponents of confrontational diplomacy during the Cold War, but in this case it was not Malik who provoked the mud slinging. I believe, to the contrary, that he genuinely wanted to (or at least was prepared to) establish normal working relations with the Chinese. When it became clear that this would not happen, it was impossible to restrain him.

The End of the Affair

After the failed attempt in the General Assembly, George Bush tried yet again to bring about a cease-fire through the Security Council. Maybe he was acting at the behest of the Pakistanis, but in any case, another meeting of the Council was called on December 12 and once again the resolution was defeated. Again, eleven members of the Council voted in favor, two countries (the USSR and Poland) voted against, and two countries (Britain and France) abstained. Malik for the third time vetoed the decision of the Security Council. Frustrated by the impotence of the Council, Bush declared that the time would come when the history of this war would be written and it would say that, despite the overwhelming will of the majority of countries, the UN could not stop the bloodshed. Bush was right. The war ended in the way the Indians wanted. The Pakistani forces surrendered unconditionally in East Pakistan on December 16. After this the Indian government declared a unilateral termination of hostilities.

The only other aspect of this political melodrama worth noting was the fact that the foreign ministers of both India and Pakistan participated in the meetings of the Security Council. I remember Singh's speeches because he delivered them drily and without any show of emotion, as though he were giving a lecture at a university. The only hint of emotion was his obvious satisfaction with the military victory over the Pakistanis. The Pakistani deputy prime minister and minister for foreign affairs Zulfikar Bhutto left a totally different impression. Educated at Oxford and Berkeley, he was a good orator whose speeches reflected his personality and obvious self-confidence. In this instance, he spoke hopefully of reconciliation between East and West Pakistan, something which we all knew was highly unlikely in the circumstances.

I also remember that Bhutto created something of a stir at the last meeting when he arrived with a retinue of three young, attractive women, who sat directly behind him. A murmur went round the room as people speculated about the identity of these women. Only later did it emerge that one of them was his daughter Benazir, the future prime minister of Pakistan. At this meeting, Bhutto reserved special indignation for Malik, once ridiculing him for behaving more like "Tsar Malik" than "Comrade Malik." Making it clear that he wanted absolutely no part of this spectacle, which had resulted in the "disgraceful capitulation of a part of my country," he stormed dramatically out of the meeting room followed by the three young women, hurrying to keep up with him.

Before the end of the final meeting, the permanent representative of Pakistan, Aga Shahi, took the floor. He acknowledged Pakistan's defeat but then took the opportunity to thank all delegations that had rendered support to his country in this time of need. He especially thanked the delegations of the United States and the People's Republic of China. His Indian opposite number, Foreign Minister Singh, also spoke but thanked no one, not even the Soviet Union—something that did not sit well with Malik or anyone from our delegation.

Although the fighting had already ended, the majority of the Security Council members wanted the cease-fire to bear the imprimatur of the Security Council, and a group of nonaligned countries submitted a formal resolution, endorsing the cease-fire between India and Pakistan and the withdrawal of the forces of each side to their respective borders. Once again we were at a loss as to what position we should take. Fortunately, this time we received instructions from Moscow not to veto the resolution. Later we learned that the new Pakistani president Bhutto (he became president upon returning from New York) had asked the Soviet leadership not to undermine the agreed cease-fire. As a result the Soviet Union ended up on the winning side. We should have been pleased, but we could not get rid of the bitter taste in our mouths.

Back in Moscow, early in 1972, I attended a meeting of the MFA. Gromyko asked Kiril Novikov and myself to report on recent events in New York. Novikov gave a generally positive account of the mission's performance but spoke critically of the Indo-Pakistan war fiasco, including the unseemly abuse exchanged between Malik and Huang Hua. He saw the fact that we had been at odds with the overwhelming majority of UN member states as a defeat for Soviet diplomacy. He added that from the reports that had reached Moscow, it was impossible to tell if the real war was between India and Pakistan or between the Soviet Union and China. He further decried the excessive vituperation and acrimony that had been bandied about in the debate. Mikhail Kapitsa, a member of the MFA collegium, and Aleksei Nesterenko, head of the economics department, both agreed with Novikov. It was obvious that Gromyko also shared this opinion.

In my report I disagreed with Novikov. I tried to argue that we should view the whole drama as a victory for the Soviet Union rather than a defeat. My reasoning was that we had found ourselves in an extremely difficult political situation where we had had to fight on two fronts at the same time—against both the United States and China. I tried to explain that being on the front lines of the Cold War meant that we were sometimes compelled "to deploy every weapon in our arsenal against our adversaries—even heavy artillery." I think what I said was true, even though it was a bitter pill to swallow and based on a distorted view of diplomacy.

Some people agreed with me. Others clearly did not, and Gromyko simply said: "Well, it's not a good idea to use artillery all the time. You'll soon run out of ammunition." In his closing statement, Gromyko tried to smooth over the differences. He agreed that the entry of the People's Republic of China into the UN had opened a "new front" in the Cold War, but he added that it was not an "act of God" and therefore it was up to us to confront the problem with cool, calm calculation. "Our people may not have been in top form, but I wouldn't be too hard on them." When I returned to New

York and described the meeting to Malik, he commended me for defending him. "Good work," he said. "Sitting back there in Moscow, they don't understand what we're up against."

The First Chinese Veto in the UN

It was not long before we had another confrontation with the Chinese in the UN. On August 8, 1972, the Security Council received a letter from the Bangladeshi minister of foreign affairs requesting that the People's Republic of Bangladesh be admitted to membership in the UN. The issue seemed quite clear. East Bengal had officially separated from Pakistan, and by the summer of 1972 more than eighty countries had recognized it.

The Security Council met on August 10, and Chinese ambassador Huang Hua was among the first to speak, making it clear that the China did not favor UN recognition of "so-called Bangladesh." He returned to the events of 1971 and repeated the Chinese position that the Indian government had waged a large-scale war against Pakistan with the "active encouragement and vigorous support of the Soviet social-imperialists," thus undermining peace in South Asia. Malik was on vacation, and I was acting permanent representative in his absence, so I was wondering how to react to Huang Hua's statement. I knew that Peking viewed Moscow's pro-Indian and anti-Pakistani stance as part and parcel of Soviet intrigues against China itself, so I realized that I had to be careful not to provoke Huang Hua into retaliation against us.

Soon after the beginning of the discussion it was clear that the majority of Security Council members were ready to support Bangladesh's application. Three nonpermanent members of the Council—Guinea, Sudan, and Somalia—hesitantly sided with China. I was not particularly concerned about the vote of these three African countries because that would not affect the outcome but it was troubling for another reason. In the past we could usually count on these African countries to vote with the Soviet Union, so it was clear that China's presence in the Security Council had changed this situation.

After two weeks of debate the Security Council was faced with two rival draft resolutions. One was the Chinese version, which would postpone consideration of the application indefinitely. The second, recommended by the

General Assembly, favored the request of Bangladesh. The delegations of India, Yugoslavia, Britain, and the Soviet Union cosponsored this draft. The Chinese draft was not approved, with only three delegations out of fifteen voting in its favor. The second draft resolution was also defeated because of the Chinese veto, even though there were eleven votes in favor, including those of Britain, the USSR, the United States, and France.

This was the first veto cast by the People's Republic of China in the Security Council. Although China got the result it wanted, Huang Hua did not look too happy after the vote, probably because China's first veto was now part of the historical record. Once again in his statement he accused the Soviet Union of aggression, incitement, sabotage, and every sin in the book. In my statement I pointed out that the Security Council was not meeting to discuss Soviet-Chinese relations but the application of Bangladesh to join the UN. Any attempts, therefore, to divert the Council from this issue should be seen as a mark of disrespect toward the Security Council and toward the UN. I then went into a rather lengthy explanation of how China's veto demonstrated that the People's Republic had in effect acted against (1) a national liberation movement; (2) the developing countries; (3) the normalization of conditions on the Indian subcontinent; (4) the universality of the UN as an organization; and (5) the very charter of the UN. I closed my speech with a standard appeal for international cooperation and expressed the hope that the People's Republic of Bangladesh would be admitted to membership in the UN.

At the time, I was pleased with my statement because I knew that Ambassador Sen and I had effectively maneuvered Huang Hua into his reluctant use of the veto. After the meeting Sen and I congratulated each other, and the Soviet press made a big thing of the Chinese veto, even publishing the text of my speech. I also remember Huang Hua's words in the Security Council: "The peoples of the world can clearly see the Soviet Union's true motives, no matter how hard it has tried to conceal them, and how it conspired with India to create by hook or by crook a situation where China was compelled to apply the veto." Of course, Huang Hua was right, and we should have been sorry that Bangladesh's application had been denied, instead of being so pleased with ourselves for forcing the Chinese into a step they desperately wanted to avoid.

This episode is a perfect illustration of the fundamental immorality of Cold War diplomacy. Its goal was often little more than to impose damaging decisions on political adversaries instead of seeking mutually acceptable solutions to real problems. This of course went against everything the diplomatic profession is supposed to stand for, and I myself was a willing offender. Unfortunately, many of the "victories" of Soviet diplomacy in the UN fall into this category.

12
TIME TO GO HOME

Soviet "Key Issues"

In previous chapters I have described the fiercest clashes in the UN during the Cold War, when I was at the Soviet mission in New York. Naturally, they reflected the realities of international life: the war in the Middle East, the Soviet intervention in Czechoslovakia, the conflict in the Indian subcontinent, and other major issues.

Many of these political upheavals occurred unexpectedly and took the UN by surprise. Other events, such as the emergence of new states as a result of national liberation movements, were inevitable and became a matter of course for the UN. The Cold War gave them a sharper edge. The confrontation between the "two camps," the rivalry of the superpowers, were thrown into sharp relief in all these conflict situations, even those that did not appear to affect their interests directly.

Malik, myself, and other political department staff who dealt with the Security Council were principally responsible for handling such conflict situations. Other diplomats rarely got involved. But there were certain matters that all of the staff of the Soviet mission had to regard as their number-one priority. I am speaking of what were known as "key issues" in Soviet policy.

Although at first I did not quite understand the overall significance of these "key issues" in the work of the mission, I soon learned how critically important they were in the eyes of a Kremlin deeply engaged in a Cold War struggle. By "key issues," the architects of Soviet foreign policy meant the USSR's proposals in international affairs, which were designed to head the agenda of international dialogue during the Cold War. The Soviet Union started putting forth these grand pronouncements as early as Khrushchev's time, but it was over the course of the 1960s that the Kremlin increasingly put forward such foreign policy initiatives as regular items of UN General Assembly sessions. As a rule, they were highly general in nature, but at the same time they were not abstract or purely academic; they took into account the specifics of the international situation.

The world at large, and even the Soviet mission to the UN, usually learned of a "key issue" only from Gromyko's speech at the opening of each session of the General Assembly. From this moment on the work of the mission and every member of it was devoted to promoting the propagation of and working to secure approval for the Soviet "key issue." Regardless of the specific area to which a given diplomat had been assigned, each was responsible for a certain number of missions of other member states and putting the case for the current "key issue" to his opposite number. If these conversations ended with promises of support for that particular "key issue," that was of course a feather in that diplomat's cap.

Under MFA instructions, the mass media persuaded Soviet readers that the "key issue" was the priority item of all meetings and the focus of attention of all delegations. If the UN voted in favor of a resolution, it was seen as both an approval of the Soviet proposal and was celebrated as a significant "victory" for the Soviet Union and all "peace-loving forces."

In the late 1960s and early 1970s Gromyko proposed the Soviet Union's "key, vital issues" in the following, appropriately titled speeches: "Some Urgent Measures on Disarmament and Halting the Arms Race" (1968); "The Strengthening of International Security" (1969); "Adopting a Declaration of International Security" (1970); "The Convening of a World Disarmament Conference" (1971); "The Non-use of Force in International Relations"; and "Banning of the Use of Nuclear Weapons for All Time" (1972). All these proposals were included in the agenda of the General Assembly and were discussed in its various committees.

Many of the provisions of these initiatives were the sort of thing that no one could object to in principle. No one objected in principle to the ending of the arms race and the conducting of appropriate negotiations, including the convening of an international conference to accomplish this end. No one opposed cooperation between and the peaceful coexistence of countries with different social systems. Many even supported in principle the halting of all suppression of national liberation movements.

Nevertheless, the Soviet tradition of submitting "key issues" to each session of the General Assembly did not usually promote the strengthening of cooperation between the countries, nor did it improve the international climate as a whole. Despite the earnest assurances of the authors of the "key issues" of their sincere and good intentions, they succeeded only in exacerbating the situation and intensifying confrontation.

The confrontational nature of the key issues was obvious. Without mentioning countries by name, the "key issues," as a rule, condemned the actions of the other superpower and its allies, the colonial powers. For example, the prohibition of the use of nuclear weapons for all time was at variance with the U.S. strategic concept, which was based on the possible use of nuclear weapons. The urgent convening of a world disarmament conference in the absence of trust between the states and without an agreement on arms control measures was unacceptable to the Western powers. The proclamation of the principle of inadmissibility of the acquisition of territory by military means was directed against Israel, which occupied a number of Arab territories.

This was the essential point of the "key issues": to put our Cold War opponents, primarily the United States and its supporters, on the defensive and place them in a difficult situation where they would be forced to oppose provisions of international law, thus ending up on the side of a conspicuous minority in the voting. And this is precisely what the authors of the "key issues" were after. As a rule this was indeed the result of most of the Soviet initiatives.

When we submitted the proposal on the non-use of force in international relations and the prohibition of the use of nuclear weapons, I once happened to ask Gromyko: "Wouldn't it be worthwhile changing the nature of our 'key issue' in light of improved relations with the U.S.?" He thought for a moment and said: "The time has not yet come. You see we have to take advantage of the rather unpopular American principal of nuclear weapons use," thus indirectly admitting that the Soviet "key issues" were a means of waging the Cold War and could be discarded with the end of Soviet initiatives.

The Americans only played into the hands of the authors by their sharply negative attitude to the Soviet initiatives and attacks on delegations of countries that supported those initiatives. If the Americans had adopted a more reserved and restrained attitude, the effect would have been quite different. We might have even lost our enthusiasm for coming up with "key issues" at every session. But this was their problem.

The confrontational motivation of the "key issues" was revealed by the manner in which they were presented. As a rule they were produced in total secrecy. We never consulted with our allies, or with other countries, who might be interested in the Soviet initiatives. The Politburo would approve the "key issue" and authorize the foreign minister to submit it to the UN in his speech at the opening of the General Assembly session. Until then nobody had access to the text except a very limited number of people from the Soviet delegation (two or three diplomats closest to the minister) and some translators and secretaries. Therefore, even the Soviet diplomats learned about the "key issue" only after its official submission to the UN.

This inexplicable secrecy not only created difficulties for the work of the Soviet delegation itself, but also aroused the undisguised discontent of our socialist allies and friendly delegations of the nonaligned countries. The theatricality of producing these "key issues" out of the hat also provoked an unfavorable response from the Western states. Many colleagues told us that if the Soviet Union was really interested in a businesslike, constructive discussion of its proposals, it should submit them before the opening of the session, thus giving other countries an opportunity to prepare for a serious dialogue.

Malik, Mendelevich, and I told Gromyko about the obvious drawbacks of the manner in which we introduced our "key issues." Only in very rare cases did he agree to make some changes, such as presenting them just before the opening of the sessions, but this cost us the surprise effect. Gromyko did not like it this and chose to revert to the old secretive approach.

The Most Honorific and Most Thankless Job

My whole diplomatic career was connected in one way or another with the UN Secretariat. Initially, when I worked in the Soviet mission in New York, and later as a member of the Soviet delegation to eighteen sessions of the General Assembly, I was in close contact with the secretariat for almost two decades. I worked with many of the highest officials of the organization, undersecretaries-general and, of course, UN secretaries-general themselves.

Some of them I knew very well, because of my meetings with them; others I knew only by reputation.

During the Cold War the international civil service—or more precisely, the secretariats of the intergovernmental organizations—represented an important theater of confrontation for the major world political forces. It is difficult to give a simple answer to the question of where exactly the interests of the Soviet Union lay in the UN Secretariat specifically, and in the international civil service in general. The latter was primarily concerned with providing effective compliance with the decisions of the international community, the Security Council, the General Assembly, and other conferences.

However, in selecting secretariat personnel, the priority of the Soviet diplomatic service was not their competence and efficiency, but rather their political allegiance, so that the secretariat would reflect the division of the world into rival camps. Indeed Khrushchev had suggested that the division of the world into socialist, capitalist, and nonaligned countries be reflected in the structure of the UN Secretariat. In fact he actually recommended having three UN secretaries-general.

The first secretaries-general Trygve Lee and Dag Hammarskjöld did not enjoy Moscow's favor. They were considered pawns of the West on the world's political chessboard and were treated with disregard by the Kremlin. The situation changed in the early 1960s. The emergence of a large group of new states on the international scene, as well as the nonaligned movement, led to a change in the role of the UN secretary-general in world politics. This became apparent during the term of office of U Thant of Burma.

During my first years in New York I frequently met with U Thant, sometimes together with Malik, sometimes alone. I was also able to observe him during numerous working meetings, protocol events, and press conferences. He made a very good impression on me. He was unassuming, quiet, and affable. He liked a good joke. When he found out that I was Armenian, he remarked with a smile: "That's very good. So you must know the Armenian Radio jokes." To this day I have no idea how jokes from Radio Yerevan, which were created in Moscow and were very popular at the time in the Soviet Union, had reached the ears of the secretary-general of the UN.

U Thant understood the complexity and responsibility of his task. He always acted in a circumspect and pondered fashion. He once rightly pointed out that the position of UN secretary-general was the most honorific and, at the same time, the most thankless job in the world. He was right. The secretary-general should embody and represent the opinion of the whole world community. Every UN member state, regardless of its size or role in international politics, expected its opinion on any matter to be heard and taken into consideration. As UN experience has shown, this was extremely difficult to achieve. Nevertheless, U Thant grappled with the problem. He showed himself to be an experienced diplomat, who possessed a very important quality for any politician and especially the UN secretary-general: the ability to listen patiently and attentively.

As time went by, U Thant demonstrated yet another rare quality. He skillfully created the impression that he sympathized with the other person's point of view. This was not a matter of facile and simulated agreeability, but rather a sincere interest in the position of his interlocutor—an interest shown by the questions he asked. He demonstrated this quality in his conversation with Brezhnev during his visit to the Soviet Union. I remember Brezhnev telling me before my departure to New York that U Thant sympathized with the Soviet position in international affairs. Later I heard similar reports from many politicians and diplomats who had met U Thant. The Indians said that U Thant supported India's position. At the same time, the Pakistanis believed that he understood and was in sympathy with their view. Of course, many representatives of nonaligned countries reported that U Thant displayed an understanding of their positions. I never heard anyone complain that he was the type who would promise support but then fail to deliver.

This previously little-known Burmese diplomat had, in the space of a few years, won international recognition and authority. The Soviet Union took a favorable view of U Thant's performance. He visited the USSR several times and met its leaders. "Leonid Ilyich [Brezhnev] is pleased with our cooperation with U Thant," Gromyko was telling me. The United States and Western countries were also well disposed toward him.

When the question of filling the post of UN secretary-general for the next five-year term arose at the beginning of 1971, none of us in New York had any doubt that it should be U Thant. And this was the recommendation we sent to Moscow. In a few days we received instructions from Gromyko to work actively to promote the candidacy of U Thant. We later learned that the decision had been taken to the highest level of the Politburo itself.

Candidates for the Post of UN Secretary-General

The first to enter the UN election campaign was Finland's representative to the UN, Max Jacobson in 1971. He was well known in UN circles and had given a good account of himself as president of the Security Council in the spring of 1970, when Finland was a nonpermanent member. He had good connections both within the organization, and within American society and business circles. Soon other names for the post began to be mentioned as candidates for the post. They were Jermakoya from Senegal, Amarasinghe from Sri Lanka, Carlos de Rozas from Argentina, and Kurt Waldheim from Austria.

The permanent representative from Sri Lanka, Amarasinghe, was particularly widely known because he was a very experienced and active diplomat, and enjoyed considerable authority among the delegations of the nonaligned countries and in the UN at large. The very fact that he was repeatedly elected president of various international conferences, of the UN General Assembly itself, and the Conference on the Law of the Sea, speaks for itself. A man of many parts, a sportsman, he always dressed to the nines, sporting his inevitable red carnation in his buttonhole. Amarasinghe lived the family-free life of a bachelor in New York, giving rise to all kinds of gossip around the UN. It was no doubt this gossip that provoked a letter from a New York women's organization that was campaigning for moral purity in the relations between the sexes. When it learned about Amarasinghe's candidacy for the post of UN secretary-general, the organization protested against his election. It argued that the election of the Sri Lankan would deal a serious blow to the morality of all member states of the United Nations. This gave rise to a great many jokes about him, which Amarasinghe himself took in good humor. However, I do think that the letter had some negative impact on his election campaign.

The other candidate, Carlos Ortiz de Rosas, was of quite a different stripe. Coming from an eminent Argentinean aristocratic family, he was an outstanding professional. He was one of the most authoritative and brilliant figures in multilateral diplomacy of the 1960s and 1970s and was an acknowledged master in his field. He usually took part in every contentious political issue in the UN and other international forums. It was de rozas who often formulated the positions of the delegations of the nonaligned countries, among whom he enjoyed unfailing authority.

Austria's permanent representative, Kurt Waldheim, was a notable figure in the world diplomatic arena too. He had been the Austrian minister of foreign affairs for a number of years as well as its representative in various UN bodies and international conferences for many years. He had accumulated vast experience in the field of multilateral diplomacy. As minister of foreign affairs he had visited the Soviet Union, and to some degree, this affected the outcome of the election of the next secretary-general.

TIME TO GO HOME

"Please, Leave Me in Peace!"

In 1971, at one of the press conferences at the UN headquarters when U Thant was asked whether he was going to run for a second term as secretary-general, he thought for a moment and said, "No. I do not have such plans." Although the time for the election of the secretary-general was approaching, the question of U Thant remained open. He was bombarded with questions about his intentions, and at this point he would answer unhesitatingly and unequivocally that he was not willing to serve as secretary-general for another term. In the fall of 1971, when Gromyko was attending the session of the General Assembly, I informed him about U Thant's position. "He's just playing hard to get," Gromyko responded, in denial.

Others did believe U Thant and started looking for alternative candidates. We, however, were locked into his candidacy, thus blocking the solution of the problem. The inconsistency of the Soviet position was obvious: we were backing a candidate who had categorically refused to be one.

At one informal meeting of the ambassadors of the permanent members of the Security Council, Sir Colin Crowe, the British representative, asked Malik to explain the inflexible position of our delegation. Malik answered that this was not the delegation's position, but the Kremlin's. "But who in the Kremlin made this decision?" asked the British representative. "The Politburo," Malik replied. "Oh really," Crowe remarked acidly. "Then why don't you tell that to U Thant. Perhaps if he knew it was the Politburo, he would change his mind."

In reply to our next request for instructions, Moscow told me to have a "heart to heart" talk with U Thant and to find out his true feelings about the possibility of being reelected. I had to go to the hospital, where secretary-general was at the time. His appearance and condition answered my questions for me. Tired and pale with a yellowing complexion, he lay in bed surrounded by innumerable baskets of flowers. U Thant asked me to thank Brezhnev, and the Soviet leadership for the trust they placed with him, but made it unmistakably clear that his physical condition did not allow him to continue working. "Believe me, I am dreaming of peace and quiet, of being left alone," he pleaded, adding, "I would rather hear an Armenian radio joke."

I was happy to oblige and improvised: Armenian radio was asked if it was possible to build communism in Burma? "Certainly, it is possible, but . . . it would be such a pity!" was the answer. "But why would it be a pity and for whom?" the listeners asked. "Why, the Burmese," explained Armenian radio. "But do you know any Burmese?" was the next question. "No. But we'd still feel sorry for them." We laughed, pleased that nobody was building communism in Burma. I wished U Thant a speedy recovery and hurried back to the mission to report the situation to Moscow.

At the end of 1971 there were a series of closed meetings of the Security Council, which settled the question of U Thant's successor. On many occasions I participated in the meetings of the council on the election of the UN secretary-general. Despite the seriousness of the matter it was impossible to banish the impression that one was witnessing a gripping political drama, whose outcome was impossible to predict. However, even with the strictest and most scrupulous rules of confidentiality in the conduct of the meetings, UN diplomatic circles and the press knew immediately after the meetings which delegation had voted for whom, and who had "vetoed" whom. How did the information come into their possession with such amazing rapidity? It had probably been leaked by the delegates themselves.

Kurt Waldheim Is Elected Secretary-General

The 1971 elections for the post of secretary-general required several rounds of voting. In the first round, there were seven candidates, none of whom won the necessary number of votes. In the second round the list of candidates had lengthened to ten names. Ten ballot papers were issued, and after the count, it was announced that none of the candidates had received the necessary support. Three of the ten received the required number of votes, but in each case one of the permanent members had voted "against."

In the third round, three of the six candidates garnered the necessary nine or more votes. However, one of the permanent members of the Council voted "against" two candidates, and only Kurt Waldheim had received eleven votes in favor, one "against" (from a nonpermanent member of the Council), with three abstentions. Thus Waldheim became the new UN secretary-general.

Waldheim's election was to a certain degree unexpected. The Austrian had joined the race rather late in the day, and his chances were not rated as high. Carlos de Rosas was thought to be the most likely winner. In all three rounds of voting he received the greatest number of votes. During the third, decisive round de Rosas received twelve votes, while only eleven voted for Waldheim. However, one permanent member of the Security Council invariably voted against de Rosas—the Soviet representative. In this the Soviet delegation was, of course, acting on instructions from Moscow. But Moscow's instructions to veto de Rosas were based on the recommendations from the Soviet delegation in New York, made on Malik's initiative.

For reasons not clear to me, Malik could not tolerate the Argentinean, and did not take much trouble to hide it. Whether Carlos de Rosas had tried to make a joke at Malik's expense at some diplomatic reception, or the Russian simply resented the prestige and popularity of the Argentinean, it is hard to say, but I remember that when we were preparing the recommendations for Moscow, Malik did not have any serious arguments against de Rosas. "Remember," he told me, "what Argentina was doing during World War II."

Although Argentina's conduct was by no means commendable, I did not think this a reason to veto de Rosas. However, it was impossible to change Malik's mind, and his was the last word. That was too bad because de Rosas could have been an excellent UN secretary-general. I was convinced of this through observing the performance of this outstanding diplomat as president of various international conferences over two decades.

This does not by any means suggest that Waldheim's election was unjustified. It was no accident that in 1976 he was elected for a further five-year term by fourteen votes, with only the Chinese delegation abstaining. Waldheim established very good working and personal relations with Malik and the Soviet mission. I kept in touch with him even after he had left the post of UN secretary-general. I feel it necessary to recount the vicissitudes of the 1971 election campaign because they illustrate how human destinies, in this case de Rosas's, depend at times on emotion, subjective factors, and happenstance that have nothing to do with the merits of the case.

The Soviet delegation voted against some other candidates too, but as a rule, this was dictated by political motives. Take the example of Jacobson. As I saw it, he too could have made an excellent secretary-general. Furthermore, he represented Finland, a country with which the Soviet Union now enjoyed excellent and neighborly relations. The president of Finland, Urkho Kekkonen, had also interceded on behalf of Jacobson's candidacy during his visit to the Soviet Union in 1971. Nevertheless, the Soviet delegation received instructions not to support him. This was because many Arab countries had urged Moscow to veto Jacobson, as he was Jewish, and his in-laws supposedly headed some Zionist organization in Finland. Whether this was true or not, it was clear that many Arab delegations to the UN were conducting a very active campaign against Jacobson. Moscow had no wish to spoil its relations with the Arabs because of him.

Between Two Stools

One of the main objectives of the Soviet mission to the UN had been "to push" Soviet staff members into the secretariat. First, we were interested in increasing our quota, that is, our total number of posts in the secretariat, and second, in promoting Soviet staff members as high as possible. Malik and his deputy Tarasov were in charge of these matters. Every additional post he managed to squeeze out of U Thant was considered a personal victory. I have to admit that Malik managed to secure dozens of posts, and we took great pride in that. Moscow was pleased with us.

We viewed every Soviet citizen working in the international secretariat, not as a highly qualified, impartial expert in his field, but as a Soviet official representing the interests of the Soviet Union. How else can it be explained that practically all Soviet staff of the UN Secretariat were members of the Soviet Communist Party and had to comply with the decisions of the bureau of party organization at the Soviet mission, even if they were grossly incompatible with the status of an international civil servant?

This meant, of course, that Soviet staff members found themselves in an extremely difficult, I would even say, a false and ambivalent position. All of them were assigned to the "special department" of the mission, in other words, they were integrated into its structure, its functional units. A senior counselor at the mission headed each of these units. If, for example, a decision of any UN body was approved despite Soviet objections, Soviet staff members were obliged to impede the implementation of this decision as far as possible. (?) As a result, most of them, despite their competence, training, and at times even good qualifications in their posts, were not trusted and were excluded from responsible and delicate assignments. These attempts to force international civil servants to serve two masters did nothing for either the standing of the Soviet Union or the efficiency of international organizations.

The Soviet Union had a number of posts in the UN Secretariat that belonged to it by tradition. The most important one was the post of undersecretary-general for and director of the Department of Security Council Affairs. The gentlemen's agreement on this matter had been reached in 1946 and it was honored, although the range of this post constantly shrank, right up to the demise of the Soviet state. Russia lost this post. Many well-known Soviet diplomats—Arkady Sobolev, Vladimir Suslov, Aleksei Nesterenko,

Mikhail Sitenko, and others—held this crucial and prestigious post, but in every case only for a brief two or three year period, since they were aware that this post did not promote their diplomatic careers.

Many Soviet career diplomats saw working in the UN Secretariat not only as very difficult, but also as unrewarding in terms of career prospects. The Ministry of Foreign Affairs and Gromyko himself shared this view. The following episode was typical. During my first year in New York, the Nigerian, Chief Simon O. Adebo, director of UNITAR (the UN Institute for Training and Research), offered me a senior post at the Institute. I seriously considered the offer. I always liked teaching and scientific research, and life in the secretariat seemed to offer more advantages. Adebo's right-hand man, an American professor named Otto Shachter, urged me to join UNITAR. Malik had no objection in principle to my transfer, but I decided to consult Gromyko.

During my next summer vacation, I told the minister about the offer made to me. This news clearly displeased him, and he fell silent. Then he said that it was of course, my business, but why then, he asked, "Did I leave the Diplomatic Academy?" It was clear that he did not approve of such a move. Gromyko condemned the ambitions "of some comrades" to settle down in the secretariat.

Nevertheless, I am firmly convinced, that some Soviet citizens, working in the secretariats of international organizations considerably benefited both themselves and their organizations. These were principally experts and authorities in their respective fields, and many of them were highly respected by their colleagues.

Summing Up

Nineteen seventy-three was my sixth year at the mission. In my time there was a widely held belief among diplomats that during his first year abroad, a diplomat acclimates himself to his environment, learns the job, and makes contacts. This period does not require any special input from him. In the second year he gains experience and gradually begins to make a contribution to the work of his embassy and mission. It is in his third and fourth years that a diplomat is most effective. It is then that the balance between fresh thinking and the mastery of the specific area for which he is responsible yields the greatest benefits. In subsequent years, some diplomats develop certain stereotypes, the sharp edge of their reactions begin to erode and responses become automatic and routine, overriding their creative impulses. Furthermore, long periods in serving the interests of his country abroad do not help the overall performance of a diplomat either.

My personal experience, as well as the experiences of many other diplomats basically confirmed this rule. I have written how difficult it was for me in the beginning, how hard it was to establish relations with Malik, with my colleagues from the mission, and also with foreign diplomats. I gradually got used to my new work and developed good and even friendly relations with many colleagues. I acquainted myself with many UN issues. I gained experience and began to enjoy my diplomatic functions. Malik happened to remark that he was thinking of asking Moscow to establish the post of first deputy permanent representative, and nominating me for the new position.

In the autumn of 1971 the post of first deputy permanent representative was established, and I was appointed. Simultaneously by a decree of the Presidium of the Supreme Soviet of the USSR I was awarded the rank of extraordinary and plenipotentiary ambassador. Practically nothing had changed in my work after my promotion. I continued to deal with political issues, Security Council issues, information, and other matters. To my great dissatisfaction Malik charged me with administrative chores, including the construction of a new large housing complex in Riverdale. I had neither the inclination for nor experience in such work.

I was, of course, pleased with the promotion. My fears about it complicating my relations with the other deputies, fortunately, proved groundless. Some deputies, with whom I began my career, had left, and Evgeny Makeyev and Vasily Safronchyuk took their places. I had known both for a long time and was happy to welcome them. They were both experts in multilateral diplomacy.

Many new diplomats joined the mission at the middle and lower levels. During my many years of work in New York I got to know many Soviet diplomats, not only those working at the mission, but also members of the many delegations which came to New York on short-term bases. By and large, they were competent, experienced, knew their jobs, and there were rarely any problems with them.

At the same time there were quite a few incidents typical of the Cold War. Among them were cases of Soviet diplomats or staff members of the secretariat who asked for political asylum and refused to return to the Soviet

Union. Such cases were not frequent in my six years of work in New York. More frequent were cases of Soviet citizens caught for shoplifting. This happened quite a lot in New York. To our shame, even the staff of the mission and members of delegations were caught committing petty thefts in stores. In such cases, one of the senior officials of the mission, including myself, would categorically deny the charge, demand the release of the accused, make a formal protest, and send the culprit back to Moscow, at once. Some of these stories were rather tragic. I remember there was one scientist, a member of a delegation, who was caught red-handed stealing from a supermarket and was so upset at the prospect of being publicly disgraced, that he attempted suicide. Fortunately, the attempt failed, and after a long hospital stay he returned home in disgrace.

There were also unpredictable situations that could ruin lives and showed how despicably human beings could behave. I will give one example. On my arriving in Moscow one summer for my vacation, I found a letter sent to me from America. The letter was in English and was signed with a completely unfamiliar Armenian name. It was a thank-you letter expressing gratitude for my speeches in Los Angeles and my "frank views" about Soviet life. At the end it contained a request for the return of three hundred dollars I had supposedly borrowed during my stay in L.A. The letter contained nothing but lies—I had never been to L.A. I decided to inform the MFA. It turned out that they were already aware of the letter, since it had been opened "by the appropriate services." After an investigation, they established that the letter had been typed in the office of a top Soviet bureaucrat working in New York, who probably wanted to discredit me by such means.

The author understood that the "appropriate services,"—the KGB—would be interested in this "tip off" about the first deputy permanent representative of the USSR who had expressed "frank views" about the Soviet Union and then took money borrowed from foreigners, something which was categorically forbidden for diplomats. Of course, the author thought the "appropriate" measures would be taken against the person concerned. Fortunately for me, he miscalculated. I had no trouble in refuting the lies, but the episode caused me a lot of trouble and unpleasantness. Especially hurtful was the fact that the dirty trick was plotted by someone whom I considered if not actually a friend, at least a decent person. I could never bring myself to speak to him about his poison pen letter. As the proverb says: "No one is a thief until he is caught."

Working Together for Common Goals

My account of my work in New York would be incomplete without the story of my cooperation with the KGB. I think that all Soviet diplomats at different stages of their careers, in one form or another, have assisted the KGB. And this is really quite natural. After all, diplomacy and intelligence work have a great deal in common.

We all had our own dealings with the KGB. Mine for example, started in Moscow. Once, a month or two before my departure to New York, an acquaintance of mine who was a member of the KGB told me that a "very interesting person" would like to meet me. The meeting took place at the Hotel Moskva. The man introduced himself as Boris Filippovich. From the way he spoke and the deferential behavior of his entourage, I understood that I was dealing with a top KGB officer. Subsequent events confirmed my impression.

The conversation was very general, and largely of a casual, social nature. The KGB official congratulated me on my assignment to New York, wished me success, talked about the close cooperation between the KGB and the MFA, and expressed the hope that I would help the KGB in its important work, since he stressed, we were all under orders from the Central Committee of our party. I, of course, agreed and promised the necessary assistance in accomplishing "our common goals." Before saying good-bye he asked me to keep our conversation secret from everybody, including my immediate superior, Malik. Then he ended our mysterious meeting with the words "Our comrades will contact you over there in New York."

Sure enough, soon after my arrival in New York, Dmitry Yakushkin, who worked in the UN, approached me. He was the son of an academician whose name was widely known in the Soviet Union. Once, Yakushkin told me, not without pride, that he was the descendant of a prominent noble family. He had not followed in his father's footsteps, but had gone into the intelligence service. I was told that he was considered a good professional and one of the leading Soviet operatives in the United States at the time.

In a bug-proof room Yakushkin informed me that the new KGB *rezident,*" or head of intelligence in the United States, who was soon to be appointed to the post of deputy permanent representative, had been delayed in Moscow and that therefore he had been instructed to establish contact with me himself. To put relations on a friendly footing he invited my wife and myself to dinner at his apartment. Just as it was at our first meeting, he did not make any requests or even mention our "special" cooperation during the dinner.

Yakushkin told me about life in New York, about work in the UN Secretariat, and advised me about life in the United States as well as UN events, and to expand my circle of American acquaintances. He talked calmly and reasonably, without using any ominous language about American imperialism and its inevitable defeat. It was my impression that his work and life in America suited him well. Gradually we established friendly relations. He had a lot of experience and was an interesting conversationalist, and I sometimes came to him for advice about practical matters.

The *rezidentura* or KGB presence in New York was the largest anywhere abroad. KGB agents included diplomats from the mission, UN Secretariat staff members, journalists, representatives of Aeroflot, Intourist, Armtorg, and all Soviet institutions in New York. I think they numbered well over a hundred. The KGB agents in the New York mission far outnumbered those in the Washington embassy. For that reason, the New York *rezident*, who was formally the deputy permanent representative to the UN, was regarded as chief of the whole KGB apparatus in the United States, although there were times when it was Washington that coordinated all Soviet intelligence work in the this country. The fact remained, however, that New York was the primary theater of operations for the vast army of Soviet agents. I knew only a few of them. From time to time they approached me with questions connected with the work of different UN bodies and wanted to know my opinion of the diplomats from foreign missions.

Shortly after the new KGB chief, Vikenty Sobolev, arrived in New York in the summer of 1968 and began work as yet another of Malik's deputies, he came to see me to tell me that Boris Filippovich sent me his regards and that he looked forward to our cooperation. I confirmed everything I had said in Moscow, and on his initiative we started meeting.

Each time we got together, Sobolev asked me to tell him about my acquaintances, my meetings with Americans, and about my impressions and observations. He asked me to take notes of the most interesting meetings, such as my conversations with David Rockefeller, Hans Morgenthau, Marshall Schulman, and with members of the Council for Foreign Relations. He also asked me not to tell anyone of these records. This is when I had my first disagreement with Sobolev. I told him that my meetings with these American personalities were done so with Malik's consent and that it was to him that I reported. The same applied to my notes of conversations, which

I sent to Moscow through MFA channels. Sobolev was most displeased. "Then how are we supposed to cooperate?" he asked. The meetings with him became less and less frequent, and I can't say that I was sorry.

"Watch Out for the CIA"

Sobolev was not too happy with some of my acquaintances, especially those among the Armenian diaspora. He advised me to keep away from some of the Armenian activists, especially from Harry Orbelyan, whom the KGB believed to be a CIA agent.

I would like to say a few words about Orbelyan. We met in the late 1960s in San Francisco, where he lived with his family. He had had an extraordinary life. Son of one of the founders of the Armenian Communist Party and one of the leaders of Soviet Armenia, who was arrested in the years of Stalin's repressions, Harry was taken prisoner by the Germans during World War II. After the war he preferred not to return to the Soviet Union. He moved to the United States and became a successful businessman in California. His mother, his brother, and other relatives lived in Armenia. His brother, Constantine, became a well-known musician in the Soviet Union. His father was posthumously rehabilitated.

Nevertheless, the road back to Armenia was closed for Harry. He repeatedly asked the Soviet embassy in Washington for help, but for many years all his efforts were in vain. The reasons had to do with an article in *Literaturnaya Gazeta*, suggesting that Orbelyan was a spy.

I met Orbelyan several times in New York, and we frequently talked over the phone. Of course, he counted on my assistance in getting a visa to Armenia or in getting his mother to the United States. It was a long time before we learned that some hack journalist had trumped up Orbelyan's espionage activities. As a matter of fact Vladimir Kazakov, who was later to become the KGB *rezident* in the United States, came to the same conclusion. Orbelyan began visiting the USSR and during Gorbachev's visit to San Francisco toward the end of 1980, he was one of the main organizers of the reception for the high-ranking Soviet guest, whom Orbelyan insisted on referring to as "my good friend."

Another of my Armenian contacts of whom Sobolev did not approve was Levon Keshishyan, a correspondent for a number of Egyptian newspapers in the UN. I met him soon after my arrival in New York. He was particularly attentive to me because of our common ethnic roots and his professional interests.

Levon grew up and received his education in Cairo, where he eventually became quite a well-known journalist. He was fluent in many languages, actively participated in the life of the New York Armenian community, and maintained excellent relations with many Arab diplomats. He had a small office at UN headquarters, where you would always meet many Arab ambassadors, and secretariat officials. Altogether, he was well connected and well informed on Middle East affairs.

I do not know why my colleagues in the KGB treated him with such suspicion and mistrust. Although I was never particularly close with Keshishyan, I never found anything "suspicious" in his behavior and continued to keep in contact with him.

In spite of everything the KGB was once compelled to ask Keshishyan for help. Oghan Dulyan, a well-known Armenian conductor who was touring internationally, appeared unexpectedly in the United States. He was hosted by the Armenian community and traveled around America, giving concerts, without permission from Moscow. Dulyan did not ask for political asylum, but neither did he show any intention of returning to the Soviet Union. As far as the Soviet authorities were concerned, his behavior had taken a decidedly undesirable turn.

Dulyan had recently gone to live in Armenia and had called on other Armenians to follow his example. Before that he had been living in one of the Arab countries. In Yerevan he was appointed principal conductor of the Yerevan Opera. He toured Russia and other countries. His "return" to Armenia was widely advertised as a triumph of "Lenin's national policy." His unauthorized stay in the United States obviously undermined Moscow's self-congratulatory propaganda.

Sobolev asked me to meet with Dulyan and to persuade him to return to Yerevan . I was authorized to assure him on behalf of Yekaterina Furtseva, the Soviet minister of culture, that he would not be punished for his unauthorized visit to America, and that he would still be able to perform abroad.

My meeting with Dulyan took place in a New York restaurant, where I was delivered like a character in a cheap detective novel. The mission driver (a KGB agent) brought me to the agreed meeting place, where Keshishyan was waiting for me. He led me through back streets and alleyways until we got to the restaurant and were shown to a private room. Dulyan was waiting for me accompanied by two hefty Armenians. He was very nervous during the whole conversation, fearing that our meeting might be part of a KGB plot to kidnap him.

He started by saying, "I am not political and have nothing against the Soviet system. It was as a musician that I went back to my native Armenia. Music is my life, and I am not interested in anything else. "But," he continued, "how come a young kid, an 'instructor' from the Armenian communist party who understands nothing about music, is giving orders to me, the musical director of the Opera, a world-renowned musician? Where does he get off telling me which singers to choose for the roles and how to interpret operatic scores?" Dulyan was outraged and indignant with the interference of party officials in his musical activities. He could not tolerate being forced to give the lead in the opera *Anush* to a stout, shapeless elderly singer instead of a young, slim beauty, just because she bore the title of "People's Artist of the USSR."

Dulyan cited other examples of boorish behavior on the part of Yerevan and Moscow party government bureaucrats, who, in his opinion, had done incalculable harm to art and music. Dulyan was very emotional and clearly felt strongly about this, and passionately resented his situation.

I sat, listening to him and not knowing how to react. One thing was clear to me, however; although Dulyan had stated that he could not care less about politics, the whole situation was essentially political. He was unable and unwilling to understand that in a totalitarian state like the Soviet Union, everything, including art and music, came under the authority of the Party. But I could not bring myself to tell him this fact of life. I started blaming everything on the "stupidity of bureaucrats" who stick their noses into other people's business. I assured him that the situation could be rectified, that Furtseva respected him, that the officials who were interfering with his work would be punished, and that he would be allowed to continue his work unimpeded and in peace. I asked him to return home.

Dulyan obviously did not believe me, and he was probably right. The Communist Party was certainly not about to give up their "leading role" in all areas of Soviet life, including music, just because of Dulyan. He did not want to return to Yerevan, where he had started a family after going to live in Armenia. Instead he asked me to help reunite him with his wife and small son who were still there. He was unhappy being separated from them, especially from his son. When I asked him how his wife felt about his decision, Dulyan was compelled to admit that she did not want to leave Armenia, where she had a large family and her work, and she was insistent that he return to them. Under these circumstances, I firmly supported the wife and refused his request. After about an hour we parted without having come to any decision.

I reported the conversation to my colleagues from the KGB and soon forgot about my inconclusive meeting with Dulyan. Two or three months later I met with Keshishyan and asked about Dulyan. I was astounded to be told that he was actually back in Yerevan. "How come?" I asked. "It is very simple" Keshishyan answered. "Recently while Dulyan was on the phone with his son, the boy started crying and asked his father to come home. Dulyan, too, burst into tears, and a couple of days later flew back to Yerevan." What can be stronger than a father's love for his son!

Upon returning to Soviet Armenia, Dulyan successfully continued his musical career and started touring again (Furtseva had kept her word). But on one of these trips, a few years after my meeting with him, he finally refused to return to the USSR.

I never had a chance to talk with Sobolev about my meeting with Dulyan, but I am sure that he was deeply dissatisfied by my failure to persuade the conductor to return to the Soviet Union. The KGB could not even take credit for his temporary return to Armenia. Once again my cooperation with the KGB had been unsuccessful.

But the final end to this cooperation came a little later, when Yakushkin came to me with a rather unusual request. Knowing that I frequently attended meetings of the prestigious New York Council for Foreign Relations and sometimes participated in them, he asked me, albeit delicately, if I would mind, surreptitiously, of course, planting a bug in the room where all the council's discussions and dinners were held. The device was no larger than a hockey puck and would enable Soviet intelligence to keep abreast of all important foreign policy discussions. He did everything he could and told me that planting the bug would be easy if I chose the right moment and just stuck it up against the fireplace.

I flatly refused and in some indignation said that I must have misunderstood the nature of our cooperation, which had to end right then. Yakushkin was a little surprised at my reaction and tried to smooth things over. In any case, a couple of weeks later at a reception, Sobolev took me aside and mumbled, "You can take it that we won't be bothering you anymore." And as a matter of fact the KGB never approached me again.

I would be telling a lie if I said that I was happy about the way it ended—far from it. I was really worried about the consequences. I remembered Malik telling me once, during a friendly conversation, that in order to succeed in any embassy, a diplomat needs to secure the support of three people: the ambassador, the chairman of the local communist party committee, and the KGB resident, with whom, of course, I had just irreparably destroyed my relations. I have to admit that to the very last day of my diplomatic career I was expecting the inevitable retribution for my "uncooperativeness" with the KGB. For all I know, both the fact and the manner of my dismissal many years later may very well have been that retribution. I do not know, but I think that the KGB must have had a hand in it.

To be fair, I must say, however, that my "uncooperativeness" with Sobolev did not affect my position or my authority at the mission. Fortunately, he was soon recalled to Moscow, and Boris Solomatin, who soon became a friend of mine, took his place. Ours was a friendship based on purely personal considerations, and he never referred to the subject of my cooperation with the KGB. I certainly never broached the subject myself.

Á La Guerre Comme á La Guerre (War Is War)

It was my sixth year in New York. Our life seemed to have settled into a comfortable routine. The deputies of the permanent representative had received permission (and most important, the money) to rent decent apartments in the city, instead of having to squeeze into the small, inconvenient rooms at the mission on Sixty-seventh Street. As a major exception to policy, Malik gave me permission to send my young sons to New York's Hunter College School, something which was technically forbidden. My wife, Alla, got a job at the mission polyclinic, which allowed her to establish professional contacts with American doctors.

Nevertheless, I felt I was ready for a change. I was beginning to feel stale in my work and sensed that it was time for me to move on, although neither Gromyko nor Malik said anything in front of me that would lead me to think that they felt the same. In fact, my fairly recent promotion to first deputy ensured that I would be staying in New York for a few more years. Nevertheless, I was clearly losing interest in many of the issues I was involved with and had begun to feel that I was simply repeating myself. With time the feeling grew stronger, even though the international climate appeared to be improving and the Soviet positions in the UN were firmly established, and no special problems had arisen.

During one of Gromyko's visits in New York, I asked him to transfer me to another job, and in the spring of 1973 I was asked if I would consider heading the MFA's International Organizations Department (IOD). Frankly speaking, I was not thrilled at this prospect and would have preferred an ambassadorship, preferably in Europe. However, to refuse Moscow's offer, knowing the importance that Gromyko attached to the department, meant jeopardizing my positive relationship with the minister. So I agreed and returned to Moscow that same summer.

Though my return to Moscow was the result of my own initiative, I felt sad to leave New York. I will not attempt to describe what I felt about New York and in any case I would not have anything original to say. I will just say I had put the same sticker on my car as millions of other New Yorkers: "I Love New York."

Having worked as one of its warriors in this unique city during the Cold War years, I nevertheless keep a very warm spot in my heart for New York. Not only did I participate in the work of many hundreds of sessions and conferences, but I also witnessed the most intense international situations and conflicts. Most of all, I remember the main participants of these diplomatic duels. Certainly the participation of the world's foremost state and political leaders in the work of the UN—presidents, kings, prime ministers, and dictators—made a huge impression on me. Their speeches garnered the world's attention. Less appreciable, but very important was the time-consuming and intensive work of other delegation members and professional diplomats. Within Cold War conditions, despite the complexity and contradictions of the international arena, diplomats aspired toward mitigation and the rapprochement of positions. They trusted that reason would triumph. Such diplomats could be found in every delegation, including the delegations of the superpowers.

Yet, I returned to Moscow feeling somewhat disappointed. When I initially set out to work in New York, I thought that I would be seeking solutions, together with diplomats from other countries, that would be acceptable to everyone. The definition of the word "multilateral" from an international law textbook which read, "any discussion, decision, or joint action of sovereign states carried out with the purpose of maintaining security and collective prosperity," was exactly how I saw it. I believed that my diplomatic performance would be evaluated based on the number of achieved agreements and treaties. This might have been the case in a world in which international relations were normal, peaceful, and civilized, but not in the conditions of the Cold War. Instead, petulance and the undermining of one's political or ideological opponents took precedence over agreements. My UN experience has shown that the Kremlin leaders expected their diplomats to use these tactics to politically combat the United States and their allies, rather than make joint efforts to achieve "mutual prosperity." Unfortunately, the White House had the very same attitude.

Á la guerre comme á la guerre. This phrase, "War is war," totally applies to the Cold War, and no weapon was spared on the UN front: provocation, slander, the imposition of unacceptable decisions, deceit, and so on. Sadly, my work in New York brought me to the conclusion that if one does not master these skills, one will never succeed in Cold War diplomacy.

The author presents a Soviet proposal at a UN meeting in New York in 1968.

The Security Council hears views on the situation in Czechoslovakia in August 1968. At the table above are Ibrahim Boye (Senegal), Yakov Malik (USSR), and Lord Caradon (U.K.). The author is seated to the right of Malik. United Nations photo.

The UN General Assembly meeting, September 1971, at which the People's Republic of China is admitted to the UN. United Nations photo.

The Security Council ails in August 1972 to accept the application of Bangladesh for membership in the UN. The author, seated third from the left above, watches with satisfaction as China makes its first UN veto. United Nations photo.

The author and the ambassador of Somalia, Abdulrahim Abby Farah, discuss the war between India and Pakistan at the UN in New York, December 1971.

Ambassador Malik and the author, together with their wives and a Russian priest, pose for a photo at the Soviet mission to the UN in New York, November 1972.

Nikita Khrushchev addresses the UN General Assembly in September 1960. During his visit to the United States, the Soviet premier promised to "bury capitalism." United Nations photo.

Soviet Foreign Minister Viacheslav Molotov, the number-one "Nyet-negotiator," addressess the San Francisco Conference in May 1945. This is where the United Nations charter and the Statute of the New International Court of Justice were agreed upon. United Nations photo.

Ernesto "Che" Guevara, Minister of Industries of Cuba, addresses the UN General Assembly in New York in December 1964. The author attended this meeting and was impressed by Guevara. United Nations photo.

U.S. Secretary of State Dean Rusk talks with the author in the General Assembly Hall in 1968.

U.S. Permanent Representative to the UN Charles W. Yost talks with the author in New York in 1971.

The U.S. Permanent Representative to the UN George H. W. Bush heads a United Nations special flight to Montreal in the summer of 1972. Next to him is the author, his wife, and the pilot.

Ambassador Malik (left) and Lord Caradon (U.K. Permanent Representative to the UN) at a Security Council meeting regarding the UN Peacekeeping Force in Cyprus, March 1968.

The author with the permanent representatives of Czechoskovakia, Zdenek Cernik, and of Hungary, Karoly Szarka, at the UN in New York in 1969. It was important to Moscow to present a united front with "fraternal socialist countries." One would never know from this photo that the Soviet Union had invaded Hungary in 1956 or Czechoslovakia in 1968.

The Soviet delegation to the UN General Assembly in New York in 1972. Permanent Representative to the UN Malik (center) jokes with Ambassador to the U.S. Dobrynin (left) while Foreign Minister Gromyko tries to listen to the speaker. The author, seated in the back, can't decide whether to listen to the speaker or to the joke.

Ambassador Carlos Ortiz de Rosas (Argentina), the recognized master of multilateral diplomacy, talks with the author in New York in 1973.

UN Secretary General Kurt Waldheim, the author, and their aids in Siberia (Irkutsk) during the Secretary General's visit to the Soviet Union in 1977.

Swedish Foreign Minister Hans Blix talks to the author at the opening session of the Geneva Conference on Disarmament in 1979 on the nonproliferation of weapons of mass destruction.

The author is president of the Geneva Conference on Disarmament in July 1985. Next to him is UN Secretary General Javier Perez de Cuellar (on the left) and the Conference Secretary, Rikhi Jaipal.

George H. W. Bush makes a statement at the Geneva Conference on Disarmament in 1985, during which he charges that the USSR is using chemical weapons. The author prepares the Soviet reply.

The author makes a statement on the nonproliferation of nuclear weapons at a meeting in Geneva in December 1986. Next to him is Valeri Loschinin, who is today the First Deputy Foreign Minister of Russia.

The famous pianist Van Cliburn talks to the author at a party in honor of Solomon Hurok in New York in 1968.

The author talks to actor Paul Newman in New York in 1972 on the occasion of the General Assembly's Special Session on Disarmament. President Nixon appointed Newman to the American delegation.

Shirley Temple Black, a member of the U.S. delegation to the General Assembly session, chats with the author at a Waldorf Astoria reception in 1969.

During the Cold War years, members of the Soviet delegation frequently lectured or took part in symposiums outside the UN. At the time this photo was taken in 1972, Dallas was off limits to Soviet diplomats, but George Bush personally intervened, making it possible for the author to visit the University of Texas at Arlington, where he spoke on Soviet foreign policy.

13

THE SOVIET DIPLOMATIC HEADQUARTERS AT SMOLENSKAYA SQUARE

Coming Home

My family's return to Moscow was marked by a memorable incident. We had decided to travel by sea. First, we would drive to Montreal, and there take the Soviet ocean liner *Lermontov* to Leningrad. From there we would take the "Red Arrow" train to Moscow. At the Canadian border I told the immigration officials that my driver would be dropping us off in Montreal and returning to New York. At the same time I asked them to inform the ship that we would be in Montreal in a few hours.

When we tried to board the ship, however, we were confronted with a strange situation. In spite of the fact that the crew had been given notice of our arrival, they not only neglected to show us to our cabins but even seemed unwilling to allow us on board at all. They kept asking me ridiculous questions, like: "Have you really decided to take your family to Leningrad?" or "Are you sure you want to live in the Soviet Union?" and so on and so forth. I was indignant. "Do you know who you are talking to? I am Ambassador Israelyan!" I responded heatedly. At this response, the first mate appeared and continued this objectionable line of questioning, although in an extremely civil manner. Again he drew our attention to the gravity of the step I was about to take. I refused to continue the conversation and demanded to speak with the captain of the ship. When he appeared, we embraced; we had known each other for many years. He burst into laughter, apologized, and personally showed us to our cabins, after reprimanding his subordinates: "What are you playing at? Don't you know that this is one of our own Soviet ambassadors!"

What had happened was that when the Canadian immigration official had reported that an Ambassador Israelyan was coming with his family and was not returning to the United States, the crew mistook "Ambassador Israelyan" for "an Israeli ambassador" who had decided to defect to the USSR and to ask for political asylum in the Soviet Union. The crew thought this would make headline news, because in view of the hostility of Moscow to the government of Israel, this event would be extremely gratifying to the Soviet government—not to mention that the *Lermontov* would be in the limelight; however, they did not dare act without the captain's approval. Later they had a good laugh over the story of their earnest preparations for this "great sensation" which, unfortunately for them, never happened. I should say that this was not the first time that my surname had lent itself to this kind of comical misunderstanding.

The sea voyage was wonderful, and my memories of the *Lermontov* could not be more pleasant, so my arrival in Moscow was something of an anticlimax. In spite of my hurried return from New York, when I reported back in late July, I discovered that Novikov, whom I was to replace, had not yet formally relinquished his duties. I had to spend a good week wandering the corridors before I could occupy the office of the head of the IOD on the tenth floor of the tall building at Smolenskaya Square, where I would eventually spend about six years.

There were about sixty people working for the department, many of whom I knew. I had done my training with some of them, and others I had worked with in New York, so I had the feeling that I was "one of them." However, it was clear that the staff of the department were not entirely happy with the fact that a relatively unknown former professor at the Diplomatic Academy had replaced their experienced and respected chief. This sentiment intensified when it became known that I had not been a member of the MFA board (also known as the Collegium), unlike Novikov, who had been a member for many years.

I must admit, though, that it was easy to adapt to the work at the department. In the first place, I was very familiar with the UN-related topics, which constituted the lion's share of the department's work. Second, my experience with the MFA Historical-Diplomatic Department helped me to navigate the labyrinths of the ministry. The presence of experienced and reliable deputies was also an advantage. After a month or two I grew accustomed to the specifics of my new job and even found time to teach part-time at the Diplomatic Academy.

A lot of time and attention was devoted to internal diplomacy, the establishment and development of contacts with the MFA authorities, senior officials of the CPSU Central Committee, and with my counterparts, the heads of other departments of the ministry.

I was lucky with the MFA management, since it was First Deputy Foreign Minister Kuznetsov who was in charge of the IOD. Foreign Minister Gromyko rarely asked to see me, and throughout the years of my tenure we spoke only rarely over the phone. As for Kuznetsov, I saw him every day. Working with him was both interesting and instructive. He would listen to people carefully and give very precise instructions. He never made excessive demands of his subordinates, while at the same time he was quite strict and exacting. But it was, above all, his compassion for which people around him respected and loved him. I benefited greatly from working with him. He was one of the few Soviet diplomats who enjoyed worldwide popularity and respect. These feelings were once very tellingly expressed in verse at a meeting of the UN Security Council by Lord Caradon.

Gromyko's other deputies—there were about ten—only rarely took an interest in IOD questions. Nikolai Firyubin, Nikolai Rodionov, Anatoly Kovalev, and Leonid Ilyichev occasionally invited me to participate in their negotiations with foreign diplomats, where UN-related issues arose. Sometimes, in Kuznetsov's absence, other deputy ministers signed instructions to Malik in New York. They did so with reluctance, as they did not really know the issues and because Malik still retained the rank of deputy foreign minister.

I would especially like to mention my friendship and collaboration with Deputy Minister Igor Zemskov. The two of us had a lot in common. We both had medical educations, both had worked for a short time as doctors, and had later studied together at the Diplomatic Academy. Zemskov's specialty was Italy, and he studied Italian and knew some German. While at the academy we both took a great interest in the history of diplomacy and shortly after graduation he completed his dissertation for the advanced degree of candidate of historical sciences.

Zemskov made extremely rapid progress in his career in the MFA, and was the only one of our large class of 1946 to become a deputy minister of foreign affairs. He was very close to Gromyko and had a great influence on his decisions on many internal matters, including promotions and appointments. It was not without reason that he was dubbed the "eminence grise" of the ministry, and he quite liked the nickname. Gromyko put Zemskov in charge of delicate and diverse contacts between the MFA and the KGB, something which Zemskov was very proud of.

Nevertheless, for all his high rank, good relations with the Kremlin leadership, and academic qualifications, I would not venture to rank Zemskov among the brightest stars of the Cold War generation of Soviet diplomats. I had the impression that the actual business of diplomacy did not interest him. He never made the slightest attempt to seek the post of ambassador, although if he had wanted to, with his connections, he would have had no trouble getting appointed to any capital in the world. Neither was he interested in multilateral diplomacy, and as a rule, chose not to participate in international conferences. But in the field of internal diplomacy he was a master. Because of our long-standing friendship, he frequently gave me useful advice about my behavior and my style of work—things very few people would have been frank enough to tell their colleagues. I have always been grateful to him for that. Zemskov had practically no personal life and died, after a serious illness, without having started his own family.

The New Generation of Realists

I found that my new colleagues—the heads of the major territorial and functional divisions of the ministry—were almost all representatives of the new, post-Stalin generation. There were fewer and fewer prewar or Second World War diplomats of the "Molotov era" left in the MFA. Novikov was perhaps one of the "last Mohicans" among the heads of the departments of the MFA from the Stalin period. There were still quite a few of them in the higher echelon of the ministry, though, at the deputy minister level. Among them were Semen Kozyrev and Vladimir Semenov. However, it seems to me that they were not the ones who "turned the pages" in Soviet diplomacy in the Cold War period of the 1970s. The lead was taken by representatives of the postwar generation.

This generation included A. Kovalev, G. Korniyenko, A. Dobrynin, V. Falin, M. Kapitsa, A. Bondarenko, M. Sitenko, Y. Dubynin, O. Troyanovsky, R.

Timerbayev, and many other diplomats who were members of the MFA board and occupied key positions in the organization in the 1970s and 1980s.

All of them, as a rule, had received a higher diplomatic education and were graduates either of the Moscow State Institute of International Relations or the Diplomatic Academy, and many of them had earned advanced degrees. They lived through the initial Stalin period of the Cold War, as well as the subsequent campaign against the "cult of personality." They went through the "thaws" and "freezes" of the Khrushchev years and trained as professional diplomats in the years when Brezhnev and his people were in power in the Kremlin. This generation of well-educated Soviet diplomats had acquired considerable experience working abroad, particularly in the United States and in Western Europe. They were not uncompromising in their commitment to the precepts of orthodox Marxism-Leninism, but tried to see the world as it was. One could call them "realists" or "pragmatists."

At the same time it did not mean that they were in any sense "revisionists." These "pragmatic" diplomats, like their predecessors, recognized that the Soviet Union under the leadership of the Communist Party had charted a course to socialism for the whole world to follow. In their opinion, many countries had already started on this course. The rest would join them very soon. The "pragmatists" believed that the USSR, faithful to the principles of proletarian internationalism, was leading the way to communism for humanity, and was strictly fulfilling its obligations to the working class and the liberation movements of other countries, and was striving for the triumph of socialism and communism throughout the world.

In terms of these basic premises there was no essential difference between the "Stalinists" and the "pragmatists." The latter, however, unlike the former, understood the tremendous difficulties, if not the impossibility, of bringing the peoples and countries of the world, and advanced capitalist countries—the United States and Western Europe in particular—to communism. In this regard the "pragmatists" gave a clear priority to securing Soviet national security interests over the fulfillment of its obligations in the area of proletarian internationalism. In support of this approach, they often quoted Lenin on the historical inevitability of a long period when socialist and capitalist states would coexist side by side. The work of Soviet diplomats came to be marked more and more by the objective of developing mutually beneficial relations between countries, instead of inciting class struggle in the international arena.

Nevertheless, the ultimate goal of the Soviet Union—to lead humanity to socialism and communism—was proclaimed in Communist Party manifestos and official documents, and was, of course, reflected in diplomatic documents as well. This idea, this myth, was the essential breeding ground for the Cold War. And the "pragmatists," as well as the "Stalinists," were warriors of the Soviet diplomatic service at the fronts of this war.

However, it would be wrong to consider the whole new generation of Soviet diplomats as an undifferentiated mass of functionaries. They included those who were liberal enough to approve of, for example, the "Prague Spring," as well as champions of Stalin's foreign policy, of his ruthless intolerance of any deviation from the Soviet course toward socialism. I already described the differing responses to the 1968 events in Czechoslovakia among the Soviet diplomats in New York and the same was true everywhere.

Among the "pragmatists" there were widely differing approaches to the implementation of Soviet foreign policy. One highly influential group believed that Soviet-American relations should take priority over relations with all other countries. They believed that the very superpower status of the two countries required primacy to be given to the question of cooperation and rivalry between the USSR and the United States. The "Americanists," as they were sometimes grandiloquently dubbed in the MFA, opposed, sometimes actively, Soviet diplomatic moves that were planned or implemented without sufficient consideration paid to their effect on Soviet-American relations. In the 1970s and 1980s the "Americanists" included Dobrynin, Korniyenko, Bessmertnikh, Komplektov, and many senior diplomats from the Soviet embassy in Washington and in the U.S. department of the ministry.

Close to the "Americanists" were the "disarmamentists." They were diplomats who were in varying degrees involved in arms control negotiations. They, too, believed that the highest priority should be given to the Soviet-American duet within the large chorus of states, which proclaimed a vital interest in disarmament. However, many of the "disarmamentists" involved in the numerous UN conferences on arms limitation had a broader outlook on the world than the "Americanists." Among them were Viktor Karpov, Yury Nazarkin, Timerbayev, Shustov, and Oleg Grinevsky.

Still another highly influential group within the MFA was the "Europeanists," who believed that Soviet foreign policy should be predicated primarily on Western Europe. In their opinion, the geostrategic position, historical connections, and traditions unequivocally predetermined the preference of developing of comprehensive ties just with West European countries. While the United States, as they saw it, would always be regarded as the main strategic adversary of the USSR, it was Germany, France, Britain, Italy, and other West-European countries that for various reasons might be interested in establishing "special" relationships with the Soviet Union. Such relationships would allow them to curb their growing dependence on the United States. In support of their thesis, the "Europeanists" pointed to the cracks that appeared from time to time in relations between the United States and their NATO partners. They sometimes represented these cracks as major breaches within NATO. The most outspoken of the "Europeanists" were Kovalev, Vladimir Suslov, Mendelevich, Dubynin, and many Soviet embassy diplomats in Western European countries and the relevant MFA European departments.

The MFA devoted particular attention to the German problem as central to the whole of Soviet foreign policy. The "Germanists," and among them I should mention particularly Falin, Bondarenko, and Yuly Kvitsinsky, were convinced that the status of the Soviet Union as a superpower would ultimately depend on its relations with Germany. Relations with the United States, arms limitation, cooperation with the Western European countries, in their opinion, would depend on whether the Soviet Union managed to preserve its influence in resolving the issue of a divided Germany.

Finally, I should mention a group of influential MFA diplomats who gave priority to relations with socialist—mainly Eastern European—countries. Their outlook derived from the ideological dogma that the main factor in international peace and progress in the world today was the worldwide socialist system, primarily, its most powerful and advanced component, the commonwealth of socialist states. They also saw the strengthening of the Warsaw Treaty Organization and the Council of Mutual Economic Aid as the highest priority for the Soviet Union. The advocates of this line of thinking were Rodionov, Loginov, Poklad, Kapitsa, and other diplomats who worked in Eastern European countries. They were not happy with the fact that the MFA paid too little attention to the countries of East Europe, "the devoted friends of the Soviet Union." They had a point, since as far back as Khrushchev, this bad practice had been established whereby not only major issues affecting the relations between the USSR and Eastern Europe, but even unimportant ones were dealt with by the Central Committee of the CPSU, while the MFA was often left on the sidelines.

There were, of course, other schools of thought about the priorities of Soviet foreign policy in the Cold War years, but I believe that these were the most widespread. However, it would be wrong to think that any lobby existed in the MFA framework that would promote the interests of this or that state. I was surprised by the depth of the hostility expressed by the "Americanists" to certain U.S. actions, and how our "Germanists" were opposed to the idea of German unification. Certainly, among the diplomats there were some who could be described as lobbyists, but behind their differing approaches to Soviet foreign policy priorities, they were all united by their concern to find the best and most effective ways of winning the Cold War.

The Beginning of the Yom Kippur War

The mid-1970s, when I worked in the headquarters of the Ministry of Foreign Affairs in Moscow, was a special period in the Cold War. It seemed to be a time when a certain equilibrium had been reached between the two superpowers, the two rival camps, capitalist and socialist. It was widely believed that a near parity, both military and political, had been established between the USSR and the United States. The positions taken by the Soviet Union in international issues had been markedly strengthened.

When I started work at the ministry, preparations for the next General Assembly session had been completed. The Politburo had approved directives for the delegation, as well as its composition. The minister's speech for the General Assembly had been prepared, and many administrative-technical questions resolved. In a word I had inherited a "going concern" from Novikov. It was agreed that I would "monitor" the work of the delegation to the General Assembly throughout the session from Moscow. I cannot speak for the delegation, but for me it was rather useful. After the delegation's departure to New York there was hardly any work left to do in the department. In the UN there was the general debate and the discussion of various organizational issues, and if there were any problems, Gromyko was there to settle them himself. Therefore, there was no need for our assistance. In the early autumn of 1973, therefore, life in the Smolenskaya Square area was pretty uneventful. But, suddenly, all hell broke loose.

Thursday, October 4, 1973, was a normal working day, filled with the usual bureaucratic bustle. There would be no reason for it to stand out in my memory any more than a thousand other humdrum working days, were it not for subsequent events. At 7 P.M., when I was ready to go home, the telephone rang. "The minister wants you right away," barked Gromyko's senior aide, Vasily Makarov, known as "Vaska the Terrible." Gromyko had come back from New York in early October. When I entered his office, I saw Kuznetsov and Korniyenko, head of the U.S. department, already sitting there. Later, Sitenko, the head of the Middle East department joined us.

Since I had missed the beginning of the conversation, I was not able to grasp the thread right away. Bureaucratic etiquette would not permit asking the minister to repeat what he had already said. Soon I understood that Gromyko had called us in to report on the final decision of the Egyptian and Syrian leadership to attack Israel on Saturday, October 6, at 2 P.M. Moscow time. He said that the Politburo had met a few hours ago and decided to order the evacuation of some of the Soviet citizens stationed in Egypt and Syria. Gromyko had given instructions to prepare the cables to that effect to Vladimir Vinogradov and Nuritdin Mukhitdinov, the Soviet ambassadors in Egypt and Syria. During the briefing Gromyko repeated that this information was strictly confidential, especially the date and time of the start of hostilities.

Gromyko was clearly disgruntled. From everything he said it was clear that he and his Kremlin colleagues had not only disapproved of the Arab leaders' decision, but they had done their best to dissuade Presidents Sadat and Assad from taking military action. Gromyko emphasized that negotiations between Brezhnev and Nixon in Washington, in the summer of 1973, had created a good basis for a political solution of the Middle East problem. A new war in the region would only damage the improvement in Soviet-American relations.

The minister was skeptical about the likelihood that the Arab military operation would succeed, though he conceded that the surprise factor would probably give them a certain advantage. When one of us asked if the urgent evacuation of Soviet citizens might tip off the Israelis and the Americans, he responded, "The lives of Soviet citizens are more important to us." Then somebody asked how we should react, in the light of our improved relations, if the Americans were to ask us to explain the reasons for the evacuation. Gromyko got annoyed and remarked that we were not in court, and were under no obligation to give explanations at every turn. Not a very compelling argument, but no one was willing to persist.

The minister dismissed us with some friendly advice: "Don't work late today, save your energy; you'll be needing it very soon." He then added that the four of us—Kuznetsov, Korniyenko, Sitenko, and I—should remain available at all times. When we left the room, I asked Sitenko, the best informed among us on the Middle East, what he thought of the whole situation. He answered, "Don't you know the Jews? They're hardly likely to allow a surprise attack on Israel. Look at what happened in 1967."

Contrary to the minister's instructions, I spent a long time studying all the cables from Cairo and Damascus. Vinogradov and Mukhitdinov had reported on their meetings with Presidents Sadat and Assad, and other Egyptian and Syrian political leaders about the tense situations in these countries, as well as their military preparations. But nowhere in the cables or other sources was there any mention of a date or time for the start of the war. That seemed very strange. Perhaps Gromyko possessed this information, and I would be able to find it out later, I thought.

The following day, October 5, passed rather quietly, although I was constantly on the alert. During a diplomatic reception at the "Arbat" restaurant that evening, I made a point of approaching the ambassadors of Egypt and Syria, and having long conversations with them. It was impossible to detect any sign of an impending war in their behavior or their words. They were in an excellent mood, they joked, and even shared their plans for an excursion outside the city. I could not tell whether they were just being discreet or simply did not know anything themselves. I certainly never brought the matter up.

After the reception I returned to the ministry and went in to see Kuznetsov, expecting some news. Vasily Vasilevich confirmed what the minister had said and told me that the evacuation of Soviet citizens from Egypt and Syria had already begun and was being carried out successfully. More than 2700 women and children and about 1000 family members of the staff of the embassies of the USSR and other socialist countries left Egypt hurriedly, in a matter of days. About the same number of Soviet civilians were evacuated from Syria. Of course, these actions taken by the USSR could not go unnoticed.

Once again I considered our reaction to possible questions by the Americans and others about the departure of our nationals. I was worried that the Americans might ask the Soviet mission in New York for explanations and that Malik would pass the question on to me. What would I do then? "What are you afraid of?" answered Kuznetsov with a smile. "Don't you think that the Americans know what the Arabs are planning?" he continued. "There are so many signs of Egyptian and Syrian military preparations that you have to be deaf and blind not to notice." He was firmly convinced that the Americans would never ask us for explanations. I do not know whether the Americans were aware of the Arabs' plans, but the experienced diplomat was right about one thing: the Americans never asked us about the reasons for the urgent evacuations.

Late that evening I once again looked through the cables from Cairo and Damascus, and again I saw the same picture. There was no mention of the date of the attack on Israel. Reports had been received from the meetings of Vinogradov with Sadat and Mukhitdinov with Assad, respectively, on October 4 and 5. Vinogradov, in particular, had transmitted Brezhnev's message to Sadat, in which the Soviet leader stated his preference for a political solution to the Middle East problem. As to Egypt's military plans, Brezhnev placed full responsibility for their implementation on the Egyptian leadership. Sadat reiterated his belief in the necessity of war, but said nothing about the date or time of the attack. The conversation between Mukhitdinov and Assad was similar. The Syrian president revealed the details of Syria's military plans, but he too was silent about when operations would begin.

It was not until early on Saturday morning, October 6, that Assad urgently summoned the Soviet ambassador and informed him of the decision to attack Israel in a few hours' time, namely, at 2 P.M. that day. On the same morning Sadat merely warned Vinogradov not to leave the embassy, and it was only after the attack had been launched, that he telephoned the ambassador to announce triumphantly that he was already on the East Bank of the Suez.

My bewilderment grew. How could Moscow have known, on the afternoon of October 4, the precise time when the war in the Middle East would begin? Neither the Egyptian nor the Syrian Presidents had disclosed the date in their conversations with the Soviet ambassadors. And it was out of the question for the information to have reached the Kremlin from intelligence sources (the KGB, the GRU) without passing through diplomatic channels. The intelligence services would never conceal information of extreme gravity, such as the timing of an invasion, from the ambassador. The information about the commencement of the hostilities was not even sent to Moscow from our KGB agents or "residents" in Cairo and Damascus.

The source that supplied the Kremlin with this top-secret data is still unknown. It was no doubt some member of the inner circle of the Egyptian or Syrian leadership, who in defiance of strict orders from Sadat and Assad had given—or sold—to Moscow the information about the date and time for the assault on Israel. Who it might have been and how it was done is still a total mystery.

On Saturday morning, October 6, I listened to the radio, watched TV, and read the papers. Everything seemed calm. There was nothing untoward in the cables from the Soviet embassies in Cairo and in Damascus. I even began to think that all our fears had been imaginary, even entertaining the notion that the threat of a new war in the Middle East had been contrived by the Arabs with the idea of hardening our position on the question of a Middle East settlement. I remembered that every year, for the last few years, had been described by Sadat as "decisive" or "critical," and that nothing "decisive" had ever happened. Could it be that 1973 would turn out to be the same? I could not imagine that the intelligence services of the United States, Israel, and other countries, plus the large corps of journalists in the Middle East could have failed to notice the military preparations of Egypt and Syria if these countries were really going to begin a war in a matter of hours. And finally, how could Sadat contemplate fighting a war after having thrown ten thousand Soviet military advisers out of Egypt in 1972?

At 2 P.M. I tuned in to the radio, but there was no sign of any war. Feeling easier in my mind, I left my staff on duty at the office and went to the Diplomatic Academy, where I was scheduled to give a lecture. I had just begun when the dean's secretary brought me a note. It read: "Victor Levonovich, you are urgently needed at the ministry." Without uttering another word I rushed back. It took me twenty to twenty-five minutes to get from the academy to Smolenskaya Square. It was about 4 P.M. when I reported to the minister. "You are late, my dear comrade," said Makarov with undisguised sarcasm. "The minister left to see Leonid Ilyich [Brezhnev] without waiting for your Excellency," he added. "What do I do now?" I asked in embarrassment. "I suggest you go back and continue lecturing—obviously that is more important to you," he continued in the same tone.

Feeling terrible, I wandered back to my office. My assistants Timerbayev and Lozinsky were waiting for me. They said that shortly the first radio reports about the start of military action had come in shortly after three o'clock, particularly from Cairo, which reported that Israeli naval forces had attacked Egyptian troops in the Suez Canal region. Damascus announced an assault by Israeli troops on Syrian positions on the Golan Heights. Cables were also received from Vinogradov and Mukhitdinov that gave a true account of how hostilities had begun and reported that Egypt and Syria had attacked Israel.

As to the time when military operations began, it was precisely at 2 P.M., but local time, not Moscow time, as Gromyko had erroneously reported on

October 4. This explained the misunderstanding that arose because of the one-hour time difference.

Armed with this information, Gromyko reported to Brezhnev, who summoned an urgent Politburo meeting. Taking Kuznetsov, Korniyenko and Sitenko, the minister left for the Kremlin. I didn't dare follow them, and in any case, as I had never been in the Kremlin before, if I appeared alone I would never have been permitted access to Brezhnev. After consulting my colleagues, I decided to wait for Gromyko to return. In the meantime we started to prepare ourselves for a possible meeting of the UN Security Council in connection with the war. We discussed the possible course of events, and the reactions to the war of the United States and other countries. The people in my department were totally unconvinced of the possibility of an Arab victory in the war. The Arab version of the "provocation" by Israel, repeated by Soviet mass media, made us smile. We were convinced that in a few hours Israel would launch a counterattack that would end not only with the capitulation of Egypt and Syria, but a change of governments in those countries and the strengthening of American influence in the Middle East.

Time passed, but Gromyko, Kuznetsov, Korniyenko, and Sitenko had still not returned. It was not until about midnight that they returned, weary and with frayed nerves, telling me what had happened at the meeting of the Politburo. But at the time, the only response they would give me to my persistent requests to fill me in on the Kremlin's decision, was Kuznetsov's curt reply: "What have they decided? To help our Arab friends. Got that?" Then, after a pause, he added in a friendly tone, "You should really drop your lecturing, and be at all meetings at the Kremlin. There's a war on, after all." I followed this good advice and thereafter, throughout the Yom Kippur War, did not miss a single, important Kremlin meeting on the Middle East.

I have published a separate book on the 1973 October war in the Middle East, *Inside the Kremlin During the Yom Kippur War*, so here, I shall confine myself to recounting some episodes of diplomatic history of this war, which have a direct bearing on the course of the Cold War as a whole.

Cooperation or Confrontation?

The Yom Kippur War has a special place in my diplomatic career. There was hardly a day when I did not meet a high-ranking Soviet official, including the general secretary of the CPSU Central Committee L. I. Brezhnev.

Brezhnev held almost daily meetings on the war. Only the inner circle of Gromyko, Defense Minister Grechko, and KGB chairman Andropov attended some of these meetings. At others, the whole Politburo was present. As a rule these inner circle meetings discussed urgent matters, such as the content of Brezhnev's messages to Nixon and the leaders of the Arab states, as well as other documents. The larger meetings discussed basic strategies of Soviet foreign policy in connection with the war and subsequent appropriate actions.

The role of the four of us (Kuznetsov, Korniyenko, Sitenko, and myself) was modest and technical. We took no active part in the discussions, except for our conversations with Gromyko. Our role was confined to the drafting of different documents: messages to heads of state and government; instructions to Soviet ambassadors; press releases; instructions to relevant Soviet organizations; and other documents. Our work was a normal part of the machinery of Soviet foreign policy decision-making.

The paramount consideration for the Kremlin was to ensure that the war did nothing to damage Soviet-American détente, which was so strikingly demonstrated during the summer 1973 meeting between Nixon and Brezhnev. The relations between the two superpowers during the Yom Kippur War were rather inconsistent in character. Despite détente, the Soviet Union and America supported the opposing parties of the conflict. Without the extensive and, above all, military support from the superpowers, neither the Arab countries nor Israel could have waged war. This was well understood by the leaders of the Middle East countries. At the same time, the Arab leaders had begun the war in defiance of the position of the Kremlin, which was clearly put out by the Arab initiative. Neither was the White House pleased by the outbreak of war in the Middle East, which came at a bad time for Washington because it coincided with the "Watergate" crisis.

In the light of all this, from the very first days of the war, both superpowers shared an interest in bringing it to the speediest possible conclusion. Therefore, the main theme of Soviet-American contacts in October 1973 was the cease-fire in the Middle East. Although Moscow and Washington pursued opposite goals in the region, they did everything in their power to prevent the expansion of the war and to avoid their own direct involvement in it.

To a certain extent the superpowers were successful in this. During Kissinger's October 20–22 visit to Moscow, a joint Soviet-American UN Security Council resolution was produced calling for a Middle East cease-fire.

I participated in the work on this document myself, and I can testify that the concern to prevent a further expansion of the war on both sides was so great that the drafting of a mutually acceptable text turned out to be relatively easy. Gromyko was so pleased with the work of the diplomats on the text that he jokingly offered Joseph Sisco, the American Middle East expert, a job at the MFA.

The UN history of the Cold War period records very few examples of such effective cooperation between the superpowers in the Security Council. Only a few hours after the tabling of the joint Soviet-American draft resolution for an immediate cease-fire, it was unanimously adopted without amendment.

It was with great relief that we learned from New York that the Security Council had approved the resolution. It had been our hope that the war would come to an end and that in agreement with the Americans we would be able to bring about peaceful settlement in the Middle East. For the first time since the beginning of the war, I managed to spend an evening at home, instead of in my office at Smolenskaya Square or at the Kremlin.

An Important Politburo Discussion

The closed and open meetings of the Politburo present the greatest interest for understanding the mentality of the Soviet leadership on international politics in the years of the Cold War. I shall briefly reproduce one such meeting.

Despite the Security Council resolution calling for an immediate cease-fire, the fighting continued in the Middle East. The Israelis were anxious to strengthen their hold on the Sinai Peninsula, having crossed the Suez Canal, thus surrounding the Egyptian army and threatening to annihilate it. Panic-stricken, Sadat persistently appealed to Brezhnev for help—even an outright Soviet military intervention—in order to throw back the Israelis.

In Moscow it had become clear that without external pressure on Israel the situation was not likely to change. On October 24, a meeting to discuss the situation went on for several hours in the Kremlin. It was decided to send Nixon an urgent message proposing the immediate dispatch of Soviet and American military contingents to Egypt, to enforce compliance with the Security Council's cease-fire resolution. The message also contained an element that threw Washington into disarray: "I have to tell you squarely and frankly," wrote Brezhnev to Nixon, "that if you do not find it possible to work together with us on this, we shall be forced to consider taking these measures unilaterally." Moscow was playing its trump card, in the belief that the Americans were not prepared to take this military step and would therefore exert the necessary pressure on Israel, and Egypt would be saved.

What actually happened was that after receiving Brezhnev's message late the evening of October 24, Kissinger could not deliver it to Nixon (since the president, it emerged later, was drunk at the time), and he called an urgent meeting of the National Security Council in his absence. Kissinger vastly overdramatized the situation, making it appear that the USSR was on the point of taking immediate military action. The Council decided to place all American armed forces, including nuclear forces, on a full combat readiness footing ("Defcon III").

Early in the morning of October 25 Moscow learned of these emergency measures taken by the American armed forces. Our group of four was summoned to the Kremlin. The Politburo was already in session. After Grechko and Andropov had reported the military alert announced by the United States, the whole Soviet leadership started a discussion that lasted for about five hours.

Brezhnev was angry with the Americans for placing their armed forces on combat readiness footing. He and his colleague characterized this decision of Nixon as irresponsible. "The Americans are claiming that we are threatening them. Where could they have gotten such an idea, and what does this have to do with the message sent to Nixon?" Brezhnev asked. In his opinion, the message simply stressed the need for joint Soviet-American action in accordance with the understanding reached during Kissinger's visit to Moscow a few days before.

As to the Soviet response to Defcon III, opinions were divided. Some argued in favor of the equivalent military measures being taken by the Soviet side. Andropov, for example, thought that the USSR should respond with total mobilization.

Grechko took the most hardest line. He insisted that the counter-action should be essentially of a military nature and recommended drafting an additional 50,000 to 70,000 thousand men for active service from the Ukraine and the Northern Caucasus. He believed that if Syria was to be saved, Soviet troops needed to occupy the Golan Heights.

Everyone there understood that the key question was Soviet readiness to confront the United States and to get involved in a large-scale war. The majority answered this question with a resounding "No." Gromyko declared:

"We should not send Soviet troops; that would lead to confrontation with the United States." Other speakers echoed, "We should not kindle the fire of World War III." Prime Minister Aleksei Kosygin resolutely opposed the idea of sending Soviet troops to the Middle East. He declared, "The United States will not start a war, and we have no reason to start one either." Grechko agreed that Soviet troops were not ready for war. He recognized that the necessary preparatory work had not been done.

While the discussion was in full swing, Brezhnev posed a question: "What if we simply fail to respond to the American nuclear alert?" Then he added, "Nixon is overreacting and we need to give him an opportunity to calm down." The majority of the Politburo meeting welcomed this proposal, and it was decided to proceed accordingly. The main reason for the Kremlin's restrained reaction to the American nuclear alert was that the Soviet Union was not prepared for military action. The General Staff had made no plans for large-scale military operations in the Middle East, and the Politburo had not approved any such plans. Furthermore, on October 25, Moscow was planning a major propaganda event, the International Congress of Peace-loving Forces, to which representatives of over seventy countries had been invited. As the leading peace warrior, Brezhnev intended to deliver a major speech at the Congress; and of course, a hard-line move by the Politburo accompanied by a show of force would be highly detrimental to this propaganda event.

The overall impression that I got from the session was that the Politburo was unanimous in its attitude to the Cold War, which was admirably suited to the purpose of the Kremlin leadership. It gave ample opportunities for implementing the principle of "proletarian, socialist internationalism," that is, the rendering of political, military, and economic assistance to states and forces opposing American-led "international imperialism." At the same time, the Cold War allowed limited cooperation with the capitalist world and principally with the United States, particularly in the field of arms control.

The Yom Kippur War demonstrated that the Soviet Union was not ready for a military showdown with the United States. Neither was Moscow prepared, on the other hand, to renounce its ideological dogmas about the inevitability of the global victory of socialism in favor of striving to build a stable world order. This war was thus a typical and striking illustration of the state of the international relations during the Cold War.

Should We Be Pleased or Sorry?

In late October, after the ending of hostilities in the Middle East, our quartet was, naturally, dissolved and each of us returned to his own business. My most pressing work was to plunge back into the depths of daily departmental chores. With the smoke just clearing from the recent General Assembly session, Gromyko once asked me how the discussion of our "key issue" was going in New York, to which I mumbled something vague about everything being under control.

In 1973 the Soviet Union proposed as an important and urgent UN agenda item the question of a "10 percent reduction in the military budgets of permanent members of the Security Council and the possible use of part of the funds so saved to aid developing countries." Gromyko submitted this proposal in late September in his speech at the General Assembly. On the whole it met with a positive response, in particular from the developing countries. Western states, however, viewed it with caution and skepticism, arguing that in view of the great secrecy of the Soviet military budget, verification would be virtually impossible and that this made the proposal unfeasible.

Then came the Middle East crisis, and the Soviet proposal was left to languish in one of the Assembly's committees. After the end of the Yom Kippur War the UN resumed its normal work and a watered-down resolution was passed on the Soviet proposal, which approved in principle of the idea of reducing military budgets, but which in practice shelved the proposal indefinitely by referring to a specially constituted group of experts.

The Middle East war ended on an evening of formal celebration commemorating the October Revolution. I will always remember the grand government reception at the Kremlin on November 7, 1973, to which my wife and I were invited for the first time. The variety, abundance, and sophistication of entertainment, food, and drink were magnificent and impressive. Everyone was in a festive mood and high spirits. The guests greeted each other warmly, and we received many congratulations on the success of Soviet diplomacy in bringing about peace in the Middle East. My response was to ask myself that same nagging question: "Had we really scored a political victory, or was it just wishful thinking on the part of our leaders and we were just their chorus of 'yes men'?" There was one person, however, who offered me no congratulations—General Sergei Akhromeyev, one of the Soviet Union's most important military experts, with whom I briefly exchanged views on the Middle East. He clearly understood that growing American activity in the region, especially in Egypt, was by no means a sign of any Soviet diplomatic triumph.

It was with these mixed feelings that we began preparations for the Middle East Peace Conference in Geneva. Basic responsibility for the arrangements was assigned to Sitenko and his Middle East department, but since the conference was to be held under UN auspices, my department was also involved in this complicated work. We were just groping our way. It was not clear who would participate in the conference, or what exactly its scope would be. How would the Soviet Union and the United States actually act on the "appropriate auspices" under whom, according to the Moscow agreement with Kissinger, negotiations between the parties should be carried out? And finally, how were we to approach the Palestinian problem, one of the thorniest and most crucial issues?

Nor were we happy about the situation developing in the Middle East. One could hardly call Kuznetsov's trip to Egypt and Syria in late October a success. In Cairo and Damascus the Egyptian and Syrian leaders delivered more complaints than thanks to the USSR for its support during the war. Assad openly accused the Kremlin leadership of violating what he described as the understanding between Moscow and Damascus about an early cease-fire in the Middle East. He repeated his objection to the Soviet-American resolution in the Security Council, calling it pro-Israeli.

For all Kuznetsov's international standing, it would probably have been more useful if Gromyko—himself a member of the Kremlin leadership—had made this difficult and delicate trip instead of one of his deputies. Our "quartet" had once mildly suggested it, but Gromyko did not like to make unpleasant visits, where he might hear some home truth about the USSR. He had no wish to go to the Middle East at the time.

Kissinger, on the other hand, was frenetically busy in that region. In early November he visited Cairo, which resulted in the restoration of American-Egyptian relations. Close personal relations between Sadat and Kissinger were quickly established, and this allowed Washington to maneuver successfully for years to come in the Middle East. As early as November it was American advisers who were behind the scenes in the negotiations on the disengagement of Egyptian and Israeli troops.

Ambassador Vinogradov, of course, continued to send cables stressing that there was no need for concern, but we in Moscow were well aware of the ambassador's propensity to embellish the state of Soviet-Egyptian relations. The MFA departments were receiving information from Cairo, especially from returning diplomats, which suggested otherwise; namely, that we should indeed be concerned about American activity in the Middle East.

A Strange Conference

On Christmas Eve, 1973, Gromyko and a group of diplomats took off for Geneva for the Middle East Peace Conference. Vinogradov, Sitenko, and I were members of the Soviet delegation. Delegations from the United States, Egypt, Israel, and Jordan also came to the conference. Despite our own effort and the urging of the United States, Assad was unwilling to attend, so the seat of the Syrian delegation at the negotiating table remained empty. UN Secretary-General Waldheim also attended the conference.

The conference was convened on the basis of a joint Soviet-American initiative. However, when Gromyko and Kissinger met in Geneva it became clear that the approaches of the superpowers to the peace settlement process were very different. The Soviet Union wanted the conference to tackle the whole range of problems of a peace settlement, including the Palestinian question, thus providing a single mechanism for multilateral negotiations. The United States, on the other hand, wanted the conference to consider separate aspects of a peace settlement, at different bilateral forums, which would only be formally linked. These fundamental differences between countries sponsoring the peace process, compounded by serious disagreements among the Arab states themselves, particularly between Egypt and Syria, made any progress in Geneva in December 1973 unlikely.

Not even the most thorough pessimist among us, however, would have thought that the Geneva conference could fail because of the most trivial of circumstances. On the day of our arrival in Geneva, Waldheim told me that difficulties had arisen in the seating arrangements for the delegations. He showed me different seating plans, which had been rejected by the delegations. "Nobody wants to sit next to Israel," he explained in some embarrassment. It appeared that even the Americans did not agree with the idea of seating the U.S. and Israeli delegations on one side of the secretary-general, who would be chairing the meeting, with the Soviet, Egyptian and Jordanian delegations on the other side. From the U.S. point of view, this would create the impression of a meeting between two opposing parties. Kissinger dug his heels in and would not budge. Because of these disagreements the start of the conference was postponed. Rumors spread around the Palais des Nations that the conference would be aborted. Waldheim invited the heads of delegations to discuss the matter with him.

Soon Gromyko came out of Waldheim's office, smiling. "The conference will take place, but we will be sitting next to the Israelis," he said. Apparently, after all the ministers had made it clear that they were unwilling to give way over the seating arrangements, Gromyko had decided to be sensible and agreed with Waldheim on the following plan: to the right of him, seated clockwise, would be the delegations of Israel, the USSR, Syria (whose seat would be empty), Jordan, the United States, and Egypt. It was with these seating arrangements that the Middle East Peace Conference opened on December 21. I do not know how the Israelis felt sitting next to us; we, ourselves, had no problems with such juxtaposition.

On the first day of the conference all heads of delegations made brief statements, setting forth their familiar positions. Gromyko paid tribute to the positive changes then taking place in the international arena, mentioning the end of the war in Vietnam, the settlement of the status of West Berlin, and the cooperation between the Soviet Union and the United States in the Middle East, reflected in the October cease-fire resolutions of the Security Council. In the light of all these changes, the continuing Middle East conflict, despite the cessation of hostilities seemed, in the minister's opinion, to be impermissible anomaly.

As to the working procedure of the conference, Gromyko proposed that all agreements reached by the participants would then be embodied in decisions of the whole conference. He gave no further details concerning the negotiating procedures and the relationships between the separate stages. I have to admit that during the preparation for the conference, we, the experts, failed to come up with a clear picture of how it was supposed work.

The other participants in the conference also chose to confine themselves to general ideas, and refrained from offering any specifics. Kissinger simply stressed the need for the interested parties to reach agreement within the framework of bilateral negotiations.

Bilateral meetings in Geneva, which the Soviet delegation held with all participants, did nothing to clarify the situation. I recall Gromyko's conversation with Egypt's Fahmy, at which I was present along with Vinogradov. It reflected the chill that had descended on our relations with Egypt. Fahmy expressed neither great delight with Soviet-Egyptian cooperation nor any gratitude for Soviet military and political assistance to Egypt. The sniping between Fahmy and Vinogradov left me, and I believe Gromyko, too, with an unpleasant impression. Every time the ambassador expressed a point of view during the conversation Fahmy would disagree with it, sometimes abrasively. It became quite clear that the new Egyptian minister and the Soviet ambassador did not get on well together.

The reason for this was simple. In the many years of his work in Cairo, Vinogradov dealt mainly with President Sadat. Vinogradov told me that in October 1973 he alone met with Sadat more than thirty times. He maintained good relations with El Zayat, the minister of foreign affairs, and barely noticed Zayat's assistant, Fahmy. He was just not important enough. Fahmy could not forget this.

I intentionally brought up this seemingly insignificant fact. Gromyko's diplomatic contacts, including his conversation with Fahmy, convinced him of the need to improve Soviet-Egyptian relations. He had come to believe that this would be helped, in particular, by replacing Vinogradov, one of the top Soviet ambassadors, who was in the habit of painting our relations with Cairo in a rosy hue. Gromyko's trips to the Middle East in the spring of 1974 were intended to improve our take on the situation in Egypt and Syria, and establish a positive dialogue in Soviet-Egyptian relations under the new circumstances. I remember that after a conversation with Fahmy, followed by a long pause of consideration, Gromyko remarked, "Clearly, it's time for me to go and pay a special visit there myself."

After two days of formal sessions of the conference and numerous bilateral conversations, both of which revealed deep disagreements that I have mentioned above, it became clear that there was no longer any point in our remaining in Geneva. It turned out to be impossible to agree on a follow-up session of the conference or to draft a future plan of action. Gromyko and Kissinger were able to agree that Vinogradov and U.S. ambassador Banker, along with their experts, would stay in Geneva as representatives of the countries sponsoring the peace conference, and would continue their consultations. They also agreed on the creation of a Military Working Group, which was to deal with questions relating to troop disengagement by the parties to the conflict. Banker stayed in Geneva for about a month, and then, on the pretext of needing new instructions, left for Washington and never returned. Vinogradov seemed to like Geneva better, and he stayed by the shores of Lake Geneva for a while, returning to Moscow in the spring of 1974.

Many years later, I was very surprised to read in Gromyko's memoirs that he considered the Geneva Middle East Peace Conference a major Soviet diplomatic success. It was neither my impression nor that of many of my colleagues that during the course of the preparation for the conference or within the session, itself, the position of the Soviet Union had become any stronger. Gromyko seemed to have forgotten that in September 1974, while speaking at the UN, he had himself expressed dissatisfaction that the Geneva conference had gone nowhere. The only thing one could really count as a success of Soviet diplomacy was, perhaps, Gromyko's flexibility in agreeing to seat the Soviet delegation—contrary to protocol—next to the Israelis at the negotiating table.

An important battle of the Cold War was fought in the autumn and winter of 1973. After the Geneva conference, we had no reason to believe that we had won it. And unfortunately, subsequent events in the Middle East proved that we hadn't.

14
AN UNEASY TRUCE IN THE COLD WAR

Preparing for the Next Session of the UN General Assembly

In spite of the sharply differing interpretations of the results of the Yom Kippur War that were revealed on Smolenskaya Square, all foreign policy specialists agreed that détente was the dominant feature of the current international scene in the early 1970s. The spring of 1974 saw the continuation of the active dialogue between the superpowers as well as constant preparations for the next U.S.-Soviet summit meeting. At the same time bilateral and multilateral negotiations were begun on creating a system of collective security for Europe. New prospects for a stable peace in Europe and throughout the world appeared to be opening up.

Many diplomats from the International Organizations Department took part in both areas of this important international political work. Nevertheless, the principal activity consisted in preparing for the twenty-ninth session of the General Assembly. For me, it was the first time I had had to prepare for a General Assembly session since I had come to work at the IOD. I knew that I would be closely observed by both by the highest authorities in the department and my own colleagues. I made a point, therefore, of working, as they say, with my nose to the grindstone.

The most important items in this six-month-long period of work, which began immediately after the New Year and had to be finished by the summer, were determining the "key international issue" to be put forward by the Soviet Union at the UN, preparing policy guidelines for the delegation on all items on the General Assembly's agenda (and there were 112 of these for the twenty-ninth session), and appointing the members of the delegation. I have to say that the most difficult and, to be frank, daunting task of all was that of determining, or rather coming up with, the "key issue." In the IOD this task was addressed with the utmost seriousness.

While, for the Politburo, the approval of the policy guidelines for the delegation and the membership of the delegations was a pure formality, the MFA proposals for the "key issue" were sometimes the subject of heated debate.

Faced with this daunting task at the beginning of 1974, I approached Gromyko for advice or instructions and was brusquely dismissed with: "That's your job!" Nor did I fare much better with Kuznetsov. When I sought the views of other leading members of the department on the subject they sometimes just laughed in my face. "That's your job; what do you think you're being paid for?" There was one thing everyone agreed on; the "key issue" had to be one that neither the West nor the United States would find highly confrontational. There was a clear preference for a disarmament theme, one, moreover, that might be described as preventive in nature. All countries at least paid lip service to the need for arms control measures.

There were many meetings on the subject of the "key issue" in the department. At one of them it was proposed that the "key issue" should be about the effects of military activity on the environment and climate and that the Soviet Union should propose a ban on damaging the geophysical environment for military purposes and prohibiting the use of the forces of nature to the detriment of international security or the well-being and health of human beings. Scientists and the public at large had long been exercised by this problem, and articles were appearing in the press with increasing frequency on questions related to military research in this field. From my time in New York I was already familiar with the interesting statements of U.S. Senator Pell on this issue.

This idea seemed to me extremely attractive as well as nonconfrontational, and I asked Gennady Stashevsky, who worked in the department, to hold the necessary consultations and to prepare material for this "key issue." I knew him from New York as an efficient and thoughtful diplomat. We had worked together for about twenty years, and after his return to Moscow he had become my deputy. I had witnessed many examples of his high level of efficiency and competence. Stashevsky and his group of disarmament people compiled all the necessary documentation to present to the MFA authorities: a draft report to be presented by Gromyko to the Politburo, a draft international convention, and other documents—all in all a pretty thick file on this "key issue."

I took it to Gromyko. He was too busy to look at the file itself but the idea interested him. Sometime later, after talking to various academics and experts he gave his approval for the presentation of the file to the Politburo, but only after warning me that all the material had to be approved by the Ministry of Defense as well. This was no easy task, and one I did not look forward to. I had no particular contacts there, and General Akhromeyev with whom I had worked at the time of the "Yom Kippur War" told me that he did not deal with matters of this kind. After lengthy inquiries, I finally found myself approaching General Nikolai Pesterev, who had often attended the Geneva Committee on Disarmament as a member of the Soviet delegation. He had submitted our material on the "key issue" to his superiors in the ministry and reported that there were no objections from that quarter. The idea of international discussions on the question of the effects of military activity on the geophysical environment was in fact of particular interest to the Defense Ministry, and the minister of Defense, Andrei Grechko, offered to sign a joint note together with Gromyko to the Politburo on the "key issue." This smoothed the way for the approval in 1974 of the initiative, which originated in the MFA. Grechko, however, had made it clear that at the talks on the proposed convention the Defense Ministry would not be presenting any material regarding any of its research activities. We in the MFA, of course, conveyed our understanding of the position of the Defense Ministry and assured them that in no circumstances would we permit anything to be done to damage the military interests of the Soviet Union.

How to Prevent Meteorological Warfare?

Now what was this initiative all about? Humanity has long striven to understand the workings of the elements and to influence the weather. It has striven to reduce to a minimum the destructive effects of inclement natural phenomena and divert them to its own benefit, and many countries have been experimenting and working in this direction. The Soviet Union and other countries, for example, have been making successful use of artificial rainmaking techniques such as the "seeding" of moisture-bearing cumulus clouds with crystals of iodized silver, which condense the moisture in the cloud thus causing rain. This technique has been widely used for agricultural purposes but also for military purposes. According to an article in *Pravda*, during the war in Vietnam the American command used rainmaking techniques in the conduct of a number of military operations. Some researchers have claimed that it would be possible to create an acoustical field on the surface of the sea as a weapon against single ships or whole flotillas.

They also claimed that it is possible to melt the ice in the Arctic and Antarctic, which could totally annihilate a potential enemy. To do this one would first have to explode a low-yield nuclear device buried deep in the ice pack. According to the scientists, this would create a water cushion between the ice and the bedrock so that a large part of the ice cover would slip into the ocean. This in turn would cause tidal waves that would obliterate many coastal cities, regions, and whole countries. Nightmare scenarios like this seem hard to imagine but reputable scientists take it quite seriously. Scientists have also contemplated the possibility of creating artificial tsunami in other ways, one of which would be to shift large blocks of bedrock from the continental shelf into deeper parts of the ocean. Another would be to artificially generate an undersea earthquake—and this, it appears, would actually be possible!

To many people these outlandish ideas seem to come straight out of the works of Jules Verne, but cynics claimed that they were nothing more than fantasies keeping Moscow awake at night. Men of science, however, including those in the West, have said that there is no guarantee that these things will not happen. It was for this reason that Gromyko, in his speech at the twenty-ninth session of the UN General Assembly, proposed an agenda item on the prohibition of activities affecting the natural environment and climate for military purposes, a proposal that was received with great interest.

The serious and nonconfrontational nature of this latest Soviet "key issue" was demonstrated by the fact that Nixon and Brezhnev discussed the problem of freeing humanity from the threat of meteorological warfare at their 1974 summit. Out of concern to limit the potential danger to humanity of potentially new means of waging war and recognizing that activities affecting the environment and climate "might have broad, lasting, and serious consequences harmful to the well-being of people," both leaders expressed their support for more effective measures designed to ban the manipulation of the environment for military purposes. Brezhnev and Nixon agreed that Soviet and American experts in the field should meet to consider the problem.

This Soviet-American understanding naturally lent further weight to our "key issue." In view of the complexity of the problem the Soviet delegation was asked to provide comments explaining of our proposal. It was quite unprecedented for the Western regional group at the UN to invite the Soviet delegation to discuss one of its own proposals at one of their closed meetings. I eagerly accepted the invitation. My brief opening remarks were followed by a host of questions. The main question was whether the Soviet Union was conducting research in meteorological warfare and whether it would be willing to present information on the subject in the course of negotiations. I had no choice but to do my level best to dodge the issue in order to avoid "damaging the military interests of the Soviet Union," as I had been so unequivocally warned in Moscow.

After a wide-ranging discussion in the General Assembly the resolution was adopted by 126 votes in favor and only 5 abstentions. The resolution called for an international agreement on the subject that would prohibit the use of the environment for military purposes; that is, the waging of "weather warfare."

We were delighted by the result, and I felt that the UN had taken a historic decision. A start had been made on erecting an international legal barrier to a colossal threat to the whole of humanity. It was a wonderful feeling. I myself became a great enthusiast and started giving lectures as well as writing articles on the subject. I even sent one to the *New York Times*, but unfortunately it was not published. Charlotta Curtis, deputy to the editor-in-chief, replied, saying that in spite their best efforts they were unable to find space for my "interesting article." This confirmed my opinion that in the Cold War even a newspaper like the *New York Times*, whose motto was "All the News That's Fit to Print," was not about to publish an article by a Soviet diplomat.

"The Delegation Must Be Chosen Intelligently"

Preparing the rest of the material for the General Assembly session, and in particular the directives for the agenda for the use of the delegation, although hard work, was essentially not too difficult. As I have said the agenda for the twenty-ninth session included more than a hundred items, such as the banning of napalm, the work of the UN University, the elimination of all forms of religious intolerance, and so on. On the basis of past practice (most items were carried over from one session to another) as well as our general approach to the various problems, our department was generally able to produce a delegation position, and approval of the directives by the Politburo was a pure formality.

An extremely delicate problem, however, was the composition of the delegation to the General Assembly session. Normally, the delegation consisted of five members and five deputies, as well as a few dozen advisers, experts, and nondiplomatic support staff. The Politburo, of course, had to approve only the senior members of the delegation. Since this was the first time I had had to make up the delegation, I asked Gromyko what the principles were on which I should base my selection. After a moment's thought he produced the following dictum: "The delegation must be chosen intelligently." Then, after a moment's further thought, he added that the delegation must include representatives of all the union republics and, preferably, some women. I was prompted to ask the minister on what principle I should base my selection of the members of the fair sex, but I checked the impulse in case he should take the question seriously and after lengthy rumination come up with another pearl of wisdom. When I suggested that he might care to name the nine persons (he himself was the tenth) he would like to see in his delegation, he simply repeated with some irritation that the composition of the delegation was a matter requiring some thought.

I then had to revert to the practice of previous years and work on the principle of rotation in the selection of the representatives of the union republics. This, however, turned out not to be so simple, since some of the republics had previously been represented in the delegation more frequently than others. How was I going to work out this rotation? Alphabetical order? By how active certain republics had been in foreign affairs? But who would decide their level of activity and how? There was another problem too. In a number of the republics the foreign ministers—and it was precisely they whom I intended to include in the Soviet delegation to the UN General Assembly were also the prime ministers and their inclusion in the delegation might cause unnecessary difficulties.

There was another thing. I happened to propose the inclusion of the foreign minister of a certain republic in the delegation but the high-ranking official of the Central Committee of the CPSU, whom I had decided to consult, objected: "What are you thinking of? Surely not the representative of a republic that hasn't fulfilled its plan for the delivery of cotton?" Realizing my lack of political sophistication, I proposed the foreign minister of another republic, which not too long before had enthusiastically welcomed Brezhnev and which the Soviet leader had commended highly for its achievements in the building of communism. I had obviously guessed right—the new name was approved.

The choice of female candidates was even harder and in the case of our IOD there were special difficulties. There were, of course, in the Soviet Union a number of women's organizations, but, for one reason or another, their representatives were not held in high esteem in the MFA, but when I proposed nominating one of our film stars for the delegation, following the example of the Americans who had appointed Shirley Temple to theirs, people just laughed in my face. Anyway, in spite of the difficulties and delicacy of the selection of the female representatives for the delegation we succeeded in doing the job. The delegation of the USSR to the regular sessions of the General Assembly, at least in my time, had always included a woman, either as a member or an alternate member, and in 1974 we were even able to include two women: Tira Tairova, the foreign minister of Azerbaijan, and K. Proskurnikova from Moscow. As a rule the women took their new diplomatic duties very seriously and made important contributions to the work of the delegation as a whole. I have very warm memories of the participation in the work of the UN of two well-known public figures, Viktoriya Siradze from Georgia and Aleksandra Biryukova from Moscow.

Personally, I found the task of selecting the delegation, especially its upper echelon, one of my most disagreeable and thankless. It is true that it won me a certain popularity. As the official in charge of the IOD responsible for deciding on the initial composition of such a high-powered delegation (the names of the members of the delegation were even published in the national newspapers), I received a lot of invitations from various republics to visit their popular resorts and take my vacation in the Baltic states, the Caucasus, and Central Asia. There is no harm in admitting that I sometimes availed myself of these invitations, although I am sure that my gracious hosts realized that my authority in selecting the members of the Soviet delegation were actually somewhat limited.

In the MFA there were also many diplomats who were anxious to work in the delegation to the UN as advisers or experts. They would apply to the IOD and we, to the extent possible and desirable, tried to accommodate requests from those best qualified. This, to my gratification, served to strengthen cooperation between the IOD and the other departments of the MFA. They were pleased to because the experience enhanced their professional skills as well as enabling them to benefit materially, and a two- or three-month stay in New York made this possible.

Of course, it was not possible to satisfy all the requests to attend the General Assembly session and there were inevitably some disappointments and at times even irrational resentment.

Anyway, when Gromyko was making his amendments to the proposed list of delegation members, he would cross out his own name as the head of the delegation and say: "Let the Politburo decide who is to lead the delegation," and then sign the list for submission to the Politburo. In the Politburo, the general secretary of the Central Committee of the CPSU, who usually chaired the meeting, would ask: "Well, comrades, shall we ask Andrei Andreyevich to lead the delegation? Any objections?" There were, of course, no objections and the matter was settled.

As a rule, other countries too named their foreign ministers to head of their delegations, and normally these ministers would stay for only the first week or two of the session. The rest of the time the delegations would be headed by the permanent representatives to the UN. Deputy permanent representatives and the heads of departments were also normally members of delegations.

Some members of the Soviet delegation—and indeed of other delegations—were not professional diplomats but members of parliaments, government representatives, and other public figures. They played a useful role both from the standpoint of national interests as well as those of the departments they represented. Sometimes I would ask Kuznetsov why certain names suddenly appeared on the list after its inspection by the minister, and he would reply significantly: "For reasons of the highest order."

A Missed Opportunity in the Cyprus Conflict

In the summer of 1974, international détente was marked by an important event—the visit to Moscow by President Nixon. As a result of this new summit meeting a number of agreements were signed. The hospitality with which he was greeted in the Soviet Union, his visit to Brezhnev in the Crimea, their trips together to the Black Sea, the intense media coverage of the president's stay in the USSR, all helped to create a climate of opinion in the Soviet Union where Nixon began to be perceived almost as a committed supporter of friendly Soviet-American relations. The acrimonious "kitchen debates" of Khrushchev's day were now a thing of the past.

I did not take any direct part in the talks and was merely invited to attend the signing of the documents and the reception in the Kremlin in honor of the president's arrival. It was the first time I had been able to see Nixon up close. In spite of the success of the talks, he looked strained, tense and absent. I got the impression that he was in no mood for conversation or banter, and he left the reception quite early. Perhaps he was already apprehensive about the possibility of impeachment.

The news of Nixon's ouster came as a complete surprise to political circles in Moscow. The view was expressed even in MFA circles that Nixon's impeachment was the work of rightist, anti-Soviet circles in the United States and was intended to punish him for his "departure from the imperialist, class struggle policy toward the USSR." One way or another, Nixon's departure from the political scene was a matter of some regret to the Kremlin, and I heard more than once that Brezhnev felt that Nixon was someone he could get along with.

Although the political weather forecast for the summer of 1974 had not predicted any storms, one did burst in the Eastern Mediterranean. The new hot spot was Cyprus. In the middle of July a group of Greek officers mutinied against the government of President Makarios. The rebel officers gained control of a large part of the island and announced their goal of "enosis," or the union of Cyprus with Greece, a member of NATO, thereby eliminating the independence and sovereignty of the Republic of Cyprus, an active member of the nonaligned movement.

A few days after the uprising in Cyprus, another member of NATO, Turkey sent troops to the island. Its justification was the need to protect the Turkish community of Cyprus. In this way, this small, defenseless country became the scene of an armed conflict. The member states of NATO tried to keep it in the family, as it were, and resolve the conflict and snuff out this military flare-up among themselves. They were unsuccessful, and the fighting spread.

This was a unique situation. It was the first time since the start of the Cold War that an armed conflict had broken out between two members of NATO, Greece and Turkey, and although the scene of the conflict was the territory of a third state, the essence of the situation in Cyprus remained unchanged. It revealed the existence of serious differences that might lead to the use of force or even outright war between two NATO allies.

The Cyprus situation could not be compared to what had happened in Hungary in 1956 or Czechoslovakia in 1968 when conflicts within the Warsaw Treaty Organization were resolved by the Soviet Union by force; nevertheless, it did give clear opening to criticism of NATO. In September 1974, Brezhnev made a point of mentioning that "the world has been given further clear evidence of the dangerous role played by the NATO bloc in international life and how the very nature of this bloc and its fundamental political goals are incompatible with the interests of the freedom, independence, and security of the peoples of the world."

The summer of 1974 was a hot one for me, in both senses of the word. At precisely the peak of preparations for the General Assembly session we were suddenly and without warning confronted with the events in Cyprus. Along with the appropriate territorial department, the IOD was instructed to draft the tactical approach to the problem. The consensus was that Soviet interests would be best served by the maximum internationalization of the Cyprus problem. The mission in New York was instructed to give its vigorous support to the representatives of Cyprus at the UN and to work for the adoption of a Security Council resolution demanding the halting of foreign military intervention and calling for the withdrawal of foreign troops from the island. With the active support of the Soviet delegation the Security Council adopted precisely just such a resolution.

The situation in Cyprus, however, remained just as tense. On the initiative of the United States and other NATO members, talks were held in Geneva attended by representatives of Cyprus and other interested parties, but they did nothing to improve the situation. It was clear that new proposals were necessary. Kuznetsov, who was acting foreign minister at the time, instructed me to submit proposals on the Cyprus question. After consulting my colleagues, I proposed that the Security Council take the initiative of convening an international conference under the aegis of the UN. Kuznetsov liked the idea, although he did express some doubt about whether NATO would agree to a conference. "They won't let us into their backyard," Kuznetsov remarked. "Well, in that case, they'll have to come up with a Brezhnev doctrine of their own," I replied.

Kuznetsov asked for detailed proposals for the conference to be submitted to the General Assembly session and told me that I would have to present them in New York. He also instructed me to prepare a directive for the mission requiring it to support a new Security Council resolution demanding the cessation of foreign intervention in the internal affairs of Cyprus. We promptly carried out both of these instructions, but, as sometimes happens with the best-laid plans, something went wrong.

That summer, Malik was on vacation in the Soviet Union and was not abreast of the diplomatic moves in the Cyprus business, including the draft directive to the Soviet delegation instructing it to support the Security Council resolution. When he flew into New York and was told by the mission people who had come to meet him that the Security Council was meeting at that very moment, he asked to be driven directly to the UN instead of the mission. Arriving at the meeting, he took over from his deputy, Safronchyuk, and announced that he was not ready to take part in the voting and intended to make a statement. He proposed that the vote be postponed until the next meeting.

Since it was an urgent matter and all delegations, including the Soviet delegation, had already spoken several times, Malik's request was denied, and the vote took place late that evening. It is hard to say why Malik, in response, voted against the resolution. Most probably he was trying to hedge his bets.

On the Saturday morning I was dismayed when I heard on the radio that Malik had vetoed the Security Council resolution in spite of the decision of the Politburo. This was something unheard of in Soviet diplomatic practice! I rushed to Smolenskaya Square. Kuznetsov was already in his office. "What are we going to do?" I asked Vasily Vasilevich. "First, call TASS and the newspapers to make absolutely sure that none of this appears in our press. Then, get in touch with Malik and find out what happened. He'd better find some way of explaining it." I proceeded accordingly.

What had happened was that the directive to support the resolution sent on Friday was waiting for Malik at the mission while he was at the Security Council meeting, and he only found out about it when he had returned from the UN after the vote had already taken place. Malik found himself in a truly difficult position. To his credit, he did not lose his head and immediately set about telephoning all the ambassadors in the Security Council, explained the situation, and asked for a special meeting of the Council to be convened urgently in order to repeat the vote.

Although it was a Saturday, all his colleagues agreed, and the vote was held over again. This was a striking example of professional solidarity and consideration among diplomats—even during the Cold War! As a result

Security Council Resolution 357 was adopted unanimously, as was reported in the Soviet press.

The Soviet proposal to hold an international conference on the problem of Cyprus was announced by Gromyko in his speech at the opening of the General Assembly. I had instructions to make a special statement on the subject in which it was proposed that the Cyprus problem be considered at a representative international forum that would reflect the political realities of the world at the time. The idea was to convene an international conference under the aegis of the UN attended by Cyprus, Greece, Turkey, and all the members of the Security Council. In order to encourage the widest possible support for the idea of the conference I stated that additional states could be invited to attend, in particular from among the nonaligned countries. An important point in the Soviet draft was the fact that any decisions taken at the conference would be guaranteed by the permanent members of the Security Council. The Soviet Union attached no validity to the London-Zurich agreements on guarantees to Cyprus, to which it was not a party.

At the General Assembly session it was apparent that the Western powers were attempting to divert the discussion of the Cyprus problem. They clearly viewed it as one that should be resolved by their own efforts without the intervention of other states, particularly the Soviet Union. Therefore, they either ignored or refused to support the idea of convening a conference under the aegis of the UN.

Nevertheless, a great many countries took part in the discussion, and the proposal to hold the conference won the support of President Makarios of Cyprus and many nonaligned delegations.

In the talks between Gromyko and George Mavros and Turan Gunes, the foreign ministers of Greece and Turkey, at which I was present, the former supported the proposal, while the latter did not oppose it. Both ministers opposed in private and in public in the General Assembly the partition of Cyprus and *enosis*, that is, annexation of part of the island by Greece and the other part by Turkey. Mavros vigorously called for the withdrawal from Cyprus of Turkish troops, whose number he put at 40,000, while Gunes justified their presence by the need to protect the Turkish population from the "atrocities of the Greek military junta."

As for the core idea of the Soviet proposal for a conference—the creation of a system of guarantees for Cyprus in which the Soviet Union itself would take part, although Mavros himself criticized the London-Zurich agreements on guarantees, he and Gunes both avoided mentioning Gromyko's views on guarantees.

In his numerous talks with other heads of delegation in New York Gromyko never missed the opportunity of pinning most of the blame for the events in Cyprus on "certain NATO circles" who were after "more and more bases" in Cyprus. "I'm sure you can guess whom I mean," he said to Mavros, implying the United States, and said frankly to the Greek that the withdrawal of "every last one" of the foreign troops in Cyprus, including, obviously in his mind, the dismantling of the British military base, was one of the major goals of Soviet policy.

Within the context of the Cold War the Soviet Union tried to exploit the Cyprus conflict to its maximum advantage in the summer of 1974. Although the conflict involved directly two members of NATO—Greece and Turkey—and considerably widened the breach between them, we were not able to weaken NATO's position in global terms. NATO simply did not allow the Soviet Union to insert itself into a solution to the Cyprus problem as a guarantor of an international agreement, something that would have been the prize of our proposed conference. At the General Assembly, all that happened was the adoption of two resolutions demanding the prompt withdrawal of all foreign forces and foreign military personnel from Cyprus, the ending of the foreign military presence on the island and indeed any military presence. The resolutions were fine, but they were not what we had been trying to achieve. That was why I was dogged by a feeling of dissatisfaction, the feeling that the opportunities offered by the Cyprus conflict had not been grasped. What opportunities and when—these were questions that were hard to answer.

Appointment as a Member of the Collegium

My first year of work in MFA headquarters was quite successful. What I found particularly valuable was my involvement in the decision-making process at the highest level during the Yom Kippur War. It was as if I were taking a doctorate in advanced political and diplomatic studies. The experience of the annual, regular sessions of the General Assembly—from working to produce the "key issue" up to taking part in the adoption of resolutions by the UN on all items on its agenda—was not attended by any special difficulties. Even acclimatizing myself to my new colleagues and the complicated bureaucratic machinery of the MFA was quite painless. When I returned from the New York sector of the Cold War front to Moscow headquarters, I did not encounter any major problems.

When, in December 1974, Vladimir Lavrov, at that time chief of the Personnel Department, told me that he was preparing the papers to be submitted to the Central Committee on my appointment to the Collegium of the MFA, it was apparent that Gromyko and Kuznetsov were pleased with my work. Although membership in the Collegium was approved by the government, candidates were invited to a meeting of the Secretariat of the Central Committee for interview. Very soon I was officially appointed by the government to the Collegium of the MFA, a position I held for twelve years.

Just a few words about the Collegium. It included the minister, his deputies, and the heads of the principal departments. In the 1970s and 1980s there were never more than twenty or so senior diplomats as members. However, I don't want to exaggerate its importance. The Collegium was not responsible for the work of the ministry as a whole and still less for foreign policy as such. The running of the ministry was solely the responsibility of the minister. The Collegium acted as the minister's consultative body.

My many years of membership did not leave me with the impression that it was a body of any great use or effectiveness. Its meetings were fairly regular—about once or twice a month and usually chaired by the minister. The questions it considered were extremely varied, ranging from relations between the Soviet Union and some other country to preparations for or the results of various conferences. Personnel matters also came up—the appointment or transfer of diplomats. The rapporteur was usually given twenty minutes to introduce the subject, and this was followed by a question and answer period and a discussion. The discussion was then summed up by the minister as chairman. There was never a shortage of speakers, anxious to get their moment in the spotlight, so to speak, what one heard was mostly a repetition of the official line and an echoing of the views of the minister. To be fair, however, Gromyko was always asking people to voice new ideas. "If only one out of ten of these fresh ideas were to prove good, we would be that much better off," he liked to say. But no one particularly wanted to be responsible for any of the other nine dud ideas or proposals for fear that it would damage his authority.

I do not mean to say that there were no fresh ideas among the diplomats who were members of the Collegium. Not at all; but for the most part they were reserved for private conversations. People were afraid of saying anything "out of line" in public that might be at variance with the official party line. This was one of the flaws in the Collegium and indeed throughout the Soviet system. For that reason, meetings of the Collegium, which at times were attended by several dozen people, including guests from the Central

Committee and the KGB, were not and could not be a breeding ground for fresh or original ideas.

Nevertheless, even this rather formalized exchange of views at least widened the range of sources of information. As they say, it is all food for thought, and in the literal sense of the word, membership in the Collegium did provide actual "food" in the sense that it entitled one to one of the privileges of the "ruling caste," that of access to the Kremlin catering service and food products, which were unavailable in the stores where "ordinary mortals" shopped. The moment, after many years, when I lost membership in the Collegium, I also lost access to "privileged" food supplies.

The Culmination of Détente

An important step toward the consolidation of détente was the creation in the 1970s of a system of stable relations among European states that set the seal on the results of the Second World War. Gromyko once described this as the number one issue in European politics. It even transcended the confines of the European continent and to a considerable extent determined the global political climate. The Pan-European Conference on Security and Cooperation, which took place in three stages between 1973 and 1975, put the copestone on the truce in the Cold War, which came to be known internationally as détente.

Both the West and the East had an interest in working together to fashion practical norms for peaceful relations among states. What the Soviet Union sought above all was recognition of the inviolability of the frontiers established as a result of the Second World War, that is, the territorial integrity of states. What the West wanted above all were confidence-building measures, the broadening of contacts among the peoples of the world, the exchange of information, and the democratization of world politics.

Initially, there was a wide gulf between the positions of the participants in the conference, but the work done by the delegations of the thirty-three European states, the United States, and Canada was impressive and could well serve as a model of constructive multilateral diplomacy. Kovalev, Dubynin, and Mendelevich were the principal Soviet negotiators. Their realism, understanding of the subject, and persistence did much to ensure the success of the second stage of the conference in Geneva, which lasted about two years and produced the conference's Final Act.

The second or working stage was, of course, decisive, and its proceedings were under the daily scrutiny of Moscow. Gromyko would report several times to the Kremlin leadership; the Collegium of the MFA discussed some specific questions that had arisen at the conference; and Kovalev and other principal negotiators appeared in Moscow from time to time for consultations. I took part in the Moscow discussions, and Gromyko invited me to attend his talks with the foreign ministers of many countries, which often focused on the Conference on Security and Cooperation in Europe. I was sometimes called upon to provide information about the progress of the Vienna negotiations on the reduction of armed forces and armaments in Central Europe as well as other UN topics and disarmament.

The main impression I retained from my participation in the negotiations on the Pan-European Conference was that the Kremlin attached supreme importance to the whole idea—I would say even more importance than our Western partners. In any case, in Gromyko's talks, which I attended, he was usually the first to touch on matters connected with the Pan-European Conference. The Soviet minister expressed his dissatisfaction at the slow pace of the Geneva talks and at time displayed what was for him an uncharacteristic nervousness. In the autumn of 1974 he told Dr. Erich Bielka, the Austrian foreign minister, "We must speed up the work of the European Conference; there's no reason for such delay." He made the same point at a dinner with Sven Andersson, the Swedish foreign minister and asked him to take a more active part and bring to bear Sweden's authority in European affairs.

The interest of the West in humanitarian problems and cultural, artistic, and scientific links was regarded by Gromyko as a desire to interfere in the internal affairs of the Soviet Union and its allies and to impose a Western pattern of life upon them. In conversations with the foreign ministers of socialist countries he talked frankly about the "hostile nature" of attempts at "ideological subversion" by the West. To Andersson, however, he explained that the Soviet Union was ready to cooperate in the area of culture, the solving of humanitarian problems, and exchanges of information but that "everything should be done on the basis of respect for domestic laws and nonintervention in internal affairs and that on this basis we would have no problems."

In response to the Canadian minister's comment that the West attached great importance to contacts between people, Gromyko said that "First we must establish a political climate, an atmosphere for the development for this kind of contact and not artificially decide on a given number of contacts." The Canadian, however, did not agree with this Soviet approach and asserted that it was precisely this kind of contact that would create the right kind of political climate. Listening to the two ministers arguing, I couldn't help thinking of the old conundrum of the chicken and the egg—which came first?

Gromyko was irritated by a French proposal to open some French libraries in the Soviet Union. "For what purpose?' he wanted to know, "we publish a tremendous number of French books here in the Soviet Union and they can be found in any library." This was the reasoning he used to oppose the French proposal.

He also found some Western proposals concerning military détente frivolous and destructive. For example, he once told his Canadian colleague that the requirement to report all troop movements was preposterous. Almost all Soviet military units are moved one or two hundred kilometers during the winter. "What kind of threat is that to anyone?" he asked. Gromyko appealed to his negotiating partners to bear the realities in mind and not to complicate further the already complex questions of military détente.

The closer the conference in Geneva came to concluding its work on the final document, the more impatient the Kremlin grew. One of the signs of this was the fact that in the summer of 1975 it became almost impossible to get to see Gromyko. He was preoccupied with the business of the Pan-European Conference. When the Final Act was ready and the delegation returned to Moscow, a reception was arranged in their honor to celebrate the occasion. Speaking at the UN, Gromyko called the Final Act "one of the most important documents of our time." The diplomats who had taken part in the Geneva negotiations were decorated with various national medals and orders. In this, Brezhnev was a lot more generous than Stalin, who did not even reward his diplomats at the Yalta Conference.

Agreeing to Disagree

In 1975, there took place another important meeting at which the spirit of cooperation prevailed. It was the first review conference of the Nuclear Non-Proliferation Treaty, which was held in May, again in Geneva. Agreement was reached on this treaty only after long and arduous negotiations, and many states, including two nuclear powers, France and China, declined to become parties to it. The work of the conference, in which I participated, was very hard, with practically every issue was deadlocked at one point or another. Nuclear powers, which in spite of their obligations under the treaty were unable to reach agreement on prohibiting nuclear tests, came in for particularly harsh criticism. Many participants were anxious to see a revision of some of the fundamental provisions of the treaty. Others—supporters of the treaty—fiercely opposed this.

The conference was drawing to a close without an agreed final document—a declaration—having been achieved. The evening before the final day of the conference Inga Thorsson from Sweden, the chairman of the conference, convened a meeting in her office of the representatives of the depository states of the treaty (the USSR, the United States, and the United Kingdom) and some of the other most active delegates. The meeting went on until 4 A.M. without our being able to reach any agreement. Despondent, we all dispersed to our hotels—the conference was clearly doomed to failure.

The next day, the last meeting of the conference was scheduled for 4 P.M.—what one delegate described as the funeral of the conference. However, at 11 A.M. Mrs. Thorsson summoned the delegates to her office and presented them with a draft final declaration, which she had prepared. The document was drafted on the basis on the various texts of the conference, and included language we had all agreed on and language we had not. On the most controversial issues Mrs. Thorsson had used her own language. As she handed round the text, she said: "This text is not ideal for any of you, but it's the only chance of saving the conference and doing something to strengthen the Non-Proliferation Treaty. I'm not prepared to change a single word or syllable of it; otherwise, it will destroy a balance which all of you might find acceptable. Please let me know your answers within the hour."

Our delegation looked at the text and certainly did not find it ideal, but agreed to accept it. Otherwise, we would not have made the slightest progress in détente, which was the prevailing trend in international life. The other delegations came to the same conclusion, and the conference ended successfully with the adoption of the document. For this, great credit must go to Inga Thorsson, the eminent Swedish public figure and diplomat. The success of the Geneva conference is due to her diplomatic skills and abilities.

We Soviet diplomats were pleased with the agreements that had been concluded as well as the truce in the Cold War and chalked it up as one of our major successes. We felt that it was the unusually active role of Soviet diplomacy that had set the seal on the easing of international tension. As Soviet leaders never tired of repeating in those years: "The process of détente is an achievement of all the peoples of the world; it is irreversible and is continually gaining momentum."

Once, for example, in Helsinki Brezhnev claimed that the results of the negotiations were such that there were no victors and no vanquished, no winners and no losers. In his view everyone won, the Eastern as well as the Western countries, the peoples of the socialist as well as the peoples of the capitalist countries, members of alliances as well as neutral countries, small countries as well as big countries. In another speech the Soviet leader expressed the view that the results of the Pan-European Conference offered nothing more or less than an opportunity for its participants to "glimpse the future of our continent and map out the routes for the development of relations between interested countries in conditions of peaceful coexistence."

So, in the view of the Soviet leaders, "the most important document of our time"—the Final Act of the Pan-European Conference—had made détente "irreversible," given it concrete form and substance, and opened a window onto the future of Europe. I think that many of us, including myself, shared that view, or at least hoped that things would turn out that way. What a serious disappointment that turned out to be! In a couple of years the international situation had once again deteriorated badly, and people stopped talking about the irreversibility of détente.

As for glimpsing the future, I am sure that even if you had read and studied the text of the Final Act a hundred times over you would never have foreseen what would happen in Europe in just fifteen years after it was signed. In any case, shortly after the Helsinki Conference renewed fighting broke out on the battlefields of the Cold War.

"This Détente Is No Use to Us"

The success of the Pan-European Conference was welcomed most warmly by the "Europeanists" and others of their persuasion in the MFA. Rumor had it within the MFA that they had coined the phrase "the irreversibility of détente," which made them very proud. The "Americanists," however, felt quite differently. They, in their turn, expressed their gratification at the results of the Helsinki Summit, since the U.S. president was one of the protagonists, but there is no harm in admitting that the United States was not as enthusiastic about the Pan-European Conference as most European countries.

Experience, however, showed that détente, the truce in the Cold War, could not halt the arms race. Here is a sample of a typical conversation that took place in the executive dining room of the MFA between the "Europeanist" Dubynin, the "Americanist" Komplektov, and myself. Dubynin criticized the United States for sharply increasing its stock of nuclear warheads during the period of détente. Komplektov, for his part, pointed out that in recent years, including the period of the Pan-European Conference, the European NATO allies of the United States had continued to increase their military budgets over previous years. I had to acknowledge, for my part, that we too had nothing particularly to be proud of on that score. During the years when détente was at its height, the number of Soviet warheads had increased by some 150 percent, I pointed out. A colleague who happened to be sitting at a nearby table overheard our conversation and remarked sarcastically: "So this is how the participants in the Pan-European Conference understand the process of making détente a reality and making their contribution to it?" This made us all feel quite uncomfortable.

We all understood very well that in spite of the principles of equal, good-neighborly and mutually beneficial relations so solemnly proclaimed at Helsinki, none of the participants in the Pan-European Conference was prepared to give up the basic premises of its foreign policy. The Soviet Union was not about to give up its own foreign policy principles any more than the United States was. This was clearly demonstrated at the Twenty-Fifth Congress of the CPSU, which was held in February 1976, six months after the Helsinki Conference, where stress was laid on the immutability of the principle of proletarian internationalism, which was central to Soviet foreign policy. "As we see it," Brezhnev declared at the Congress, "giving up proletarian internationalism would be tantamount to stripping the Communist Party and the workers' movement as a whole of a powerful, tried and trusted weapon and would be giving a gift to the class enemy."

Accordingly, when, in the mid-1970s during the civil war in Angola, a People's Republic was proclaimed, with the pro-Soviet A. Neto as its head, the Soviet Union started to provide him and his supporters with every possible kind of assistance. The new regime was supplied with the necessary modern weaponry, and it was given direct military assistance in its operations against the adversaries of the regime. Thus, no "gift was offered to the class enemy," and proletarian internationalism was given free rein.

For their part, the "class enemy" and its major supporter, the United States, roundly condemned the actions of the Soviet Union and opposed them in every possible way.

At one of the meetings of the Collegium of the MFA the question of the civil war in Angola and détente unexpectedly claimed everyone's attention during the discussion of the results of the thirtieth session of the General Assembly. In my report I mentioned the strong statement of Daniel Moynihan, the permanent representative of the United States at the UN, at a plenary meeting of the General Assembly in which he attacked the Soviet Union for its intervention in the affairs of Angola and contended that the Soviet actions were contrary to the policy of détente. I also quoted from another U.S. statement that read: "If the (Soviet) intervention in Angola continues, no government in Washington can remain passive and its reaction will have serious long-term consequences." It also stated that the dubious advantages the Soviet Union hopes to derive from its actions in Angola will be nothing compared with the difficulties they will provoke. These American statements angered many of those attending the meeting of the Collegium.

The head of one of the African departments, Aleksei Shvedov, called Moynihan's statement provocative and said that Soviet support for Angola was decisive for the fate of Africa as a whole. Another member of the Collegium, Mikhail Kapitsa, an eminent diplomat, known for his ultrapatriotic, anti-American views, sharply condemned Moynihan as "the mouthpiece of American imperialism," and said that détente, which was weakening the influence and authority of the Soviet Union in the developing countries, was something we had no use for. Other participants shared this view.

Gromyko, in his summing up, confirmed the vital importance of the principle of proletarian internationalism and attempted to wax philosophical. He said that détente and the position of countries on this subject was the focal point on international politics. This very fact, according to him, showed that it was not just a myth or a flashy slogan, but that behind it lay a real switch from confrontation and brinkmanship to mutually beneficial cooperation among states. He unreservedly justified Soviet assistance to Angola and dodged the question of how to reconcile that with détente and mutually beneficial cooperation between the Soviet Union and the United States. Instead, he brushed it off with some generalization about the need to make this cooperation more and more of a concrete reality. When the minister mentioned the subject of making détente a concrete reality, those of us who had taken part in the conversation in the dining room looked at each other and smiled.

"Please, Don't Panic!"

The most obvious symptom of a new flare-up of the Cold War, which showed that détente was not just marking time but beating a retreat, was a noticeable cooling in Soviet-American relations. Although at the meeting with President Ford in November 1974 in Vladivostok reconfirmed the determination of the two powers to implement unreservedly the agreements and commitments entered into over the past few years, the actual working negotiations between the diplomats of both sides were getting nowhere. When, soon after the Vladivostok meeting, I asked Viktor Sukhodrev, the brilliant interpreter, who was an unfailing presence at every single Soviet-American summit, about his impressions of the meeting with Ford, he replied very briefly, but significantly: "Well, he's no Nixon!"

The relations established between the Kremlin and the Carter administration were no improvement. For some reason, the proposals on arms control and disarmament brought to Moscow in March 1977 by Cyrus Vance, the new U.S. secretary of state, were rejected out of hand. I had met him a few times in New York before he took over the State Department. He had always had a keen interest in the Soviet Union and never gave me the impression of being fiercely anti-Soviet. Nevertheless, his proposals for arms limitation were dismissed by Gromyko as an attempt to "undermine serious dialogue" between Moscow and Washington by brandishing "populist slogans" with the idea of using our rejection of them against us. "Basically, the Americans are trying to shift the blame for everything to us," he remarked after the end of the talks with Vance.

In those years I met Gromyko quite a few times. He was ruffled by the slightest suggestion that détente had fizzled out and that it had not lived up to expectations. He would always interrupt anyone who expressed disappointment with the results of Helsinki with "Please, don't panic!" When one of his speechwriters included a critical judgment about progress in the implementation of the Helsinki agreements in the text of his speech to the UN General Assembly, Gromyko deleted it.

However, in his speech at the UN in 1977, Gromyko devoted a good deal of space to an analysis of the process of détente. Indeed, on this occasion he himself even somewhat strengthened the language of his text. For the first time in many years he uttered a warning that " in the present situation with its complex tissue of pluses and minuses 'the process of détente' was still not proof against hold-ups or even reversals." He condemned "certain circles" which were prodding the world back to the times of the Cold War. As for the formula of the "irreversibility of détente," Gromyko was now, of course, no longer using it.

Grasping at Straws

In 1977 I was instructed by the minister to prepare some "unprovocative, constructive proposals" for the UN General Assembly. Accordingly, the IOD drafted the Declaration on the Deepening and Consolidation of Détente. With this document we intended to halt the drift toward confrontation. According to the terms of our draft the Soviet Union was to call on all states to support the declaration and thus demonstrate their readiness to end the Cold War. Moreover, on my own initiative we also prepared a draft resolution on the prevention of nuclear war, which we also planned to submit to the General Assembly.

Both texts were based on the language of the UN Charter and other documents approved by the overwhelming majority of states. We included, of course, language about respect for human rights and fundamental freedoms, the encouragement of mutual understanding among people by the development of contacts between them, language which was so important to the Western countries, as well as many other points which were normally approved without difficulty.

These regular initiatives of ours at the thirty-second session of the General Assembly (which, of course, bore the title of "key issues") were met around the world with little enthusiasm. This was not because they contained any unacceptable or controversial points, but because they were being put forward by a country that many thought was one of those primarily responsible for the decline of the policy of détente.

The discussion of the Soviet proposals in New York was quite uninspired, and there was the danger that our declaration on détente would be stillborn. Those of us in New York began to show signs of alarm. Oleg Troyanovsky, our new permanent representative to the UN, was particularly worried. For him this session of the General Assembly was a kind of debut. I don't remember which of us in these difficult circumstances got the idea of persuading one of the nonaligned or neutral countries' ambassadors who enjoyed particular respect and authority to take on the role of coordinator or even principal negotiator of the text of the declaration. It was the permanent representative of Iran, Fereydun Hoveida, who expressed an interest in this role. He was very well known in New York. He was wealthy, married to a young American woman, and frequented the highest echelons of New York society. He was the brother of the Iranian prime minister who was executed a year after Khomeini took power, and liked the idea of being the center of attention in the General Assembly. He set aside the Soviet draft declaration on détente and substituted his own text, which became known as the "Hoveida document."

The Iranian ambassador borrowed a good deal of language from the Soviet text. Other language was included at the request of the delegations of other countries, and he strengthened the language about human rights and fundamental freedoms. We understood that this was done to please the Western delegations, but for the sake of salvaging the idea of the declaration, we decided to ignore what was for us a drawback. The Americans and their allies, who were generally negative toward the Soviet initiative, were not inclined to obstruct the work of the ambassador of Iran, a country which at that time was governed by an openly pro-American regime. The West trusted Hoveida and regarded him as their man. It was no accident, therefore, that after the establishment of the Khomeini dictatorship he was immediately removed from the post of permanent representative and was forced into hiding from the retribution of Iran's new rulers.

We were pleased that the idea of using Hoveida had worked so well and that the Declaration on the Strengthening and Deepening of Détente had been adopted by consensus. One of us, half-joking, suggested that Hoveida should be awarded some Soviet decoration. Of course, that did not happen, but he was the guest of honor at a lavish dinner organized at the Soviet mission, where he was presented with a special gift to mark the occasion.

Our other proposal—on the prevention of nuclear war—was in effect a total failure. The General Assembly was not prepared to spawn yet another abstract document on such an extremely complex subject. On the pretext that many delegations "were unable to study thoroughly" our draft resolution, we did not press it to a vote. At best it might have passed by a bare majority, which would have been tantamount to a rejection.

I was particularly put out, since the idea of proposing this resolution was my own. My dominant motive was probably a desire to put our Cold War adversaries in an awkward position by forcing them into a discussion of a subject they found "distasteful." In the end it was we who wound up in the awkward position. However, I was not in the least fazed by this and was not deterred from asserting in an article in *Pravda* on the results of the General

Assembly session that "the Soviet proposal on the strengthening and deepening of détente and preventing the outbreak of nuclear war had aroused particular interest. Decisions were made on these subjects and the initial drafts of these decisions were submitted by the Soviet Union." (I did this against my own conscience.)

I remember one of my younger colleagues commenting on my article with a smile: "I have to hand it to you, Victor Levonovich, for the way you summed up the discussion of our 'key issues'!" I detected in his tone more of a reproach than a compliment, so I didn't reply. However, I could not help noticing that from time to time some of my bright young colleagues would venture comments and questions which in "the good old days" junior diplomats who were just starting out would never have dared to utter. The new, young generation who entered the foreign service in the 1970s were of a different mold, and I would like to say something about them.

The Young "Sovki"*

Once, one of my young colleagues, known for his acerbic wit, joked to me: "If your generation is called the 'sovki,' ours should be called the 'young sovki.'" I had never liked this sobriquet, but the prefix "young" did highlight a clear difference between the generations.

The young or third generation of Soviet diplomats in the Cold War period, unlike the "Stalinists" and the "pragmatists," were born either during the Second World War or shortly afterwards and so only knew about the war at second hand. They had no personal experience of the privations, horrors, and upheavals it had brought with it. Their attitude to questions of war and peace was based not their personal experience or feelings but on historical accounts and prevailing sentiment.

Nor, fortunately for them, had they been exposed to Stalin's terror and the mass repressions of the 1930s. The "cult of Stalin" was for them an academic notion. Disobedience to or failure to conform to the Soviet regime did not necessarily earn you a death sentence as it had under Stalin, but rather meant the ruin of your career or ostracism. Thus even Soviet diplomats could breathe a little easier.

---

* Sovok (*pl.*, sovki). A disparaging term for an establishment-minded Soviet citizen of unswerving ideological orthodoxy.

Furthermore, the younger generation started out on a diplomatic career with much greater knowledge of the outside world than their elders had had. During their training at the Moscow State Institute of International Relations (MSIIR) and the Diplomatic Academy, students even received on-the-job training in Soviet embassies and missions. Also, most of the new entrants in the MFA had already been abroad either as tourists or members of sports teams. All of this gave the "young sovki" undoubted advantages.

As for the academic education of the third-generation diplomats, it was of an extremely high level. As a rule they went through a five-year course of study at the MSIIR often supplemented by a two-year course at the Diplomatic Academy. Young diplomats were expected to possess a working knowledge of two foreign languages. There was also another accomplishment that gave them a clear advantage over the older generation of career diplomats; namely, their acquaintance with advanced information technology.

In short, they were highly educated young people who no longer saw the world through the blinkers of Marxist-Leninist dogma. They were, of course, all members of the CPSU, but I do not recall a single committed champion of communist ideology among the third-generation diplomats of my acquaintance.

For the most part, these "young sovki" were the scions of affluent families whose parents were high officials of the CPSU Central Committee, the MFA, the KGB, or other ministries and party organs. There were, it is true, some rare exceptions, young men with no high-level connections, but they had a more difficult time of it, although one or two of them did succeed in attaining high diplomatic rank.

Toward the end of the 1970s, in the IOD, as well as in the delegations which I headed, there were quite a few representatives of the third generation. Gradually they came to play a key role in our diplomatic work. The "young sovki" became the workhorses who pulled the load of negotiations, and I grew to rely on them increasingly, as did, I observed, my colleagues, the heads of departments and ambassadors. Among the members of this generation of the 1970s and 1980s the following names stand out: Sergei Batsanov, Grigory Berdennikov, Sergei Kislyak, Andrei Kozyrev, Eduard Malayan, Georgy Mamedov, Sergei Ordzhonikidze, Vladimir Toitiov, Vasily Sidorov, Nikita Smidovich, and Vasily Sredin, among others.

By the 1990s they had almost completely replaced the representatives of the "pragmatist" generation in the senior posts of the MFA. They had climbed to the peak of the diplomatic Olympus, and others were not far behind them. It should be stressed that what was probably the most difficult and dramatic period of the Cold War—its conclusion—took place on their watch. It so happened that it was Andrei Kozyrev, who was to become the foreign minister of the Russian Soviet Federal Socialist Republic (RSFSR) at the age of thirty-nine, who found himself in the very thick of events, so I would like to say a few words about him.

The Rise of Andrei Kozyrev

As the head of the IOD, I was able to observe the work of Andrei Kozyrev, a junior member of the department, on a daily basis for almost five years. Later, right up to the time of my retirement in 1987, I used to meet him regularly at the sessions of the General Assembly in New York, so that I was able to get to know him even better.

Kozyrev's fifteen-year journey along the thorny path of a diplomatic career progressed with remarkable speed and regularity. After graduating from the MSIIR, he joined the MFA in 1974. He ascended all the rungs of the diplomatic ladder, eventually being appointed head of the International Organizations Department. His whole diplomatic career right up to his appointment as foreign minister was in the area of multilateral diplomacy, that is to say, UN affairs. He never spent any extended period of time abroad, although he was sent to New York and other centers of multilateral diplomacy for short-term missions and in the course of his career had spent time in many of the world's capitals.

In Kozyrev there were two attributes which stood out, industry and ambition. In the IOD I put him in charge of Security Council affairs, and he was quick to master the varied and quite complicated political problems involved; he did his homework well and absorbed the background to the issues. However, his great strength was not so much his ability to store information but rather his analytical ability. In the documents he prepared he always made a point of including elements of analysis and displayed the ability to draw conclusions.

Although Kozyrev, like any other official in a hierarchy, was anxious to please his superiors, at the same time he had a sense of his own merits, which he lost no opportunity to demonstrate. On the surface, the future minister behaved with great modesty and humility and gave the impression of being a mild and self-effacing person, but in fact this was far from the case. He was very well aware of his own worth, which at times he overrated, and as he moved up the ladder he made sure that it was properly appreciated. He defended his views firmly, sometimes fiercely. Depending on the level in the hierarchy to which he had risen at the moment, he calculated his interests quite carefully and nearly always successfully.

There is one typical episode, dating back to the mid-1970s, I will never forget. I once gave him a task that clearly interfered with his plans, and he expressed his displeasure. Wishing to emphasize the importance of the work, I pointed out that the reputation of the department and indeed my own professional reputation depended on his prompt and efficient performance of the task ordered by the MFA authorities. In response, this very junior diplomat calmly remarked that, while he understood my concern, nevertheless his own interests and career must come first. In the end, Kozyrev did do what was asked of him, but I was struck by his candor.

I also remember attempts by members of Kozyrev's family to interfere in his career. Soon after Kozyrev was appointed to the IOD, his former father-in-law, a senior official in the MFA, an ambassador, came to me to complain about his son-in-law's behavior toward his wife from whom he was ultimately divorced. He wanted to get Kozyrev dismissed from the MFA. Naturally, I refused and said that the family affairs of my young colleague were no business of mine.

Kozyrev had a flair for writing. He enjoyed writing, and it came easily to him, and what he wrote was always interesting. I was less familiar with his abilities as a speaker, although I doubt that he was a good debater. He basically lacked the appetite for the kind of polemics that were so characteristic of the Cold War.

In the early years of Kozyrev's career I saw no sign that his analyses and judgments about the international situation and the foreign policy of the Soviet Union in any way criticized or deviated from the official line. Many of his papers were published in political science journals. The articles he wrote in the 1970s were on UN-related themes. His dissertation for his candidate's degree or doctorate in historical studies was titled "The Role of the UN in the Development of Détente."

At that time his writings reflected the standpoints of communist ideology. The author himself acknowledged that the methodological basis of his dissertation was "the works of the founders of Marxism-Leninism, Marx, Engels, and Lenin, the policy documents of the CPSU and the world communist movement."

During Gorbachev's "perestroika" in the late 1980s, Kozyrev was quick to become one of its most zealous advocates, and the leitmotif of his writings became the idea that developing the full range of relations with the civilized West, primarily the United States, should be the first priority of Soviet foreign policy. It was through this same prism that he saw questions of confidence building, the balance of interests and unilateral actions likely to promote the process of rapprochement between East and West, and so on.

Of course, after the dissolution of the Soviet Union and after Gorbachev, the father of perestroika, had stepped down, Kozyrev started to see perestroika in a new light. According to him, the "new thinking" was largely an incompletely thought out philosophical concept and amounted to nothing more than a change of label. He now became an outspoken opponent of "renewed socialism." It is hard to say whether this was some miraculous change of heart or simply a change of tactics.

But still, how did it come about that Kozyrev was appointed foreign minister of the Russian Soviet Federated Socialist Republic in 1990, *before* the dissolution of the Soviet Union? Formerly, this had been a post reserved for retired worthies who were drawing their pensions. Foreign ministers of the RSFSR had never had any say in the formulation of Soviet foreign policy, and the whole ministry had a staff of barely two dozen people, whose only dream was to be transferred to or to return to the hub of affairs—the MFA. Needless to say, the RSFSR had no representatives of its own posted abroad.

The best that the foreign minister of the RSFSR could hope for would be to be included—maybe once in ten years—in the Soviet delegation to the UN General Assembly. Kozyrev's immediate predecessors in this post, Vladimir Vinogradov and Mikhail Yakovlev, distinguished diplomats who had served as ambassadors in many countries, were evidently satisfied with their lot.

After Yeltsin was elected president of the RSFSR, Vinogradov, a typical representative of the Soviet school of "nay-saying" negotiators, was no longer considered a suitable candidate for the post of foreign minister of Russia. Apparently, no one in Yeltsin's immediate entourage was anxious to take what at that time was a low-prestige, subordinate post. Yeltsin needed someone who was dynamic and reasonably experienced, yet without ties to the old party structures.

On the other hand, Shevardnadze, who was foreign minister of the USSR at the time, did not want some outsider or intruder in the Russian Foreign Ministry who might create problems for the Soviet Foreign Ministry. What he wanted there was one of *his* men, never mind if he was young and active, and that was how the idea of putting Andrei Kozyrev, the head of the International Organizations Department, in the post arose. Within the MFA it was widely rumored that this name had been suggested to Shevardnadze by Kovalev, his first deputy, who had at one time been a favorite of Gromyko, but after his departure had quite quickly succeeded in winning the confidence of the new minister, Shevardnadze, especially when it came to personnel matters. In the absence of any other serious candidates, Shevardnadze recommended Kozyrev to Yeltsin, who was favorably impressed by this obliging young man.

The appointment of Kozyrev drew mixed reviews. While some approved the appointment of the young diplomat, others expressed doubt about his capacities and his lack of experience and authority. In the MFA it was widely felt that he would not last long in the ministerial post and that at best he would succeed in parlaying it into a humble ambassadorship in some small African country or, if he was lucky, somewhere in Latin America.

Later, Kozyrev himself came to favor a somewhat different version of his elevation to the post. In an interview he claimed that the reason for his leaving the Soviet MFA was simply that his political views clashed with those of its leadership. How precisely his views differed from those of Shevardnadze and his colleagues was something he did not explain, and to be frank, I myself never heard anything to suggest any difference of view between Kozyrev and the leadership of the MFA, otherwise he would not have had the ghost of chance of being appointed a minister.

Shevchenko's Defection

During the Cold War there were quite few Soviet diplomats who were aware of the failures, errors, and organic flaws in Soviet foreign policy, but in all my years of service only a few actually left the MFA for this reason. The fear of official retaliation, the prospect of public opprobrium and social ostracism on the one hand, and concern for their material well-being and faith and hope for some change for the better in the future on the other—all these things kept most diplomats within the pale of the government bureaucracy. There were some, however, who made a clean break with the Soviet Union and sought political asylum in other countries. Compared with people from other professions, such as artists and performers, scientists, and intelligence agents, the number of diplomats who took this course was rather small.

In the 1970s, the case that attracted the most publicity was the defection of Arkady Shevchenko. His action, naturally, had a particular impact in Smolenskaya Square. This was, after all, a betrayal by an important diplomat with the rank of ambassador who was at the very pinnacle of the Soviet diplomatic service.

I had worked with Shevchenko for ten years beginning in 1968. At one time we worked together at the Soviet mission to the UN in New York where he was the senior counselor. During the period 1973 to 1978 when he occupied the post of undersecretary-general at the UN my work in Moscow made me privy to the information we received from him, and I met him on a number of occasions both in Moscow and in New York. I should add that we were also neighbors in Moscow. There was also another link between us, namely, that his son, Gennady, worked in my department and from time to time his work required my attention.

My personal relations with Arkady Shevchenko were quite good. I valued his knowledge and experience, and we worked together quite frequently, although we were never friends. For some years he was one of Gromyko's assistants and became a familiar figure to the leadership. The minister was well disposed to Shevchenko, trusted him, and advanced his career.

Along with his professional qualities as a diplomat and an official (he was a good speechwriter and drafter of documents and was good at grasping the ideas of his superiors and also, at times, of formulating them effectively), he had one serious—and ultimately ruinous—weakness: he was too fond of the bottle. What started out for him as innocent, friendly get-togethers, would gradually develop into serious drinking bouts that sometimes knocked him out for days on end.

There is one incident I particularly remember. In May 1975 in Geneva there was a review conference on the Non-Proliferation Treaty. I happened to be the Soviet delegate at the conference, and Shevchenko was sent from New York as the personal representative of Secretary-General Kurt Waldheim. This was an extremely important position, and our delegation was looking forward to business-like cooperation with him. Since Shevchenko had reported sick on his arrival in Geneva, I went to visit him in the apartment where he was living. Also I happened to have a package for him from Moscow. When I got there, I found him in a dazed condition, eyeing me with a vacant look and quite unable to focus on anything I was telling him about events in Moscow or the work of the conference. When I offered to send for a doctor, he would not hear of it and assured me that he would be at the conference the next day. In spite of his promise, in the entire four weeks it lasted none of the participants in the conference laid eyes on the personal representative of the secretary-general even once. In response to the numerous questions from delegations, secretariat officials invariably replied with a grin: "His Excellency is indisposed." These "indispositions" occurred with increasing frequency, and practically everyone who came into contact with him knew about his drunken escapades.

Many of us among his colleagues reported these drinking bouts to the MFA authorities. During these episodes Shevchenko would give free rein to his tongue and free play to his imagination. Did these reports reach Gromyko's ears? I think some word of it must have got through but probably after the event and considerably watered down—"old Arkash's boyish pranks." Everyone remembered that Shevchenko was Gromyko's protégé. Shevchenko also possessed another quality—he was an accomplished courtier. He and his wife pulled out all the stops when it came to endearing themselves to their superiors or anyone who could be useful to them. Because of this the people "up there" turned a blind eye to much of Shevchenko's aberrations, and he enjoyed a great deal of indulgence.

In 1978 Judy Chavez, a member of one of the world's few professions older than diplomacy, published a tell-all book titled *Defector's Mistress*, which became a best-seller in the United States. Chavez, who was hired by the FBI as a companion for Shevchenko right after his defection, had little interest in the political views of her client, and in her book she gave a rather caustic account of certain of Shevchenko's more unsavory habits, including his drinking bouts. Shevchenko's downfall was also helped along by his exaggerated opinion of himself, his overambitiousness, and his know-it-all attitude. These characteristics were also exhibited in his book, *Breaking with Moscow*, where the author at times wildly exaggerated his influence in the formulation of Soviet foreign policy and his connections with the Kremlin leadership.

These characteristics combined with his frequent drinking bouts made him relatively easy prey for American intelligence services, which, as one of Shevchenko's American partners has acknowledged, had been keeping him under surveillance for a long time. Shevchenko knew, of course, that once he had compromised himself by speech or act in the course of one of his regular foolhardy escapades, he would be in for it as soon as word reached Moscow. There was no way that the former secretary of the communist party organization of the minister's secretariat, the post held by Shevchenko before he was sent to New York, would be allowed to continue his vertiginous career ascent.

By 1978, the storm clouds were beginning to gather around his head. Even the KGB had begun to draw Gromyko's attention to Shevchenko's behavior, and in any case his term of office as UN undersecretary-general was drawing to an end. At the beginning of April 1978 he was called back to Moscow by Gromyko for a meeting of the Collegium of the MFA to consider the question of the Special Session of the General Assembly on Disarmament scheduled for May that year. This summons to Moscow came as a surprise to Shevchenko. When I had met him in New York not long before, he talked about his plans to go to Moscow after the Disarmament Session. Nevertheless, after receiving the telegram from Gromyko, he reserved an airline ticket for a flight to Moscow on April 9.

Something happened, however, to change the situation radically. In fact, there were no plans whatsoever for a meeting of the Collegium on the subject, and neither the IOD, which was responsible for UN matters, nor I myself knew anything about Shevchenko's recall to Moscow. So that when Shevchenko on the day before he was due to fly to Moscow asked my deputy, Stashevsky, who had just arrived in New York, about the preparations for the meeting of the Collegium, he quite truthfully replied that there were no plans for a meeting of the Collegium to consider the matter. This revelation, as Shevchenko himself acknowledged, gave him a fright. He assumed that Moscow had learned of his American intelligence connections, and he decided there and then to run to the Americans for protection.

I learned of his defection from General Vladimir Kazakov of the KGB, who was shortly to become the Soviet *rezident* in the United States. He telephoned me and announced dramatically: "Your"—to use his very words—"your Shevchenko has cleared out." My heart skipped a beat. I assumed that "my" Shevchenko was the Gennady Shevchenko who worked in my department and who happened to be on a short-term mission in Geneva at the time. Since I had been the one to recommend him for the mission, I was the one directly responsible. When it became clear that it was his father who had absconded, I was greatly relieved. I was not the one responsible for Shevchenko the elder. Kazakov asked me to recall Gennady to Moscow immediately in case, God forbid! he followed his father's example. I did as I was asked, and Gennady returned to Moscow at once.

In the first few days after Shevchenko's defection, Gromyko and some other high-ranking officials thought he might return. Indeed, the brief announcement in the Soviet press was worded in such a way as to create the impression that Shevchenko had been forcibly abducted by the American "special services" and members of his family were encouraged to send messages to him expressing the hope that they would soon be reunited.

In fact, Shevchenko's "break" with Moscow led above all to the ruin of his own family; the suicide of his wife a month after his defection; and devastating effects, both moral and material, on his children, his schoolgirl daughter, and his son Gennady, who was dismissed from the MFA. As their neighbors in the same building we had a front-row seat at this family tragedy.

Shevchenko did enormous and lasting harm to his former friends and colleagues, who, of course, had no idea of his espionage activities. They hid nothing from him and freely shared news and official information with him. Many of them suffered serious consequences. There was one in particular I remember, the late Ambassador Stashevsky, an eminent Soviet disarmament expert, who in spite of his high rank and post was classified as "banned from traveling abroad" merely for being frank in conversation with Shevchenko. I will not touch on the legal aspects of Shevchenko's action. I was not invited to his trial and cannot really judge whether his sentence in absentia to death by firing squad was warranted. In any case he has never been able to return to his country and died in the United States a few year ago.

The course of breaking with Moscow chosen by Shevchenko was wrong principally because it was immoral, inhuman, and did irreparable harm to his nearest and dearest—such was the verdict of many of his former colleagues. They felt that changes in the country, including the area of foreign policy, should not be brought about by actions of this kind for which scores of people had to pay dearly, but through the persistent efforts of all sectors of society to reform the existing order, structures, and policies.

The Special Session on Disarmament

All international conferences held during the Cold War attended by the two superpowers followed the same scenario. The Soviet Union would take one position and the United States the opposite one, and their respective friends and allies would align themselves accordingly. Sometimes a third position was taken by the nonaligned countries, who would ultimately veer in the direction of one side or the other.

It was expected that the Special Session of the UN General Assembly on Disarmament would take the same course. Disagreements about the very idea of an international conference on the subject had emerged as far back as 1971 when the Soviet Union proposed convening a world disarmament conference. The United States vigorously opposed this idea as untimely and useless. When a committee was nevertheless set up to study the possibility of holding such a conference, the United States even refused to take part in its work or cooperate with it. The Americans were, however, unable to prevent the convening of the Special Session because the proposal came from the nonaligned movement and was supported by the overwhelming majority of the member states of the UN.

During the preparations for the Special Session, which lasted for almost a year in the committee set up for the purpose, the U.S. delegation was extremely passive and maintained an obstinate silence. It submitted no documents to the preparatory committee. Finally, shortly before the opening of the Special Session, they published a paper titled "The U.S. View of the Agenda and other Issues Relating to the Special Session." Washington expressed the hope that the UN Conference on Disarmament "would provide a genuinely new stimulus for productive multilateral negotiations on disarmament."

Further evidence of what was, to say the least, the skeptical attitude of the United States toward the Special Session was the NATO summit meeting held in Washington at the same time, which took a decision foreshadowing an arms buildup by the members of that block over the next few years. This approach was diametrically opposed to the goals and objectives of the UN Special Session. This was acknowledged by the *New York Times*, which wrote on May 25, 1978: "Next week at the NATO meeting in Washington, Carter will be discussing an increase in American arms shipments to Europe; this will make it difficult for him to go to the UN at practically the same time and proclaim an arms reduction."

The Soviet delegation to the preparatory committee, which I headed, was very active. It submitted a document titled "Practical Ways and Means of Halting Arms," which was circulated at the session itself. In preparing the document, we in the IOD tried to cover all the areas of disarmament and make it as concrete and noncontroversial as possible.

Nevertheless, the principled approach to the international disarmament conference and the level and nature of participation in the preparatory work for it on the part of the two superpowers made it very likely that, in the context of the Cold War, we would be seeing yet another duel between the United States and the Soviet Union.

The Special Session lasted for almost six weeks (May–June 1978), and great interest in it was shown by a majority of member states and international nongovernmental organizations. Probably never in the history of the UN had the voice of public opinion made itself heard so loudly. Many nongovernmental organizations were given the right to speak at the session. Representatives of major scientific research institutions, including the Stockholm Institute for the Study of Peace Problems, the Vienna International Peace Institute, and many others came to New York for the session. The meeting rooms were flooded with petitions, brochures, and documents from independent and nongovernmental organizations. Most of them were of undoubted value, and we returned to Moscow with our luggage bursting with disarmament literature.

Hardly a day passed without demonstrations, sit-ins, and gatherings of groups of people right outside the UN building in New York where the delegates were meeting, protesting against war, and calling for international cooperation. The organizers of one of these rallies invited some important delegates to the Special Session to speak. I took advantage of the opportunity to explain for the Soviet document, which had been submitted to the session, and did my best to embellish the Soviet position on disarmament matters. To the chagrin of the participants in the rally, which took place in a basically friendly atmosphere, no representatives of the American delegation were present.

After the general debate in which the heads of delegation spoke, the real work began on the Final Document, the outcome of the conference. This work went on in a number of subordinate bodies of the session, the committee of the whole, and its subcommittees and drafting groups. All kinds of informal meetings were also held. The work grew more intensive every day; indeed, during the last two weeks it continued over the weekends and usually well beyond midnight. Agreement was reached on the final text of the Final Document only on the very last night of the conference, June 29.

Thanks to the work of three men in particular—Lazar Moisov, Carlos Ortiz de Rosas, and Alfonso García Robles—the Special Session ended in success. Lazar Moisov, the permanent representative of Yugoslavia to the UN, was the president of the conference. He had worked as ambassador to Moscow and went on to become deputy minister and minister of foreign affairs of his country. He enjoyed authority with the nonaligned movement, for which he often acted as spokesman.

Carlos Ortiz de Rosas and Alfonso García Robles were the chairmen of the working groups. De Rosas, an Argentinean, was the chairman of the General Committee of the Special Session on Disarmament. His talent in multilateral diplomacy shown brightly during these negotiations. When the delegates needed to speak, he would give them the opportunity. He did not care about time, as long as the discussions were useful and productive. However, when the time came to make decisions, he would apply the necessary pressure on the delegates, limiting opportunities for repetitive discussions and skillfully pushing them to a consensus. The only time he "spared us" was the day Argentina played a world championship soccer game. It was Sunday, and the game was supposed to be on in the evening, so he called a recess. Being a tremendous soccer fan, he couldn't deprive himself of this one pleasure.

The name of Alfonso García Robles will no doubt go down in history as one of the great heroes in the struggle of humanity against war and for arms control. García Robles devoted his whole long and interesting life to this noble purpose, and his work in this area was recognized with the Nobel Peace Prize in 1982. We, his colleagues, always marveled at (and envied) the freedom he enjoyed when staking out his own position at any negotiations. His authority and competence were seemingly so great that his government thoroughly trusted him to choose the right side of an issue. The proposals he submitted were even called the Robles proposals rather than the Mexican proposals.

Through the efforts of these three grand masters of multilateral diplomacy and the innumerable committed supporters of disarmament, both inside and outside the conference, the Special Session ended in success.

What was so unusual about the conference was not the traditional confrontation between the superpowers but the convergence of their interests and their cooperation. The reason for this was that even during the general debate at the beginning of the session the feeling prevailed that it was the two superpowers, the Soviet Union and the United States who bore particular responsibility for the arms race and its grave consequences for all the peoples and countries in the world. The delegates of practically all the non-aligned countries as well as many Western countries insisted that disarmament, or rather curbing the arms race, was essentially the job of the two superpowers.

We in the Soviet delegation were distinctly put out by this turn of affairs. We had expected that the Special Session would be marked by the singing of the praises of the Soviet Union for the disarmament initiatives we had been feeding the UN every year. The reality was very different indeed from our fantasy. When the Final Document began to take shape and many delegates were trying to include these insidious ideas about the special responsibility of the two superpowers we began to be seriously alarmed.

At a meeting of the delegation we agreed to maintain close contact with the U.S. delegation in order to find out their reaction to the attempt to pin the blame for the arms race on the superpowers. We were delighted to learn that the Americans did not care for the idea either. Consequently, we began to consult and coordinate our actions. I started to have regular meetings with ambassadors Harriman, James Leonard, and Adrian Fisher, as well as other members of the U.S. delegation. We gradually came to understand each other better and to realize that our interests converged.

When France, Pakistan, and some other countries tried to include in the Final Document the notion of the special responsibility of the Soviet Union and the United States for solving the problems of nuclear disarmament, thus at the same time relieving other countries of responsibility, both the American Leonard and I, separately and jointly, had to spend many hours working to produce a compromise document that would be acceptable to all parties. The text reflected the responsibility of all nuclear powers for the achievement of nuclear disarmament and in particular those nuclear powers who "possessed the most significant nuclear arsenals." This made both ourselves and the Americans feel a little better.

Mexico, Yugoslavia, and certain other countries worked to ensure that the language referring to the Soviet-American talks on the limitation of strategic armaments stipulated the manner in which they would be conducted and the possible results of further negotiations on the subject. There were also attempts to place the talks under the control of the UN. We and the Americans both were offended by these proposals and when we were discussing them with each other on one occasion I could not refrain from paraphrasing the words of a well-known character from a Soviet novel and said jokingly: "Perhaps they would like the keys to our safes too?" The proposals for meddling in the Soviet-American talks were rejected, and the text finally adopted contained an appeal to the United States and the Soviet Union to reach agreement as soon as possible at the SALT talks.

The superpower delegations also jointly resisted the numerous attacks on the Nuclear Non-Proliferation Treaty. Here, our fiercest opponents were India and Brazil. They directed their fire mainly at the principle of the universality of international treaties in the area of disarmament on the pretext that the adoption of such a principle would mean recognition by all countries of the Non-Proliferation Treaty, even though many countries were not parties to it.

I had quite a few conversations with the Indian ambassador, Chinmoy Garekhan, as did the Americans with the Brazilians, in an attempt to produce an acceptable formula: "The universality of disarmament agreements will foster trust between countries."

However, the most curious situation arose during the discussion of the machinery for disarmament negotiations. In the view of the Soviet Union, the United States, the United Kingdom and a number of other countries, the existing machinery, in particular the Geneva Committee on Disarmament, was adequate for the scope and nature of the many and varied problems of disarmament and should therefore continue to be used for the work on the necessary international agreements. France had a different view of the matter and proposed the creation of an entirely new negotiating body, which would replace the existing Geneva committee. The French indicated that they would not join the Geneva committee in whose work they had refrained from participating for many years. This created a deadlock that threatened to scuttle the conference. García Robles offered his services as mediator to attempt to break the deadlock. The French agreed and said that they were ready to negotiate with only one delegation, which would represent the position of those opposed to the French proposal. After consultations it was proposed that I should be the one to negotiate with the French. In order to check on the terms of the agreement I asked the American, Fisher, whether my understanding was correct and that in fact I would also be representing the United States in my negotiations with the French. Fisher confirmed this. I was pleasantly surprised by the situation; it was the only time ever in my diplomatic career that I found myself negotiating on behalf of the United States, albeit on a matter of secondary importance.

The negotiations with the French were very difficult. For some reason or other Jacques Leprette, the French ambassador to the UN, was unwilling to sit down with his negotiating partner, that is to say myself, in the same room. So García Robles had to run back and forth between the room where the Frenchman was sitting and the one where I was sitting. The negotiations were based on a draft prepared by García Robles. The Frenchman and I took turns amending the document. This exhausting work took hours, and it was not until very late at night that we reached agreement on a text. This was very much to García Robles's credit. He worked hard at persuading us not to dig in our heels and often came up with his own balanced language. The fundamental principles of the Geneva Committee on Disarmament were preserved: the taking of decisions by consensus, limited membership, and special status vis-à-vis the UN, among others. There were certain changes in procedure, but the committee remained essentially unchanged.

The ambassadors who had been awaiting the outcome of the negotiations congratulated García Robles, the Frenchman, and myself, and when Fisher told me how pleased he was with the agreement, I joked that I was now entitled to part of his salary.

Finally, a few words about the Soviet delegation. It was headed by Gromyko, and its members included his deputy, Kovalev, Troyanovsky, Academician Nikoilai Inozemtsev, and myself. After Gromyko's departure, Kovalev took over as head of delegation. All the time we worked together, Kovalev persistently stressed that our main goal was to see to it that the Soviet document "Practical Ways and Means of Halting the Arms Race" was mentioned in the Final Document of the conference. The Special Session decided to send all the proposals, which numbered several dozen, submitted by governments to the conference to the various discussion and negotiating bodies. Accordingly, the Soviet proposal was, of course, included. Everyone was pleased, especially Kovalev, who had apparently been promising the minister that the Soviet document would be "properly reflected" among the decisions of the conference.

Personally, I had thought that the more points and concrete proposals submitted to the conference by the Soviet Union that ended up in the Final Document, the better. So it was with this aim in mind that I conducted the negotiations at the session, and my colleagues and I were pleased that we had been to some degree successful in this. At the end of the session we returned home. I was happy that the UN Special Session on Disarmament had not degenerated into just one more clash between the two superpowers in the context of the Cold War. As a matter of fact, the event was marked by a certain convergence of interests between the Soviet Union and the United States, and in this sense the Special Session was a rare occurrence of the Cold War. I even had the illusion that perhaps the UN Disarmament Conference would open a new chapter in the history of the Cold War and would mark a return to the time of détente at the beginning of the 1970s. How wrong I was! Within a year after the conference Soviet troops had entered Afghanistan.

15
THE APOTHEOSIS OF THE COLD WAR

New Appointment

My optimistic assessment of the Special Session of the General Assembly on Disarmament was shared by many of my colleagues both in the delegation and back in Moscow. The discussion of the results of the session in the Collegium of the MFA in the summer of 1978 was equally upbeat. Naturally, all those who took part in the discussion attributed the good results principally to the persevering and persistent "struggle for peace and disarmament" of the Soviet Union. Gromyko struck the same note. There began to be talk around the ministry about some members of the delegation to the session being recommended for decorations, as had happened in the case of Helsinki. To our disappointment this did not happen. We were just given a monetary reward, and we were grateful for this.

Both in public statements and in discussions of the results among colleagues attention was drawn to the essentially constructive dialogue with the American delegation and to the mutually acceptable understandings reached on a wide range of disarmament questions. I made a point of emphasizing the positive role played by Harriman, a veteran in the area of Soviet-American relations, as well as the initiative taken by Paul Newman, the American movie star who was so ready to promote contacts with the Soviet delegation. Gromyko, to whom I reported in detail about our dealings with the Americans, listened with interest to what I had to say, but I do not believe he shared my optimism about the possibility of a serious breakthrough in Soviet-American relations as a result of the Special Session.

One of the direct results of the session was a change in the nature of the Geneva Committee on Disarmament. For the first time it was attended by all five nuclear powers, and the committee undertook to work to bring about general and complete disarmament under effective international control. Many people began to believe that the committee with its new composition would succeed in producing positive results.

This overoptimistic assessment of the results of the first Special Session of the UN on Disarmament on which I had had a direct bearing persuaded the MFA authorities that there needed to be a new Soviet representative in the Geneva committee. Viktor Likhachev, who had been our representative there since 1976, was an experienced diplomat but was not sufficiently accustomed to working in a multilateral diplomatic environment and had never before dealt with disarmament matters. It was proposed that I should become the new Soviet representative in the reconstituted committee.

My reaction to this proposal was mixed. On the one hand, my more than five years in a senior administrative post at MFA headquarters had not been all that interesting. I had vastly preferred my work at the Soviet mission in New York. "Office diplomacy" with its subservience to rank, sycophancy, and toadying went against my grain. I saw many examples of this kind of "diplomacy" among my colleagues, and it was not an example I was inclined to follow. Therefore, I was delighted to get this opportunity to return to multilateral, conference diplomacy. Moreover, having been exposed to various disarmament problems, I had to some extent succeeded in mastering them. I had also gotten to know the leading figures in disarmament diplomacy from different countries and was on friendly terms with them, and this was another important factor in my decision.

On the other hand, the post of representative to the disarmament committee was not exactly a high-prestige appointment. Although the Soviet Union had been represented on the committee in the 1960s by Gromyko, Kuznetsov, and Zorin, they had combined those functions with their other posts and only attended the Geneva negotiations for short spells. The first permanent representative appointed was Semen Tsarapkin, although he did not stay long in the post. With the start of the bilateral Soviet-American negotiations on strategic armaments the scope of the Geneva committee was reduced and its authority somewhat diminished. The post of representative to the committee had also lost some of its standing in Smolenskaya Square, but I could not start thinking in those terms.

Accordingly, upon my appointment as representative to Geneva my tenure as a member of the Collegium was confirmed and in addition to becoming the Soviet representative on the Disarmament Committee I was also given responsibility for conducting the Soviet-American negotiations in Geneva on the prohibition of new types of weapons of mass destruction and the prohibition of chemical weapons. Furthermore, on my appointment by Gromyko I was instructed "in the time between sessions to take part in the work going on at MFA headquarters of preparing documentation and proposals" in the area of disarmament.

Thus my appointment to the committee was not just a change of watch but a move designed to equip the Soviet representative with wider powers. This was stressed by Gromyko in a conversation with me as I was leaving for Geneva. He advised me not to confine my activities within the strict framework of the committee's agenda, but to take an interest in the whole range of disarmament problems. He recommended that I give priority to cooperation with the American delegation, something which in his estimation would be critical for the success of the committee's work. "Well, it was you who convinced me at the Special Session in New York that Soviet-American contacts were a good thing," he said with a smile, "now's your chance to prove it." Of course, I had no choice but to make him a promise of fruitful cooperation, but as events proved during my years in Geneva, it was not a promise I could keep.

A Painful Change of Name

The Geneva Disarmament Committee was not only a one-of-a-kind negotiating forum during the Cold War years but also one of the very few relatively effective channels of Soviet-American cooperation available at the time. The existence of the committee was itself the result of a joint initiative of the Soviet Union and the United States. It was created by a UN General Assembly resolution in 1968 with a membership of eighteen countries. In 1969, the membership was increased to twenty-six and that was when what had been the Committee of Eighteen became known as the Conference of the Committee on Disarmament. In 1975 the membership rose to thirty-one and finally, in 1978, to forty.

From the very outset, membership in the committee was linked to the political orientation of the country in question. For example, the original Committee of Eighteen was made up of six Western, six socialist, and six nonaligned states. The same ratio was preserved when the membership of the committee rose to forty.

In 1984, the committee was renamed the Conference on Disarmament, a move preceded by a typical piece of downright comic Cold War diplomatic farce, in which I was directly involved. The person who originally came up with the idea of renaming the committee and calling it a conference was the ambassador from the Netherlands, Richard Fine,—who argued in support of the proposal that disarmament problems were of great importance in international politics and was a subject of major concern to the world community. In private conversation I expressed my approval of the idea, but without instructions from Moscow I did not express this view in the committee.

Very soon, representatives of the nonaligned countries began to insist on replacing "committee" by "conference." Then, however, delegations of Western countries came out against the idea, arguing that such a step was untimely. I was told privately that the main reason for the opposition of the Western countries was that they claimed that the change of title was politically advantageous to the Soviet Union and its allies. Interestingly enough, Moscow too had actually considered renaming the committee but decided against it when it was learned that the initiator of the proposal was the representative of the Netherlands. That, in the opinion of the Soviet MFA, testified to the political motives of the United States and its allies. I was advised from Moscow not to take any initiative in the matter.

However, it was now too late to oppose the change of title, since the nonaligned countries had begun to view the issue as a matter of principle and were pressing for a positive solution. In the circumstances, the Western countries did not think that it was worth provoking a confrontation with the nonaligned ones on such a secondary issue. Moscow came to the same conclusion.

In brief, it took three years for the Dutchman's sensible proposal to be acted on. Since then the standing multilateral negotiating forum on disarmament and arms control has borne the name of "Conference on Disarmament" and this is the title I shall be using for it henceforth.

The living and working conditions of Soviet diplomats assigned to the conference, namely, the heads of delegations and their colleagues, are worth looking at more closely. They let us see the conditions under which, so to speak, these individuals waged the Cold War. I spent no more than five or six months a year in Geneva; the rest of the time I was in Moscow, New York, and other capitals, where I was often sent on short-term assignments.

There was no permanent mission. The number of staff varied between five or six in the first year of my assignment to the conference and twenty to twenty-five at the end. This increase was entailed partly by the increasing complexity of the negotiations and partly, I have to confess, by considerations of a different order altogether. I had no wish to be outstripped by the more "go-getting" Soviet heads of delegation, including those who had worked in Geneva, who contrived to include on their staffs cooks, maids, and even personal physicians, not to mention secretaries. I think I am safe in saying that in the period of the 1960s through the 1980s there was no country which had such a large contingent of nondiplomatic service personnel on the staffs of their missions as the Soviet Union.

Normally, there were two sessions of the Conference on Disarmament a year, a spring or winter session and a summer session. This meant that a delegation had to be put together twice a year, comprising both diplomatic and auxiliary personnel. The first criterion of selection was that of professional and job qualifications. However, I have to admit that considerations of "domestic or office diplomacy" had to be taken into account. At various times I had working for me on my nondiplomatic staff a distant relative of the minister, the son-in-law of the secretary of the Central Committee of the CPSU, the nephew of the head of a KGB Department among others. I could not say no to a friend and took on his girl friend, later to become his wife, I hasten to add, as delegation secretary. So there was always "ballast" on board the delegation.

Before leaving for Geneva, the staff were always warned about certain practical inconveniences they would be encountering. As a rule, their living conditions would be unusual, and there were the extra problems created by their ignorance of the language, customs, and traditions of the place.

In spite of all the difficulties, inconveniences, and problems of working in the delegation, I do not remember anyone ever refusing an invitation to join it—for a number of reasons. An important factor was that of professional advancement. Participation in international negotiations and conferences was always looked good on the record of any official of the MFA, diplomat and nondiplomat alike. The subject of disarmament was very much in vogue during the Cold War and had a great attraction for many diplomats, especially of the younger generation, and they were very eager to attend the Geneva negotiations. It was both interesting and prestigious to work in Geneva, which was one of the nerve centers of multilateral diplomacy, and that too was a powerful inducement for joining the delegation to the Disarmament Conference.

Last but not least, the material conditions enjoyed by Soviet delegation members were extremely advantageous. It was not so much a matter of the subsistence allowance paid in Swiss francs, which was not really that high, but rather the privileges that accrued; free housing, medical care (the mission's own clinic in Geneva with access to Swiss doctors if necessary) and transportation, plus, and this was what was really important, their ruble salaries were accumulating for them intact back in Moscow.

Most of the staff of the delegations, including my own, were wizards at economizing. First, they brought with them vast quantities of nonperishable foodstuffs from Moscow—canned food, cereals, dried fruit, smoked sausage, and so on, and this always made life difficult for the Swiss customs officials who, surprised as they were, always let these products through in the belief that Soviet diplomats thought that people were starving in Geneva. Second, Soviet citizens always saved money by using shops and markets where food prices were lowest. This enabled my compatriots to spend most of their subsistence allowance on durable goods (always, of course, the lowest-priced), either for their own use or for resale in Moscow. This in turn allowed many in the delegation, both diplomatic and nondiplomatic staff, to maintain a relatively high standards of living in the Soviet Union. My drivers, for example, managed to save enough money to buy used cars in Geneva. What I have described here applies in varying degrees to all staff of the Soviet delegation in Geneva as well as in other international centers.

One last point. The work in Geneva was extremely multifaceted. It was very important to be able to speak in public, to be able to argue your case in negotiations, to be able to formulate your position in treaty language, and to be familiar with the background of the issue and the positions of at least the major negotiating partners and to keep on good, if not friendly terms with them. Equally important, of course, was the ability to report promptly and authoritatively to headquarters. Only some ideal of a diplomat could possess all these attributes and in fact every diplomat has only some of these qualities; one, for example, would be a good speaker and would enjoy speaking in public, another would be a better at drafting documents and formulating proposals, and so on. When I assigned the various tasks to my subordinates, I tried to do so in the light of individual talents and abilities.

Generally speaking, I look back on working with my delegation colleagues with a great deal of warmth and satisfaction. In my long career I must have worked closely with more than a hundred different people, both diplomats and nondiplomatic associates. I believe I can say that, for the most part, they were first-class professionals. It was only on the rarest occasions that I was guilty of misjudgment in my selection of the members of a delegation. We worked and lived in Geneva like one big happy family, and because of the wholehearted support of my colleagues I never experienced any difficulty in carrying out the formidable and important tasks assigned to me by Moscow. I do not remember a single case where anyone refused even what were at times major extra workloads, and I will never forget the trips we took together through the spectacular landscape of Switzerland. I formed friendships with many of my colleagues at the Disarmament Conference, friendships that I maintained for many years afterwards.

But Why Do We Need Negotiations?

In spite of the storm clouds gathering on the international horizon, the solemn opening of the reconstituted Conference on Disarmament in January 1979 was a festive occasion. Many delegations were led by foreign ministers and other important officials. The foreign minister of Algeria, who presided over the opening, together with practically all speakers, expressed the hope that the conference would prove to be an effective negotiating forum on disarmament.

The first month was truly extremely effective. Under the experienced leadership of the familiar figure of Carlos de Rosas from Argentina the conference adopted its agenda, its program of work, and its rules of procedure. It decided to deal with the questions of halting the arms race and disarmament and other relevant measures in the following areas: nuclear weapons in all aspects; chemical weapons; other weapons of mass destruction; conventional weapons; reduction of military budgets; reduction of armed forces; disarmament and development; disarmament and international security; related measures and, in particular, verification measures; in short, it had decided to adopt a comprehensive program oriented toward complete and general disarmament under effective international control.

I have described the conference's program of work to give the reader an idea of the ambitiousness of the goals it had set for itself. Hans Blix, the foreign minister of Sweden, who was sitting next to me and who subsequently became director of the International Atomic Energy Agency for many years, remarked with feeling: "This is tremendous! If we complete this program, we'll be living in a completely different world!" "I'm afraid," I responded skeptically, "we won't live long enough to see that never-never land!" "Everything depends on you, the superpowers," said the Swede quite rightly.

In fact, throughout the years of the Cold War the United States and the Soviet Union continued to play their crucial and dominant role at the conference. Initially, a system of Soviet-American cochairmanship was instituted so that even matters of procedure could not be decided without their approval. Later the practice was abolished, but during my time there it was the position of the two superpowers that unquestionably determined the whole course of negotiations on practically all subjects dealt with by that important forum of multilateral diplomacy. Sad as it is to acknowledge, it fell to my lot to work at the conference during what was probably its least effective period at the height of a major Cold War crisis. At the end of the 1970s and the beginning of the 1980s after the Soviet intervention in Afghanistan and after President Reagan took office, the rivalry of the superpowers reached its peak. On the surface, there did not seem to be any particular reason for such a deterioration in relations between the superpowers. In March 1977, an important agreement was reached on holding a whole series of bilateral negotiations on arms limitation, but they produced no meaningful results. Work on a new strategic arms limitation treaty (SALT 2) was hampered by major obstacles and moved forward very slowly until it was finally signed in 1979.

Naturally, the United States laid the blame for the slow progress in negotiations on key international issues, particularly in the area of arms limitations, on the actions of the Soviet Union in Afghanistan, Angola, Ethiopia, South Yemen, Cuba, and elsewhere, but this was viewed as the normal and inevitable background music to the Cold War. All of Reagan's speeches, both during the electoral campaign and in the first years of his presidency, breathed his ultra-anticommunism and hostility to the Soviet Union.

I first heard one of the president's speeches in 1982 at the second UN Session on Disarmament. Although he was an excellent speaker, I was disappointed. In spite of the subject of the Special Session, anyone hearing him was left without a shred of hope for a constructive dialogue on disarmament with representatives of his administration. The bulk of Reagan's speech was devoted to harsh criticism of the Soviet Union, expressed at times in a highly prejudiced manner. As a Soviet representative I was naturally offended by what he said, and I thought that Gromyko who was at the meeting had every right to walk out in protest against the speech. He, however, chose not to.

Statements in the same spirit were made by Secretary of State Haig; Secretary of Defense Weinberger; the directors of the Arms Control Agency, Eugene Rostow and Kenneth Adelman; and other Washington officials. They all felt that the best way to protect the national interests of the United States was from " a position of strength." While paying lip service at times to the possibility of diplomatic dialogue, they stressed at the same time that if diplomacy was not backed by strength, it was not for them. Once in Geneva I happened to be talking to Rostow and asked him: "Why are you Americans so strongly opposed to negotiating with us?" "What good does it do us?" was the question with which the Director of the Arms Control and Disarmament Agency answered my question. My conversation with Rostow made it clear to me that the very possibility of any joint Soviet-American action at the Conference on Disarmament was out of the question for Washington at that time.

For its part, the Kremlin gave as good as it got. The Soviet Union accused the United States of attempting to interfere in the internal affairs of other countries, striving to roll back national-liberation and revolutionary movements throughout the world and turning its back on the policy of détente, and so on. One of the most bitterly contested and confrontational subjects was that of disarmament. In the UN, at the Disarmament Conference, and at other international meetings, the representatives of the Soviet Union and the United States missed no opportunity to inflict damage on and score points off their fellow superpower.

For example, in 1982 at the General Assembly, the American delegation submitted a draft resolution titled "The Movement for Peace and Disarmament." It contained the entirely legitimate point that "an informed discussion and consideration of all points of view on disarmament could have a positive influence on achieving meaningful measures on arms limitation and in other areas."

On the surface, the U.S. proposal looked nonconfrontational. However, in his introduction, Adelman, who at that time held the post of deputy permanent representative of the United States to the UN, focused on human rights violations in the Soviet Union and other countries and the inability of the peoples of those countries to express their views on disarmament and other questions. Seen in this light the U.S. draft resolution took on an anti-Soviet resonance. The expectation was that this slant would inevitably antagonize the Soviet Union and compel it to vote against the resolution. A negative vote would cast the Soviet Union and its allies as opponents of the worldwide campaign for disarmament, while the United States, on the other hand, would be seen as its zealous champion.

I had the task of replying to Adelman's speech with the standard clichés about the supposed complete freedom of speech in the Soviet Union, while at the same time accusing the American government of all the mortal sins. In the light of the situation and also because the actual wording of the American draft contained nothing unacceptable and drew no objections from a considerable number of delegations, the Soviet delegation decided to support the resolution with one small amendment. We proposed the addition of the single word "truthful" so that the relevant provision in it would read: "Calls upon member states to promote the flow of a broad range of truthful information on disarmament questions."

We resolved to enter this amendment in the belief that it would be extremely difficult to reject it. Anyone who opposed it would inevitably be placed in the position of favoring the dissemination of slander. The Soviet amendment came as a complete surprise to the Americans. Sitting behind Adelman in the seats reserved for the American delegation were a host of legal experts, State Department representatives, and what have you.

When the chairman asked the U.S. delegation whether the Soviet amendment was acceptable, Adelman said that he needed to consult his experts and the other cosponsors of the draft and asked for a recess. The Americans understood that adoption of the Soviet amendment might be interpreted as acceptance of the Soviet viewpoint expressed in the course of the discussion on their draft and indeed that the whole point of the American initiative, which was to isolate the Soviet Union on the question of the worldwide campaign for disarmament, would be defeated.

In order to blunt the effect of the Soviet proposal, the U.S. delegation and their allies started to propose various synonyms of "truthful." They argued that in the context of the American draft the English adjectives "reliable," "accurate," or "precise" would be more appropriate. The Western diplomats ransacked the vast lexicon of the English language just to prevent the word proposed by the Soviet delegation from appearing in the text of the resolution. The feverish search for the right word took up a good hour of the meeting's time.

In the midst of this search, I said that the Soviet delegation had proposed an amendment in Russian, one of the official languages of the UN, and that *pravdivy* was a perfectly legitimate Russian word. As for the proper English translation of the word, that was a matter for the translators, the experts in the English language. The Soviet delegation, therefore, asked the chairman to put the matter to a vote without further delay. There were no objections, and the committee, and later the plenary of the General Assembly, approved the text of the resolution originally proposed by the Americans as amended by the Soviet delegation. Adelman and his team sat there looking gloomy after discussion of the question of the worldwide campaign for peace and disarmament. Many felt that the adoption of the resolution was a Pyrrhic victory for the American delegation.

I met Adelman on frequent occasions. He was undoubtedly a person of ability and had had a successful career; he had taken part in many important Soviet-American negotiations on arms limitation. I did, however, get the impression that he was not only an arch-anticommunist and anti-Soviet, although no different in this regard from other American officials, but also a Russophobe. My attempts to persuade him that Russians had many good sides such as friendliness and decency fell on deaf ears.

Richard Perle, assistant secretary of defense in the 1980s, proved to be an official out of the same mold, and also took an active part in the disarmament battles of those days. My contacts with him were sporadic, but his input to the formulation of the American position was clearly designed to provoke a negative response from the Soviet Union, if not open confrontation. Viktor Karpov, one of the leading Soviet negotiators on strategic armaments, called Perle the evil genius of the negotiations. In the 1980s, the disagreement between Perle and the State Department over the question of verification of compliance with the treaty banning chemical weapons was public knowledge. The State Department believed that the Soviet Union would never agree to the adoption of unwarrantably strict standards and the negotiations would fail. Nevertheless, Perle managed to get his way and frankly admitted that "we will never get an agreement on that basis."

The "strong-arm" tactics that formed part of the Reagan administration's policy were backed by an arms buildup that was supposedly necessary to preempt possible action by the Soviet Union and intimidate it with the prospect of "irretrievable" damage. We Soviet negotiators were disheartened by the military doctrine of direct confrontation set forth by the Pentagon in 1982 in "Defense Directives for 1984–8."

The height of anti-Soviet rhetoric was reached with Reagan's phrase "the evil empire." More than enough has already been said and written about this expression. I recall that it so happened that on the very day after Reagan's speech, our delegation was to meet our American colleagues at the bilateral negotiations in Geneva. When we asked how we should take the, to put it mildly, unfriendly remark of the president, our American colleagues explained it away with some embarrassment by saying that the president was being "overemotional," and some even thought that he had simply misspoken.

Well, of course, he wasn't and he hadn't and that made it harder to take. The president, by using this phrase, had lumped together a long-suffering people who had sacrificed tens of millions of their lives for the sake of the victory over fascism and had suffered the horrors of starvation and terror along with many other hardships. Suddenly all the people of the Soviet Union were being branded with the same stigma, the same evil. My countrymen were deeply offended by that epithet.

There Does Not Have to Be a Conflict Because of Missiles

Rhetoric is one thing, but at the end of the 1970s and the beginning of the 1980s things were clearly moving in the direction of increased danger of a real conflict between the superpowers, the threat of the Cold War turning hot. I and many of my Soviet colleagues understood that the deterioration of the international situation was due solely to Washington's anti-Sovietism. Some of our own military moves, which caused considerable alarm in the West, were also disturbing.

I am thinking particularly of our SS-20 medium-range missiles, which were produced and then deployed in 1976. In response, the Council of NATO decided in December 1979 to deploy new American medium-range missiles in Europe. Although it was at about the same time that the SALT 2 Treaty was concluded, it was clear that the deployment of new medium-range missiles would create enormous difficulties for the bilateral negotiations on arms limitation as a whole.

As a representative to the Conference on Disarmament I had no direct connection with the problem of missile deployment, but it was something that affected every aspect of the relations between the two superpowers, particularly in the area of disarmament, and many delegations referred to it at the conference.

In my statements I confined myself to repeating the official Soviet position and tried to avoid going into detail. In a conversation with the delegation's military expert, a colonel from the General Staff, I asked him to enlighten me on the subject. He told me that the old Soviet SS-4 and SS-5 medium-range missiles were hopelessly antiquated, since they ran on first generation liquid fuel. Production of them stopped, according to him, in the mid-1960s. The SS-20 missiles were a modernized version, and their deployment, in his view, would not be an addition to the Soviet medium-range missile arsenal so much as a replacement of the old ones by a new generation. He saw no particular reason for concern on the part of the United States and its Western allies, since different types of weaponry were constantly being modernized by both sides.

My colleague was unable to answer to my question about whether the deployment of the SS-20s would mean an increase in missiles in terms of warheads. At the same time he expressed the conviction that if the Americans and their allies had been given guarantees that the deployment of the SS-20s would not change the existing balance of forces, then it would not have aroused all this concern.

Many years later I discovered that one of our leading experts on military political questions, Deputy Foreign Minister Korniyenko, was of the same opinion. He thought that it would have been possible to reach a compromise with the West on the question of medium-range missiles by informing the Western countries that the deployment of the SS-20s was not designed to secure any one-sided advantages for the Soviet Union. In that case the question of the deployment of new American missiles in Europe might well not have arisen and all the tension generated by the deployment of the SS-20s would have been dissipated. That this was a genuine possibility at that time was shown by an opinion expressed by the chancellor of the Federal Republic of Germany, Helmut Schmidt. Yet when Korniyenko expressed this view at a meeting of the Politburo, he recalls that it drew a sharp rebuke from the defense minister, Dmitry Ustinov: "I can't believe what I'm hearing! It's not enough that you're giving away our plans to the other side, now you want to tinker with them! And what makes you so sure they'll give up their own plans after that anyway?"

Granted that the colonel from the delegation knew his minister's position, but he was much more sober and realistic and, more important, a lot more peace-loving than him. Ustinov, one of the most powerful members of the politburo, was a Soviet policy hard-liner, and this came out particularly clearly in this question of the medium-range missiles.

Korniyenko points out in his memoirs that there were other mistakes too in the handling of this matter, such as the refusal to sit down at the negotiating table "until NATO rescinded its decision to deploy the new American medium-range missiles," followed by "until the deployment is halted," and finally "slamming the door" on negotiations. I must say that I and many of my colleagues in Geneva felt exactly the same way. However, I would not describe them so much as mistakes as a flawed policy that led inevitably to a further exacerbation of the Cold War.

The Sverdlovsk Incident

The strained relations between the two superpowers and the East and the West became apparent at the first review conference on the Convention on the Prohibition of Bacteriological Weapons held in Geneva in the spring of 1980. Although it did not fall within the framework of the Conference on Disarmament, practically all the protagonists were the same, as was the political climate at both conferences.

A few days before the end of the review conference, the head of the U.S. delegation, Charles Flowerree, told me that the U.S. government had doubts about the nature of the outbreak of anthrax that had occurred in Sverdlovsk in April and May of 1979, and that it was awaiting an explanation. Flowerree also told me that the American embassy in Moscow had made a similar demarche and added that the final position of the United States on the Final Document of the conference would depend on the response.

I immediately reported the conversation with Flowerree to Moscow and voiced my misgivings about the prospects for a positive outcome to the conference, which was already under way. There was an immediate reply from Moscow. It confirmed the outbreak of anthrax in Sverdlovsk, but claimed that it had nothing to do with the bacteriological convention. I was informed that a reply to this effect had been given to the American embassy in Moscow. I met with Flowerree at once and transmitted the information from Moscow.

At the closing session of the conference, Flowerree once again raised the matter of the anthrax outbreak but did nothing to prevent the adoption of the Final Document by consensus. The Final Document gave an overall favorable assessment of the bacteriological convention and mentioned no instances of violation of it. In my statement I also supported the Final

Document and referred briefly to the Sverdlovsk outbreak, repeating the version I had received from Moscow.

Although I hoped that this would be the end of the "Sverdlovsk incident," the matter continued to be investigated and discussed for decades. At the beginning of that lengthy period, as official representative (I was also the head of the Soviet Delegation at the second review conference in 1986), and later as a private individual, I was involved in and followed the evolution of this mysterious problem.

Washington was not, of course, satisfied by Moscow's answer to its demarche, and the United States continued to press for a more complete explanation of the Sverdlovsk incident. Although I was not formally responsible for this question, the subject of the anthrax outbreak inevitably came up in conversations with various experts on the subject. As a result of these conversations, I resolved to express my views on Sverdlovsk to Gromyko. My first suggestion was that it would be well advised to hold formal consultations among experts pursuant to Article 5 of the Convention on the Prohibition of Bacteriological Weapons. I thought that such consultations would dispel all doubts that had arisen in the minds of the Americans because of the incident. My second proposal was that reputable medical journals should publish articles containing appropriate data that would shed light on the anthrax epidemic in Sverdlovsk.

The answer to my first suggestion was negative. Moscow believed that the very fact of our agreement to consultations would be an acknowledgment that the epidemic in Sverdlovsk was directly connected with the bacteriological convention, and this had been categorically rejected in the initial Soviet reaction to the American demarche. My second proposal, however, found support, and two Moscow journals—*The Journal of Microbiology, Epidemiology, and Immunology* and *Man and the Law*—soon published articles on the anthrax outbreak in Sverdlovsk. At first I was pleased by this development, but when I actually read the articles my medical education and some previous experience with bacteriology led me to conclude that the articles failed to answer the numerous questions the American government had raised about Sverdlovsk. The articles were not very professional, and they were couched in general terms without any of the necessary data. In fact, the articles only raised more questions and doubts.

When I was appointed head of the delegation to the second review conference on the bacteriological convention in 1986, I asked for expert epidemiologists to be included in the delegation. One such expert, Professor

N. Antonov, disclosed that anthrax quite frequently attacked people and animals not only in the Sverdlovsk region but throughout the whole of Siberia. It was for this very reason that anthrax became known in Russia as Siberian ulcers or sores. In fact we learned that from 1920 to 1960 there were 865 recorded cases of anthrax among humans, and in the period from 1936 to 1968 the number of cases among animals was 160. It had been discovered that the frozen soil of Siberia contained widely scattered spores of anthrax bacteria, which entered the organism through food, infecting them. In turn, the consumption of meat from infected animals caused serious illness to humans. Other sources of anthrax infection among humans are inhalation, where anthrax bacteria enter the human organism through the lungs, and cutaneous or skin anthrax, where the infection enters through the skin.

Soviet medical experts claimed that in the spring of 1979 the relevant services of the Sverdlovsk region decided to permit the sale of fertilizer that later turned out to contain anthrax spores. As a result sheep and cattle were infected and were slaughtered and sold on the private market. The first patients suffering from anthrax were hospitalized on April 4, and patients continued to come in until May 18. All told, ninety-six hospital patients were diagnosed with anthrax, and despite intensive treatment sixty-four died. The Soviet experts claimed that, on the basis of careful epidemiological analysis and the results of bacteriological studies of meat and meat products taken from households whose members had suffered from anthrax, it had been established that in April and May 1979 there had been an outbreak of an intestinal form of anthrax.

The American version of the Sverdlovsk incident was quite different. According to it, the epidemic in Sverdlovsk broke out because of an accident in a local military bacteriological laboratory, which released anthrax spores into the air that subsequently spread around a wide area a pulmonary form of anthrax. According to American data, as a result of the Sverdlovsk outbreak thousands of people were stricken by the disease and there were several hundred deaths because of the inhalation of bacteria of the anthrax bacillus.

In the ensuing argument, both the Soviet and American sides stood stubbornly by their positions. At meetings of experts as well as in the course of visits by groups of Russian specialists to the United States at the end of the 1980s, additional data was produced confirming the claim that the outbreak took the form of intestinal anthrax. However, American officials remained unimpressed by these additional explanations by the Soviet side.

Soviet diplomats, including myself, supported the explanation by Soviet medical experts. On the basis of this information and materials from medical experts, we in Geneva tried to convince our U.S. colleagues that the Soviet version of the Sverdlovsk incident was the correct and true one. The U.S. government officials with whom I spoke said they had gained information from confidential sources that differed significantly from our explanation of the Sverdlovsk incident. I had established good working and personal relations with the U.S. representatives and tried several times to find out what sources they had in mind, but I never succeeded.

The twentieth century came to an end, but the secret of the Sverdlovsk incident remained. The Soviet story had in fact been a fabrication. An explosion in a military laboratory in Sverdlovsk, which led to the aerosolization of anthrax spores in the air and thus a pulmonary form of the disease, caused the epidemic. A missing air filter at the laboratory is believed to have been to blame. During one shift a clogged filter had been removed, and a note was left for incoming workers on the next shift to replace it, but the task was delayed.

One thing is clear however: The Sverdlovsk incident was a luminous display of the Cold War. The main reason Soviet authorities conspired to prevent an investigation into the case was the Soviet Union's involvement in activities incompatible with the Convention on the Prohibition of Bacteriological Weapons. The investigation could have disclosed crude Soviet infringement of its international obligations and its preparation for waging bacteriological war. As head of the Soviet delegations to the review conference on the bacteriological convention, I had many talks with experts from the Ministries of Defense and of Public Health, but I never asked delicate questions about their activity or about the Sverdlovsk laboratory. From their comments, however, I have concluded that they either knew very little or hid many things from me.

My experience with the Soviet military and the frequency with which they had violated international law gave me reason to believe that the Sverdlovsk incident was directly connected to the Soviet's infringement of the bacteriological weapons convention.

In 1992, after the collapse of the Soviet Union, President Yeltsin said of the Sverdlovsk incident, "The KGB admitted that our military development was the cause." Yeltsin's statement did not elaborate, however, on what kind of military research the laboratory conducted, nor did it explain the connection between the laboratory's activity and the outbreak of anthrax among the population of the city.

The Sverdlovsk incident was a display of the mistrust and deception that characterized the Cold War. The aspiration of the United States and the

Soviet Union to outwit each other in this incident and their readiness to break obligations and international contracts was representative of the ugly dispute between these civilized countries. Such a lack of transparency can have dire consequences in this new era of terrorism. Whenever questions about Sverdlovsk arose, American representatives would refuse to answer them on the grounds that revealing the sources of their version would be prejudicial to the security interests of the United States.

On the other hand, the Soviet authorities did their best to protect the Sverdlovsk military laboratory from any possible inspection connected with the outbreak of anthrax in the city itself. At the end of World War II and in the years immediately following it, I was in contact with many Moscow bacteriologists (at the beginning of these memoirs I mentioned that as a young man I was very interested in bacteriology and worked as a bacteriologist for a short time), and I knew that in some Moscow scientific institutions and in particular at a major institute in the nearby town of Zagorsk, research was going on into bacteriological warfare. Many of my friends would describe with great enthusiasm the prospects of their research and of its great importance for defensive purposes. Of course, this was long before the conclusion of the Convention Prohibiting Bacteriological Weapons, but I never had any reason to believe, even much later, that their work had stopped or even changed in any significant way. I did not ask them anything about the nature of their work; and they, of course, generally evaded answering questions about it.

It is now impossible to completely understand the details of the anthrax outbreaks in Sverdlovsk. The aerosolization of anthrax spores was undoubtedly the actual cause of the epidemic. At the same time it is quite possible that, in the spring of 1979, there were some isolated cases of intestinal anthrax. In December of 2001, for example, a woman in Russia's remote far northern Yakutia region was being treated in hospital for suspected anthrax linked to deer meat she was given instead of wages.

After the Sverdlovsk incident had become an issue, I had many occasions as part of my job as head of the delegation to talk to bacteriologists and experts from the Ministries of Health and Defense. Here again I made a point of not asking dumb questions such as what the Sverdlovsk laboratory did, but from their standard and unvarying answers, which were extremely vague and general, even during private conversations among friends, to the questions that were asked, I concluded that they themselves either knew very little or were covering up a great deal.

A Colleague's Gloomy Prediction

At the end of the 1970s and the beginning of the 1980s we saw another example of the political failing that was to lead to the doom of our Soviet, socialist system as a whole—the urge to impose on other peoples an alien and unacceptable political regime.

When at the end of April 1978, a report came in of a coup in the Afghan capital, Kabul, I, like most of my fellow countrymen, did not attach any particular importance to that event. Since, from its very foundation the Soviet Union had always enjoyed excellent relations with Afghanistan, relations, be it said, buttressed by many international agreements, it appeared that the new regime would not mean any substantial change in relations between the two friendly countries.

I do recall, however, a conversation in the spring of 1978 with a colleague at the Diplomatic Academy, Professor Enver Aliyev, who occupied the chair of oriental languages. Aliyev was an outstanding philologist and knew a number of oriental languages. Because of his linguistic expertise the Soviet leadership systematically employed him at all Soviet-Afghan and Soviet-Iranian summit meetings. He was quite rightly considered a star of his profession and enjoyed not only an excellent reputation in the Kremlin but also the warm regard of the royal families of Afghanistan and Iran. King Zahir-Shah once even invited him to Afghanistan as his guest and as a token of his goodwill presented him with an automobile. I note in passing that the royal gift caused Aliyev no little grief. It transpired that a rank-and-file member of the CPSU needed special authorization from the Central Committee to accept a gift from the king.

In a word, Aliyev was well acquainted with the situation in Kabul as well as the political mood in the country under Zahir-Shah and under Daud and, above all, the attitude of the leadership of the country toward its giant neighbor. At the time of the coup in Afghanistan, Aliyev was deeply depressed and disturbed by the changes taking place in that country. Naturally, he did his best not to betray any trace of these feelings and publicly welcomed the "national-democratic revolution" in Afghanistan, but among friends he spoke his mind. He told me with great conviction that the so-called people's democratic revolution and the plans for building socialism in Afghanistan would come up against a brick wall and that there was "great trouble" in store for the Soviet Union in that country. I was reluctant to believe him and thought that Aliyev was being excessively pessimistic about the situation there. How wrong I was and how quickly events vindicated his prophecies!

The first bad news about the situation in Afghanistan began to come in the spring of 1979, and by the autumn of the same year the situation had deteriorated even further. Because of the nature of my work in the disarmament field I was not directly confronted with these troubling events. In December 1979 I was undergoing treatment in a Moscow hospital. In a neighboring ward was our ambassador to the United States, Dobrynin, who had returned from Washington for a medical checkup. Sometimes we would walk together in the hospital park, chatting about this and that. Once, it was December 28, during one of these walks, Dobrynin told me about a report he had just heard on the radio about Soviet troops going into Afghanistan.

This news came as a complete surprise to me, but what I found even more surprising was that this was news to Dobrynin as well. It was hard for me to believe that, having taken such a grave decision which would undoubtedly have a serious influence on Soviet-American relations in particular, the Kremlin leaders had not felt it necessary to invite the opinion of their ambassador in Washington, especially since he was close at hand here in Moscow. I even entertained the possibility that Dobrynin was privy to the preparations for the military intervention but was not at liberty to share this information with others. However, Dobrynin's assurances that the decision of the Soviet leadership was a complete surprise to him sounded so sincere that I ended up believing him, my old schoolmate. Dobrynin refrained from comment on the decision, although he could not hide his concern at the sending of what was described in the official document as "some contingents of Soviet troops" into the territory of Afghanistan. I too was alarmed by this move.

This fateful decision by the Kremlin leadership to send troops into Afghanistan thoroughly embittered the Soviet Union's relations with the Western powers, especially with the United States. Soviet-American relations had already taken a serious turn for the worse as a result of the deployment of the SS-20 missiles and the retaliatory decision by the Council of NATO to deploy new American missiles. Now, with the invasion of Afghanistan, dialogue with the United States practically petered out, and this affected us, the disarmament people, directly. The bilateral talks on the limitation of the arms trade were cut short and the negotiations between the Soviet Union and the United States on antisatellite weapons and making the Indian Ocean a zone of peace were broken off. Finally, in May 1980, a halt was called to the Soviet-American negotiations on the prohibition of chemical weapons in which I had participated, as were, at the end of the year, the tripartite Soviet-Anglo-American talks on a total and complete ban on nuclear weapons testing.

The Failed Peace Attempt in Afghanistan

The sending of Soviet troops into Afghanistan was not, of course, an item on the agenda of the Conference on Disarmament. Nevertheless, when the winter session of the conference opened in February 1980, most delegations stated their views on this Soviet action. I had to "put up some kind of defense" and resorted to the official arguments, which I am afraid convinced no one. In private conversations I tried to persuade my fellow ambassadors not to allow themselves to be diverted from the subject of disarmament by what I described as "fruitless wrangling" over Afghanistan.

In spite of my appeal, Ambassador Jamsheed Marker of Pakistan in April 1980 suddenly called for an urgent meeting on the Afghan question. He reported that the Pakistani government was proposing that the Soviet government hold unofficial talks with a view to bringing about a withdrawal of Soviet troops and a peaceful settlement in Afghanistan. Marker said that these talks should be confidential and could be held in any place the parties found convenient. Pakistan continued to stress the negative consequences of the Soviet Union siding with those in power in Afghanistan at that time and expressed the readiness of Islamabad to promote the "normalisation" of the situation in the region. He stressed that the Pakistani initiative came from Foreign Minister Aga Shahi himself, who, knowing me from our work together in New York, was looking forward to my cooperation.

I urgently transmitted the Pakistani proposal to Moscow. The reply came back at once. It was flatly and even brusquely negative. The message was that if Islamabad was really interested in strengthening peace and security in the region, then Pakistan and "certain" other powers for which it was fronting should cease their meddling in the internal affairs of Afghanistan.

I was instructed to invite Marker to meet me and to read him this answer, something which, I must admit, I did not relish. Marker expressed his regret at Moscow's response and repeated his negative view of the events in Afghanistan. On that note we parted, both understanding that there was no further point in our returning to the subject.

To my regret, Moscow had no wish to make use of the Pakistani initiative, if only for the purpose of putting out diplomatic feelers.

Three months later Marker invited me to lunch at a fashionable Geneva restaurant, the "Puss in Boots." The two of us were seated at a separate table, chatting. The subject of the war in Afghanistan naturally came up. I was frank with Marker about my opinion of the war and said that there were many in the Soviet Union who did not approve of sending Soviet troops to Afghanistan and were worried about the deterioration of the international situation. We both expressed regret that the Pakistani initiative had gotten nowhere. Then we turned to other topics and parted. I soon forgot about the lunch and generally lost sight of him in the busy round of official diplomatic events in Geneva, that focal point of multilateral diplomacy.

A couple of weeks after my lunch with Marker, I received an unusual telegram from Gromyko. It read: "Do you think you could hop back to Moscow for a couple of days without hurting the work of the conference?" Well, of course, I could. The unusual terms in which the invitation was couched set me thinking some rather optimistic thoughts. I felt that the proposals which the delegation had put forward at the negotiations at the conference must have attracted Gromyko's interest, and I even entertained the possibility of my promotion to a more responsible diplomatic post.

On my arrival, before my meeting with Gromyko I tried to find out from friends the reason for being called back to Moscow, but no one knew anything.

My conversation with Gromyko started out in the usual way: he asked about the negotiations in Geneva and how the conference was going and I could not for the life of me make out why it was necessary to call me back to Moscow for a conversation like this. However, just as I was about to leave, Gromyko handed me a five or six page document and asked me to read it. When I tried to leave with the document, Gromyko stopped me and said: "No, read it here, I don't want you to take it away!"

The document was an official memo from Andropov to Gromyko forwarding a copy of a report from Marker to Islamabad about our lunchtime conversation in the "Puss in Boots" restaurant and giving a detailed account of my views on the war in Afghanistan as well as the negative view of it prevailing in some quarters of Soviet society.

I must say that the Pakistani ambassador gave a pretty accurate account of what I had said. For a brief moment I toyed with the idea of admitting what I had said and telling him everything that I thought about the criminal adventure in Afghanistan. However, I knew that Gromyko was himself one of the principal initiators of it and it would have meant my immediate dismissal from the MFA—in Stalin's day it would have meant my arrest. No, I was not ready for that.

I handed back Andropov's document to Gromyko and said that it conveyed a false impression of my remarks on that occasion and expressed the hope that the minister trusted me more than the Pakistani ambassador. After a moment's silence, Gromyko agreed and suggested that I return to Geneva. I gave a sigh of relief. I am sure that if Andropov and Gromyko had not been on such good terms, and Gromyko had not been reluctant to make an issue of my conversation with the Pakistani, I would not have gotten off so lightly. As it was, this episode really put the fear of God into me. How could Marker's report have fallen into the hands of the KGB? Who was the Pakistani in Geneva or Islamabad that was cooperating with our intelligence services? Was the KGB really that omnipotent and omniscient? Such questions haunted me.

Divergent Opinions About the Afghanistan War

There were quite a number of occasions when the question of the war in Afghanistan came up in conversation with Gromyko. I was always struck by his failure to see how ruinous the Afghan adventure would be for the authority of the Soviet Union, and also his intransigence. I remember once after my return from New York where I had gone for a regular session of the UN General Assembly, he asked me to tell him my impressions about the discussion of our "key issue" as well as the overall situation in the UN in New York. He was in a good mood and ready to listen to what I had to say.

I decided to be frank and told him that the main topic of discussion was not, unfortunately, our propagandist proposal, but the Afghan question. Without overdramatizing the situation, I tried to describe the atmosphere surrounding the discussion in the UN of our actions in Afghanistan. The overwhelming majority of delegations took part in the debate and, for the most part, condemned the policy of the Soviet Union. Moreover, among our critics were the delegations of friendly nonaligned countries. I told him that our attempts to explain our position and influence opinion in our favor had been a failure. More than a hundred delegations voted in favor of the resolution condemning the policy of the Soviet Union and only a handful of delegations of the socialist countries along with India and Bhutan voted against.

As I spoke Gromyko's mood darkened; he began to interrupt me and finally said the bad results of the voting were due to the poor performance of the Soviet delegation, including my own. He curtly dismissed the idea that the debate on the Afghan question could be described as the keynote of the General Assembly session, referring to it disparagingly as political shortsightedness. The minister scornfully dismissed the debate as "a storm in a teacup." He was really annoyed. After that I tried to avoid conversations with him on the subject of Afghanistan. I never could tell if Gromyko would ever be capable of grasping the irreparable harm done to the Soviet Union by the decision to send Soviet troops into Afghanistan, a decision for which he shared direct responsibility.

My colleagues and I discussed this question over and over again, but I have to say that there was never a consensus among us on this issue, either at the time the troops were sent in or later. Once at the beginning of the 1980s I happened to be on the same plane to Geneva as Ambassador Yuly Kvitsinsky. He was on his way to one set of negotiations and I to another. We were discussing the "bad behavior" of our American negotiating partners and their bid to use the entry of Soviet troops into Afghanistan as a pretext to undermine all the ongoing negotiations. As I saw it, the Afghanistan business had no bearing on our negotiations, and I expressed my regret about it. Kvitsinsky, one of the most capable Soviet diplomats, totally disagreed with me. He sincerely believed that the presence of Soviet troops in Afghanistan was fully justified and only strengthened the authority of the Soviet Union as a superpower which would not permit undesirable maneuvering in the vicinity of its frontiers. As for the Americans, it was his view that our action would also have a sobering effect on them. Kvitsinsky even entertained the notion that the presence of Soviet troops might even force the Americans to seek an early agreement with the Soviet Union.

This was pretty much the same view as that of Shalva Sanakoyev, the editor of the journal *International Life*, who was usually very well informed about international affairs and was close to Gromyko. For him, the theory underlying his judgments about the responsibility of the Soviet Union in international politics was the necessity of relentlessly and systematically resorting to acts of force in order to keep "reminding" the rest of the world "who is who." In his view, action to prevent Afghanistan becoming a base for anti-Soviet operations in Central Asia was entirely justified.

My colleague Ambassador Vasily Safronchyuk, with whom I had worked in New York, also had an interesting approach to the matter. He had been posted for some time in the 1980s to Kabul as special adviser to the Afghan foreign minister. I will not attempt to evaluate the usefulness of Safronchyuk's advice for the foreign policy of the Afghan authorities, who were entirely dependent on Moscow, but this experienced Soviet diplomat knew more about the situation than many of the Kremlin leaders. He once told me in a conversation that sending in troops had, no doubt, not been a good idea, but now that they were there, the Afghan problem, in his view, could and must be resolved by the *total* occupation of the whole country. At the time, he felt that the sooner and more decisively we did that, the better.

However, I think I can safely say that most Soviet diplomats, both those in Smolenskaya Square and those posted abroad, did not approve of and regretted the sending of Soviet troops into Afghanistan. Those who were for quitting that country were in the majority and in time their number grew.

I have to mention here the extremely difficult task assigned to another eminent Soviet diplomat, Vladimir Shustov, who at that time was deputy permanent representative of the Soviet Union to the UN. He was instructed to work for a change in the extremely unfavorable attitude of member states of the organization toward the position of the Soviet Union in Afghanistan. Shustov was undoubtedly one of the most popular Soviet diplomats in New York. He was an extremely personable, witty and affable diplomat, and he did his best to carry out his mission. His best efforts, however, led nowhere. The world community condemned Soviet policy in Afghanistan and demanded a change in it.

It was in this international atmosphere that I had to start work at the Conference on Disarmament. The first session of the year, the spring session of 1979, had already been a disappointment. Although most participants had expressed dissatisfaction at the fact that too much time had been spent on producing the conference's program of work and resolving organizational matters, when the conference finally did get down to the substantive work, it turned out that delegations were not ready for negotiations. Most of the meeting time was spent in mutual recriminations about stoking up the arms race.

On my return to Moscow after the first session of the conference I reported my impressions to the minister and the Collegium. It emerged from my contacts that the situation in other areas of foreign policy was no better at all. I was chagrined to see that the discussion of the results of the conference did not lead to the production of any new positions on specific disarmament issues. The document issued by the Collegium on my report spoke only of various propaganda exercises. In particular, embassies and missions were asked to carry out "an information campaign with as many countries as possible with a view to securing support for our positions on disarmament questions." The other points covered in the document were equally devoid of substance.

I have to admit that I myself was one of the authors of this empty document. Our delegation made some attempt to give it some positive substance, but feeling as we did about the general political climate in Moscow and the reluctance and inability of the Kremlin leadership to revise old positions that seemed hopelessly immovable, we gave up even these tentative attempts. The prospects for progress in multilateral and bilateral Soviet-American negotiations grew worse and worse as the differences over medium-range missiles and the war in Afghanistan deepened. Our delegation was leaving for Geneva deeply dispirited.

16
MARKING TIME

The Resolution That Had to Be Called Back

The Soviet representatives at the Conference on Disarmament—and I think that this applies to all representatives there—were sincerely interested in the success of the Soviet-American negotiations on nuclear weapons, particularly because progress in other areas of arms limitation and disarmament depended on their success. Particular importance was attached to the talks on the limitation of nuclear weapons in Europe. Everyone understood that the failure of these talks might have unforeseeable consequences and lead to the inevitable escalation of the Cold War. The following unusual episode attests our readiness to everything in our power to prevent the talks failing.

In the autumn of 1983 an extremely tense situation arose in and with regard to these talks. While negotiating with the Soviet Union, the United States simultaneously was preparing to deploy Pershing-2 medium-range missiles and cruise missiles in Western Europe by the end of 1983. The Soviet Union, for its part, had repeatedly stated that if the United States deployed new nuclear armaments in Europe, there would no longer be any point in proceeding with the talks.

At the same time, it was public knowledge that there was no progress in the Soviet-American talks in the autumn of 1983, and this was causing widespread concern. It was not surprising, therefore, that the question of bilateral negotiations on nuclear weapons should have become the focus of attention at the session of the UN General Assembly, which was then under way. After lengthy discussion, in which all delegations spoke against the breaking-off of negotiations, a number of draft resolutions were tabled on items of the agenda of the First Committee. The first draft to be submitted was that of Romania, followed by drafts from Mexico, Sweden, Yugoslavia and a number of other countries. These documents all reflected the approach to the bilateral negotiations of the neutral and nonaligned countries. A group of Western countries—the United Kingdom, Belgium, Italy, Canada, the Netherlands, and Japan—also introduced a resolution reflecting their view of the negotiations.

We in the Soviet delegation had no instructions to present a draft resolution on the subject. The delegations of the socialist countries were in favor of submitting a resolution, but for obvious reasons, asked the Soviet representatives to decide on the matter. I, the representative on the First Committee, and my colleagues racked our brains: was it a good idea to submit a resolution calling for the talks to continue in a situation where the Soviet Union had clearly stated that there was no point whatsoever in proceeding with negotiations, if the United States were actively to deploy its missiles in Western Europe, and there was no reason to suppose that Washington and its allies would back off from their decision to do so?

In the circumstances, we decided on a risky step. Without asking Moscow, we advised the delegations of the socialist countries to submit their own draft resolution calling for the talks to continue. We were well aware that a breakdown in the negotiations would only do harm to the Soviet Union, and we still held out a slender hope that an appeal from our "brothers" from the socialist countries, would help to cool down some of the hotheads in Moscow.

In response to our advice, the delegations of Bulgaria, Hungary, Vietnam, the German Democratic Republic, Laos, Mongolia, Poland, and Czechoslovakia introduced their draft resolution, which expressed their conviction that it was possible to achieve an acceptable agreement at the Geneva talks on the basis of the principle of equality and equal security.

The United States and the Soviet Union, as the parties to the Geneva negotiations, did not cosponsor the resolution, although both the U.S. delegation and particularly our own delegation together with our allies took an active part in the work on the various drafts.

Finally, there were four drafts on the table, all calling for the talks to continue. The First Committee took a vote on all the draft resolutions, all of which, including, of course, that of the socialist countries, were approved by sizable majorities and sent, in accordance with the UN rules of procedure, to the plenary of the General Assembly for its approval. However, at the end of November, the United States began deploying the new American medium-range missiles on the territory of the Federal Republic of Germany, the United Kingdom, and Italy. In the circumstances, the Kremlin announced that any further participation by the Soviet Union in the negotiations with the United States had now become impossible, and they were called off.

The meeting of the General Assembly to approve the draft resolutions was to have been held about a week after the Soviet government had called a halt to the talks. In the new circumstances, the impression might be created that the socialist countries—the cosponsors of the draft resolution—might be in disagreement with the Soviet government and were calling on the Soviet Union and the United States to return to the negotiating table. In short, the unilateral decision of the Kremlin to call a halt to the talks, a decision that, quite frankly, aroused bitter disappointment and did nothing to help a speedy resolution to the question of the elimination of medium-range missiles, threatened, apart from anything else, to cause naked diplomatic disarray.

I felt personal responsibility for the ensuing situation, since I had been an outspoken proponent of placing the draft resolution by the socialist countries on the agenda. My colleagues from the delegations of these countries did not attempt to conceal from me the fact that they feared trouble with their capitals over this unprecedented incident where all the socialist countries had, in essence, condemned a decision of the Soviet government. After consultation, we decided that the draft resolution of the socialist countries should not be brought to a vote at the plenary of the General Assembly.

This decision was communicated to the president of the General Assembly. He, however, stated that the request of the cosponsors could only be granted with the approval of the plenary itself, since, after the adoption of the draft resolution of the socialist countries by the First Committee, it had ceased to be "the property" of its sponsors and now "belonged" to the committee that had transmitted it to the General Assembly for its consideration. There was quite a heated argument with the president (the post was occupied at that time by the representative of Panama), but he stood firm.

The delegations of the Western countries, which had voted against the socialist draft in the First Committee, learning of the unusual request of its cosponsors, staunchly defended it and demanded that it be voted on in the plenary too. They did not conceal their glee at the awkward situation in which the delegations of the socialist countries and, first and foremost, the Soviet delegation found themselves, knowing full well, as they did, that it was behind the action taken by its allies.

Within the "fraternal family" of socialist countries a row was brewing. It was urgent to prevent the socialist draft being voted on in the General Assembly, particularly because it had come to my ears privately that the authorities in Moscow were incensed at the situation resulting from our actions, which had not been authorized by the ministry

One can imagine my relief when, after numerous meetings, principally with representatives of neutral and nonaligned countries, which were, on the whole, sympathetic to the request of the cosponsors of the socialist countries' resolution, and after all kinds of procedural wrangling, we finally succeeded in preventing the resolution from being put to the vote in the plenary and thereby becoming a decision of the General Assembly. When I returned to Moscow from New York, I was reprimanded for my unauthorized initiative in instigating the socialist countries' draft resolution, but not as severely as I would have been if the General Assembly had taken the unwelcome decision.

This was a very unusual case, but none the less extremely enlightening. It showed how many unexpected twists and turns lay on the tortuous path of multilateral diplomacy; yet one had to be ready for them. Also, it was typical of Cold War diplomacy that the slightest slip-up, even of a procedural kind, by one side was immediately seized upon and exploited to the limit by the other.

As to the substance of the incident of the draft resolution of the socialist countries, our attempt to influence the position of the leadership of the Soviet Union by trying to get a "socialist" resolution passed by the General Assembly was, to say the least, naïve, and it did betray a certain thoughtlessness and undoubted indiscipline on the part of my colleagues and myself. On the other hand, I have to say that we were so anxious to get the Moscow leadership to view world developments and specific international situations in a more realistic and pragmatic way that we were unwilling to pass up the slightest chance of doing so.

Trust, but Verify

Our hope that the Kremlin would take a more pragmatic line was encouraged by the fact that the sheer facts of life sometimes forced it to rethink its orthodox reactions to events and to adapt them to the realities. This happened, for the most part, as a result of pressure from the other side in the Cold War. Experience proved that even the negotiators themselves were sometimes instrumental in bringing about a certain evolution in Kremlin attitudes. One example was the shift in Soviet views on the key disarmament issue, that of verification.

In the Cold War period the conceptual differences between the two sides were particularly contentious. The Western approach was based on establishing a system of arms control or verification, which extended to cover the effective monitoring of essentially the entire range of a country's military activity. The Soviet approach was based on the concept that only disarmament measures should be subject to verification and that they should be confined exclusively to areas of military activity specifically covered by a given disarmament agreement.

To prevent verification extending beyond the framework of a disarmament agreement, it was our view that its scope should correspond strictly with practical disarmament measures. In our statements at the Conference on Disarmament, we Soviet representatives constantly stressed the need for the organic interdependence of verification measures and disarmament, and we described the Western approach as an attempt to interfere in the internal affairs of other states and an out-and-out means of spying on them.

On the other hand, the Soviet approach was unacceptable to the West. From their standpoint, this approach left open considerable opportunities for carrying out activities prohibited under the agreement on the pretext that such activities did not fall under its terms. The Western powers believed that the Soviet approach created favorable conditions, not only for violating the agreement in specific areas of arms limitation, but also for the overall growth of a state's military potential.

The discussion of verification issues during the Cold War at the Conference on Disarmament among other forums made it abundantly clear that the factors underlying the problem were primarily political. In the context of the bitter rivalry between the two superpowers and their allies, it was extraordinarily difficult to find mutually acceptable and fair agreements on the verification of disarmament agreements. The main reason was the absence of trust.

Even at the time of the Second World War, when the Soviet Union the United States, and Britain were allies, they strove to guard their most important advances in the field of armaments and military technology as closely as possible and did not trust each other. After the war, the distrust was many times greater. The former allies did everything possible to overtake each other and achieve military superiority.

It became clear that in order to make the slightest progress in arms limitation and disarmament a minimum of trust had to be created. This was to be done by means of expanding contacts between nongovernmental organizations and summits, at which leaders began talking about "the spirit of Geneva" and the "spirit of Camp David."

During the Cold War, and not only then, trust was extremely elusive and ephemeral. It was for precisely this reason that the Russian proverb: "Trust but verify!" became very popular. It became universally familiar because at the end of the 1980s President Reagan became very fond of using it in connection with the arms limitation talks and international relations in general.

For me this proverb always had a different association. At the height of the purges and the reign of terror in the 1930s, Stalin was very fond of using it, although what his satraps understood by it, was the use of any means to attain their ends. Did Reagan know of Stalin's fondness for this proverb and how its meaning was distorted during Stalin's dictatorship? I don't know. I even felt like bringing it to the president's attention and told Louis Fields, an American colleague at the Disarmament Conference about this fact of history and asked him to convey it to the president. After returning from one of his trips to Washington, Fields told me that he had done as I asked. "And . . . ?" I asked. He smiled and said: "The president still likes the proverb anyway." And indeed the president went on using it.

Control, or verification, and its forms, content, and methods have always been and, no doubt, always will be, a constantly evolving process. It should be viewed in conjunction with the transformation of international legal, technical, organizational, administrative, and other norms. During the years I was associated with disarmament negotiations, the most important methods of control were the use of national technical means, the submission of information, the exchange of seismic and other data, consultations, testing and examination, a complaints process against suspected violators of an agreement, and finally, on-site inspections.

The most highly controversial of these was on-site inspection. The differences in approach were very marked, ranging from Khrushchev's "You check yourself and I'll check myself" to the proposal of the extremists who demanded inspections anywhere, at any time, and under any circumstances. Time was passing, but still no compromise on the question of inspections could be reached, although in circumstances of total distrust so typical of the Cold War, it was precisely this that seemed to be the most reliable method. The failure to reach agreement on on-site inspections prevented, for example, agreement on a comprehensive nuclear test ban treaty, a convention on the prohibition of chemical weapons, and a number of other treaties.

The question of a comprehensive test ban treaty was one of the core issues on the agenda of the Conference on Disarmament. After the Soviet-American-British negotiations on this subject had been broken off, many countries began to urge insistently that the conference get down to practical negotiations. It was proposed that a special working group of the conference be established to prepare a draft treaty on the subject. A number of countries, including Sweden and the Soviet Union, submitted draft treaties but no progress was recorded. However, as in previous years, the stumbling block was the problem of verification; that is, on-site inspections.

At the end of the 1970s and the beginning of the 1980s the problem of verification grew into quite a fierce internal argument in Moscow itself, both within the MFA and between departments (the Ministry of Defense and the Ministry of Medium Engineering). One side, principally the military, believed that the use of national technical means together with the establishment of an appropriate system of seismic stations would be quite sufficient for ensuring verification of compliance with the comprehensive test ban treaty. In their view, on-site inspection was unnecessary. The other side believed that without such inspections there would never be agreement on a treaty. The proponents of this view, myself among them, believed that the question of inspections had now become a matter of principle and that the Western powers would never come to an agreement in the context of the prevailing distrust.

Consequently, experts were assigned the task of producing a formula that would make it impossible to use inspections for intelligence or espionage purposes. After considerable effort the experts finally came up with a formula that provided that if a state-party to the treaty had doubts about the nature of a seismic event occurring on the territory of another state-party, it could raise the question of an on-site inspection in order to ascertain the true nature of the event. In such a case, the experts proposed, the necessary justification for the need to carry out such an inspection would have to be produced. The key sentence of this clause, whose wording we labored over for so many days and nights, was as follows: "The state-party in respect of which doubts have been expressed as to its compliance with the present treaty, understanding the significance of the question, may take a favorable position with regard to the conducting of an inspection on its territory if it deems that the justification advanced is cogent, or may take a different decision. Such an inspection shall take place in a manner to be determined by the inviting state-party."

This formula, thrashed out as the result of arduous interdepartmental negotiations and representing a difficult compromise between different points of view, was not, of course, properly appreciated in the West and failed to produce progress in the talks. Nevertheless, it did reflect growing awareness on the part of the Soviet ruling elite of the importance of on-site inspections in the implementation of arms limitation measures. In essence this was an acknowledgment of the necessity for inspections limited neither in number nor in location. The formula did, of course, contain various restrictions, principally in providing for the refusal of the request for an inspection. Nevertheless, the positive evolution in the Soviet position was clear, if we recall the original Khrushchev formula of let each side inspect itself. In one of our discussions, Gromyko acknowledged that although the Soviet formula made on-site inspection voluntary, it would actually be very difficult, if not impossible for the state-party, whose compliance with the treaty was in doubt, to refuse such a request, unless of course, that state was willing to risk a confrontation with international law. In general, then, the position of the Soviet superpower, on questions of international verification in particular, was becoming more realistic. This was encouraging.

Important steps had been taken in the right direction. At the Disarmament Conference a special working group was set up and was able to start work on negotiating a nuclear test ban treaty.

But Does the Soviet Union Possess Chemical Weapons?

When I came to work at the Disarmament Conference, our delegation was conducting separate negotiations with the United States on the prohibition of chemical weapons, radiological weapons, and new types of weapons of mass destruction. The most arduous and important, of course, were the negotiations on chemical weapons, and in Geneva we gave priority to these negotiations. As head of the Soviet delegation I took part in the bilateral and multilateral negotiations on the prohibition of chemical weapons for almost ten years. That might appear a rather long time, but if one realizes that the first attempts to ban the use of chemical agents in warfare were made as long ago as 1874 at an international conference on the laws and customs of war in Brussels and subsequently repeated on a number of occasions at other forums at the end of the nineteenth and the beginning of the twentieth century, and that formal multilateral negotiations to prohibit chemical weapons had taken place at the League of Nations between 1926 and 1930 and at the Geneva Conference on Disarmament at intervals between the end of the 1960s and 1992, when a convention on the subject was finally signed, my measly ten years does not seem so long by comparison.

The first question with which I was confronted was: "Does the Soviet Union possess chemical weapons?" Well, this seems to be a pretty naïve question, to say the least. Of course, it does. But it was impossible for me as the chief Soviet negotiator to give such a categorical reply. When I was appointed head of the delegation to the bilateral talks on chemical weapons, I put this question to Korniyenko, my immediate superior at the MFA. Instead of giving me a direct answer, he simply said that my job was to conduct negotiations on the prohibition of these weapons—period. I once raised the question with General Vladimir Pikalov, commander of the Soviet chemical forces, with whom I happened to have a good personal and working relationship. His answer was more or less the same as Korniyenko's, but he did stress that the role of the chemical forces was that of defense against chemical warfare. Chemical experts both from the Ministry of Defense and the Ministry of Chemical Industry who were well acquainted with the kinds and amounts of chemical weapons in the arsenals of the United States and other countries, said that Soviet activities in this area were purely defensive.

My position as negotiator became at times complicated and ambiguous. I was urging my negotiating partners, first and foremost the Americans, to negotiate frankly and honestly, while I myself was not in a position to give an answer to the key question about whether the Soviet Union possessed chemical weapons.

In response to the queries of my opposite numbers, in particular Foreign Minister Hans Dietrich Genscher of the Federal Republic of Germany during my visit to Bonn in the summer of 1986, I urged Moscow to tell me how to react to the persistent inquiries received by the Soviet delegation; should I firmly deny possession, or acknowledge in some general fashion that the

Soviet Union did have chemical weapons? I received strict instructions to do neither, but to say that the Soviet Union would be ready to answer that question after the conclusion of a treaty banning chemical weapons. There is no denying that an answer of this kind had a negative effect on the negotiations and did nothing to build trust between the parties to them.

Of course, my fellow diplomats and I, both Soviet and foreign, understood that the Soviet superpower, which possessed all the very latest types of weaponry also had chemical weapons in its arsenals, but I, as the official government representative, needed to be able to operate not on the basis of guesswork but rather on the basis of a formal acknowledgment by the leaders of our country of the existence of chemical weapons. One of my colleagues, sympathizing with my position, advised me to search for some acknowledgment of this kind in statements by Soviet leaders and use it.

I decided to examine the statements of Soviet leaders made during the Second World War and after it and came across a curious fact. In the spring of 1942, Stalin, through Ivan Maisky, our ambassador in London, passed on to Churchill some information obtained by the Soviet government about the possible use by German forces of poison gas against the Soviet Union. The British prime minister thereupon informed the Soviet leader of the decision of the British government to treat any use of poison gas against the Soviet Union precisely as if that weapon had been used against Britain herself.

"I have accumulated vast stockpiles of gas bombs which can be dropped from aircraft," Churchill wrote to Stalin, "and we shall not hesitate to drop them on all appropriate targets in Western Germany from the moment when your army and people are attacked by these weapons." A similar statement was also made by Roosevelt when he learned of the use of chemical weapons by enemy powers. "The government," he stated in the summer of 1943, "has received reliable reports of the use by the Japanese armed forces of poison and toxic gas in various parts of China. I want to make it unequivocally clear that if Japan continues to practise this inhuman form of warfare against China or an other member of the United Nations, such action will be viewed by the government of the United States as an attack on the United States and all-out retaliatory action of the same kind will be taken."

The leaders of Britain and the United States thus unequivocally announced the possession by those countries of chemical weapons and their willingness to use them in the event that enemy powers were to resort to kinds of warfare proscribed by international agreements. And what about Stalin? He too acknowledged possession of chemical weapons by the Soviet

Union, but did not say in what circumstances he would be willing to use them. He just expressed his interest in cooperating with his allies in the production of these weapons. That was, of course, in time of war and invoking Stalin's admissions would not have been entirely appropriate. Other Kremlin leaders, however, civilian and military alike, never subsequently referred to that matter.

Before my resignation as head of the Soviet delegation at the negotiations, I undertook one more attempt to overcome the "silence conspiracy" surrounding the issue of chemical weapons. At the beginning of 1987, the delegation indirectly admitted to Soviet possession of chemical weapons. However, hardly anyone paid attention to this vague declaration; everyone waited for a precise and authoritative explanation.

It was only in April 1987 that Gorbachev acknowledged possession by the Soviet Union of chemical weapons, when he said that the Soviet Union had stopped production of them and that it had no chemical weapons outside its own borders and that work had begun on the construction of a special facility for the destruction of chemical weapons. At the end of the same year Gorbachev announced that stockpiles of these weapons in Soviet arsenals did not exceed fifty tons.

Alas, I was unable to make use of these hopelessly tardy admissions, since I was no longer participating in negotiations on the prohibition of chemical weapons. I really envied my successor, who no longer needed, as I had for so many years, to dance around the question of whether the Soviet Union possessed chemical weapons or not.

"The Adzhimushk Incident"

Everyone, of course, knew that chemical weapons had first been used by Imperial Germany in the First World War. As to the use of poison gas and other chemical agents in warfare by Britain and France, also in the first World War; by Italy against Ethiopia in 1935 and 1936; by Japan against China on the eve of the Second World War; and by the United States in Vietnam, a great deal had been written about all this in the Soviet press and timely use was also made of this information by the Soviet delegation.

As for the use by the Soviet Union of chemical agents against the civilian population and military personnel of the enemy, far from conceding that there had been any actions of this kind, I "categorically rebuffed" any claims to this effect. One attempt at such a "categorical rebuff" rebounded in the most unexpected way.

It all began at the Geneva conference at the beginning of 1983 with a speech by the then vice president of the United States, George Bush. In his speech, Bush, talking about the cruel nature and immorality of the use of chemical weapons, claimed that they had been used by the Soviet Union and its allies in Afghanistan and Southeast Asia, in violation of the 1925 Geneva protocol prohibiting the use of asphyxiating gases. Naturally, he said nothing about the use by American forces of chemical weapons for more than a decade in the war in Vietnam.

The Soviet delegation, of course, could not let that "thrust" by Bush go by without a riposte and in a brief "right of reply" pointed out that the Geneva protocol of 1925 had indeed been violated on several occasions, and I listed the offenders, highlighting the United States. I also mentioned that German forces had used chemical agents against Soviet troops in the Crimea in 1942. I described the allegations of the use of chemical weapons by the Soviet Union as pure slander.

A few days later, I received a letter from the representative of the FRG to the conference, Ambassador Wegener. In it, the West German diplomat wrote that he was "surprised" to hear the statement of the Soviet delegation about the use by the Hitlerites of chemical weapons, since it was the first time he had heard such a claim. He said that he believed we must have made some mistake which needed to be corrected. He expressed the hope that I would find some appropriate way of reestablishing the truth. He added that the question of identifying the true offenders was an extremely serious one and should leave no room for doubt.

I discussed the letter with the delegation and, without attaching any great importance to the matter, we decided to confirm the use by the Nazis of poison gas in one of our statements. We were concerned that we might provoke an argument about whether the Soviet Union had been one of the violators of the Geneva protocol; and there was a danger of that.

In one of my statements I repeated that fascist forces had used chemical gases on a number of occasions. I mentioned specifically that in 1942 gas had been used in the Crimea during military operations against Soviet units and civilians who had taken up positions in the Adzhimushk stone quarries near the town of Kerch. This was a definite violation of the Geneva protocol, and I thought that would be the end of the matter.

From time to time Wegener had been privately expressing his dissatisfaction with my explanation, and a few months after I had mentioned the incident in the Adzhimushk quarries I received a long letter from the German ambassador. In it he said that he had carefully studied the military history of that time and had made a point of consulting the military archives and particularly the military log books in the Bundesarchiv in Freiburg, and had come to the conclusion that in the spring of 1942 German troops had not used any chemical weapons during the fighting in the area of the Adzhimushk catacombs or inside them. He claimed that the German High Command had decided to observe the Geneva protocol of 1925. At the same time he acknowledged that " in order to make life unpleasant for the regular forces and partisans on the Soviet side, German troops had from time to time thrown into the catacombs various types of conventional weapon such as smoke grenades, devices for creating smoke screens as well as the decomposing corpses of animals in order to create a sickening stench. All these attempts to smoke out the people in the catacombs, although they had cause discomfort to those fighting on the other side, had had absolutely no lethal effects."

Ambassador Wegener stated in his letter that his delegation had no brief for defending the actions of the German army during the National-Socialist period and that this response was dictated solely by his "commitment to the ideals of historical truth." He once again advised me "to find an appropriate opportunity to correct 'the false allegations' so that the correction could be reflected in the records of the Disarmament Conference."

I was outraged by Wegener's letter. My first impulse was to deliver an angry denunciation at one of the meetings and accuse the fascists of a whole range of crimes, including the use of gas in their numerous gas chambers and embarrass Wegener for his attempts to rehabilitate the Nazis.

However, some of my colleagues advised me to keep my temper and to hold back with the denunciation. The delegation's adviser, Lev Naumov, an extremely well informed diplomat, expressed the view that the use by the Germans of smoke and foul-smelling objects in the catacombs in order to smoke people out, while undeniably barbaric, could not be described as using chemical weapons. Therefore, he argued, Wegener might well be technically correct. Moreover, some of my colleagues pointed out that not even at the Nuremberg trials or in any of the historical records had the German fascists been accused of using chemical weapons during the Second World War, and advised me to bear this in mind.

These arguments curbed my ardor, and I decided not to go on the warpath, especially since Wegener's objection was a private one. At the same time I did feel the urge to investigate more closely what had actually happened in the Crimea in the summer of 1942. I wrote to the Military History Institute of the Ministry of Defense in Moscow and asked them to send me in Geneva any material they had on the subject. Quite soon I received a package containing an answer as well as articles, reviews, references and other material.

Using this information, I was able to put together the following picture of what had happened in the area of the Adzhimushk quarries. In the second half of May 1942, a Soviet unit on the Crimean front found itself surrounded during fierce fighting around the town of Kerch and took up defensive positions in the quarries. The unit numbered more than 10,000 men and shared the quarries with the local civilian population, which had also taken refuge in them. In spite of all the hardships—lack of water, food, medical supplies, and ammunition—the troops of the garrison, operating from their underground positions, carried out repeated, daring raids and did a great deal of damage to the enemy, capturing ammunition, food, and water and thus claiming the attention and energies of considerable numbers of fascist troops. Hitler's troops surrounded the quarries with several rows of barbed wire fencing, blocked the entrances and exits to the quarries by explosions, and bombed and shelled them.

Anxious to put paid to the defenders in the catacombs, the German forces attacked both the military personnel and the civilians with poison gas. According to the testimony of the victims and records, it was asphyxiating gas with yellow fumes and a strong smell of chlorine. Smoke was pumped into the quarries through hoses and piped in from special cylinders.

Here are some eyewitness accounts I was sent from the Military History Institute from soldiers and civilians who were in the catacombs. A Private Kaznacheyev wrote in his diary: "Today the enemy's chemical weapon took a heavy toll on the underground garrison. Many people suffocated and did not survive the second gas attack." Also: "Many people, overcome by the fumes, fell and choked to death, tearing off their undershirts; the only sounds that could be heard were those of the gas-mask containers clattering to the ground and the gasps of the dying. They were struggling for breath and writhing in spasms. . . . It was possible to get away from the smoke, but there was no escaping this gas."

Another soldier, Private Efremov recalls: "The galleries and tunnels gradually filled with asphyxiating gas. It moved in thick columns, driven by the air currents, and licked the walls and ceilings. It got denser and denser. It became impossible to breathe. People's throats were racked with spasms. The lanterns and oil lamps went out. Even the gloom itself became thicker and darker."

A woman named Sarikova testified: "I began to feel pressure in my chest; there was no air to breathe. All around me I hear cries and noise. The catacombs fill with poison gas. Little children are crying piteously and calling for their mothers. But it was horrible; there they were lying dead on the ground, their little shirts ripped open on their chests and blood pouring from their mouths."

These barbaric gas attacks of the German troops were repeated many times over and were organized by a special SS detail with the help of a field engineer battalion. A representative of the Wehrmacht Staff, Chemical Forces General Ochsner reported to his headquarters in June 1942 the participation in the battle for Kerch of a chemical unit. Some of the thousands who died in the fighting around Adzhimushk were killed by the effects of asphyxiating gas. More than three thousand bodies were found in the catacombs after the liberation of the Crimea from the German occupiers.

Anyway, to return to Wegener's letter. During our meetings, the ambassador repeatedly reminded me of it and once, in front of all the guests at a diplomatic reception, reproached me for not having had the elementary decency to reply to his letter. I riposted heatedly: "Those are not the kind of letters I have any intention of replying to!"

Wegener, in turn, announced that in that case he reserved his right to circulate his letter to all the other participants on the conference. And indeed, on the last day of the session just before a five-month long break he sent letters to all heads of delegation containing more or less the same text of his letters to me.

However, at the last meeting of the session I had with me the text of a statement on the Adzhimushk incident, which I had carefully prepared against just such an emergency. On the basis of the documentation I had received from Moscow, I described in my statement the horrible scene of the agonizing death of thousands of people, including young children, who were struck down by the asphyxiating gas released by the German forces, the effects of which had been described by Wegener as designed to make life "unpleasant" for the defenders of the stone quarries.

Although I kept to my prepared text for most of my speech, I could not help giving way to the emotions aroused by my personal memories. It goes back to the summer of 1942 when I was serving in the armed forces. We were deployed on the shore of the Black Sea to the south of Tuapse. The Nazis had driven the Soviet forces out of the Crimean peninsula, and they had sustained major losses during the crossing of the Kerch strait. The enemy were bombing and strafing Soviet forces remorselessly as we crossed the strait, and many of our ships were sunk. For a long time afterwards the bodies of Soviet soldiers kept washing up on shore.

The retreating troops told stories about the ruthlessness of the Nazis in the Crimea, and it was then that the first rumors began to circulate about the use of gas by the German forces. After this we began to be much more careful about using our gas masks.

At the end of my speech, I said that anyone claiming to want to set the historical record straight should get to know the primary sources at first hand—the documents, testimony, and the other evidence provided by the victims—and not the records of the violator, the criminal perpetrator. I went on to stress that, in spite of the assurances contained in Wegener's letter, failure to acquaint oneself with this evidence would be tantamount to defending the crimes of the Nazis. Wegener sat there, frowning and red in the face. No other delegation rose to his defense.

In this unusual way, Bush's charge that the Soviet Union had used chemical weapons ended up as a bitter dispute over whether or not the Nazis in the Second World War had violated the Geneva protocol.

"I Will Not Sign These Instructions"

Fisher, my negotiating partner, who had headed the American delegation to the Disarmament Conference from the very beginning of the bilateral negotiations on chemical weapons told me just before my debut: "Just accept our proposals for declaring stockpiles of chemical weapons and their elimination, the destruction of their production facilities and the establishment of international supervision, and we can agree on the entire convention tomorrow." Although I realized that we could not accept any of these proposals, I never imagined that it would take almost fifteen years to achieve agreement.

I demonstrated my optimism by making my first statement very businesslike and avoiding recriminations and ideological clichés. I devoted most of it to the problem of verification. Fisher warmly welcomed my choice of this topic, although, after hearing my statement, he could not conceal his disappointment at the absence of any sign of agreement to international inspections, the chief prerequisite for effective control.

In 1979 and 1980, Fisher and I (later he was replaced by Flowerree) presented to the Disarmament Conference various joint reports on the course of the bilateral chemical weapons negotiations, and they were generally favorably received. In a resolution the conference expressed the hope that the "U.S.S.R. and the U.S.A. would make every effort to conclude the negotiations as soon as possible and submit a joint initiative on the subject."

The noble hopes expressed by the conference were, however, far removed from reality. Inevitably, the problem of banning chemical weapons proved far more difficult than it had seemed when the diplomats started work on the text of a convention. Suffice it to say that the draft convention on the subject submitted by the Soviet Union in 1982 was barely ten pages long, while the initial draft with its only partially agreed language submitted in 1986 contained more than a hundred pages. I am sure, however, that the main reason for the delay was not that it was a difficult problem (although certainly it was) but rather a lack of interest in and readiness, especially on the part of the superpowers, to reach agreement on the banning of chemical weapons.

As far as the Soviet Union and its leadership was concerned, the banning of chemical weapons was for a very long time just a propaganda slogan. I myself helped to draft quite a few Politburo decisions on the subject. These were issued at least once or twice every year and were drafted in a working group composed of representatives of the Ministries of Foreign Affairs, Defense, and the Chemical Industry and the KGB.

From my many years of association with people who were directly involved in the chemical weapons area, I got the distinct impression that they were not ready for an agreement in the 1970s and the early 1980s. To my great regret, Gromyko showed no particular interest in the banning of chemical weapons. Whenever I attempted to explain the difficulties arising in the negotiations and the weakness of our position, he would listen to me indifferently and practically never offered any help. I even noticed that he was rarely interested in grasping the substance of the reports of the working group and always signed them if the other ministers had already done so.

Once, something happened that troubled and delighted me at the same time. It happened in the autumn of 1985, after Shevardnadze had been appointed foreign minister. In keeping with a practice of many years standing, I presented to Shevardnadze for signature the letter which had been agreed on by the working group, containing the usual proposed instructions for the delegation to the negotiations, and which had already been signed by three ministers. I expected that, like his predecessor, Shevardnadze would sign the document just to get it out of the way, especially as it already bore the signatures of the other more experienced ministers. I could not conceal from him the fact that these instructions contained nothing that would help us with our difficulties, and Shevardnadze responded by saying that he would not sign these instructions. I did not know what to think. It had taken us, the members of the working group, more than a month to iron out our differences and come up with a consensus that, although it contained no real improvements, at least provided some minimal movement in the right direction. Suddenly all this was to be nullified—and we were due at the negotiations in just a few days. There was even the danger that the delegation would end up with no instructions at all. As a matter of fact, this had already happened before, but it was hard to imagine a worse situation.

After I had urged him not to postpone approval of the instructions, Shevardnadze signed the letter but asked me to send him some radically new ideas from Geneva. I was delighted to give him my promise, which with help from the delegation I kept.

Looking Over Our Shoulders at the Pentagon

The attitude of the Kremlin leadership to the banning of chemical weapons changed according to the time. It depended to a large extent on the position of the White House. In February 1970, the Nixon administration announced that it was halting production and stockpiling of chemical and bacteriological weapons and was willing to negotiate on the limitation and banning of these weapons, the reaction of Moscow was largely one of satisfaction. Representatives of the Soviet military explained this decision by the fact that existing stocks of traditional, unitary chemical weapons were now sufficient for the needs of the Pentagon. What did concern the Soviet military-industrial complex were the American plans for creating a new generation of chemical weapons—binary, and multiple chemical compounds. The essence of binary or multi-chemical compounds is that two or more relatively nontoxic chemicals can be separately stored, transported, produced, and assembled into chemical weapons. Immediately after firing or launching of a shell or a missile, the chemicals combine and, in the course of flight and before reaching the target, combine to form highly toxic, deadly chemical compounds that have a paralyzing effect on the nervous system.

Soviet intelligence took a particular interest in the development of binary weapons in American laboratories. This work began in the 1950s, particularly around the time when the United States started to develop the "Big Eye," a binary weapon in the form of a bomb that paralyzed the nervous system. At the meetings of our working group in Moscow on chemical weapons, our colleagues from the Ministry of Defense constantly stressed the importance of preventing a large-scale binary weapon production program; and that was about the only thing that interested them.

It is true that they had formed the impression that the modernization of the American chemical arsenal was still at the experimental stage, and this gave them reason to hope that it could still be stopped or at least delayed.

Beginning in 1983, the situation began to change when the United States started a broad program of renovating its chemical arsenal that was designed to bring about a thoroughgoing modernization as well as an increase in the quantity of its chemical weapons, bringing their number up to five million units over the next five years. In July 1985, Congress decided to appropriate the funds necessary for the production of binary chemical weapons, and this seriously worried our military and military-industrial complex.

The attitude of the Soviet Union toward the banning of chemical weapons was also somewhat influenced by the fact that George Bush, the U.S. vice president, became involved in the negotiations. In February 1983 and April 1984, Bush made a special trip to Geneva to take part in the Conference on Disarmament. He devoted another speech in 1984 exclusively to the question of banning chemical weapons. In private conversations Bush said that he also had a personal interest in banning chemical weapons; his mother had made him promise to work for the elimination of this barbaric weapon of mass destruction of human beings.

I reported to Moscow that, as I saw it, the reason for Bush's visit was the genuine wish of the U.S. government to eliminate chemical weapons, which were not that effective in conditions of modern warfare. Nor did I rule out the possibility that humanitarian considerations had also influenced Washington's position. The minister agreed with me. "Well," he allowed, "it looks as if the Americans might really be taking the problem seriously." It was the sheer logic of the negotiating process, which made it clear that a convention was now in the national security interests of the Soviet Union.

In the document presented in April 1984, the Americans couched their position in treaty language with regard to all substantive provisions of a future convention, the fundamental elements of prohibition, definitions, permissible types of activity, declaration of stockpiles, chemical weapons production facilities, inspection, and so on, as well as the procedural and legal aspects, such as amendments, duration, signature, ratification, entry into force, and so forth.

On the whole, the American documents were quite impressive. They contained a number of provisions taken from the joint Soviet-American reports of 1979 and 1980 and reflected some of the results of the multilateral negotiations at the conference. Speaking at the conference after Bush, the Soviet delegation stated that the document introduced by the vice president would be thoroughly studied by the Soviet Union. Even this natural reaction was unusual for the Cold War. It might have been expected that the Soviet delegation would reject the American document out of hand as a product of "U.S. imperialist forces."

Unfortunately, consideration of the American draft convention by our delegation in Geneva and the relevant departments in Moscow led to the conclusion that, although it contained quite a few acceptable provisions, it could not serve as a basis for a future convention. The major flaw in the American document, as we saw it, was that it discriminated against states-parties with state ownership of property or partially nationalized industry and put them on an unequal footing with states where privately owned industry predominated. The negative attitude of the Soviet Union was provoked by the "new concept" of the United States, which consisted in establishing a system of control on the basis of a "standing invitation to inspect." In effect, it meant giving unrestricted access to inspectors to any plant, storage, or other facilities, something that might lead to the uncovering of states-parties' military or commercial secrets which had nothing to do with the production, stockpiling, or storage of chemical weapons. Such "standing invitations," however, applied only to plants owned or controlled by governments.

This "new concept" of the United States with regard to questions of control met with unqualified opposition in the working group from the representatives of the Ministries of Defense and the Chemical Industry as well as the KGB. The Chemical Industry minister, Leonid Kostandov, after hearing my report on the American initiative, said that if the "new concept" were adopted, he would be unable to prevent the Soviet Union falling behind the United States in the area of chemical weapons.

After the American draft convention had been studied in Moscow, I received instructions to produce arguments against it and "to show that the draft did not offer any constructive advance over the work already done in Geneva, but rather, in fact, widened the differences between delegations on a number of issues, particularly those relating to control and detracted from the progress already achieved on those issues." Moscow's particular displeasure was provoked by the fact that the American document was essentially silent on the question of the prohibition of binary chemical weapons, a question that, in the Soviet view, should be the focal point of a future convention.

I repeated this criticism on a number of occasions both in Geneva and New York and also stressed that the U.S. document contained a number of clauses providing for unjustified interference in the internal affairs of states and violations of their constitutional processes. I referred in particular to the fact that the draft contemplated the violation of the Fourth and Fifth Amendments of the U.S. Constitution.

To be fair, I should add that it was not only the Soviet Union and its allies which voiced criticism of the American draft, but also a number of nonaligned countries and China. Also, outside the conference rooms, certain Western countries such as the Federal Republic of Germany, France, and the Netherlands expressed their disapproval of certain provisions. It was felt that the American draft went too far in certain areas and especially in matters of control and that this was detrimental to the commercial and defense interests of a large number of states.

What was particularly interesting, however, was that when the Convention on the Prohibition of Chemical Weapons, which had been signed by the U.S. government, came up for ratification in the U.S. Senate at the end of the 1990s, many leading senators, Senator Jesse Helms in particular, severely criticized it for much the same reasons that Soviet representatives had criticized it in the mid-1980s. These senators made precisely the same points about the Fourth and Fifth Amendments of the Constitution.

As the Soviet representative to the negotiations on the chemical convention, my own contribution to this vast construct was, I fear, extremely modest. In February 1984, for example, I found myself stating the readiness of the Soviet Union to establish permanent international control by means of on-site inspection at the specialized facilities for the destruction of chemical weapon stocks. This was a small step, but a very important one. For the first time in its entire history, the Soviet Union was agreeing to the establishment of some form of permanent international control. I remember how, at the meeting of the working group in Moscow under the chairmanship of Akhromeyev, I succeeded in persuading its members to agree to this step. The argument that helped us to take this decision was basically that international control would allow the interested Soviet departments to keep their fingers constantly on the pulse of what was going on at the American specialized facility. This Soviet decision came in for special mention in a speech by Reagan, who made a point of commending Konstantin Chernenko, the then Soviet leader, for his "bold" move.

Some time in 1986, I was instructed to state the new Soviet position on a number of important issues. We agreed that the destruction of chemical weapon stocks should begin no later than six months, and the destruction or dismantling of production facilities no later than one year, after entry into force. We also made some other important proposals.

When I made these statements, I thought we would need another year or two and a lot of hard work at the negotiations before achieving final agreement on and the signing of a convention on the prohibition of chemical weapons. I was also expecting to be present for the final phase of negotiations. Fate had a different plan. It took another six or seven years before the final phase was completed, and I was not there to see it.

17
THE BEGINNING OF THE END OF THE COLD WAR

Gorbachev—Your Next Leader

General Edward Roney, the well-known American arms limitation expert, once wrote: "There is no such thing as a really friendly Soviet negotiator. At least I have never met one in ten years." On the other hand, another American disarmament negotiator, Louis Fields, had a different view. On the photograph he presented to me, he wrote the following inscription: "To Ambassador Victor Israelyan, a worthy opponent and respected colleague, with best wishes and deepest respect." I felt the same way about Louis.

During my time in Geneva, there were four different American representatives at the Disarmament Conference: Andrew Fisher, Charles Flowerree, Louis Fields, and Donald Lovitz. Before their appointment the first two had worked at the Arms Control and Disarmament Agency, Fields in the State Department, and Lovitz in a law firm. They were all good representatives of the United States who threw themselves into the work of the conference and enjoyed the respect of their colleagues.

I was able to establish a good working relationship and good personal relations with all of the American representatives. Outside the conference, we went on sightseeing trips together and visited sporting events around

Switzerland. We also got to know each others' families. With some of the American representatives, these contacts were maintained even after they had left Geneva, and we continued to correspond. Fate was not kind to them, and all four passed away at relatively young ages.

It so happened that the instructions to the delegation from Moscow almost always included orders to cooperate with the U.S. delegation on the questions under discussion at the conference, particularly those that were also subjects of negotiation at the bilateral, Soviet-American talks. At the same time, Moscow was equally insistent that we criticize American policy "from the standpoint of principle" and "duly rebuff" the anti-Soviet attacks of the American delegation. We, of course, dutifully carried out both orders, the first whole-heartedly and the second, without relish. I have no doubt that my American colleagues had similar orders.

Our good personal relations with the American ambassadors to the conference accounted for our use of this channel of communication for the discharge of certain, what were to us, unconventional functions.

In March 1984, for example, Fields returned to Washington for consultations. On his return he asked me to meet him on a matter of some urgency. I invited him to our delegation's residence, but he preferred to meet on "neutral territory" in a restaurant outside the city. During the meal, Fields said nothing of particular interest. He said that in April Vice President Bush would be coming and would personally present the American draft convention on the prohibition of chemical weapons. As to its content, the ambassador spoke only in general terms already familiar from the press. I was puzzled: why had Fields been at such pains to meet me alone and why didn't he want to tell me about Bush's arrival at our delegation's residence? What was such a big secret?

"What's so confidential about all this, Lou?" I asked the American. "Let's take a walk in the park, you'll soon understand. I don't trust the walls of the restaurant," he replied. "Washington would like to establish a serious working contact with the Kremlin leadership," Fields began, "and Vice President Bush is ready to meet one of the new Soviet leaders during his visit to Geneva. The meeting must be strictly confidential and no one must know about it." In answer to my question whether the Americans had any particular Soviet leader in mind, Fields simply answered that the vice president would like to meet Mikhail Gorbachev, who would most probably be the next leader of the Soviet Union.

I immediately started wondering why the Americans were so interested in the candidacy of Gorbachev, who dealt essentially with agriculture and ideology, and why this proposal was not being made through the usual diplomatic channels—through Dobrynin in Washington or Hartman in Moscow—rather than through representatives at the Conference on Disarmament. Fields was unable to give me any meaningful answer to these questions and simply said that he was just carrying out orders.

I promised Fields that I would inform Moscow of our talk, but I was deeply troubled by it. On the surface it all looked very simple. It was my duty to convey this American idea to Moscow and that was all there was to it. In fact, it was even good for my diplomatic standing that Washington should have chosen to channel such an important proposal to the Kremlin leadership through me. However, the more I thought about the possible reaction to my telegram back in Moscow, I began to get cold feet. After all, Andropov had just passed away and Chernenko had taken his place as leader of the CPSU and the state in February 1984. My report to Moscow about the plans for a meeting with "the next Soviet leader" might seem, to say the least, a little premature. It was not difficult to imagine Chernenko's feelings when he was shown my report.

I was also worried about the fact that the American idea might be taken in Moscow as an act of provocation designed to split the Soviet leadership and that this would exacerbate the already strained relations between our two countries. I therefore decided to temporize about reporting to Moscow and await developments. Strictly speaking, this was a breach of diplomatic discipline but I told myself that it was justified in order to prevent a possible deterioration in Soviet-American relations.

Fields never mentioned the subject of a Bush-Gorbachev meeting again. Meanwhile, in mid-April Bush arrived in Geneva. His speech on the subject of the prohibition of chemical weapons at the conference, which I mentioned in the previous chapter, was scheduled for April the eighteenth. The day before I was called at home by Sadrudin Aga Khan and told in confidence that "our common friend" wanted to meet me on the evening of the seventeenth. Aga Khan was a well-known international political figure who for many years had been carrying out important and delicate missions on behalf of the world community and was a friend of Bush's of long standing.

The conversation began with the three of us together. Bush referred briefly to the main purpose of his visit to Geneva—to introduce the draft convention on the prohibition of chemical weapons—and reminded me of our cooperation at the UN. When we turned to other topics, Aga Khan left us alone, and Bush immediately raised the subject of a possible unofficial Soviet-American meeting. The vice president confirmed the instructions he had given to Fields and added that the time and place of the meeting would depend on the wishes and convenience of both sides. As to the content of the conversation, in the light of the informal nature of the proposed meeting, each of the participants would be free to raise any subject he chose. As for his interlocutor, he mentioned only one name, and that with some confidence, "your next leader, Gorbachev." Those words left a lasting impression on me. I had a momentary impulse to ask Bush how he could be so sure, but I suppressed it.

Bush reminded me that he had been to Moscow twice (in 1982 and 1984) for the funerals of Brezhnev and Andropov and that he might well be visiting our capital again in the same capacity. And indeed Bush did return to Moscow—for Chernenko's funeral.

I promised Bush that I would report his proposal to Moscow. However, for the same reasons that I had refrained from reporting my talk with Fields to Moscow, I decided to defer reporting my meeting with Bush until I could do so orally to Gromyko, since I was due to return to Moscow in the near future. In the meantime, I mentioned the meeting in a private letter to Korniyenko. Bush had expressed concern at the current international situation and stressed his loyalty to Reagan, although his conversation betrayed a glimmer of regret with regard to certain steps taken by his president in connection with us. As I stressed in my letter to Korniyenko, "Bush seemed obsessed by the idea—to which he returned over and over again in the course of the conversation—of having an informal conversation, verging on a secret meeting, with a Soviet leader at the same level as himself. Reagan, of course, knew about this and no doubt supported the idea. My feeling was that Bush was ready to travel anywhere at any time."

Even in this private letter, I decided not to mention the name of Gorbachev, but to leave that for my oral report. There were several reasons for this. I knew from casual conversations around the MFA that the situation at the very top of the Kremlin pyramid was very complicated and that there were several contenders for the leadership: Gorbachev, Romanov, and Grishin were among the names mentioned. I certainly did not want to be on record as appearing to support anyone, even obliquely, in a document that would become known to all the members of the Politburo. Moreover, Gorbachev was not particularly popular with the MFA people at that time. He was not well known, and he had been variously dubbed "the provincial," "the upstart" and " the farmer" by certain diplomats. Something else that the MFA did not like was that Gorbachev took too great an interest in foreign policy and took too active a part in discussions of international matters in the Politburo. There was one incident that became public knowledge which, according to certain sources, had taken place in the Politburo. At one of its meetings, Gromyko was reporting at great length and not without pride on the meetings he had had with presidents, prime ministers, and other world leaders in New York at the General Assembly when Gorbachev intervened with a caustic reminder: "Andrei Andreyevich, don't forget that Soviet foreign policy is made here in Moscow and not in New York!" This story was galling to diplomats who considered Gorbachev's remark the impertinent interference of a "know nothing" in affairs of state at the highest level.

Another unflattering story that made the rounds in Smolenskaya Square at that time was that Gorbachev had been instrumental in the replacement of our ambassador in Britain just because his wife had not been sufficiently attentive to Gorbachev's wife, the all-powerful Raisa Maksimovna, during her visit to Britain with her husband in 1984. Such antipathy to Gorbachev, which I generally shared, although I had no particular reason for it, helped to restrain any enthusiasm I might have felt for broadcasting my conversation with Bush, which could only have enhanced Gorbachev's standing.

In any case, once I had returned to Moscow, at my first meeting with Gromyko, I reported Bush's proposal to him. The minister listened to my report without a single interruption or a single question and an awkward silence ensued. Gromyko just looked away from me and appeared to be thinking hard about something. Finally, he turned to me and said: "So, how are things going at your conference over there?" It was clear that the conversation was at an end.

Whether the Americans were also sounding out the possibility of a confidential meeting with Gorbachev through other channels, I just do not know. Nor do I know whether the Kremlin leadership ever discussed the matter. Probably not.

Did the American proposal for a meeting with "the next leader of the Soviet Union" made by Bush in 1984 have any influence on Gromyko's own position? Well, it was none other than Gromyko who nominated Gorbachev as general secretary of the Central Committee of the CPSU, and only he could answer that question. I wanted to raise the subject with him after we had both retired, but the opportunity never arose.

There were also questions I wanted to put to the Americans. Wasn't Washington afraid that their undisguised preference for Gorbachev as leader of the Soviet Union might actually prove detrimental to him and be used against him by his adversaries in the Politburo?

After deciding to reveal this episode from the end of the 1980s, I wrote to Bush, who by now was president of the United States, and he had no objection. I published an article on the subject first in the Soviet Union and later in the United States, and it provoked quite a number of extremely varied reactions. Some made the assumption that Washington was banking on Gorbachev because it had grounds for believing that he would be likely to make major concessions to the United States. There were also those who even suggested that Gorbachev had been cooperating with the CIA, and Bush knew about it and singled him out precisely for that reason. There was no end to this kind of idle speculation.

After my article was published I didn't much think about the episode until a few years ago when I came across George Bush's published memoir, *All the Best: My Life in Letters and Other Writings* (1999). In it, I was very interested to find on pages 333–34 a "Memorandum of Conversation . . . with Ambassador Viktor Israelyan" in which Bush describes our "very frank, very friendly discussion" in Geneva in 1984. For the most part, the memorandum accurately represents the substance of our conversation, which lasted about an hour and a half. But I was surprised to see no mention whatsoever of Gorbachev or of a possible Soviet-American meeting—even though Bush had persisted in raising this subject during our conversation. This is no accident, I am sure, but I could never understand the reason for the omission until just recently when I raised the subject with one of my American colleagues. A former CIA expert on the USSR, he told me that during the early 1980s the CIA had analyzed the situation inside Andropov's Politburo and determined that Gorbachev would soon emerge from the pool of potential candidates to become leader of the Soviet Union. Why Gorbachev in particular? I do not know, but it now seems clear that Mr. Bush was acting on this intelligence when he met with me in Geneva.

The New Foreign Minister of the Soviet Union

By the early 1980s, we Soviet citizens had become so used to the swift succession of our leaders that the death of Chernenko in March 1985 was regarded as nothing out of the ordinary and aroused no particular feelings. Recalling, as I did, those same cold March days back in 1953 when Stalin died after his dictatorship of almost thirty years and so many Soviet citizens were in unfeigned mourning for him, I could not help being struck by such a steep decline in the authority of the supreme governmental leadership of the Soviet Union. Our delegation was in Geneva at the time and the death of Chernenko, apart from a brief formal memorial meeting, had no effect on our life and work. Gorbachev's appointment was also no great surprise and was calmly accepted.

Of course, I remembered my talk with Bush the year before and could not help marveling at his clairvoyance. There was another piece of news that did astound me after Gorbachev came to power. In the summer of 1985 in Geneva, Datcu, the Romanian ambassador, came to me and asked me an unexpected question: "Do you know that you have a new foreign minister?" I thought he was joking, but he convinced me that he was serious, when he told me that he had just heard the news on the radio. "Would you like to try guessing?" he asked. I tried out a few names, including Korniyenko, Dobrynin, Maltsev, and other diplomats, and Datcu suggested I try the names of some leading party figures, so I came up with a dozen names of officials prominent in party circles in Moscow and the republics—but none of them were the right one.

That the post of foreign minister might go to the first secretary of the Central Committee of the Communist Party of Georgia was something I could never have imagined. He was widely known within and outside the MFA as one of Brezhnev's men, a man who had been nominated for the post of head of the Georgian communists by Nikolai Shchelokov, the minister of internal affairs and one of the most odious figures of the Brezhnev era. No one knew much about any close ties between Shevardnadze and Gorbachev.

Everyone in the MFA found the appointment of Shevardnadze baffling. Hardly any of the senior officials—deputy foreign ministers or members of the Collegium—knew anything about him. Gromyko's departure after almost three decades as foreign minister left people largely unmoved. His career had run its course, and it was simply time for him to be replaced. Indeed, he himself felt it was time for him to move on, but no one expected him to be replaced so suddenly. When in the summer of 1985 in the conference hall of the MFA on Smolenskaya Square, the new minister was formally presented, Shevardnadze modestly remarked that in comparison with the outgoing minister, Gromyko, he felt like a small boat alongside an ocean liner—"but a boat with a motor!" he added significantly. How powerful and unpredictable this "motor" turned out to be became evident soon after the "boat" was launched.

On the whole, my reaction to Shevardnadze's appointment was favorable. I happened to have heard a great deal about him and to have met him quite a few times before his appointment to his post in Moscow. A native of Georgia, I had many friends and relations there and always maintained an interest in events in Georgia. I grew up in Tbilisi and when I went back from time to time I heard a lot of talk about the local party bosses at various times—Beria, Charkviani, and Mgeladze. Most of the talk was about Shevardnadze. I approved of his attempts to battle corruption, which had assumed fantastic proportions under his predecessor, Mzhavanadze, to restore a minimum of order in various institutions and industrial enterprises and to carry out some reforms in the Georgian economy. There was much talk about his initiative, personal courage, and relatively modest lifestyle. He liked to show up unannounced and incognito at stores and markets to find out for himself what unsavory practices were going on and attempt to deal with them. Once at a soccer match in the Tbilisi stadium a pack of enraged fans invaded the field, threatening to beat up the referee, and Shevardnadze, who was among the spectators, rushed onto the field himself and, single-handedly, succeeded in restraining the crowd. This act earned him a lot of respect.

However, it was also public knowledge that while he was minister of internal affairs of Georgia, Shevardnadze actively cracked down not only on common criminals and corruption, but also on law-abiding citizens because of their political convictions; he was also ruthless in settling his own personal scores. Shevardnadze was considered to be Moscow's man and at times even he overdid his sycophancy toward "big brother." He became notorious in Georgia for his fawning and obsequious utterances, such as, for example, "For us Georgians, the sun rises not in the east, but in the north," that is to say, in Russia. In terms of boot-licking, Shevardnadze rivaled even Geidar Aliyev, the then first secretary of the Communist Party of Azerbaijan, who turned the visits of the Kremlin bosses to Baku into Soviet versions of a Bacchanalian orgy.

I met Shevardnadze quite a few times in the late 1970s and early 1980s. It happened that both of our families took our vacations at Pitsunda, a Black Sea resort. The sanatorium where we were staying belonged to the government of Georgia and was very small but extremely comfortable. Shevardnadze occupied an individual dacha, but apart from that did not enjoy any special privileges. All the vacationers took their meals in the same dining room, and we had the table next to the one reserved for the

Shevardnadze family. I could not help noticing that our neighbors were served from the same menu as everyone else, unlike the members of the Moscow Politburo, who normally enjoyed a special cuisine.

Generally speaking, Shevardnadze and his family, on both occasions when we were there at the same time, behaved very discreetly and modestly and did not throw their weight around or try to impose themselves. Although there was heightened security in the sanatorium for the occasion, its presence was hardly noticeable. It was only when Shevardnadze went for long swims that his bodyguards showed any sign of perturbation, but they were strictly forbidden to accompany him.

A couple of times, I attempted to strike up a conversation with him and interest him in my diplomatic work, but it led nowhere. He had no interest in getting to know people who were of no use to him—a category to which I clearly belonged. He did, however, pay a great deal of attention to Shchelokov's son, who was on vacation there at the same time. His wife, Nanuli, was more sociable and was not averse to chit-chatting with my wife.

On the whole then, my chance contacts with Shevardnadze left me with a good impression, and that is why I was basically pleased by his appointment as foreign minister, although I realized that from a professional standpoint he might leave something to be desired.

In the summer of 1985, I was in Geneva when reports reached us that the new minister was to be found in his office day and night, Saturdays and Sundays included, studying documents and acquainting himself with his staff. For all practical purposes, during Shevardnadze's first few months in office, the MFA was run by his first deputy, Korniyenko, who even chaired the meetings of the Collegium. However, the ministries grapevine had it that it was his other first deputy, Kovalev who had more influence with him, especially when it came to personnel matters.

A Conference with Gorbachev

It was in October of 1985 that I reported for the first time to the new minister. Shevardnadze greeted me without giving any sign that we had already met. I reported in detail on the work of the Conference on Disarmament and the problems facing our delegation at the negotiations. Shevardnadze listened to me attentively, but asked no questions. He seemed particularly interested in my comment that the conference seemed powerless with respect to the most important disarmament issue—nuclear weapons limitation and reduction.

I described our proposal for all the nuclear powers to hold talks on this subject as doomed, since it lacked support even among many nonaligned countries. I told him about my talks with representatives of those countries, especially Garekhan from India, and said that they considered that it was unfair to lump all the nuclear powers together because the nuclear arsenals of the Soviet Union and the United States were incomparably superior to those of Britain, France, and China and that one could not expect them to sit down at the negotiating table on an equal footing with the superpowers.

Under the circumstances, it seemed to me that it would be fairer and more pragmatic to propose stage by stage negotiations. At the initial stage, the question would be that of reducing the nuclear arsenals of just the two superpowers, and only after agreement had been reached on an intermediate level of nuclear armaments between them, as a step on the way toward nuclear disarmament, would the other three countries, Britain, France, and China, join the negotiations. The ultimate target of zero nuclear armament would be achieved by a certain deadline by all the nuclear powers together.

Shevardnadze liked this idea and instructed me to put it in writing and submit it to him. As I was about to return to New York, he asked me to send it to him from New York without any unnecessary delay. Although I did not have high hopes that the idea would work, I did what the minister had asked. A great deal of the credit for the work of formulating the idea of stage by stage nuclear disarmament belongs to Nikita Smidovich, a colleague working with me in New York.

On paper the nuclear disarmament program formulated by Smidovich and myself looked something like this. The entire process of worldwide nuclear disarmament was to take fifteen years, starting in 1986 and completed by the beginning of 2000. There would be three stages, each taking about five years. We described in concrete detail the role of each nuclear power at each stage. All negotiations were to take place within the framework of the Conference on Disarmament and under the strict control of the world community. We told many of our colleagues about the idea and they, for the most part, approved. Buoyed by this support, we sent the paper to the minister.

It is true that subsequently Korniyenko claimed that the idea of stage by stage nuclear disarmament belonged to Akhromeyev and himself, and I have no doubt that this was an idea that could have occurred to many people. As I have already mentioned, the Indian, Garekhan had expressed this idea in a general way at the Conference on Disarmament as far back as 1979. As for the development of the idea, Akhromeyev and Korniyenko certainly had a very active hand in it.

When we returned to Moscow, Shevardnadze said that he liked the proposal and that it would be useful to convey it to Gorbachev personally. At the end of 1985, the minister raised the subject again and said that I should get ready for a meeting with Gorbachev at which the general secretary wanted to discuss the whole question of disarmament, with special emphasis on nuclear disarmament, together with all the leading experts on the subject.

The meeting with Gorbachev took place on December 30. Attending the meeting were Shevardnadze; Zaikov, the Politburo member responsible for defense matters; Karpov, our negotiator at the Soviet-American talks on nuclear and space armaments; Mikhailov, our negotiator at the Vienna talks on the reduction of arms and armed forces in Central Europe; Grinevsky, our representative at the Stockholm conference on confidence-building measures, security, and disarmament in Europe; and myself, as well as Petrovsky, my successor at the IOD.

At Gorbachev's request, each of the negotiators reported on the most contentious issues in his area and proposed ways of resolving them. We were all, of course, a little nervous, and most of us were meeting Gorbachev for the first time. He impressed me considerably with his businesslike, no-nonsense approach. He was also straightforward and direct, not betraying any signs of warmth or geniality. I do not recall any joking or easing up in the course of what was quite a long conversation. My dominant impression was one of exceptional concentration on the business at hand. One small detail was the large birthmark on Gorbachev's forehead, which one could not help noticing. In the photographs that appeared in the Soviet press every possible technique was employed to eliminate it.

Each of us, of course, strove to make the best possible impression on the general secretary, but at the same time, I must say that everyone there was highly critical of the Soviet position on disarmament matters, especially in the area of control. I remember, for example, Mikhailov quite heatedly complaining that he felt himself to be in an invidious position in the negotiations, since he was constantly forced to manipulate the facts and to dissemble. Others also spoke in the same vein. We all assured Gorbachev that if we did not change our position on the problem of verification, it would be impossible to make progress in the negotiations.

I wanted to confine myself essentially to the subject of the banning of chemical weapons, but Shevardnadze, who was sitting next to me, whispered to me that I should go into detail about the idea of stage by stage or staggered nuclear disarmament. So I found myself summarizing the contents of my telegram from New York. Gorbachev responded with interest to the idea of staggered nuclear disarmament and asked the other disarmament people, and Karpov in particular, to give their views on the subject. Sensing that the idea appealed to the general secretary and Shevardnadze, they all took a positive line on it. Summing up, Gorbachev ordered that a special statement on disarmament be prepared, with special focus on the idea of staggered nuclear disarmament. Gorbachev firmly rejected my proposal to make the idea the keynote of the general secretary's report to the Twenty-Seventh Congress of the CPSU, which was to meet in February 1986. "For the Congress I have a different idea," he said. "For nuclear disarmament we need to have a special declaration."

When we had left Gorbachev, my companions ribbed me: "So now your Conference on Disarmament is going to be the center of the universe and the fate of humanity will hinge on your negotiations there." We were pleased with the meeting. The general secretary had heard us out without interrupting with the ripostes and comments that became increasingly common toward the end of his tenure, and, what was particularly appreciated, he paid attention to the many different ideas and suggestions voiced at the meeting.

In compliance with Gorbachev's instructions, a special interdepartmental working group was set up, which prepared a Special Declaration of General Secretary of the Central Committee of the CPSU for January 15, 1986. It was mainly devoted to a program for the phased elimination of nuclear weapons throughout the world by the end of the century. The document detailed the measures related to all types of nuclear weapon—tactical, medium-range, and strategic for all five nuclear powers. It provided, for example, for the reduction of the strategic offensive weapons of the Soviet Union and the United States to 6,000 nuclear warheads in the initial phase of the program, that is, by 1990. At the same stage, medium- and short-range missiles would be subject to elimination. An indispensable part of the program would be a ban on the production, testing, and deployment of space strike weapons, and this was essentially one of the basic goals of the initiative, namely, to do everything possible to prevent the American strategic defense initiative or "star wars." The document was drafted in the proper technical terminology with the help of many military and other experts.

The dissemination and elucidation of the Gorbachev Declaration became the primary task of the Soviet media. Book stores, libraries, and reading rooms were deluged with articles, pamphlets, posters with catchy titles such as: "Into the Twenty-First Century Without Nuclear Weapons!" "The Atom—for Peace Only!" "Space for Peace Only!" and "For a World Free from War and Weapons!" Akhromeyev and Korniyenko held a press conference. Arbatov, Primakov, and Zhukov, as well as other eminent political commentators and journalists, wrote articles in the press. Foreign language versions of all this material went to countries abroad. Soviet embassies received instructions to give maximum publicity to the Gorbachev Declaration, and ambassadors themselves were made personally responsible for this work.

Finally, the Politburo decided to send special representatives of the MFA from Moscow for meetings with the leaders of other countries devoted exclusively to the question of the significance of the Gorbachev Declaration. Some Moscow emissaries were even named special representatives of the General Secretary of the Central Committee of the CPSU. Diplomats that had specialized in disarmament matters, including myself, were entrusted with this mission.

In the first three months of the year I went on this mission to Finland, Sweden, India, and Bulgaria. As I rule, I met the foreign ministers, or sometimes other members of the government, members of Parliament, and well-known political and public figures. In some countries I was invited to speak on radio and television. In India, I was able to publish a long article in the New Delhi daily, the *National Herald*, titled "The Soviet Position on Disarmament: A Safe World by the Year 2000."

On the whole, the response to the Gorbachev Declaration was one of great interest, as was demonstrated by the number of questions and amount of comment it aroused. What was of the greatest interest to our audience was the soundness of the concept and the concrete proposals accompanying it as well as the seriousness of intent shown by the new Soviet leadership in coming forward with the idea of phased nuclear disarmament. I do not know how successful I was in convincing my audience of the realism and pragmatism of the Soviet idea of a nuclear free world, but no one had any doubts about the appeal of a world without nuclear weapons. My most successful visit was to Finland, where the press gave it a lot of coverage. Vladimir Sobolev, our ambassador in Helsinki, had taken his instructions about the significance of the Gorbachev Declaration extremely seriously.

Of all those consulted, the only one who was pessimistic about the idea of a nuclear free world was the Indian foreign minister, B. R. Bhagat. He received me at home in his residence and, after listening to what I had to say, took my breath away by suggesting that we should talk about something "more serious." I did not know what to say. Luckily, at that moment, the foreign minister's little granddaughter came running into the room, and I was able to save the situation with a little joke: "Then let's talk about her— let's hope for a nuclear free world for her sake."

I was in India after the Twenty-Seventh Congress of the CPSU at which Gorbachev made his proposal for the creation of a comprehensive system of international security, an idea he had mentioned obliquely at the December meeting in his office. This made it necessary for me also to give an account of the relevant part of Gorbachev's report in my meetings in New Delhi. However, this proposal of Gorbachev aroused much less interest than his Declaration of January 15. Many people, including myself, found themselves wondering how a comprehensive system of international security would differ in principle from the articles contained in the UN Charter; and indeed how would this system look in practice? Would it operate within the framework of the UN Charter, or would a new organization be set up, would it involve the conclusion of one, or a whole series of international treaties? Gorbachev's report contained no answers to these questions. The proposal for a new system of international security was a typical Soviet propaganda exercise, and in spite of strenuous efforts on the Soviet side, it was swiftly forgotten like dozens of other Soviet foreign policy initiatives. Gorbachev's January 15 Declaration, however, was a document of a different order. It contained concrete proposals that took into account the security interests of our negotiating partners and made it possible to achieve mutually advantageous agreements. Many of the key provisions of the document facilitated the conclusion in the years to come of important international agreements on reducing strategic offensive weapons (START-2), the prohibition of chemical weapons, a comprehensive nuclear test ban, and many others. The Soviet declaration of January 15 will go down in the history of international relations as a document that does credit to the period of perestroika which brought the Cold War to an end.

Academician Primakov in Geneva

The questions aroused by Gorbachev's exceptionally energetic activities gave rise, during the period of perestroika, to a new form of Soviet foreign policy promotion. The Politburo decided to send to the capitals of major powers and centers of multilateral diplomacy, eminent academics and political scientists to elucidate and provide a commentary on Kremlin policy. In the spring of 1986, we in Geneva were visited for a week by a group consisting of the Academicians Evgeny Primakov and Vitaly Zhurkin and Nikolai Shishlin, a journalist and an official of the Central Committee. We welcomed their visit, not only because we counted on their help in our propaganda efforts, but also because our guests from Moscow were very well known figures, especially Primakov.

Primakov and I had known each other since childhood. Zhenya Primakov and I attended the same high school in Tbilisi. His uncle, Dr. Kirshenblat, was a friend of my father; they were both successful pediatricians. After leaving school we both went to college in Moscow, but specialized in different subjects. Zhenya graduated from the Oriental Studies Institute and began work as a *Pravda* correspondent in various Middle Eastern countries. His excellent knowledge of Arabic and his firsthand acquaintance with the area soon made him a leading Soviet orientalist. He established personal contact with many Middle Eastern leaders, including Saddam Hussein. These contacts turned out to be quite useful when Primakov became a political figure himself.

While I was working in New York, we would meet during his visits to the United States. Primakov showed great interest in a broad range of international problems, including those discussed in the UN, and also in the work of practical diplomacy. It seemed that he would readily join the Foreign Service. He gave up journalism in favor of academic research and was brilliantly successful in this area, earning a doctorate in economics. He published a great deal and was appointed director of one of Moscow's leading academic institutions and was elected a full member of the Soviet Academy of Science. I once tried to talk to Malik about the possibility of transferring Primakov to work in our mission, but Malik didn't like the idea. "He won't make it," he said. "You have to think like a diplomat; he is merely a journalist." Malik passed away almost two decades ago, so unfortunately he didn't live to see the "journalist" Primakov rise like a meteor to the top of the diplomatic profession and became prime minister of Russia in the 1990s.

I remember one unpleasant episode, which unfortunately was typical of the man and the times. As a young academic, he published an article on the problem of disarmament in a Moscow journal. While I was a department head at the MFA, some members of the Soviet delegation to the UN General Assembly in New York showed it to me, claiming that it distorted the Soviet position on disarmament. They insisted that we should send a collective letter to the editor of the journal, drawing his attention to the errors. One of this group was Ambassador Aleksei Roshchin, a well-known expert on disarmament whose opinions carried considerable weight, and, I have to confess, I signed the letter, even though, of course, it contained nothing at all seditious. When we returned to Moscow, I was told that the letter had made a bad impression in academic circles and certainly did not please Primakov. Our common friends reproached me and said that Primakov would never forgive me for my unfriendly action. The editor of the journal, by way of response, simply said that the publication of the article was justified. To his credit, Primakov never brought up the subject of my signing that wretched letter that I would prefer to forget.

Primakov is congenial, good-hearted, and an excellent companion, and he and his charming wife, Laura, were always surrounded by a crowd of friends. We were among them and used to meet the Primakovs either in Moscow or in Georgia. His family was not free from adversity and loss. He lost a young son, full of promise, and later his wife, Laura.

Returning now to Primakov's visit to Geneva: we organized a number of meetings with foreign ambassadors for him and his colleagues. Everyone they talked to was interested in the new Soviet position on arms limitation, a comprehensive system of international security, and of course, the personality of Gorbachev, the new Soviet leader. The members of the Moscow group were able to satisfy their questioners with the quality of their answers. One of these questioners was particularly intrigued by the personality of Primakov himself. This ambassador told me that he had been deeply impressed by Primakov's erudition and particularly by his talent for disagreeing with you with such a disarming smile that you might go away with the impression that he had just agreed with you. Diplomats were also charmed by his humor, straightforwardness, and genuine interest in dialogue.

In my view, Primakov was rather sharp in his criticism of American policy in conversation and expressed himself particularly forcefully against U.S. imperialism when talking to ambassadors of socialist countries. In private conversation with him I would express my preference for a less belligerent approach, but he would disagree and say: "In politics, Victor, one has to be assertive." The visit by these academics and political scientists figures was frequently referred to at the Conference on Disarmament, but, of course, it never entered anyone's head that one of them would one day become the prime minister of an independent Russia.

The political rise of Primakov began in the second half of the 1980s, and in those years I saw him mostly on television. However, a little more than ten years after that visit to Geneva, at the end of 1997, I met Primakov in the by now familiar office of the Russian foreign minister on the seventh floor of the tall building on Smolenskaya Square. What changes there had been in that time! A second "Russian revolution," the disappearance of a government under which we had both been born and which we had both served. We were also ten years older, of course and he had finally scaled—and deservedly so—the heights of his ambition, he had become head of the diplomatic service of the Russian state.

On the subject of Russian-American relations, Foreign Minister Evgeny Maksimovich Primakov said that after the end of the Cold War, the strategic relationship between the former superpowers had begun to take the form of a relationship between "the leader and the led." "Russia has not and will not stand for that. We want a relationship of equality with all regardless of who is stronger and who is weaker," Primakov asserted. In these words I recognized my old friend, Zhenya Primakov.

An Important Conference

On May 23 and 24 of 1986 a major conference took place, bringing together officials of the Central Committee of the CPSU, the MFA, foreign trade organizations, and other departments. It was called and organized by Shevardnadze and held at MFA headquarters on Smolenskaya Square. Among those attending were several secretaries of the Central Committee, ministers, and the chairs of government committees. Also invited were leading Soviet diplomats, all Soviet ambassadors abroad, consuls general, heads of delegations, and senior officials from MFA headquarters. The lists of invitees and participants were approved by Shevardnadze himself. He took particular care in selecting those who were to speak at the conference, and only those speakers who had something to say of interest to the minister were chosen. To my satisfaction I was one of those chosen.

This conference in Moscow was, as it were, the culmination of a yearlong preparatory period during which Shevardnadze got acquainted with the complex Soviet diplomatic machine, its leading figures and their views, and most important, produced, in close cooperation with Gorbachev, a new perestroika-based Soviet outlook on international political issues in the final phase of the Cold War.

Shevardnadze lost no time in making a clean sweep of the upper echelons of the MFA, removing those of Gromyko's deputies with whom, for one reason or another, he was not comfortable, and in the spring of 1986 he appointed in their places new ones. Ambassadors and the heads of major departments were also replaced. Shevardnadze must be given his due for appointing, for the most part, highly competent professionals to the top posts, officials who had proved themselves under Gromyko. In spite of this, they appreciated their advancement, which they owed to the new minister, and served him loyally and faithfully for a number of years. They were good civil servants and knew how to keep their opinions to themselves when these did not coincide with those of their masters. Shevardnadze could not abide people whose views differed from his own. This was the reason, for example, why he got rid of Korniyenko and, with Gorbachev's support, excluded Dobrynin, one of our most experienced diplomats, from the decision-making process on major foreign policy issues.

The principal event of the conference, was, of course, Gorbachev's speech. This was probably the first time ever in the seventy-year history of the Soviet Union that its supreme leader had spoken before a special diplomatic audience, and Shevardnadze was proud of this. Although the common report on MFA activity was delivered by the minister, it was Gorbachev's speech that was the focus of attention, and it was Gorbachev's favorite theme, "new thinking in the nuclear age," that constituted the keynote of his speech. What held the attention of the audience, however, was a critical evaluation of the past performance of Soviet diplomacy. Gorbachev gave no concrete examples, but his appeal for searching, critical scrutiny of recent Soviet diplomatic practice made it clear to everyone that what he had principally in mind was the Soviet position on strategic arms limitation and reduction and the withdrawal of Soviet troops from Afghanistan. He also condemned the negotiating stance taken by the Soviet Union of invariably rejecting any proposal made by the other side. This was the first time a Soviet leader had ever said this aloud and publicly deplored the "nay-saying negotiators," a nickname that had become firmly associated with Gromyko.

In America there had even been a highly successful play titled "A Walk in the Woods." In it the American negotiator tells his Soviet opposite number: "You are a very good negotiator. That's why they keep you. You can say 'no' longer than other people. You can say it with a frown, you can say it with a smile, you can say 'no' and still be so charming, we'll think you said 'yes.' You dress well, speak English well, you are good with the media. Most of all you know how to take orders—at least, when it really counts. And the orders are nearly always the same: say 'no' and look good doing it."

In his speech Gorbachev called the diplomats to improve all practices in their work, to deviate from the "old thinking," to achieve the implementation of a new strategic line directed at the termination of the Cold War. In his memoirs Gorbachev assesses the meeting at the MFA. "The essence of my speech was reduced to attract the attention to inability of our international establishments, to keep up with the policy and practical steps, undertaken by the political leadership of the country." Now I consider this meeting as a starting point of a complete realization of our "new thinking." Of course, the overwhelming majority of us at the conference welcomed Gorbachev's speech. It struck a responsive chord and was in line with our own wish to see diplomacy fulfilling its natural function—that of working for honorable, mutually acceptable agreements with our opposite numbers.

This was the note struck by most of the speakers at the conference. Many interesting proposals were put forward, and there was also a good deal of criticism. In my own statement, for example, I complained about the unwarrantable length of time taken by the Soviet side to respond to the proposals of our negotiating partners. The work of coordination, sifting, harmonization among departments, and office diplomacy all took too long in my view. I also stressed that the Soviet side was particularly remiss in delaying for months at a time its stands on the various proposals and initiatives of our socialist friends—and there were many instances of this. The effect of this, I said, was not only detrimental to negotiations but also left our friends justifiably aggrieved. Many of the other diplomats made similar remarks.

On the whole, it was a successful conference and demonstrated the willingness of Soviet diplomats to support the strategic line of Gorbachev and his associate, Shevardnadze, which meant an end to confrontational diplomacy and was designed to bring the Cold War to an end.

18
FEIGNED FRIENDSHIP

A Monolith with Cracks

A full, comprehensive picture of the Cold War and the way it evolved and ended is impossible to convey without giving a true insight into the nature and character of relations between the Soviet Union and its allies. The Cold War was a war of coalitions in which two "camps," the capitalist and the socialist, were pitted against each other, with the advantage passing back and forth between them. Problems were also constantly arising within the "camps." Because of their refusal to acknowledge total subordination to Moscow, Yugoslavia and Albania were expelled from the "socialist camp" in the 1940s and the 1960s. On the other hand, certain developing countries in Africa, Asia, and Latin America joined it.

The "coalitional" nature of the Cold War was particularly marked in the area of multilateral conference diplomacy. In the first few years after the end of World War II, the Soviet Union found itself distinctly in the minority in the UN and normally lost in the voting on resolutions in the General Assembly. Later, from the 1960s on, it was the United States's turn to find itself in the minority. A large group of new, nonaligned states preferred to vote with the Soviet Union and its allies on many political and colonial issues.

This was interpreted by the Kremlin leaders as irrefutable evidence of the growing influence of the socialist camp on world developments and as an indicator of its stability. In fact, however, conference diplomacy revealed perhaps more starkly, than any other form of international interaction the weakness, vulnerability, and even the flawed nature of the relations between the Soviet Union and its allies.

Throughout the Cold War, the Kremlin leaders regarded the preservation and strengthening of the unchallenged domination by the Soviet Union of the countries of Eastern Europe as one of the most vital tasks of Soviet foreign policy. This was stressed by all Soviet leaders, beginning with Stalin under whom these countries began to call themselves "peoples' democracies," and ending with Gorbachev when they came to be described as "socialist."

Soviet leaders were convinced that the establishment of a "worldwide socialist system," whose core was the Warsaw Pact Organization, had led to a radical and irreversible change in, and the emergence of an entirely "new kind" of, international relations. "The extraordinarily rich and constantly growing cooperation with the fraternal socialist countries," Brezhnev once declared with pride, "is our permanent number one priority in the external relations of our party and state."

Soviet propaganda claimed that socialist international relations were "not only relations of peace and genuine equality, but also the fraternal mutual assistance of free and sovereign countries," an expression of their unity of action in the realm of international affairs. Of course, the "monolithic unity" of socialist diplomacy was somewhat breached, beginning in the 1960s, by the "special position" of Romania. The Kremlin hoped that in due course it would become possible to return the Romanian mavericks to the herd.

Eastern Europe was the sphere of influence of the Soviet Union—this was one of the most significant outcomes of World War II, and the result of one of many decisions made at the Yalta Conference and elsewhere by the "Big Three," Stalin, Roosevelt, and Churchill.

In this connection, I recall a conversation I had after the war in Oxford in the spring of 1958 with the rector of St. Anthony's College, Frederick Deakin. A historian by profession, he was close to Churchill, who appointed him his personal representative to Tito, since he was an expert on Yugoslavia and spoke Serbo-Croatian. He did an outstanding job and earned the trust and esteem of Tito as well as Churchill. Deakin showed me a sheet of paper given to him by Churchill. On it Churchill had written: "Romania: Russia—90%; others—10%. Greece: Gt. Britain (with the agreement of the U.S.)—

90%; Russia—10%. Yugoslavia—50–50%. Hungary—50–50%. Bulgaria: Russia—75%; others—25%."

Churchill had noted down this list during his visit to Stalin in Moscow in October 1944. This list, which the prime minister had included in his memoirs, was meant to be a reflection of the Anglo-Soviet understanding concerning spheres of influence in southern and eastern Europe. "And why aren't Poland and Czechoslovakia on this list?" I asked the professor. "Stalin signed a treaty of friendship and cooperation with Poland and Czechoslovakia in Moscow during the War, and this made the situation obvious," he answered. Churchill handed the list to Stalin, who as a mark of his consent, ticked the edge of the page with a blue pencil. (Stalin was in the habit of marking documents with bold ticks of a red or blue pencil to signify his approval.)

Deakin added by way of commentary that Churchill was a great realist and put forward the idea of dividing up certain southern European countries into spheres of interest in order to prevent conflict between the two allied powers. He thought that the establishment of Moscow's domination over the countries of Eastern Europe was the inevitable outcome of the Soviet Union's military victories. Deakin claimed that Churchill saw nothing unnatural, still less tragic, in this. He thought that everything would depend on the Soviet Union's influence over neighboring friendly countries. If this influence was going to promote the prosperity and the development of democratic institutions in these countries and prove to be mutually advantageous, then Britain would only welcome it. But, to his great regret, said Deakin, things did not work out like that at all. He referred to the events in East Berlin, in Poland in the early 1950s, and in Hungary in 1956. So, Deakin concluded, the problem did not arise at the time when Eastern Europe fell under the influence of the Soviet Union, but at the time when, and because of the way in which, the Soviet Union actually came to exercise this influence. This talk with Deakin has often come back to me. However, I think Churchill just didn't care what happened to the people of Eastern Europe.

Colleagues of Unequal Status

In spite of hopes for a stable democratic world, the Soviet Union began to exercise its influence over the Eastern European countries, not for their benefit, but rather to their detriment—and to its own. The imposition by force on the countries of Eastern Europe of a Soviet-style system began in the first days after their liberation from fascist occupation. Even the trials of "enemies of the people" in the late 1940s were modeled on the Stalinist purges of the 1930s in the Soviet Union. Moscow thwarted the slightest attempt to honor the national customs, traditions, or histories of these countries. I have already had occasion to mention the pernicious consequences of Soviet actions in Hungary in 1956 and in Czechoslovakia in 1968. Kremlin leaders certainly understood the need to improve relations between the Soviet Union and its allies. Even during the tense moments in 1956, the Politburo adopted a special declaration on the "further" strengthening of cooperation and friendship between the Soviet Union and other socialist countries. This was the kind of statement that was issued from time to time, but did nothing to change the essence of the unequal, one-sided relationships within the Warsaw Pact Organization that reflected the mentality of the Kremlin leaders. From the vantage point of my work in diplomacy I was able to observe this mentality at work.

It was illuminating in this regard to observe the disdain and condescension that Soviet foreign ministers displayed toward their colleagues from the socialist countries. I remember Molotov's distrust for the Czech foreign minister, Vlado Klementis, calling him a "shady character." Molotov did not like to meet with the foreign ministers of Eastern European states; and when he did so, the meeting usually consisted of a querulous monologue delivered by Molotov with the ministers expected to listen intently and carry out any orders they were given to the letter.

Gromyko paid more attention to his colleagues from the socialist countries than Molotov had. Bilateral meetings, mainly in Moscow, meetings of the Committee of the Foreign Ministers of the Warsaw Pact, and multilateral conferences in New York were held regularly and to some extent served to coordinate the foreign policies of the socialist countries, although they too bore the imprint of lectures from "big brother." Nevertheless, Gromyko regarded his opposite numbers at these foreign policy meetings not as foreign ministers but rather as the leaders of their countries, and he accorded them the same respect whenever he visited their capitals. The equality did not always exist between "big brother" and his socialist colleagues.

The following story well illustrates Gromyko's mentality. In the summer of 1964, the Cuban government invited the deputy foreign ministers of the socialist countries to a conference on UN issues in Havana. The Cubans attached great importance to this meeting, and it was designed to enhance the international standing of Cuba and demonstrate great interest in the UN. Vasily Kuznetsov received a personal invitation to the conference. The hosts had planned a meeting for those attending the conference with Fidel Castro.

However, at the last moment Gromyko changed his mind, telling Kuznetsov to remain in Moscow and me, as the head of the Soviet delegation, to go to Havana . Although the Cubans repeated their invitation, we could do nothing to persuade Gromyko to send one of his numerous deputies. His only response was: "A head of department of the MFA is easily equivalent to a deputy foreign minister of any socialist country." I felt very bad at the Havana conference. This was a serious breach of diplomatic protocol. Although our Cuban hosts tried to conceal their disappointment, they were clearly offended and the meeting with Castro was canceled.

Shevardnadze's arrival at the MFA foreshadowed a kind of warming of relations among the heads of the diplomatic services of the socialist countries. The characteristic smile and the ostensible straightforwardness of the new foreign minister were in clear contrast to the unbending sullenness of his predecessor. Initially, he made it a priority to improve relations with our socialist partners and held frequent meetings with his communist colleagues, but soon Gorbachev's "new thinking" began to assign different priorities in Soviet foreign policy, and the minister began to turn more enthusiastically to other problems, putting the serious problems of the socialist fraternity on the back burner. I remember the foreign minister of an Eastern European socialist country saying ruefully in a private conversation: "If Eduard Amvrosiyevich [Shevardnadze] only spent as much time with us as he does with Shultz [the U.S. secretary of state] and other Western foreign ministers, he and the other Soviet leaders would have a much better understanding of the problems of our region." It would be difficult to disagree with this. It is enough to look at the memoirs of Gorbachev and indeed of Shevardnadze himself, to realize how superficial was the knowledge of the Kremlin leadership of the real state of affairs in Eastern Europe. Shevardnadze, for example, writes that his colleagues from the socialist countries "were seriously alarmed at the situation in their countries and spoke to me frankly about it." And that was it. What exactly it was that alarmed them, what advice he gave them, what his reaction was—about all this he says exactly nothing. He doesn't even mention a single one of his colleagues in his book, except for his friends, George (Shultz) and Jim (Baker).

No, Shevardnadze had absolutely no friendly relations—personal or professional—with his colleagues from our socialist allies. I was therefore not surprised to learn that in 1990 he declined a private meeting with his "good friend" Bohuslav Khnyoupek, the former Czech foreign minister, when he came to Moscow.

Extraordinary and Plenipotentiary Nonprofessionals

Deliberately or otherwise, the Kremlin treated the development of the sovereign, socialist states of Eastern Europe the same way as they treated the Soviet republics and regions, and this dictated the pernicious manner in which they appointed Soviet ambassadors and consuls general to Eastern European countries. The secretaries of the central committees of the communist parties of the republics, the regional committees, and senior officials of the secretariat of the Central Committee of the CPSU—this was the list from which were drawn Soviet ambassadors to the socialist countries.

At first these appointments were isolated cases, but by the middle of the 1950s, on Khrushchev's initiative, they became the rule. Sometimes these appointments were dictated by a kind of regional principle. Thus, the leaders of Byelorussia were appointed ambassadors to Poland, senior party officials of the Ukraine were appointed to Romania, and those from the Irkutsk region to Mongolia, and so on. The idea was that similar economic and geographical conditions and historic ties would help these neophyte ambassadors discharge their functions effectively. Of course, it is hard to see in this context what Armenia and Vietnam have in common, but it was the first secretary of the communist party of Armenia, Karen Tovmasian, who was appointed ambassador to Vietnam, and this was by no means the only oddity of its kind.

The logic of these appointments was simple. Inasmuch as the country concerned had proclaimed its goal as communism, those accredited to the governments of these countries should, of course, be exclusively senior officials of the CPSU. Some Soviet ambassadors, even though they were in sovereign foreign countries, felt just as if they were back home in their own republics or regions, and thought that their advice, which they issued in the form of instructions, should be followed unswervingly by the leaders of these socialist states. They dealt almost exclusively with the top leaders of the countries to which they were posted and, in the foreign ministries, with the foreign ministers themselves. For the ambassadors of the socialist countries in Moscow the situation was reversed, and only in the most exceptional circumstances were they vouchsafed the honor of being received by the Soviet foreign minister, and they had to be content to deal with the appropriate heads of department of the MFA or officials of equivalent rank in the Central Committee secretariat.

When I was the head of the IOD in the MFA, I quite often invited representatives of the embassies of socialist countries in Moscow to come to my department for explanations of Soviet initiatives at the UN and briefings on disarmament matters. With the rarest of exceptions it was ambassadors who responded to my invitations, although counselors could very well have done the job of listening to what I had to say.

The attempts of our ambassadors to use the same methods and approach in their posts in the socialist countries as they had in their former party functions, created a situation where many of them were forced to leave at the request, or even the demand, of the leadership of the host country. Hungary was particularly unlucky in this respect. In a relatively short space of time in the 1950s and 1960s, there was a swift succession of Soviet ambassadors in Budapest as, one after another, they were as good as declared persona non grata by the Hungarian authorities. One particularly notorious figure was General Terenti Shtykov, a political officer in the Soviet Army, who for unknown reasons, was appointed, albeit for a very short time, Soviet ambassador to Hungary.

I believe that the unprofessional, clumsy, and disrespectful conduct of some Soviet ambassadors in socialist countries, as well as their interference in their affairs, thwarted the development of truly friendly and equal relations with the Soviet Union. I am not saying, of course, that the collapse of the political and economic systems of the Eastern European countries was due to the amateurish work of Soviet ambassadors in those countries, because the same system proved untenable in the Soviet Union itself and its forcible imposition on the Eastern European countries stood even less chance of success. In any case, the highest Soviet diplomatic representatives in those countries refused to look the realities of those countries in the face.

This bad practice of appointing senior party officials to diplomatic posts persisted throughout the Cold War and even into the perestroika period. In some cases, it even extended to Soviet ambassadorships in capitalist countries. At one time, for example, the Soviet ambassador to France was a former secretary of the Central Committee, Yakov Ryabov. Under Gorbachev, another Central Committee secretary, Oleg Razumovsky was appointed consul general in Shanghai, and Aleksandr Kapto, the head of one of the departments of the Central Committee, was named ambassador to North Korea.

Past experience over many centuries shows that the appointment of people to diplomatic posts without the necessary specialized training never pays. The higher the post, the greater the damage. The experience of Soviet diplomacy in the countries of Eastern Europe provided further striking evidence of this.

You Need Good Eyes and Quick Hands

The inconsistent and flawed policy of the Kremlin leadership toward the Eastern European countries, and indeed all the socialist countries, was particularly conspicuous in the area of multilateral conference diplomacy, where mutual understanding and respect are especially important. As someone who spent many years working in precisely this area, I witnessed and, regrettably, participated in this kind of dysfunctional cooperation with the former socialist countries. In the UN the Soviet Union had in practice, not three votes (USSR, Ukraine, Belorussia)—as had been agreed in Yalta by Stalin, Roosevelt, and Churchill—but ten to twelve, those of the socialist countries. From the mid-1950s on no socialist country failed to vote on the side of the Soviet Union in any meeting. The only exception on occasion was Romania. In any case, the Soviet Union was never totally isolated—something that sometimes happened the United States.

Generally speaking, it is only natural for members of military political alliances to share the same positions. What was *unnatural* was the total, invariable show of unanimity of the socialist countries, which did nothing to enhance the authority and standing of either the Soviet Union itself or of the other members of the Warsaw Pact. It was never the result of coordinated efforts to work out a common position, but simply the imposition of the Soviet position on the other socialist states.

My Czech colleague told me that before his appointment as permanent representative to the UN, Bohuslav Khnyoupek, the Czech foreign minister, when he was seeing him off said to him only half-jokingly: "You'll need two things in your new job: good eyes and quick hands. Good eyes to see how your Soviet comrade is voting, and quick hands to make sure you vote at the same time. So, watch out for both and don't fall down on the job!" I do not recall any socialist country diplomat ever "falling down" on that job and failing to vote with the Soviet representative.

Another feature of the "new type" of relations was the machinery of consultation among socialist countries. There were more than enough of these consultations, and they took place at all levels—from meetings of the leaders down to conferences of experts. Their procedure was always and everywhere exactly the same. The chairman, usually a representative of the host country, would open the meeting with a brief formal statement. Then the floor would be given to the Soviet representative, who would set forth the Soviet position on the agenda item. Then it would usually be the turn of the representative of Poland, except for those occasions when the representative of the GDR competed successfully for second place, followed by the rest. All the participants in the discussion uniformly approved the Soviet position, each one finding his own way of lauding the timeliness and importance of the Soviet proposal.

Sometimes innocuous questions were put to the Soviet representative, which he would have no difficulty in fielding. Normally, there was no actual discussion at these meetings. In conclusion, the chairman would thank, first and foremost, the Soviet representative and then the others and would then adjourn. Of course, every conference was accompanied by protocol events, including lavish receptions where endless toasts were pronounced to "the great Soviet Union and eternal and indissoluble friendship among the socialist countries."

At an international meeting of experts and diplomats in Sicily in 1984 on the American "Star Wars" project, Pierre Trudeau, the Canadian prime minister, was invited to speak. He asked me what the political consultations among the Warsaw Pact members were like and stressed that the NATO meetings at all levels took place in an atmosphere of a free and frank exchange of views which sometimes grew quite heated. I am afraid I did not give him a frank answer and told him that our meetings of the socialist countries were also open and constructive. I don't know whether the prime minister believed me, but if there was any truth in what I had said, it only applied to secondary procedural and organizational matters. And only then on rare occasions.

I took part in innumerable consultations among the socialist countries as head of delegation and head of department in the MFA. Sometimes I tried to change established practices at them. I refused, for example, as the Soviet representative, always to be the one to speak first and proposed the normal democratic practice whereby speakers took the floor in the order they had asked for it. I urged people to express their views freely. At the Disarmament

Conference, on my initiative, we distributed the agenda items among the socialist delegations, so that in certain cases each delegation could speak on behalf of the whole group.

Unfortunately, however, I soon realized that I was just being quixotic. The fact is that the socialist delegations had strict instructions from their capitals to support the Soviet position. Any sign of the independence I was urging on them, on the part of those delegations, could only complicate relations between their capitals and Moscow. So my colleagues held their tongues for fear of appearing to oppose "big brother" and courting punishment from their authorities.

My friends from the socialist countries persuaded me to stick to established practices. My idea of distributing the agenda items did not fare any better either, because the delegations of the socialist countries did not possess the necessary documents or information to respond in a serious or constructive manner. The same difficulties emerged even with respect to positions already agreed upon within the Warsaw Pact Organization on various arms limitation and disarmament issues. For this reason, they were constantly relying on the Soviet delegation to select the necessary documentation, draft information papers, and even write their speeches for them. We had no problem with this, believing, as we did, that this was our sacred duty, but in all this there was not even a hint of the expression of their own interests, equality, or any real constructive pooling of ideas. My good intentions conflicted with the "big brother" policy.

Don't Keep Your Allies in the Dark

One of the shortcomings of the "new type" of relations among the socialist countries was the absence of any organized, effective machinery for the sharing of information by the Soviet Union with its allies about international political and diplomatic issues. A certain amount of information was channeled at various levels through the Central Committee, the MFA, and other departments, but it was irregular, late in coming, and in most cases extremely superficial (sometimes the content of the "confidential information" sent to the leadership of socialist countries could have been published in *Pravda* or *Izvestiya* editorials). Worst of all, however, was the fact that the Soviet Union's allies as often as not were kept in the dark about the various diplomatic moves of "big brother."

Take, for example, the annual Soviet initiatives at the UN. As I have said, they were mostly designed for propaganda purposes and were fully part of the pattern of the confrontational diplomacy of the Cold War. These Soviet proposals were designed by the Kremlin to win wide support from "the whole of progressive humanity" and "the peace-loving states of the UN." Naturally, at the bilateral and multilateral consultations of the socialist countries on the eve of the UN General Assembly session, their representatives were mostly interested in knowing what the next Soviet initiative in the series would be. This was not, of course, just idle curiosity; this was information they needed because of the severe pressure they were under to demonstrate the "total and vigorous support" of the whole socialist camp. However, the minister and the other diplomats were under strict orders from the Politburo not to give a straight answer to that question before the proposal had been formally introduced. At the very outside, in spite of the risk I knew I was running, I would reveal the barest outline of the issue that would be the subject of the Soviet proposal.

Just the day before his speech at the UN, Gromyko, who was already in New York, sent copies of his speech to his colleagues, the foreign ministers of the socialist countries, who felt it was their sacred duty to be in the UN to hear the speech of "big brother," the Soviet foreign minister. Gromyko frequently put me in charge of circulating the text of his speech to the foreign ministers. And an unenviable task it was! While formally expressing their gratitude for our kindness, the foreign ministers in one way or another made it apparent that they were disappointed at receiving this information so late in the day. The Polish foreign minister Stefan Olshovsky once told me frankly that the late arrival of Gromyko's speech caused him personally and his whole delegation serious difficulties because he was schedule to speak on the same day as the Soviet foreign minister. He confessed his annoyance at having to amend the text of his own speech at the last moment in the light of the contents of Gromyko's. I should point out that because of this, to put it mildly, strange Soviet tradition, the foreign ministers of the socialist countries preferred to speak a few days after Gromyko.

What was particularly intolerable was the fact that members of NATO, through their American colleagues, were better informed about the Soviet position at various bilateral negotiations than the members of the Warsaw Pact, who never received this information from the Soviet representatives—and these were by no means just a few isolated cases.

In 1985, I was at the consultations on disarmament in Budapest. In response to the tired clichés I was mouthing about the ever closer cooperation among the socialist countries and particularly between the Soviet Union and Hungary, in the realm of disarmament, the Hungarian foreign minister, Frigyes Puja, replied in a pretty abrasive, undiplomatic manner that it was impossible to talk of effective cooperation among the socialist countries in the realm of disarmament as long as the Soviet Union insisted on keeping its own allies in the dark about their own interests in this area as well as the progress of the negotiations with the United States and other countries. I am sure I was not the only one to whom this kind of resentment was expressed. In the late 1980s, at the time of "perestroika," the situation with regard to the sharing of information improved somewhat and the heads of Soviet delegations were instructed by Moscow to brief their colleagues from the socialist countries about the results of Soviet-American negotiations on various subjects. But this was too little too late. The cracks that had appeared in relations between the Soviet Union and its allies toward the end of the Cold War were now too great to be repaired by mere palliatives.

Deterioration, Not Improvement

The rise of Gorbachev and his people to the leadership of the Party and the state gave grounds for hoping for an improvement in the Soviet Union's relations with its allies. The familiar doctrine of the paramountcy of cooperation within the socialist fraternity could be found in all Soviet political documents of the time of "perestroika." Gorbachev's report to the Twenty-Seventh Congress of the CPSU stressed the vital importance of more active concertation among the socialist countries. Soon after Gorbachev came to power, a summit meeting of leaders of the member states of the Warsaw Pact was held in Sofia at which it was decided to extend the treaty (it was to last for only a few more years!). The traditional bilateral and multilateral talks within the socialist camp were also held. Shevardnadze even felt it necessary to make Pyongyang the destination of one of his first trips abroad. There the "parties noted with satisfaction that the ironclad principles of Marxism-Leninism, socialist internationalism, and the relations between the Soviet Union and the Korean People's Democratic Republic were constantly developing and becoming closer." Ultimately, however, the posturing and the forms, which were properly observed, were not what it was all about.

In practice, the communist leadership of the countries of Eastern Europe did not share Gorbachev's "new thinking" and did not understand the nature and purpose of perestroika in any respect, including that of international politics. As mutual understanding between superpowers grew, so relations between the Soviet Union and its Warsaw Pact allies, far from improving, actually and perceptibly cooled. Even the reference in Gorbachev's report to the Twenty-Seventh Congress of the CPSU to the allies of the Soviet Union occupied a far less prominent place than it had in the reports of previous general secretaries to previous party congresses.

Gorbachev and his people found that their Warsaw Pact allies were beginning to become a something of nuisance and to create more problems for them in the larger strategy embraced within their "new thinking." For example, the frequent and rapid changes in the stance of the Kremlin leadership in international affairs and the growing number of Soviet-American meetings all required explanation, and the Kremlin simply did not have the time or inclination for this. This open disregard for the position and interests of their allies on the part of Moscow could not help offending the leaders of the Warsaw Pact countries. The countries of Eastern Europe now found themselves on the sidelines of world politics.

Gorbachev and his people saw no place for the participation of the Warsaw Pact countries in the rapid process of change sweeping over the world. This was apparent to me even in terms of the relatively narrow problem of the prohibition of chemical weapons. For a number of years, the delegations of the socialist countries at the Conference on Disarmament were extremely active and quite competent in the work of negotiating a treaty on the subject. We had excellent cooperation with them, and between us we often set the tone in the working group. We also came up with joint initiatives. We made proposals to Moscow for coordinated action, which would help the negotiations along. Unfortunately, our authorities showed no interest in our proposals, and inevitably our colleagues felt this and took offense.

At the same time the situation in the Eastern European countries was steadily deteriorating and tensions were rising—particularly in Poland. In spite of the Berlin Wall, the stream of Germans fleeing from East to West Germany was becoming unstoppable, and the economic situation in most of these countries was bad and the standard of living in decline. All this damaged the authority of the ruling communist parties of these countries, encouraged the growth of widespread opposition, and exacerbated relations within the Warsaw pact.

Moving as I did in diplomatic circles in Geneva, I was often involved in discussions about the situation in the Eastern European countries. Many diplomats, and particularly those from socialist countries, were quite alarmed by events in those countries, especially in Poland. Outwardly, there was no change in friendly relations between the ambassadors and the diplomats from the socialist countries, but behind it all one sensed their concern at the situation back home.

I spent hours at a time talking to the Polish representative in Geneva, Bogumil Suika. We had developed a friendly and cooperative relationship when our countries were allies and maintained this relationship even many years later when our countries came to belong to different military-political alliances. Suika was one of the most skillful conference diplomats I have ever met. As a matter of fact, he played an extremely important part in negotiating and producing the convention on the prohibition of chemical weapons. The profound knowledge, persistence, and patience he displayed as chairman of the working group on chemical weapons at the Conference on Disarmament made a great contribution to the conclusion of this highly important international treaty.

Suika described to me the complex political situation in Warsaw and shared his thoughtful analysis of the lineup of political forces in Poland. He was firmly opposed to the idea of sending additional Soviet troops to Poland, something he foresaw would lead inevitably to war. Basically, he thought that intervention in any shape or form, be it political, economic, diplomatic, let alone military, by the Soviet Union in Poland, could only exacerbate the situation. He believed that the dramatic step taken by General Jaruzelski— the declaration of martial law—was the only possible way of maintaining order in the country. To his credit, his prediction about the development of events in Poland proved largely correct.

For my part, I agreed fully that there must be no repetition of the Hungarian and Czech scenarios of 1956 and 1968 in attempting to resolve the Polish situation. I have to confess that this possibility could not be entirely ruled out. Some of my colleagues in the delegation voiced their apprehensions about the possibility of a Soviet invasion, pointing to certain reports that had appeared in the media as well as the increased frequency of contacts between the Soviet and Polish leadership, which to judge by the Hungarian and Czech precedents, they felt boded no good.

In spite of our friendship, or perhaps even because of it, Bogush was very often critical of Soviet moves both within the Soviet Union and in foreign policy. He foresaw profound changes in Soviet-Polish relations, which should be built on the basis of equality and mutual benefit. He welcomed

Gorbachev's "perestroika," I believe, although a lot of it was not clear to him—or to me, for that matter.

I also spent a lot of time talking with Milos Veivoda, the Czech representative in Geneva. He too was worried about the situation in Eastern Europe. Having served for several years as deputy foreign minister, he knew his way very well around the maze of Prague politics. His assessment of the situation in the country was also not very optimistic for the future of the then current regime in Czechoslovakia.

Talking with the representatives of the GDR and observing their behavior, I detected a certain embarrassment on the part of the Germans about the growing number of refugees from the East flooding into West Germany in the early 1980s; and this time it was largely through the territory of their Hungarian ally, something which caused problems in relations between the two countries. It did not escape my notice that my colleague from the GDR was reluctant to touch on the question of perestroika in his conversations with me and gave me to understand that the government in Berlin, and the leader himself, Erich Honnecker, disapproved of many of Gorbachev's ideas.

The representatives of the socialist countries in Geneva took every convenient opportunity to express to me their puzzlement at the policies of the Gorbachev leadership in international affairs. As they saw it, it would end up weakening the position of the socialist camp as a whole. Some of them also stressed that this line would ultimately and inevitably be damaging to the interests of the Soviet Union, which, in effect, was encouraging the Eastern European countries to broaden their contacts with the West and tending to isolate itself in the process.

I recall a frank conversation in the spring of 1986 in Sofia with Petr Mladenov, the Bulgarian foreign minister. He was very well informed about the Soviet Union and had graduated from the Moscow State Institute of International Relations. He expressed a lively interest in news from the MFA, the "new thinking," and the status and authority of the new minister, Shevardnadze. He was not all that free in expressing his views, but he gave me the feeling that he was somewhat worried about the current "cooling" of "fraternal cooperation," the growing problems in the socialist camp, and the ever growing cracks in the monolith which might very well crumble one of these days.

I discussed with the minister the prospects of more active cooperation with the socialist countries within the significantly improved climate of superpower relations. Bringing the Warsaw Pact members into these positive processes, we thought, would not only give the Soviet Union a more powerful hand to play with, but would also strengthen the position of the communist parties in those countries as well as their domestic stability. The minister warned that if the Eastern European countries and their ruling regimes were denied an active role in world events, it would be a political death blow to them.

It was typical of those times for my colleagues from the socialist countries to be anxious to clear every step they took with their capitals. I remember the Hungarian ambassador Meisner, at a conference of the regional group, asking for a postponement of a decision of what was really only a matter of secondary importance, until he had received instructions from Budapest, even though all the other representatives, including the representative of the Soviet "big brother," supported it unanimously. On another occasion, a problem arose about the reaction of the socialist delegations to the visit to Geneva of Lech Wałęsa, the leader of the Polish opposition. Many questions also arose, relating to the growing influence of the West on the Eastern European countries, in particular with regard to their negotiating position on various subjects.

The logic of events, even within the relatively narrow framework of the Geneva Conference on Disarmament, dictated a serious reappraisal of relations among the Warsaw Pact countries and between the Soviet Union and the countries of Eastern Europe.

In conclusion, I would like to say a word about the relations between diplomats from the socialist countries and their Soviet colleagues. There was, of course, no prevailing uniform pattern to these relationships. Many Soviet diplomats had genuinely friendly feelings and sincere respect for these colleagues, they cooperated and shared information and experiences with them, and consulted them, and this treatment was reciprocated. I personally have taken part in negotiations and had conversations with the foreign ministers and leading diplomats of all the socialist countries, many of them were highly professional diplomats, highly cultured, with a broad outlook, and enjoyed the high esteem of the diplomatic corps. I enjoyed working with them and learned a lot from them. I have mentioned some of them in the pages of this book.

As a rule, diplomats from the socialist countries were highly professional men as well as patriots. They were proud advocates of their countries and their history, art, and traditions. They would bristle at any sign of disrespect or disregard for their countries—as I had good reason to know and rue from my own experience. It was in May 1985, just before day of the Fortieth Anniversary of the Victory over Fascism. I was speaking at the Conference on Disarmament and quoting figures showing the destruction caused by Germany and its allies in World War II. I was using data contained in the documents of the Paris Special Reparations Commission and describing the extent of the damage done to a number of countries. The document contained no specific figures for Poland, simply stating that it had lost 38 percent of its national income, and this was the figure I used in my speech. Soon afterwards I was in Moscow, and my boss in the MFA made a point of calling me in and asking me how I felt about Poland. I was somewhat taken aback by the question and said I had great respect for that country, which was one of our loyal allies. I added that I had many friends in Poland and that I was fond of Polish literature and music. I in turn asked what was the reason for the question and whether it was my appointment to Poland.

The minister explained that President Jaruzelski had told the Soviet ambassador in Warsaw that he was unhappy about the fact that the Soviet representative at the Conference on Disarmament, namely myself, had failed to describe the magnitude of the damage done to Poland in World War II. I explained that I was relying on the data of the international commission; there was no other source available to me. Of course, I regretted that, without meaning to, I had offended the Poles, and on my return to Geneva, in one of my statements, I made a point of dwelling on the tremendous toll taken on Poland during World War II and its great contribution to the victory over fascism. Happily, my relations with the Polish representative did not suffer as a result of this misunderstanding.

Generally speaking, my relations with the representatives of the socialist countries were informal, friendly, and warm. I very much appreciated the friendliness extended toward me by my colleagues from those countries and treasure as a cherished possession the letter they wrote to me when I was forced into retirement. There were, of course, some Soviet diplomats who treated their socialist colleagues with disdain and only ever spoke to them in a hectoring manner, on the rare occasions they deigned to make contact with them. It is not difficult to imagine how diplomats from the socialist countries felt about this attitude.

In a word, the 1980s were a fateful decade for the whole "socialist camp." Just as a fish rots from the head, so the collapse of the famous "socialist fraternity" started with the Soviet Union. The socialist system as such, and its economic and political infrastructure, went bankrupt and the military-political alliance forcibly erected on this foundation was doomed to go down with it.

As early as the first years of perestroika it was clear that Moscow could not be bothered about the fate of the socialist camp and showed little concern for the position of its allies—a position for which Moscow itself was to blame. There had been a time when the peoples of many Eastern European countries, liberated from fascist occupation by the Soviet army, looked forward to the development of lasting friendly relations with their great neighbor and their watchword was "With the Soviet Union—for Eternity!" The Soviet Union did not appreciate this. Unable to build its relations with the countries of Eastern Europe on a foundation of equal, mutually beneficial cooperation, respect, and democracy, the Soviet Union chose a self-defeating course. Its policies brought down on itself hostility, followed by outright fear and hatred.

I will never forget the genuine friendliness and hospitality with which a small group of Soviet tourists with which I was traveling, was greeted in Romania and Bulgaria in the 1950s and how ashamed and pained I was to hear my Hungarian friends advising me, when I was on a visit to Budapest in the late 1980s, not to speak Russian on the street.

Perestroika in the Soviet Union created an opportunity to work together to solve the many problems facing all the Warsaw Pact countries. The opportunity was missed. To make things worse, the Soviet Union proved to be a bad ally, abandoning its friends when things were difficult. The end result of this Soviet policy was to make the countries of Eastern Europe look elsewhere for more loyal allies—by joining NATO.

19 FAREWELL TO THE COLD WAR

A New Year's Surprise

The year 1987 began like any other year. My wife and I went to our dacha outside Moscow to celebrate with our two sons. The setting was spectacular that New Year's Eve as the snow had fallen on the woods surrounding the house, making it unusually quiet and beautiful in the evening light. After a short house-concert and the unwrapping of gifts, we shared stories of the previous year and expressed hopes for the coming one, as most families do. My younger son, Levon, was pleased that he was doing well in his studies at the MSIIR and was looking forward to a career in the diplomatic service. Karen told us about his life in the army (he was serving in the Soviet Army) and how he was looking forward to coming home. Alla and I told family stories. Dinner passed in a cheerful, festive mood. At midnight we set off fireworks in our garden and watched the New Year's concert on TV. There was nothing about that evening which gave a hint of the trouble to come in the next few months.

After spending a few more days relaxing at the dacha I returned to Moscow. It was then that Alla told me an unsettling story. In December the prosecutor's office (PO) had twice asked her to testify in a case involving one of her acquaintances, who had been arrested on suspicion of a number of crimes. The charges included fabrication of documents and participation in currency frauds. Alla had avoided telling me about this until after our New Year's celebration so that it wouldn't spoil the holiday spirit.

At first I wasn't terribly troubled by the news because it was only a deposition. However, the more I thought about the nature of the conversations in the prosecutor's office the more they worried me. Alla was planning to join me in late January in Geneva, where I was to head the Soviet delegation to the Conference on Disarmament, so I decided it was best to notify my MFA superiors. Technically speaking, the PO could have prevented my wife from leaving the country on the pretext of the investigation.

I met with Vladimir Petrovsky, deputy minister of foreign affairs and responsible for the work of the delegation to the Geneva Conference on Disarmament. After we had discussed various professional matters, I told him the story of the prosecutor's office. Petrovsky, who knew my wife, reacted to this news with great caution and informed me that he had no authority in this area and suggested that we go to see the deputy minister for personnel, Valentin Nikiforov.

I should say a few words about Nikiforov. He joined the MFA in 1985 with little or no previous experience in foreign affairs or diplomacy. For a time he had worked in Soviet Georgia as a senior official of the Party and during those years he had become the protégé of Eduard Shevardnadze. When Shevardnadze went to Moscow in 1985, he took Nikiforov with him, knowing that he would be a loyal supporter. Shevardnadze appointed him director of personnel—a major post in the MFA even though it did not directly involve questions of foreign policy. This meant that Nikiforov, with his lack of experience, never enjoyed any authority in foreign policy matters with the professionals in the ministry. Nikiforov understood this well, keeping to himself and not developing any genuine rapport with his new colleagues.

Prior to our meeting in 1987, my relations with Nikiforov had been restricted to professional matters. We never had any disputes or confrontations, and he generally agreed with me whenever I had occasion to express my views on personnel matters. When I entered his office, therefore, on that January day I did not quite know what to expect. Nikiforov was very formal with me. He told me that Petrovsky had informed him beforehand of the purpose of my visit. "Yes," he said, "we have received a letter concerning your wife." He then pointed to a document lying on his desk—a typical bureaucratic gesture, which made me bristle with anger. Who did he mean by "we" and what kind of "letter" could it possibly be? Did it originate from an official source or was it some anonymous denunciation? And what could it possibly say? These were the questions that crowded into my mind. I expected that Nikiforov would next hand me the letter and let me read it but not only did he not offer to show it to me, he even refused when I asked. This infuriated me even more.

I then informed Nikiforov that I was about to leave in a few days for Geneva, where I would be participating in long and complex negotiations and that such unpleasant conversations just before a crucial mission were hardly likely to help my performance. Nikiforov replied that he was not prepared to discuss the matter any further and that it was up to the minister to decide whether I would be sent to Geneva. Shevardnadze was not expected in Moscow for a few days so Nikiforov and I agreed that upon his return we would both "consult" with him.

A Meeting with Shevardnadze

I left Nikiforov's office in a state of anxiety. I was coming to the realization that I was facing the gravest crisis of my career. This was not a small matter that could be brushed aside easily; my entire career in the MFA was hanging in the balance. My friend Petrovsky, who had heard my conversation with Nikiforov, kept silent, and that only made matters worse. Somehow I knew that my only hope was that my meeting with Shevardnadze would resolve the issue in my favor.

I now began to see previous incidents in a whole new light. For instance, on New Year's Eve just before leaving for the dacha, I had had a brief talk with Shevardnadze in which I suggested that we devote part of the MFA board meeting in early January to discuss the upcoming negotiations on chemical weapons in Geneva. Shevardnadze had agreed and instructed the secretary to put this on the agenda for the meeting. After my conversation with Nikiforov, however, I had called the secretary to inquire about preparations for the discussion of my topic, and he told me that the item had been removed from the agenda. When I asked who had removed it, he answered, with some reluctance, that it had been the minister himself.

I also recalled that at one of the recent board meetings Shevardnadze had persistently ignored me when I raised my hand during a certain discussion.

I had been in New York for several months so I joked that it was dangerous to be away for a long time because the board forgets who you are. I noticed that Shevardnadze winced ever so slightly at my remark. At the time I hadn't attached any special significance to the incident, but now I began to see it differently. I knew I was in trouble.

Nikiforov and I met Shevardnadze at his office at 10 A.M. on Friday, January 9. The meeting of the Collegium was scheduled to start an hour later, and my flight to Geneva was planned for Saturday. Shevardnadze rose from his chair and greeted me with a smile and a friendly handshake. His first words, however, made it clear that our conversation was not to be a friendly one. He said that he had always read my reports with "great interest" but that now he found himself in a "very difficult position." When I asked him what had put him in such a position, Shevardnadze referred to a "letter" concerning my wife that had been sent to the MFA.

I was surprised by this comment and responded that, as far as I knew, my wife had been called as a witness in a criminal case and that no charges had been brought against her. To this Shevardnadze shrugged, replying that there was much more to the case than this. I answered that I had complete faith in my wife and that I did not see what this had to do with my work at the MFA. He obviously felt uncomfortable with the conversation, and I could sense that he had nothing to back up his charges so he began talking vaguely about relations between husband and wife in a way that made no sense to me and simply goaded me into losing my temper. I responded heatedly that I had been a loyal employee of the MFA system for over four decades, that I was not an amateur, and that I enjoyed the trust of both my colleagues and my superiors. Clearly, Shevardnadze did not like my use of the word "amateur," which he took as a swipe at him as a newcomer to the ministry. I was, of course, angry with Shevardnadze, although that was not the point I was making, but just as he was getting ready to retort, the Gorbachev hot line rang. Shevardnadze signaled for us to leave his office as he prepared to take the call.

When Nikiforov and I returned a few minutes later, Shevardnadze was clearly ready to end the conversation. He said that it was not his intention to level any charges against me; he would leave that to "the courts." "And you certainly must know," he said menacingly, " Soviet courts are the fairest of all courts." This statement stunned me. What did "courts" have to do with it? All I could think of, hearing these words come from a member of the Politburo who spoke with a distinctly Georgian accent, was Comrade

Stalin, whose "fair" Soviet courts had slaughtered millions of people in the terrible 1930s. I responded in the only way I knew how to at such a moment. "Eduard Amvrosiyevich," I said, "we are obviously talking about trust here. If you, as minister of foreign affairs and as a human being, trust me, then I am prepared to take off for Geneva tomorrow to continue negotiations. If there is no trust, I am ready to tender my resignation right here and now." Hearing this, Shevardnadze thought for a few moments and then muttered, "The second option is obviously the more acceptable one." "In that case, there is no point in my being present at the board meeting," I said. It was clear that Shevardnadze agreed with me, and that our conversation was over. Nikiforov and I left the room.

Resignation for "Family Reasons"

I went into the anteroom and wrote my letter of resignation, which I then handed to Nikiforov. It was very brief, citing only "family reasons" for my decision. Then I informed the assistant that my trip to Geneva had been canceled and left the building. I decided to walk home so that I could think about what had just happened.

I have to say that my dismissal from the ministry came as a complete surprise to me. This is not to say that I had never thought of a time when my career as a diplomat would come to an end. As a matter of fact, in recent years I had occasionally thought about retiring from the MFA and returning to Moscow, most likely to resume my teaching. Frankly speaking, I knew that at my age my chances of being appointed to a major ambassadorship were not good. The post of rector of the Diplomatic Academy, which I was familiar with at one time, had always appealed to me. While in Geneva I even tried to win over Gromyko to this idea, but to no avail.

In 1986 I also signed contracts with three publishing houses—International Relations, Progress, and Mysl'—for three different books on the history of diplomacy to be published in the late 1980s. While still in Geneva, I even began working on one of them, but it would have been impossible to meet my contractual obligations in the course of an active diplomatic career. Nonetheless, all of this was evidence that I had been mentally contemplating a career change.

Despite all of this, there is no question that I wanted to leave with dignity and in a manner befitting my standing and accomplishments instead of being virtually kicked out. As I walked home that day, stunned by my conversation with Shevardnadze, I was overwhelmed by a feeling of resentment. What had I done to deserve such shoddy treatment by the MFA authorities? I racked my brain, but for the life of me I could not come up with an answer that made sense. Of course, I may well have done something to displease Shevardnadze, and my actions or remarks may not always have concurred with his plans or intentions. Nevertheless, I was a loyal soldier of my country—a soldier in World War II and later a warrior of the Cold War, who served my country for almost half a century.

My wounded feelings, however, soon gave way to feelings of fear. I was afraid of possible punitive measures against myself and my family. The first move might be disciplinary action against me by the Communist Party in the form of expulsion. Reasons were neither here nor there, since the sorry history of the CPSU is marked by innumerable examples of groundless expulsions, which were invariably followed by violations of basic human rights. Sometimes these culminated in arrests, which in the 1930s were often followed by execution. In this case, I hoped that my fears were groundless and that everything would be put right and the truth would come out. After all, this was the time of Gorbachev's perestroika. Unfortunately, this was not to be the case.

Soon after my resignation I was called by the chief editor of the International Relations publishing house, a Ms. Zavalnaya, who asked under what pseudonym I was going to publish my article in the 1986 annual journal, *Diplomatic Bulletin*. I was surprised by the question and asked her in turn why I would want to use a pseudonym when in the previous yearbooks I had used my own name. In some embarrassment she answered that "under the new circumstances" the publishing house couldn't release the book with the article signed by me. "That's your problem," I responded angrily. "I absolutely refuse to be published under a pseudonym." Obviously my situation had created a dilemma for the publishing house. It was practically impossible not to include an article on disarmament, and it was too late to replace it with another one. To jeopardize the release of the yearbook at this late date meant considerable financial costs for the publishing house. Fortunately, the director Vadim Kozmin turned out to be a reasonable man and took personal responsibility for publishing the yearbook with my name attached to my article—even though Ms. Zavalnaya thought it a "suspect" name.

It was the same story with *Izvestiya*. On the eve of my resignation one of the people from the paper's international department asked me to write an article about chemical weapons. I agreed and submitted the article. However, time passed and it was not published, and the person who had commissioned the article persistently avoided me. Petrovsky, whom I asked to talk to the chief editor, claimed that he was simply unable to contact the paper. Considering that both of them were on the direct hot line, this explanation was not too plausible, to say the least. Rather, it was very clear that these officials were afraid to have anything to do with me.

Even more worrisome were the demonstrative avoidance by friends and acquaintances of any association with me or to my family. For example, I had had a long association with a deputy head of delegation, Boris Prokofiev. We were on a first-name basis and knew each other's families, especially during our time in Geneva. Boris would call me for no other reason than just to chat. Then suddenly, after my unexpected "resignation"—silence! My "friend" totally disappeared from my life.

Fortunately, there were not many others who behaved like Prokofiev. Some of our acquaintances, who had, at least superficially, been on friendly terms with us, dropped us entirely, declining our invitations and not returning our phone calls. I was especially worried by the change in attitude toward me of people I knew who were "close to the top." I could only view their "boycotting of me" as a sign of future punitive measures in store for me.

There were even more disturbing signs. Malignant rumors spread about the "hostile activities" of myself and my family. I had a driver, a very good-natured and loyal person, who once told me in strict confidence that a senior official of the ministry for whom he was driving, had told him, "Israelyan is finished because of his American connections. He has been cooperating with them for ages." A well-known broadcaster, who had once invited me to participate in a program on disarmament, started to spread malicious rumors that I was a "provocateur" posing as a disarmament expert.

However, there were also many people—true friends and acquaintances—who were unhappy about my dismissal. They did not believe the slander spread by our enemies. These people consoled and encouraged us, offered us advice and compassion, and above all, their support.

The Verdict of the Moscow Prosecutor's Office

What happened after my resignation? My wife Alla was invited to the prosecutor's office once again, and once again she was questioned about her relations with the woman who had been arrested. The prosecutor was specifically interested in a note that had been confiscated from her. Attached to the note was a receipt for about 600 Swiss francs for articles of woman's clothing (blouses, skirts, lingerie). The woman claimed that Alla had sent the note to her in Geneva so that she would purchase these items and bring them back to Alla when she returned to Moscow. Knowing that such things are forbidden in the Soviet Union, my wife denied it, saying that she had nothing to do with the note. The investigators from the Moscow prosecutor's office could not prove the contrary.

After that point I am not sure what happened, but I presume that the investigators, having received instructions to disgrace my family, came up with another "terrible" accusation. Relying on the same source (the accused woman), they accused my wife of having shown a video of the movie *Emmanuelle* in our apartment to several guests during my stay in Geneva. The investigators described this as distribution of pornography. The charge was true, but I should point out that my wife watched this film in Moscow with several friends of mature years. In the eyes of the investigators, however, this did not change the "criminal" nature of the act. In fact, the charge of pornography was never pursued any further, most likely because this was the time of glasnost when videotapes of movies more explicit than *Emmanuelle* were becoming readily available in Moscow video stores.

In time my wife stopped getting these invitations from the prosecutor's office so she contacted the investigator herself to find out if the investigation was still going on. She was told that it was not and that she could resume her normal life. Alla was shocked. "How can we return to our normal lives when this investigation had resulted in the firing of my husband from the MFA?" she asked. "That's the business of the MFA authorities, not ours!" was the only response. It made sense but there was nothing we could do.

We found ourselves in a ridiculous situation. On the one hand, the prosecutor's office had dropped its charges against my wife. Yet, on the other hand, the manner of my resignation together with the rumors surrounding me left the impression that my wife and I had committed some crime. From our point of view, those responsible for the injustice of which we were victims should do something at least partially to compensate us for the moral injury we had suffered. Our friends, in particular Valentin Loshinin, who was then deputy chief for personnel at the ministry, convinced us that we should seek redress. So we approached the prosecutor's office and succeeded in obtaining a document that cleared Alla of any and all charges. It declared that under paragraph 2 of article 5 of the Criminal Code of the Russian

Federation all criminal charges against my wife were dismissed for lack of evidence of any criminal offense.

Incidentally, we learned during the process of obtaining this document that according to the official records Alla had in fact been summoned to the PO not as a witness but as a suspect. Thus for reasons that still remain unclear to me, we were never told the real truth behind this painful episode.

Shevardnadze's Response to My Request

Meanwhile I was relieved of my duties at the ministry, ordered to surrender the keys to my office, and stripped of a number of perquisites. At the same time, Nikiforov was in no hurry to process my pension. It was explained to me that because of my professional status, I was supposed to register as a retiree of "national importance," but I suspect that Nikiforov was unwilling to recommend me for this status for fear of appearing to support a person whose conduct had come under official suspicion. Nonetheless, it was only four months after my resignation that my pension status was finally clarified. When the MFA officially gave me the news, I asked if my departure would be accompanied by a traditional retirement party. One of my former assistants replied with some embarrassment that the authorities were not planning a party because of the "special" circumstances of my retirement. Indeed, my case was truly special.

To set the record straight, I wrote a letter to Shevardnadze telling him that the slander against my wife had officially been dismissed by the prosecutor's office. I also wanted him to know that my resignation, which he had forced me to tender, had resulted in malicious and defamatory rumors about myself and my family. In the letter I asked the minister to see me and to consider the opportunity of making use of my diplomatic and academic experience within the MFA system. In conclusion I reminded the minister that in our last conversation he had expressed his faith that in the land of the Soviets truth would always prevail. I urged him to "bring to bear his authority in giving me an opportunity to continue to do the work to which I had devoted my life."

Shevardnadze's reaction to the prosecutor's document and to my letter was, I'm afraid, typical of him. One would expect him to be pleased that all attempts to tarnish the reputation of a subordinate had failed. It would also be natural for the minister to make an effort to restore the reputation of a veteran of the diplomatic service. All he needed to do was say one word at any ministerial meeting or, failing that, simply make an effort to meet with me and hear me out. Nothing of the sort happened. As an eyewitness told me, when Shevardnadze read the document from the PO, he was livid. He summoned Mikhail Kurishev, from the Special Department (the KGB representative in the MFA), and expressed his extreme displeasure at the "poor quality" of work of the investigators. Shortly thereafter the PO received instructions to reopen the criminal case against my wife. I did not learn of this until later. I first became suspicious when I attempted to communicate with Kurishev, who made no effort to hide his displeasure at being reprimanded by the minister on my account. I then spoke with Shevardnadze's secretary to confirm receipt of my letter, but he referred me to Nikiforov for a response. He tried to avoided meeting with me but finally brought himself to offer me on the telephone the tight-lipped comment: "Your wife's case is not yet closed."

Shevardnadze, known in the West as a "champion of democracy and justice," had given instructions that resulted in the USSR Prosecutor's Office overriding the decision of the Moscow PO and referring my wife's "case" to the RSFSR PO for a new investigation.

The investigation was entrusted to the public prosecutor of the Russian PO. Knowing that Shevardnadze had a personal interest in the case, he pursued the matter with great zeal. He summoned a large number of witnesses, including myself, many of our acquaintances, and even people we did not know. It is hard to describe the ordeal inflicted on my friends, my family, and myself by the interrogations to which we were subjected. In one instance, two of our friends who had watched the movie *Emmanuelle* (he was in his seventies, she was in her sixties) told us the details of the interrogation during which they were required to watch the video again. They were asked absurd questions about what they felt watching the movie and whether they would like to see it again. Their story would have been funny had it not been so ludicrous.

Despite the prosecutor's fervor he was eventually compelled to halt his investigation and in essence confirm the decision of the Moscow PO. In his letter dated late September 1987 he wrote that with regard to the charges of "breaking the rules and regulations governing currency operations," of the "distribution of videotapes containing pornographic content," my wife had committed no offense. We were greatly relieved to receive this letter, although after the ordeal of the previous ten months, we had no confidence that that we had heard the last of the matter. We certainly had no intention of contesting the findings of the PO, but one never knew what to expect from that "champion of democracy and justice."

My Case Goes to the Board

Since no one contested the decision of the prosecutor, it became official. What was I to do? I could not ignore the injustice done to me, which essentially meant letting the authorities off the hook. How could it happen that in a civilized age there was still a country where one citizen could not ask another to bring back insignificant articles from another country without special permission from the government? After all, it should not be forgotten that all of this was happening at the height of perestroika, when Shevardnadze and other top-ranking Soviet leaders were extolling the virtues of the "human factor" in Soviet society. In such a climate it seemed absolutely unthinkable to me that the Soviet state should be oppressing its own citizens with total impunity. It all seemed to me to be an utter disgrace to our society and its political system.

Pondering this whole chain of events I could not help concluding that what I had just experienced was typical of Soviet life during the Cold War. Certainly it had nothing to do with the international policy of the Soviet state, but it did reflect the basic immorality of the totalitarian Soviet system, even at a time when reform was in full swing. Perestroika had brought about some modest reforms in our jurisprudence and legal system, but the very fact that "criminal cases" such as mine could still be prosecuted showed that the icy winds of the Cold War were still blowing from on high.

After the PO had dismissed all the charges against my wife, I wrote to Shevardnadze again in November. "Since I failed to receive a response to my letter sent to you personally on June 24, I am writing to you again to request a meeting with you to discuss my forced resignation, precipitated by the slander against my wife." I emphasized my long years of service in the MFA in the hope that he would at least be influenced by my excellent record. Shevardnadze did not answer. In fact, his staff told me, he was annoyed at my persistence and was not prepared to meet with me. Nonetheless, he did agree to bring my case before the MFA Collegium, probably out of fear that I would persevere in my appeals to him.

The meeting of the Collegium at which my case was reviewed was held on December 29, 1987. I asked if I might be permitted to attend the meeting but my request was denied. The members of the board were informed of the decision of the Russian PO and then asked to consider possible redress. I was never shown the text of the board's decision but Nikiforov relayed its contents to me. He explained that it contained a request to the minister of foreign affairs that he express regret and offer an apology to me for the events that had led to my forced resignation. The board further recommended me for a post in the Diplomatic Academy and petitioned for an increase in my pension.

This news reached me on New Year's Eve 1987, thus ending a tumultuous year in my life and the life of my family. Nikiforov assured me that Shevardnadze would soon see me to apologize personally on behalf of the board, but I never heard from him again nor did I ever meet with him.

A Silver Lining

Though I was not completely satisfied with the board's decision, I decided not to challenge it, and in February 1988 I returned to work as a professor in the Diplomatic Academy, where twenty years before I had headed the department of history and diplomatic sciences. The episode, however, had one valuable outcome. It showed us who our friends really were. It pained us that some of our acquaintances had found it impossible to at least show us some sympathy and to show some belief in our integrity. After all, the same thing could have happened to anyone.

At the same time it was with pleasure and pride that we thanked our many true friends for their support. Among those who never lost faith in us were Valentin Loshinin, Valery Savitsky, Evgeny Primakov, Valentin Berezhkov, Aleksandr Kashirin, Vsevolod Oleandrov, Vitaly Ganzha, Valentina Gromyko, and Viktor Popov, among others.

After returning to teaching, which I dearly loved, I nevertheless regretted that I was no longer privy to the momentous events of the late 1980s and early 1990s that brought an end to the Cold War. It reminded me of when I was given a medical discharge from the Army at the end of World War II. To me it was embarrassing and in some ways shameful that I could not personally fight in the final battles of the war. Many decades later I felt much the same. I was proud and happy to have participated in some of the most important negotiations between the Soviet Union and the United

States. I hoped that the Cold War would culminate the victory of reason over madness, order over chaos, and creativity over destructiveness, and I dreamed that I would somehow play a role in that final victory. Things, however, did not work out the way I had hoped.

CONCLUSION

It is as difficult to name the day the Cold War ended as it is to establish the date when it began. For me it ended when I was compelled to leave diplomatic work and retreat from the "front" to "the second echelon." I returned to teaching at the Diplomatic Academy, became active in a number of public organizations, headed the International Dialogue Association, and participated in numerous conferences, symposiums, and meetings devoted to world policy. I even considered creating an international organization of Cold War veterans.

However, it was not the level of activity I'd gotten used to in the years of the Cold War. I had been demoted from warrior to mere witness. To my disappointment, the MFA management did not find it necessary to use my services in any capacity, even as an expert or an adviser, though professor-adviser was my official title at the Diplomatic Academy.

This exclusion, however, did not reduce my natural professional interest in the foreign policy of my country. I used every excuse to visit my alma mater at Smolenskaya Square. I especially appreciated the contacts with my friends and diplomatic colleagues—who readily shared information and their ideas with me. These personal communications as well as the press and other sources informed my opinions on the ending process of the Cold War.

The conversion of a total confrontation between the two superpowers into a reasonable, mutually advantageous cooperation at the end of the 1980s enjoyed my unequivocal understanding and approval. In turn I established working contacts with my American counterparts. I took active part in the joint research by the Diplomatic Academy and Harvard University into the theory and practice of diplomatic negotiation. In 1990 Professor Roger Fisher of Harvard and I organized an international seminar for UN diplomats in New York. This seminar was widely considered a perfect example of the efficient new methods in international politics, which are so different from the practices of the Cold War.

Nevertheless, I failed to understand many things that occurred in diplomatic negotiations of that period. I could not comprehend the extremes to which the Soviet leadership rushed to from time to time. Here are two examples.

The German problem was one of the central themes of negotiations of that period. When the will of the German people was finally realized, when the inevitable unification of the two German states finally happened, a new and most difficult question arose: what would the international-contractual position of a united Germany be? Life demanded the revision of the decisions reached by the Big Three at the Potsdam Conference. However, for this purpose the participants needed to agree on a position that was both a natural extension of the Potsdam Agreement and reasonable. The Kremlin however, failed to do so. Within less than a year, from late 1989 through mid-1990, Gorbachev made various proposals, some of which were mutually contradictory. He believed that a united Germany could become a member of the Warsaw Treaty Organization (then still existing), and possibly retain membership in NATO at the same time. Gorbachev also proposed that Germany be neutral or nonaligned.

However, at a meeting with an East German governmental delegation in March of 1990 Gorbachev "with all definiteness" declared that NATO membership for a united Germany would be unacceptable, "regardless of any conditions." Yet, after having made these categorical declarations in March, he reversed himself completely and gave final consent to a united Germany joining NATO in the summer of the same year.

Explaining the transformation of the Soviet position, Gorbachev loved to refer to the irregular, stormy development of the political situation in Germany. This excuse only raises one other important question: why could our Western partners foresee such a development and thus avoid swaying from one opinion to another while we could not? How could the unrealistic Soviet proposals that Germany join the Warsaw Treaty Organization or both NATO and the Warsaw Treaty Organization simultaneously promote international agreement?

There were no answers to these questions. One could only hope that the interests of Soviet security would be considered while determining the new international-contractual status of Germany. In those years none of us, professionals and nonprofessionals alike, could imagine that Germany's membership in NATO would logically result in NATO's absorption not only of a number of East European states but also some former Soviet republics. Anyone who would have allowed such a possibility would have been called a madman.

Here is another example—issues of chemical disarmament. Guided by the spirit of the Cold War, the Soviet Union rejected the inspection methods the Americans offered during negotiations on a chemical convention in the early 1980s. Indeed, for some reason many nonaligned and even some Western countries rejected the U.S. proposal as well. The American authors of the proposal had submitted what was an obviously unacceptable plan to the Soviet Union to prevent a chemical convention from being reached. However, in the late 1980s the Soviet side unexpectedly changed its position, though all other participants in the negotiations had maintained their reservations. Many years later at the ratification of the chemical convention by the U.S. Senate some senators raised the same objections to the convention that the Soviet delegation had voiced at the Conference on Disarmament in the early 1980s. Why did Moscow abandon a position that it (and others) had considered reasonable?

Gorbachev and Shevardnadze were as inconsistent and controversial in their dealings with other socialist states, in the Middle East crises, in the Iraqi war of 1991, and on other international issues.

It is widely believed both in the West, and in Russia, that Gorbachev's "perestroika" and "new thinking" played a decisive role in the ending of the Cold War, resulting in the disintegration and collapse of the Soviet Union with all its consequences. In the West this statement is made with satisfaction and praise of the Soviet leader, in Russia with disgust and condemnation.

Time will judge Gorbachev's actions. His resolute rejection of confrontation in the Cold War was without doubt a huge step forward, but his fluctuations, his inconsistency, his posturing, and at times his diplomatic illiteracy did a lot of damage.

The truth is that the decline and fall of the Soviet Union was historically logical. The dogma of classical Marxism says that the victory of socialism and communism on a global scale is inevitable. Such a primitive, utopian approach to social evolution was replaced under Stalin with the postulate that socialism could be built in one separate country. By becoming a superpower in the years of the Cold War, the Soviet Union was expressing a resolute adherence to the orthodox Marxist dogmas concerning world socialist revolution. In the historical rivalry between socialism and capitalism the Kremlin believed the only logical outcome would be the victory of the socialist camp over the Western world.

This vile mentality was the primary reason for all internal and external Soviet failures. The Kremlin was forced to lie to itself and the rest of the country about conditions at home and abroad in order to fit the diverse, complex events of the world into the narrow framework of the friend-foe stereotype.

CONCLUSION

The wretched trend to make the information reported to Moscow fit the "truth" coming from the Kremlin became a habit in the work of Soviet missions abroad. I believe that it was for this reason that so many Soviet diplomatic initiatives were not based on reality. Nevertheless, Soviet diplomats abroad, including myself, reported back that Soviet initiatives and offers that could scarcely be taken seriously were "attracting general interest" or "in the center of public attention." The simplistic analysis of world prospects very frequently led the Soviet Union into international deadlocks.

Soviet foreign policy was probably the only field of the USSR's activity where the decisions on vital questions, which as a rule had long-term and at times tragic consequences, were made so secretively and ambiguously. The role of the Soviet parliament—the All-Russian, and later the All-Union Soviet, the Supreme Soviet—was insignificant in the development of foreign policy. In the years of the Cold War the Supreme Soviet would sometimes listen to reports from the foreign minister on the international situation; however, the ensuing "debate" was never more than "a unanimous approval of the Leninist foreign policy of the USSR" and praise for the Soviet leader. During the Cold War the parliament played no role in the decisions on such vital issues as the suppression of the revolt in Hungary, the Berlin blockade, the Caribbean crisis, and the sending of troops to Czechoslovakia and Afghanistan. At best the Politburo was the deciding body, but in some cases the Soviet leader and two or three of his closest associates made the decisions that the people paid for with their blood.

Sometimes at the late-night dinners in his summer residence Stalin might touch on isolated questions of foreign policy with his guests. After listening to their opinions, he would summarize the discussion and make a final conclusion. Khrushchev, on the other hand, loved external matters, at times passionately and discussed them in detail at the Politburo and sometimes even with family members. Under Brezhnev, however, even some of the members of the Politburo did not find out about the order to send troops to Afghanistan until after Brezhnev together with the ministers of defense and foreign affairs and the chairman of the KGB had already made the decision. Gorbachev initially listened to the opinions of those around him. However toward the end of his career he made at times unreasonable decisions, ignoring the considerations of experts and advisers. The dictatorship of the Soviet system led to genuine blunders in world affairs.

The military potential of the Soviet Union influenced its foreign policy directly and fatally. Throughout the existence of the Soviet state, including the years of the Cold War, its leaders asserted that the Soviet armed forces did not have a single unnecessary soldier or shell, that a failure to keep up with the West would lead to war. Soviet diplomats, myself included, echoed them at all international crossroads in every possible way supporting this statement with figures borrowed from the defense ministry brochures. Then suddenly the whole world, including the Soviet people learned from Gorbachev's UN speech on December 1988, that if the Soviet armed forces were reduced by 500 thousand men, nothing special would happen. The economic and social consequences of this declaration were not seriously researched; otherwise, I am sure, Gorbachev would have quoted a much higher figure. Certainly, the impact of such an unexpected declaration was great. The UN applauded Gorbachev, but once again he demonstrated the equivocal nature of his decisions on an arsenal inflated totally out of proportion with the valid requirements of national security.

This hyperbole in military matters was based on the same notorious theory of world revolution and the principle of proletarian internationalism. The growing Soviet military power was quickly exhausting the country. The country was a giant with legs of clay, which had to collapse sooner or later. The Soviet Union's international partners, including allies and friends, began to understand that.

One can name a number of Soviet actions, including those in the field of foreign policy, that undermined Soviet unity. During perestroika in the late 1980s the Kremlin was finally compelled to admit that in 1939 Stalin and Hitler had agreed to divide the territory lying between the Soviet Union and the Third Reich into spheres of influence; yet it denied the fatal consequences of the act. Known as the Molotov-Ribbentrop Pact, this agreement not only crushed the independence of many countries and peoples, it also violated international law and irreparably damaged the authority of the USSR and the ideas of socialism and communism. It revealed what the true face "of the free entry into the family of the Soviet peoples" really was—mass exile to Siberia. That is why, when there was the slightest opportunity to leave this "family of peoples," the republics of the former Soviet Union took it immediately. Indeed, it makes sense to assert that the Soviet-German pact of 1939 was an important part in the chain of events that resulted in the dissolution of the Soviet Union in 1991. And it is the present generation of Russians that have to pay for its consequences: Russia is smaller now than it has been for centuries and not on the best terms with its new neighbors—former Soviet republics, and members of the Commonwealth of Independent States.

I came to such conclusions when answering the questions about the place and role of foreign politics in the disintegration of the Soviet Union. Being on the fronts of the Cold War, I regarded various events in the manner described on the pages of this book. I want to emphasize, that the capitulation of the USSR in the Cold War and more so its disintegration, were almost as much of a surprise to me as they were to the rest of the world. I could never have predicted that in a few days the CPSU would be outlawed in the USSR, and the Soviet Union itself would disappear by year's end.

By and large the first attempt to build a righteous society on Marxist principles failed. Would it be possible to for another country to succeed where the Soviet Union failed? Perhaps China? I do not know.

In my long life I have lived in many countries, at times for many years. I cannot say that I have ever seen a country with an ideal political regime, free from any social or economic afflictions. Probably, mankind will always be striving for an unattainable perfection. That is why it is important to learn from the errors and especially the crimes of the past. In this respect the study of Soviet experience is vitally important for the future of mankind, and with this in mind, I humbly present my memoirs.

INDEX

Page numbers in *italics* indicate photographs.

Abrasimov, Peter, 94
Acheson, Dean, 14–15
Adebo, Simon O., 209
Adelman, Kenneth, 307–8, 309
Adzhimushk incident, 335–40
Adzhubei, Aleksei, 72
Afghanistan
  coup in, 317–18
  failed peace attempt in, 319–21
  opinions about war in, 321–24
  Soviet invasion of, x, xi, 318–19
Aga Khan, Sadrudin, 349
Akhromeyev, Sergei, xii, 253–54, 261, 345, 356–57, 359
Alarcon, Ricardo, 183
Albania, 179, 180–81, 366
Aleksandrov-Agentov, Andrei, 100
Alekseyev, Aleksandr, 75
Aliyev, Enver, 317
Aliyev, Geidar, 354
allies
  cooperation during World War II, 39–40
  diplomacy of confrontation with after World War II, 29–30
  distrust and, 330
  publication of documents after World War II, 27
  relations between after World War II, 23–25
All the Best (Bush), 352
Amarasinghe, 204
"Americanists," xiii, 241, 243, 277
American-Soviet relations. *See* Soviet-American relations
Amin, Idi, 108
Andersson, Sven, 274
Andropov, Igor, 60–61
Andropov, Yuri
  as ambassador to Hungary, 56, 57, 58–59
  Kadar and, 61
  uprising in Hungary and, x, 59–60
  Yom Kippur War and, xi–xii, 249, 251
Angola, civil war in, 278–79
annexation, 42–43
anthrax outbreak, 312–16
"The Anti-Hitler Coalition" (dissertation), 72–75
The Anti-Hitler Coalition (Israelyan), 75, 98

anti-imperialist solidarity, principle of, 42
anti-Semitism, 7, 123
anti-Stalin campaign. *See* "struggle against the cult of Stalin"
Antonov, N., 313–14
Arab countries, 163–64, 169–73
Arbatov, Georgy, 99, 121–22, 359
Archive Department, Ministry of Foreign Affairs, 26–27
Armenian activists, 214–18
Armenian foreign ministry, 35
arms control. *See also* Geneva Committee on Disarmament; Treaty on the Non-proliferation of Nuclear Weapons
  chemical weapons, 398–99
  meetings in Boston regarding, 121–22
  negotiations regarding, 128, 129–30
  nuclear weapons limitation and reduction, 355–57, 358–60
  strategic arms limitation treaty, 306
  UN Special Session on Disarmament, 292–98, 299–300
  Vance and, 280
  verification issues, 329–32
articles and reviews
  in *Diplomatic Bulletin*, 389
  in *Izvestiya*, 389–90
  in *National Herald*, 359
  for *New York Times*, 263
  while teaching, 37
Assad, Hafez, 244, 245, 246, 254, 255
asylum, political, 210–11, 288–89

bacteriological weapons, 312–14, 315–16
Ball, George, 135, 150–51, 154, 155–56
Bangladesh, 187, 191, 195–96
Barudi, Jamil, 149, 171–73, 173, 183
Bashkin, Lev, 92
Berezhkov, Valentine, 395
Beria, Lavrenty, 3, 4, 44
Bessmertnykh, Alexander, xiii, 241
Bevin, Ernest, 11–12
Bhagat, B. R., 359–60
Bhutto, Zulfikar, 193, 194
Bidault, George, 12
Bielka, Erich, 274
binary chemical weapons, 342–43

403

INDEX

Biryukova, Aleksandra, 265
Black, Cyril, 121
Black, Shirley Temple, *235*
Blix, Hans, *232*, 306
Bohlen, Charles, 14
Bondarenko, A., 239–40, 242
Borisov, Yury, 91
Boye, Ibrahim, *222*
Brazil, 296–97
Breaking with Moscow (A. Shevchenko), 290
Brezhnev, Leonid
　anti-Stalin campaign and, 87
　on détente, 277
　foreign policy of, 400
　meeting with, 99–103
　on NATO, 268
　Nixon and, 128–29, 262–63, 266–67
　on proletarian internationalism, 278
　Sadat and, 246
　on socialist countries, 367
　on Stalin, 90
　Thant and, 203
　Yom Kippur War and, xi–xii, 248–49, 250–51, 252
Brown, George, 170
Brykin, Vladimir, 56, 61
Brzezinski, Mrs., 125
Brzezinski, Zbigniew, 116–17, 125
Budapest University, 64
Buffum, William, 154
bug, planting of, 217
Bukharin trial, 14
Bush, George H. W.
　chemical weapons and, 336, 343, 348
　China and, 179–80, 181, 182, 184
　at Geneva Committee on Disarmament, *233*, 349
　Indo-Pakistani war and, 187, 189, 192–93
　Israelyan and, 349–50
　memoir of, 352
　as permanent representative to UN, 137–40, 141–42, *229*
　on Soviet mission being fired on, 140–41
Byelorussian SSR, 181
Byrnes, James, 115
Campbell, George, 98
Caradon, Lord
　Czechoslovakia debate and, 150–51, 153
　Kuznetsov and, 238
　on Malik, 107
　Non-proliferation Treaty and, 130
　Resolution 242 and, 160
　at UN Security Council, *222*, *229*

Carter, Jimmy, 280
Castro, Fidel, 76, 370
Central Intelligence Department of the Defense Ministry (GRU), 111–12
Cernik, Zdenek, *230*
Chatorday, Karoly, 64–65
Chavez, Judy, 290
chemical weapons
　Adzhimushk incident, 335–40
　American document on, 343–45
　Bush and, 336, 343, 348
　Geneva Committee on Disarmament and, 332–35, 340–42
　Soviet attitude toward, 342–46, 398–99
Chernenko, Konstantin, 346, 349, 352
China, People's Republic of
　Indo-Pakistani war and, 191–92
　Soviet mission and, 184–86
　Soviet relations with, 175–78
　United Nations and, 177–84
　veto in UN Security Council by, 195–97
Churchill, Winston
　on chemical weapons, 334
　Deakin and, 367
　Iron Curtain speech of, 24, 29
　Molotov and, 11, 13
　note of, 367–68
　opinion of, 19
　"Unity in Peace, and in War" declaration, 19
Cliburn, Van, *234*
Cold War
　"coalitional" nature of, 366–68
　conceptual differences between sides in, 329–32
　diplomacy in, 196–97, 219–20
　end of, 397
　first icy gusts of, 24
　period of optimism during, 128–30
　specter of, 40–41
　transition to, 28–32
Collegium of the Ministry of Foreign Affairs, 272–73, 301, 394–95
Columbia University, 116, 117
Communist Party of the Soviet Union (CPSU)
　appointment of members as ambassadors, 7, 371–73
　Department of Propaganda, 38, 53–58, 79
　headquarters of, 53
　methods of, 31
　mission to UN and, 111
　secretary for ideology, 74–75
　"The Struggle Against the Cult of Stalin," 49–50

INDEX

Twentieth Congress, 176
Twenty-Second Congress, 73
Twenty-Fifth Congress, 278
Twenty-Sixth Congress, 180
Twenty-Seventh Congress, 360, 377, 378
comprehensive nuclear test ban treaty, 331
Conference on Disarmament. *See* Geneva Committee on Disarmament
Convention on the Prohibition of Bacteriological Weapons, 312–14, 315, 316
Convention on the Prohibition of Chemical Weapons, 345
Council of Ministers of Foreign Affairs, 11, 12
CPSU. *See* Communist Party of the Soviet Union (CPSU)
criminals, trainload of, 2–3
Crowe, Colin, 137, 183, 205
Cuba, conference on UN issues in, 369–70
Cuban missile crisis, 75–79
Cuellar, Javier Perez de, 232
Cutujian, Ibrahim, 95–96
Cyprus, Republic of, 267–71
Czechoslovakia
  debates on, 145–47
  Five States' Letter and, 144–45
  leadership of, 156–57
  in 1980s, 380
  "Prague Spring," 143
  repudiation of actions in, 156
  response in UN of, 152–54
  Soviet actions in, x, 129, 136, 148–52
  Soviet-American relations and, 147–48
  Soviet Union and, 143–44, 157–58, 368

Daniel, Yuly, 87
Datcu, 353
D-Day landing, fiftieth anniversary of, 40
Deakin, Frederick, 367–68
Deborin, Grigory, 118
De Calliers, François, 16
defection of Soviet citizens, 94–95, 288–92
Defector's Mistress (Chavez), 290
Dekanozov, Vladimir, 3–4, 5–6, 11, 34
Department of International Relations, Moscow State University, 5
Department of the History of International Relations and Soviet Foreign Policy, 22
de Rosas, Carlos Ortiz, 204, 206, 231, 294, 295, 305
détente, 276–77
  Angolan civil war and, 279
  culmination of, 273–75
  irreversibility of, 277

Khrushchev and, 68–69
in 1970s, 259
Nixon-Brezhnev meetings and, 128–29
Non-proliferation Treaty and, 130
retreat of, 280–81
as truce on Cold War, 278
Yom Kippur War and, 249–50
diplomacy, 8–9
  Cold War, 196–97, 219–20
  confrontational, 29–30, 134–35
  contacts with foreigners, reprisals for, 31–32
  dedication to career in, 24, 25
  multilateral, 104, 219–20
  "office" type, 300
  in socialist countries, 373–75
  Stalin and, 73
  at United Nations, 114–15
  of World War II, 39
Diplomatic Academy, 6, 7
  atmosphere of, 36–37
  as classified establishment, 95
  deputy dean position offer for Israelyan, 35
  history of, 5
  Israelyan as teacher at, 238, 395–96
  Israelyan graduation from, 20, 21–22
  Israelyan position at, 36–39, 41
  Israelyan studies at, 6–8, 18–19, 284
  Research Council, 38
  training program of, 97
diplomatic careers, 113–14
Diplomatic Dictionary, 79, 80, 83
"The Diplomatic History of World War II" (course), 39–41
disarmament. *See* arms control; Geneva Committee on Disarmament
"disarmamentists," 241
dissertations, 22, 37–39, 72–75
Dmitriyevna, Lidya, 98
Dobrynin, Anatoly
  on Afghanistan, 318
  as "Americanist," xiii, 241
  Cuban missile crisis and, 75
  graduation from Diplomatic Academy, 21
  hospitalization of, xi
  Kuznetsov and, 130
  as member of postwar generation, 239–40
  Shevardnadze and, 364
  at UN General Assembly, 230
Domokos, Matyas, 64
Doty, Paul, 121
Dubček, Alexander, 143, 153
Dubynin, Y., 239–40, 242, 273, 278
Dulles, John, 12, 13
Dulyan, Oghan, 215–17

405

Dzhugashvili, Gulya, 46, 47–49
Dzhugashvili, Yakov, 45–47
Dzhugashvili, Yevgeny, 46
Dzhugashvili, Yuliya Meltser, 44–49

Eastern Europe, 367–71, 372, 378–81, 383
Egypt, 167–69, 244, 256–57
Eisenhower, Dwight, 41
El Farra, Mohammed, 169–71
El Kouni, 167
El Zayat, 166, 167–68, 257
Emmanuelle, 391, 393
enlistment, 2
environment, military use of, 260–63
"Europeanists," 241–42, 277
European politics, 273
"The Events in Hungary" (Leonov), 61
expulsion, fear of, 389

Fahmy, 256–57
Faisal (king), 171
Falin, V., 239–40, 242
Falk, Richard, 121
Farah, Abdulrahim Abby, 224
Fedorenko, Nikolai, 101, 106
Fields, Louis, 330, 347, 348–49, 350
Filippovich, Boris, 212, 213
Fine, Richard, 302
Finland, 359
First Moscow Medical Institute, 1, 33
Fisher, Adrian, 296, 297, 298
Fisher, Andrew, 340–41, 347
Fisher, Roger, 397
Five States' Letter, 144–45
Flowerree, Charles, 312, 347
food supplies, 273
Ford, Gerald, 280
foreign minister, swift succession of, 352–53
foreign policy. *See also* "Lenin's foreign policy"
  of Brezhnev, 400
  development of, 400–401
  of Gorbachev, 360–61, 364–65
  in international organizations, 122–24
  "key issues" in, 198–201, 253, 260–63, 281–83
  of Khrushchev, 51–52, 63, 66–70, 84–85, 400
  military and, 400–401
  "pragmatists" and, 241–42
  of Stalin, 49–50, 51, 66, 400
  theoretical foundations of, 41–44
  "young sovki" generation and, 283–85
free expression, 86–87, 89

Fulbright Foundation, xvi
Furtseva, Yekaterina, 215, 217
"The Future of International Order" (research project), 121–22

Gadzhiev, Surchai, 33
Gaek, Jiri, 152, 153–54
Ganzha, Vitaly, 395
García Robles, Alfonso, 294, 295, 297–98
Garekhan, Chinmoy, 297, 356
Gasparian, Sergei, 35
Geiger, Boris, 55–56
Geneva Committee on Disarmament, 301–2
  American representatives to, 347–48
  chemical weapons and, 332–35, 336–37, 340–42
  comprehensive test ban treaty, 331
  first statement to, 340
  Israelyan as representative to, 300–301, 323
  missile deployment and, 325–28
  opening of in 1979, 305–6
  opening session of (1979), 232
  principles of, 298
  purpose of, 297, 300
  Soviet-American relations and, 306–7, 347–48
  Soviet diplomats assigned to, 302–5, 325
Genscher, Hans Dietrich, 333
"Germanists," 242, 243
German problem, 398
Germany, 27–28, 380
Ghandi, Indira, 188
Goldberg, Arthur, 130, 135, 162
Golikov, Filipp, 89
Gorbachev, Mikhail. *See also* "perestroika"
  American preference for, 351–52
  appointment of, 353
  Bush and, 348
  on chemical weapons, 335
  coup against, xii
  foreign policy of, 360–61, 364–65
  Germany and, 398
  meeting with, 357–58
  military and, 401
  Ministry of Foreign Affairs and, 350–51
  socialist countries and, 377–81, 383
  speech before diplomats, 364–65
  views of, 399
Gorbachev Declaration, 358–60
Gori, Georgia, 34
Gospolitizdat, 79
Gozochov, Ivan, 93
graduation exams, 20

INDEX

"The Great Decade," 79–80, 84
Grechko, Andrei, xi–xii, 249, 251, 252, 261
Grinevsky, Oleg, xiii, 241, 357
Gromyko, Andrei, 71
   Afghanistan and, 321–22
   on assistance to Angola, 279
   chemical weapons and, 341
   Cyprus and, 270–71
   as delegate to UN, 266
   departure of, 353
   Diplomatic Dictionary and, 80
   Fahmy and, 256–57
   on fresh ideas, 272
   Geneva Committee on Disarmament and, 300, 301
   Gorbachev and, 351
   on Indo-Pakistani war diplomacy, 194
   Israelyan and, ix, 97–99, 320–21
   Kissinger and, 255
   Litvinov and, 71
   Middle East and, 254, 257
   Middle East Peace Conference, Geneva, 256, 257–58
   as minister of foreign affairs, 71–72
   Ministry of Foreign Affairs International Organizations Department, 219
   Molotov and, 13, 50
   "nay-saying negotiators" and, 364–65
   Pan-European Conference on Security and Cooperation and, 274–75
   on selection of delegation for UN, 264
   Shevchenko and, 289, 290, 291–92
   socialist countries and, 369–70
   Soviet-Indian treaty and, 186
   Soviet "key issues" and, 199, 200, 201, 253, 261, 262
   speech to UN, 280–81, 376
   on Stalin, 49–50
   transition to Cold War and, 29
   U-2 incident and, 69–70
   at UN General Assembly, *230*
   UN Special Session on Disarmament and, 298, 299, 300
   on Vance, 280
   Yom Kippur War and, 244–45, 248, 251–52
   Zemskov and, 239
Gromyko, Valentina, 395
Guevara, Ernesto "Che," 227
Gunes, Turan, 270
Gusev, Fedor, 13, 29, 32, 49
Guzikov, Mikhail, 44
Guzikov, Rosalia Meltser, 44, 45
Haig, Alexander, 307

Halperin, Morton, 177
Hammarskjöld, Dag, 202
Harriman, Averell, 41, 296, 299
Harvard University, 397
Helms, Jesse, 345
Historical-Diplomatic Department, 26–28, 32
The History of Soviet Foreign Policy (Nekrich and Ponomarev), 89, 90
"History's Falsifiers" (brochure), 28, 95
Hitler, Adolf, 10, 11
Hollai, Imre, 64, 65
Horthy, Regent, 22
Horthyites, 8
Hoveida, Fereydun, 282
Huang Hua, 184–85, 186, 191, 192, 195–96
Hulinsky, Ilya, 145, 146
"Hungarian Foreign Policy on the Eve of World War II" (dissertation), 22
Hungary
   anti-Stalin campaign and, 62
   articles and pamphlets on, 37, 53–54, 58, 61
   Foreign Ministry and, 55–56
   Kadar government of, 61
   similarity of Czechoslovakia situation to, 157
   Soviet ambassadors to, 372
   uprising in, 54–55, 57–58, 59–60, 61–64
   visits to, 56–57, 64–65

idols, medical profession, 1
Ilyichev, Leonid, 74–75, 238
India, 186–90, 192–95, 296–97, 359–60
Inozemtsev, Nikoilai, 298
The Insecurity of Nations (Yost), 136
Inside the Kremlin During the Yom Kippur War (Israelyan), ix–x
inspections, on-site, 331–32, 344
Institute of History, 89
International Congress of Peaceloving Forces, 252
International Organizations Department of MFA, Declaration on the Deepening and Consolidation of Détente, 281–82
International Organizations Department of Ministry of Foreign Affairs
   Cyprus and, 268–70
   Israelyan internship at, 103–5
   Isrealyan as head of, 219, 237–39, 271–72
   Kozyrev and, 285
   preparations for UN General Assembly and, 259–62
   selection of delegates to UN, 264–66
International Relations, 72–74, 75, 83, 388, 389

INDEX

Iran, 282
Isaakian, Avetik, 35
Israel, 173–74. *See also* Yom Kippur War
Israelyan, Alla, 218, *225, 229*, 384–85, 387, 390–92
Israelyan, Karen, 384
Israelyan, Levon, 384
Israelyan, Victor
  birth of, 1
  education of, 20, 22, 32–33
  father of, 1, 3, 34
  photos of, *221, 222, 224, 225, 228–35*
Izvestiya, 72, 389–90

Jacobson, Max, 203–4, 207
Jaipal, Rikhi, *232*
Jarring, Gunnar, 161, 162, 163
Jaruzelski, General, 379, 382
Jiao Huanhu, 184
Johnson, Lyndon B., 128, 148
Jordan, 169
Jou Enlai, 127
June 22, 1941 (Nekrich), 89–90

Kadar, Janos, 59, 61
Kaluga, 2
Kapitsa, Mikhail, 194, 239–40, 242, 279
Kapto, Aleksandr, 372–73
Karpov, Viktor, 241, 309, 357, 358
Kashirin, Aleksandr, 395
Kazakov, Vladimir, 214, 291
Kekkonen, Urkho, 207
Kennan, George, 14
Kennedy, John, 76, 77
Keshishyan, Levon, 214–15, 217
KGB
  cooperation with, 212–18
  Diplomatic Academy and, 7
  mission to UN and, 111–12
  presence in New York, 213
  train incident and, 4–5
  as UN deputy permanent representatives, 109
Khachatrian, Robert, 35, 77
Khilchevsky, Yury, 140
Khnyoupek, Bohuslav, 371, 373
Khrushchev, Nikita
  China and, 176
  criticism of, 86
  Cuban missile crisis and, 75–79
  death of Stalin and, 44
  foreign policy of, 51–52, 63, 66–70, 84–85, 400

Gromyko and, 71–72
Hungary and, 56–57
Kistyakovsky on, 122
Molotov and, 13, 63
ouster of, 82–83
speeches of after travels, 67
Stalin, report on, and, 49
style of, 67–68
at UN General Assembly, *225*
as World Youth Forum, 82
Khulchevsky, Yury, 111
Khvostov, Vladimir, 26–28, 32, 41, 87, 88
Kissinger, Henry, 121, 249, 251, 254, 255
Kistyakovsky, George, 121, 122
Klementis, Vlado, 369
Klusak, Milan, 113, 146
Komives, Imre, 64
Kondakov, German, 111
Korniyenko, G.
  chemical weapons and, 333
  letter to about Bush proposal, 350
  missile deployment and, 311, 312
  nuclear disarmament and, 356–57, 359
  as "pragmatist," 239–40
  Shevardnadze and, 355, 364
  Yom Kippur War and, 244, 248, 249
Kosciusko-Morizet, Jacques, 137, 185
Kostandov, Leonid, 344
Kosygin, Aleksei, xi–xii, 82, 128, 252
Kovalev, Anatoly
  as "Europeanist," 242
  as Gromyko's deputy, 238
  Pan-European Conference on Security and Cooperation and, 273, 274
  as "pragmatist," 239–40
  Shevardnadze and, 355
  Special Session on Disarmament and, 298
Kozmin, Vadim, 389
Kozyrev, Andrei, 284, 285–88
Kozyrev, Semen, 239
Kral, Carel, 145
Kun, Bela, 8
Kurishev, Mikhail, 393
Kutakov, Leonid, 26
Kuzmin, Vyacheslav, 177
Kuznetsov, Vasily
  on appointments to UN, 266
  career of, 70–71
  Cyprus and, 268–69
  detainment of, 129–30
  Geneva Committee on Disarmament and, 300

408

Israelyan and, 238
Middle East and, 254
as "troubleshooter," 78–79
UN General Assembly and, 57
Yom Kippur War and, 244, 245, 248, 249
Kvitsinsky, Yuly, 242, 322

"Labor Sundays," 30–31
languages, 6
Lannung, Hermod, 18
Lashkaradze, David, 26
Lavrishchev, Aleksandr, 13, 26
Lavrov, Vladimir, 272
Lebedev, Viktor, 50
lecture tour, 93–97
Lee, Trygve, 202
"Lenin's foreign policy," 41–42, 66
Leonard, James, 296
Leonev, V. (pen name), 61
Leprette, Jacques, 297
Lermontov, 236–37
Levini, Yaguda Leub, 123
Libya, 11, 115
Liebknecht, Sofia and Karl, 6
Ligachev, Yegor, ix
Likhachev, Viktor, 300
Lisov, Gennady, 134
Litvinov, Maxim, 9–10, 13, 20, 71
Lobanov, Ivan, 15
Loschinin, Valeri, *233*
Loshinin, Valentin, 391, 395
Lovitz, Donald, 347
Lozinsky, Valentin, 110, 135
Lozovsky, Solomon, 22, 31

MacCloy, John, 78
Macmillan, Harold, 69
Maisky, Ivan
  as ambassador to London, 71, 334
  arrest of, 31
  career of, 106
  Council on the History of Soviet Foreign Policy and International Relations and, 88
  Nekrich and, 91
  transition to Cold War and, 29
Makarov, Vasily, 243–44, 247
Makashev, Boris, 69–70
Makeyev, Evgeny, 110, 210
Makhailov, 357
Maksimovna, Raisa, 351
Malik, Yakov (Jacob), *222, 225, 229, 230*
  on Ball's remarks, 156

on Bush, 138, 142
China and, 178–79, 181–82, 184, 191–92
Crowe and, 205
Cyprus and, 269
Czechoslovakia and, 149, 151, 154
de Rosas and, 206–7
Huang and, 185–86, 191
Indo-Pakistani war and, 188–89
Israel and, 166
Israelyan and, 110, 210
Kuznetsov and, 130
in Miami, 119–20
Middle East and, 159, 160, 162, 164–65
Molotov and, 13
on Primakov, 361
Security Council meetings and, 137
Soviet mission attack and, 141, 183
Soviet mission to UN and, 106–7
on Stalin, 50
on success, 217–18
Tekoah and, 164–65
UN and, 101
Vyshinsky and, 17
Yost and, 134
Manasarian, Levon, 35
Manchukuo, 191
Mao Zedong, 175–76
Marker, Jamsheed, 319–20
Marshall Plan, 30
Marxist-Leninist dogma, 89, 399
Mavros, George, 270
medical profession, 1, 2, 3
Megid, Abdel Ismat, 167, 168–69
Meisner, 381
memoirs, role of, ix, xvi
Mendelevich, Lev, 81, 83, 108–9, 159, 242, 273
Meshera, Vladimir, 21
meteorological warfare, prevention of, 261–63
Middle East
  American activity in, 254–55
  Arab countries, 163–64, 169–73
  Egypt, 167–69, 244, 256–57
  hard line toward Israel, 165–66
  Israelyan and, 159–60
  June 1967 war, 129
  Syria, 171, 183, 244
  UN Resolution 242, 160–63
  Yom Kippur War, 243–52
Middle East Peace Conference, Geneva, 254–58
Mikoyan, Anastas, 56–57, 63, 82
military and foreign policy, 400–401

INDEX

military service, 2–3, 4–5, 33–34, 339–40
ministries of foreign affairs in republics, 21
Ministry of Defense, 261
Ministry of Foreign Affairs (MFA). *See also* International Organizations Department of Ministry of Foreign Affairs
   Archive Department, 26–27
   arrests in, 31–32
   Collegium of, 272–73, 301, 394–95
   Cuban missile crisis and, 78–79
   Dekanozov and, 4
   Diplomatic Academy and, 7
   end of World War II and, 20
   External Planning Department, 88
   foreign policy planning proposal of, 87–88
   generation of pragmatists in, 239–43
   Gorbachev and, 350–51, 365
   Historical-Diplomatic Department, 26–28, 32
   Hungarian Division, 55–56
   Israelyan exclusion from, 397
   "key issues" and, 199, 260–63, 281–83
   Shevardnadze and, 363–64
   "Stalin Tribe," 69
missile deployment, 310–12, 325–26
Mladenov, Petr, 380
Moisov, Lazar, 294
Molotov, Vyacheslav, 10–13
   anti-Soviet demonstrations, view of, 63
   Diplomatic Academy graduates and, 21–22
   dissertation and, 38
   as foreign minister, 52
   German attack and, 1
   Gromyko and, 50
   on Klementis, 369
   Marshall Plan and, 30
   as model of diplomacy, 9
   on "Motherland," 12
   negotiating style of, 11–12
   removal of, 66
   at San Francisco Conference, *226*
   Stalin and, 9–10
   trip to U.S., 23
Molotov-Ribbentrop Pact of 1939, 10–11, 42–43, 95, 401
Morgenthau, Hans, 98, 118, 147
Moscow, Israelyan return to, 218–20, 236–37
Moscow Club of Scholars, 91–92
Moscow State Institute of International Relations, 284
Moscow State University, Department of International Relations, 5
Moscow U.S. Institute, 121
Mosley, Philip, 98

"Motherland," concept of, 12
Moynihan, Daniel, 279
Mukhitdinov, Nuritdin, 244, 245, 246, 247
Muzic, Jan, 146, 152–53, 157

Nagy, Imre, 56–57, 59–60, 61, 62
Narochnitsky, Aleksei, 88
Nase, Neshti, 180–81
"national minorities," 33
NATO, 267–68, 271, 293, 310, 383
Naumov, Lev, 337
Nekrich, Aleksandr, 89–91
Nesterenko, Aleksei, 194, 208–9
Neto, A., 278
Newman, Paul, *234*, 299–300
New Year's celebration of Israelyan family, 384–85
New York, 218, 219
New York Council for Foreign Relations, 217
New York Times, 263
Nezhinsky, Leonid, 37
Nikiforov, Valentin, 385–86, 387, 392, 395
Nixon, Richard
   Brezhnev and, 128–29, 262–63
   chemical and biological weapons and, 342
   impeachment of, 267
   Khrushchev and, 51
   rapprochement and, 128
   Vietnam War and, 131, 132
   visit to Soviet Union, 133, 266–67
   Yom Kippur War and, 250–51
Non-proliferation Treaty. *See* Treaty on the Non-proliferation of Nuclear Weapons
Novikov, Kiril, 103–4
   on Indo-Pakistani war, 194
   Israelyan as replacement for, 237
   Molotov and, 23
   as Stalin's generation, 13, 103–4
   transition to Cold War and, 29
   on troika, 68
nuclear war, proposal to UN on, 282–83
nuclear weapons limitation and reduction, 355–57, 358–60. *See also* Treaty on the Non-proliferation of Nuclear Weapons

October Revolution, commemoration of, 253
October War of 1973. *See* Yom Kippur War
Oleandrov, Vsevolod, 110, 135, 395
Olshovsky, Stefan, 376
Orbelyan, Constantine, 214
Orbelyan, Harry, 214
Order of the Red Labor Banner, 103

Pakistan, 186–90, 192–95, 319–20

INDEX

Pan-European Conference on Security and Cooperation, 273–75, 277–78
Panyushkin, Aleksandr, 88, 97, 102
Paris Peace Conference, 27, 29, 37–38
peaceful coexistence, principle of, 42, 67
pension status, 392
"perestroika," 287, 377–78, 383, 394
Perle, Richard, 309
personal file on Israelyan, 5–6
Pesterev, Nikolai, 261
Petrovsky, Vladimir, 357, 385, 386, 390
Phillips, Christopher, 185
Pikalov, Vladimir, 333
Piñes, Jaime, 173
Pinhez, Haim, 149
Pirlin, Evgeny, 166
Podtserob, Boris, 19, 49
Poklad, Boris, 78
Poland, 368, 378–80, 382
Politburo, 250–52, 400
Ponomarev, Boris, 88, 89
Popov, Victor, 43, 395
Potsdam Agreement, 398
Primakov, Evgeny, 359, 361–63, 395
Prokofiev, Boris, 390
proletarian or socialist internationalism, principle of, 42, 278, 401
propaganda machine
 activities outside UN, 116–18
 anti-Stalin, 49–50
 on capitalist world, 24–25
 International Congress of Peaceloving Forces, 252
 Marshall Plan and, 30
prosecutor's office, 384–85, 390–92, 393–94
Proskurnikova, K., 265
Puerto Rico, 116
Puja, Frigyes, 377
Pushkin, Georgy, 13, 55

Rahman, Mujibur, 186–87
rainmaking, artificial, 262
Rakosi, Matyas, 7–8, 59, 62, 63
Razumovsky, Oleg, 372
Reagan, Ronald, 306–7, 309–10, 330, 346, 350
Recent Hungarian History (Israelyan and Nezhinsky), 37
resignation of Israelyan, 388–89
responsibility for evil, xv–xvi
Ribbentrop, Joachim von, 3–4, 11. *See also* Molotov-Ribbentrop Pact of 1939
Rice, Eugene, 117
Rogachev, Igor, 177
Rogers, William, 139

Romania, 367
Roney, Edward, 347
Roosevelt, Franklin
 on chemical weapons, 334
 death of, 23
 Gromyko on, 98
 popularity of, 19
 on Soviet offensive, 40–41
 "Unity in Peace, and in War" declaration, 19
 Vyshinsky and, 17
Roshchin, Aleksei, 362
Rostow, Eugene, 307
Rusk, Dean, 130, 151, *228*
Russell, Richard B., 151–52
Russian Soviet Federated Socialist Republic (RSFSR), 287
Ryabov, Yakov, 372

Sadat, Anwar
 Kissinger and, 254
 Soviet relations with, 168–69
 Vinogradov and, 257
 Yom Kippur War and, 244, 245, 246, 250
Safronchyuk, Vasily, 110, 210, 322–23
Salim, Salim, 184
Sanakoyev, Shalva, 322
San Francisco Conference, 226
Sarian, Martiros, 35
Saudi Arabia, 171, 183
Savitsky, Valery, 395
Schmidt, Helmut, 311
Schulman, Marshall, 116
secretariats of intergovernmental organizations, 201–3, 208–9
Semenov, Vladimir, 13, 50, 116–17, 166, 239
Sen, Samar, 187–89, 190, 196
Shachter, Otto, 209
Shahi, Aga, 193, 319
Shawcross, Hartley, 17
Shchelokov, Nikolai, 353
Shepilov, Aleksandr, 70, 159–60
Shepilov, Dmitry, 51–52, 56
Shevardnadze, Eduard
 appointment of, xii–xiii, 353–54
 chemical weapons and, 341–42
 conference called by, 363–65
 impressions of, 354–55
 Israelyan and, ix, 386–87
 Israelyan letters to, 392–93, 394
 Israelyan meeting with, 355–56, 387–88
 Kozyrev and, 287–88
 Nikiforov and, 385

411

Shevardnadze, Eduard *(continued)*
   nuclear disarmament and, 357
   socialist countries and, 370–71
Shevchenko, Arkady, 110, 289–92
Shevchenko, Gennady, 289, 291, 292
Shevel, Grigory, 181
Shishlin, Nikolai, 361
shoplifting, 211
Shtykov, Terenti, 372
Shustov, Vladimir, 110, 241, 323
Shvedov, Aleksei, 279
Sikachev, Nikolai, 56
Silin, Mikhail, 38, 53
Singh, Svaran, 187, 188–89, 193
Sinyavsky, Andrei, 87
Sippols, Willi, 26
Siradze, Viktoriya, 265
Sisco, Joseph, 250
Sitenko, Mikhail
   Middle East Peace Conference, Geneva, 255
   as pragmatist, 239–40
   UN Secretariat and, 208–9
   Yom Kippur War and, 244–45, 248, 249, 254
Smidovich, Nikita, 284, 356
Snow, Edgar, 17
Sobolev, Vikenty, 109, 213–14, 215, 217, 218
Sobolev, Vladimir, 359
social-economic experiment, tragedy of, xv
socialism
   collapse of, 382–83
   immorality of in USSR, 394
   Marxist-Leninist dogma, 89, 399
   unpopularity of Soviet-style, 157
socialist countries
   ambassadors and consuls to, 371–73
   diplomacy in, 373–75
   diplomats from and Soviet colleagues, 381–82
   Gorbachev and, 377–83, 383
   resolution of, 325–28
   sharing of information with, 375–77
   Soviet Union and, 367, 368–71
Soldatov, Aleksandr, 88, 100
Solomatin, Boris, 109, 218
Solzhenitsyn, Alexander, 123
Soviet Academy of Science, Council on the History of Soviet Foreign Policy and International Relations, 88–89
Soviet-American relations. *See also* détente; Geneva Committee on Disarmament
   Afghanistan and, 318–19
   confrontational diplomacy, 134–35
   at end of World War II, 19–20

   "key issues" and, 200–201, 260–63
   "Prague Spring" and, 147–48
   U-2 incident, 69–70
   as unstable and inconsistent, 130–34
   Yom Kippur War and, 249–50, 250–52
Soviet-Arab relations, 163–64
Soviet Foreign Policy (textbook), 79–80, 83–84
Soviet-German Pact of 1939. *See* Molotov-Ribbentrop Pact of 1939
Soviet-German relations, 27–28
Soviet-Indian treaty on peace, friendship, and cooperation, 186
Soviet Information Bureau, 22
Soviet mission, attack on, 140–41, 183
Soviet Union
   American interest in, 117–18, 124
   decline and fall of, xvi–xvii, 399–402
   June 1944 offensive, 40–41
   negative reactions to, 124–25
   socialist system, immorality of, 394
   ultimate goal of, 241
speeches
   of Churchill, 24, 29
   in Dallas, 120, 138–39, *235*
   on foreign policy, 122–24
   of Gorbachev, 364–65
   of Gromyko, 199, 280–81, 376
   of Khrushchev, 67
   lecture tour, 93–97
   in Miami, 118–20
   at Moscow factory, 19
   of Reagan, 306–7, 310
   of Stalin, 18, 34
   of Vyshinsky, 16–18
Stalin, Joseph. *See also* "struggle against the cult of Stalin"
   birth place of, 34
   on chemical weapons, 334–35
   Churchill and, 368
   death of, 43–44
   Dekanozov and, 4
   diplomacy and, 73
   documents regarding, 27
   family of, 44–46
   foreign policy of, 49–50, 51, 66, 400
   Litvinov, Gromyko, and, 71
   Marshall Plan and, 30
   Molotov and, 9–10, 11
   Orders of Suvorov, Kutuzov, and Nakhimov, and, 33
   publication of wartime documents and, 27, 28
   on role of superpowers, 127

Soviet boycott of UN Security Council and, 179
speeches of, 18, 34
stories about, 49–50
style of, 50
Tehran Conference and, 5
"Trust but verify!" proverb and, 330
on UN, 127–28
"Unity in Peace, and in War" declaration, 19
Stalin's generation, 13, 69, 103–4
Stanford, Henry, 119
Stashevsky, Gennady, 110, 135, 260–61, 291, 292
Stevenson, Adlai, 78
strategic arms limitation treaty, 306
Strock, Felix, 177
"struggle against the cult of Stalin," 49–51, 52, 72–75, 84, 90
Suika, Bogumil, 379–80
Sukhodrev, Viktor, 67, 280
Sukhumi Border Guards, 2
Supreme Attestation Commission, 90–91
Supreme Soviet, 400
Suslov, Mikhail, 56–57
Suslov, Vladimir, 242
Svanidze, Katerina, 45
Sverdlovsk incident, 312–16
Svoboda, Ludvik, 153
Syria, 171, 183, 244
Szarka, Karoly, 64, 65, *230*

Tairova, Tira, 265
Taiwan, 179–80, 181, 183–84
Tarasov, Nikolai, 109, 208
Tbilisi, Georgia, 1, 32–33, 354
Tehran Conference, 5, 40
Tekoah, Joseph, 164–65, 171, 173, 174, 183
territorial disputes, 80–83
Thant, U, 101, 145, 149, 185, 202–3, 205
Thorsson, Inga, 276
Timerbayev, Roland, xiii, 110, 239–40, 241, 247
Tito, Josef, 367
Tomeh, George, 171, 183
Tovmasian, Karen, 371
Treaty on the Non-proliferation of Nuclear Weapons, 129, 130, 275–76, 296–97
Troyanovsky, Oleg, 239–40, 281, 298
Trudeau, Pierre, 374
Trukhanovsky, 88
Truman, Harry, 23–24
"Trust but verify!" proverb, 330
Tsarapkin, Semen, 300
tsunami, artificial, 262

U-2 incident, 69–70
Ukrainian SSR, 181
uniform of diplomat, 20–21
UNITAR (UN Institute for Training and Research), 209
United Nations General Assembly. *See also* Thant, U; United Nations Security Council
Afghanistan and, 321
Bush appointment to, 137–38
China's admission to, 180–82, 183–84
delegates lounge of, 112–13
delegation to, 107–12, 209–11, 243, 264–66
deputy permanent representatives to, 108–10
Geneva Committee on Disarmament and, 301–2, 325–28
International Organizations Department preparations for, 259–62
Israelyan as delegate to, 81–82, 83
Israelyan as deputy permanent representative to, 99, 100–103, 109–10, 115–16
Israelyan as first deputy permanent representative to, 210, 211
Israelyan experience in, 219–20
Khrushchev and, 68–69
meeting of, *223*
"The Movement for Peace and Disarmament," 307–9
"post inflation" and, 107–8
propaganda activities outside, 116–18
Soviet-Chinese relations and, 177–80
Soviet "key issues" and, 198–201, 253, 260–63, 281–83
Special Session on Disarmament, 292–98, 299–300
superpowers and, 126–28
troika and, 68
twenty-ninth session of, 263–64
Vyshinsky and, 16
United Nations Secretariat, 201–4, 208–9
United Nations Security Council
conflict situations in, 198
Cyprus and, 269–70
Czechoslovakia and, 149, 150–55
Indo-Pakistani war and, 186–88, 192–95
meetings of, 136–37, *224*
Resolution 242, 160–63
Soviet boycott of, 178–79
successor to Thant and, 206
veto cast by China in, 195–97
vetos cast by Soviet Union in, 155, 189–90
Yom Kippur War and, 250

United States "Defense Directives for 1984–8," 309
"Unity in Peace, and in War" declaration, 19
Urbanovich, Vladislav, 33
Ustinov, Dmitry, 311

Vance, Cyrus, 280
Veivoda, Milos, 380
Vietnam, war in, 129, 130–33
Vinogradov, Vladimir
  as Ambassador to Egypt, 168, 244, 245, 246, 247, 254
  Fahmy and, 256–57
  Middle East Peace Conference, Geneva, 255
  Russian Soviet Federated Socialist Republic and, 287
Vorontsov, Yuly, xiii, 122–23
Voroshilov, Klim, 55
Vyshinsky, Andrei, 14–16
  Dekanozov and, 4
  dissertation and, 38
  as foreign minister, 52
  hypocrisy of, 114
  as model of diplomacy, 9
  publication of wartime documents and, 27, 28
  speeches of, 16–18

Waldheim, Kurt, 204, 206, 207, *231*, 255–56, 289
Warsaw Pact Organization, 367, 369, 373, 374, 375, 377
Wegener, 336–37, 339, 340
Weinberger, 307
West
  references to Soviets by, 40

views on verification of disarmament by, 329
Wiesner, Jerome, 121
Wise, Wes, 120
World War II. *See also* allies; Yalta Conference
  awakening among Soviet people after, 25
  celebration of end of, 19–20
  D-Day landing, fiftieth anniversary of, 40
  diplomacy of, 39
  writers, persecution of, 86–87

Yakovlev, Mikhail, 101, 287
Yakushkin, Dmitry, 212–13, 217
Yalta Conference, 17, 18–19, 29, 181, 367
Yeltsin, Boris, 287, 315
Yelutin, Vyacheslav, 91
Yerevan, Armenia, 32, 34–35
Yom Kippur War
  beginning of, 243–48
  daily meetings on, 248–49
  Politburo and, 250–52
  Soviet-American relations and, 249–50, 250–52
  as turning point, xi–xii
Yost, Charles, 117, 134, 135–36, 137, 162, *228*
Yugoslavia, 366

Zahir-Shah (king), 317
Zaikov, 357
Zakharov, Aleksei, 108
Zamyatin, Leonid, 81, 83
Zeder, Fred, 120
Zemskov, Igor, 26, 238–39
Zhemchuzhina, Polina, 10
Zhukov, 359
Zhurkin, Vitaly, 361
Zorin, Valerian, 13, 75, 300

www.ingramcontent.com/pod-product-compliance
Lightning Source LLC
Chambersburg PA
CBHW021928290426
44108CB00012B/758